Photographer's Guide to the Fujifilm X100S

Photographer's Guide to the Fujifilm X100S

Getting the Most from Fujifilm's Advanced Digital Camera

Alexander S. White

WHITE KNIGHT PRESS
HENRICO, VIRGINIA

Published by
White Knight Press
9704 Old Club Trace
Henrico, Virginia 23238
www.whiteknightpress.com
contact@whiteknightpress.com

ISBN: 978-1-937986-20-9 (paperback)
       978-1-937986-21-6 (e-book)

Printed in the United States of America

To my wife, Clenise.

Contents

CHAPTER 3:
The Shooting Modes   51

CHAPTER 4:
The Shooting Menu   79

Chapter 5:
Physical Controls

CHAPTER 6:
Playback

CHAPTER 7:
The Setup Menu — 286

CHAPTER 8:
Movies   314

CHAPTER 9:
OTHER TOPICS   328

APPENDIX A:
Accessories   353

APPENDIX B :
Quick Tips

APPENDIX C:
Resources for Further Information

Author's Note

In November 2011, I published Photographer's Guide to the Fujifilm FinePix X100, a guide to the earlier version of the X100S camera. After that book, I moved on to write about other cameras from Fujifilm, Sony, Canon, and other makers. When the X100S was released, I did not immediately decide to do a new book about it, because it was difficult to fit into my schedule. I kept receiving questions from readers about whether I would be doing an updated book, though, and the more I heard and read about the X100S, the more it seemed that a new book would be a good idea.

I went ahead and started this book, and as soon as I spent some time with the new camera, I became very glad I was doing this project. The newer model has several welcome improvements over the FinePix X100, and the X100S has turned out to be a great pleasure to work with.

I would like to express my appreciation to Jill Cooper, who was unfailingly patient and thorough as she helped me navigate through the complexities of the Adobe InDesign software package to accomplish the design and layout of the book.

Finally, as with my earlier books, the greatest support in every possible way, from joining me on trips to take photographs for this book to editing and proofreading the final text, has come from my wife, Clenise.

Introduction

This book is a guide to understanding the controls, menus, and features of the Fujifilm X100S, one of the most desirable advanced compact cameras in the marketplace today. Although the X100S, likes its predecessor, the FinePix X100, attracts a lot of its attention because of its stunning "retro" appearance, looks alone do not tell the story of this camera. The X100S is one of very few compact cameras that are equipped with the same large (APS-C) size of image sensor that is found in many mid-range DSLR (digital single-lens reflex) cameras, such as the Canon EOS 70D, the Nikon D7100, and the Sony Alpha A3000.

With this sensor, which is several times larger than the one found even in high-quality compact cameras such as the Canon PowerShot S120 and the Panasonic Lumix LX7, the X100S takes images of superb quality that can produce prints at substantial sizes. And, besides the quality made possible by the large sensor, the X100S offers an excellent lens with a very fast f/2.0 aperture. With that wide aperture, the lens of the X100S gathers light efficiently, allowing you to shoot high-quality images in fairly dark areas. In addition, the wide aperture gives you the opportunity to produce photographs with the pleasing look provided by blurring the background while leaving the foreground sharp.

The X100S also offers sophisticated features, including drive modes for burst shooting and bracketing; a useful set of film-simulation options that let you vary the look and color density of your images with in-camera processing; shutter speeds as fast as 1/4000 second and as long as 60 minutes using the Bulb setting; a built-in flash; Raw format; and just about every feature a serious photographer would ask for in a camera of this class. Along with its standard LCD display screen, the camera offers a bright optical viewfinder as well as an excellent electronic viewfinder, giving you three options for viewing your scene. The camera is equipped with a hot shoe that accepts external flash units, and the X100S even has a shutter release button that is threaded to accept a traditional cable release, allowing you to trigger the shutter without shaking the camera. The camera also offers a good set of options for capturing high-definition video clips.

Of course, as with all cameras, there are some trade-offs with the X100S that could be considered drawbacks, depending on your needs and preferences. The lens, while excellent in quality, is non-interchangeable, and has a fixed focal length of 35mm equivalent. Thus, the photographer has no ability to zoom or to vary the focal length in any way; you are limited to taking photographs with what could be considered a wide-angle lens. Also, although many photographers may not consider this point a negative one, the camera offers no fully automatic mode of shooting, and does not offer any "scene" modes that are oriented to particular types of subject, such as portraits, sports, beach, landscape, or fireworks. The X100S does, however, offer an excellent array of menu options and controls that will let you deal with such subjects with no problem; you will just have to figure out what settings to use to get optimal results for any given subject. One other limitation is that the camera does not offer any type of image stabilization system to counter camera shake.

This discussion of the camera's features is, of course, not complete, but it serves to illustrate that the Fujifilm X100S is equipped with features that should be attractive to serious photographers—those who want numerous options for creative control of their images in a camera that is small enough and light enough to be carried around at all times, so they will be ready for action when a picture-taking opportunity arises. The X100S should be of particular interest to those photographers who have an interest in street photography and other forms of candid shooting, but it also is an excellent choice as an all-around photographic Jack of all trades.

My goal with this guide is to provide a thorough introduction to the camera's features, explaining how they work and when you might want to use them. The book is aimed largely at beginning and intermediate photographers who are not satisfied with the technical documentation that comes with the camera and who would like a more user-friendly explanation of the camera's many controls and menus. For those who are seeking more advanced information, I provide some discussion of topics that go beyond the basics, and I include in the appendices information to help you uncover additional resources. I will also try to provide updates from time to time at whiteknightpress.com.

One note on the scope of this guide: I live in the United States, and I bought my camera in the U.S. market. I am not familiar with variations (such as different chargers) for cameras sold in Europe, Asia, or elsewhere. The photographic functions are not different, though, so this guide should be useful to photographers in all locations, apart from that narrow range of issues. I have stated measurements of distance and weight in both the Imperial and metric systems, for the benefit of readers in various countries around the world.

The photographs in this book that illustrate the capabilities of the X100S are ones that I took with that camera, using firmware version 1.03. The menu illustrations and photographs of the X100S and its accessories are images that I took using a Sony Alpha SLT-A99 camera with a Sony f/2.8 50mm macro lens and a Sony 24 -70mm f/2.8 zoom lens.

There is one minor point to note for those who pay attention to fine details. The predecessor camera is officially called the Fujifilm FinePix X100; for some reason, Fujifilm dropped the "FinePix" part of the label for this model, which is known simply as the Fujifilm X100S.

Finally, I would like to encourage readers to provide feedback about this book and about White Knight Press in general, such as suggestions for future books and for ways to increase the usefulness of these guides. Also, if you find this book and other books from White Knight Press to be useful and would like to see more books written, it is very helpful when readers spread the word about the books, through online reviews and discussions. Like other authors who publish their own books, I do not have the resources to conduct advertising campaigns, and I rely on readers to bring the books to the attention of others who might benefit from them.

Please send feedback to contact@whiteknightpress.com. I respond to all messages, usually within 24 hours.

CHAPTER 1:
Preliminary Setup

Setting Up the Camera

When you receive your Fujifilm X100S, the package should include the battery, battery charger with power cord, USB cable, shoulder strap, printed user's manual, CD with owner's manual and software, and a clip-attaching tool with clips for fastening the shoulder strap to the camera. There also should be a warranty card and one or two other items, such as an advertising sheet or safety notice.

It is generally a good idea to attach the shoulder strap to the camera right away, which requires that you use the clip-attaching tool to attach a metal clip to each of the metal eyelets at the sides of the camera; then thread the strap through those clips, using protective covers to insulate the camera body from the clips, as shown at pages 9-10 of the user's manual. You might want to consider alternatives, though, such as the SnapR 35 strap and case combination, discussed in Appendix A. If you should decide to purchase the official Fujifilm leather case, also discussed in Appendix A, that case comes with its own leather strap, which you can attach to the camera using the clips provided with the X100S.

CHARGING AND INSERTING THE BATTERY

The battery model for the X100S is the NP-95. The only way to charge the battery is with an external charger such as model BC-65N, the Fujifilm charger supplied with the camera. Unfortunately, the battery and charger are designed so that it is possible to insert the battery into the charger in the wrong direction, which would result in an uncharged battery. If you are using the official Fujifilm battery, it has arrows pointing the correct direction in which to insert it into the charger. If you're using a replacement battery from another company, though, such arrows are likely to be missing. Personally, I prefer to look for the three gold-colored metal contacts on the battery and to insert the battery so those three contacts come into contact with the three metal prongs inside the charger, as shown in FIGURE 1-1; that way, you know you have the battery inserted correctly.

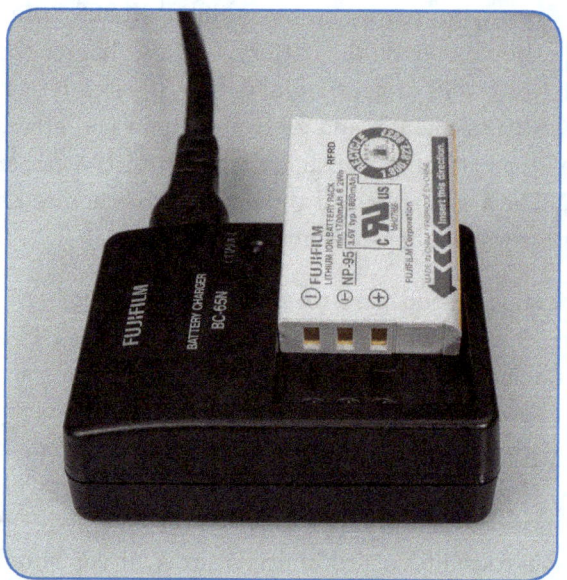

Figure 1-1. Battery Going into Charger

There is one fact you need to be aware of about the charger that comes with the camera: This charger has a small plastic piece attached to the end opposite the contacts; that piece evidently is included in order to make the NP-95 battery fit snugly into the charging compartment. When that charger shipped with the FinePix X100 model, the additional piece was not permanently attached to the charger, and that small piece could easily fall off and get lost. The charger that I received with my X100S had the extra piece firmly glued in place, but you might want to make sure that the piece is solidly attached, especially if you are using an earlier model of the charger.

With the battery inserted into the charger, plug the charger's power cord into an electrical outlet. (If you prefer not to have to deal with the somewhat bulky cord, see Appendix A for a way to use the charger without the cord.) The light on the charger should be a solid green, to show that charging is taking place. A full charge of a depleted battery should take about 210 minutes, after which the charging light will turn off to indicate that charging is complete.

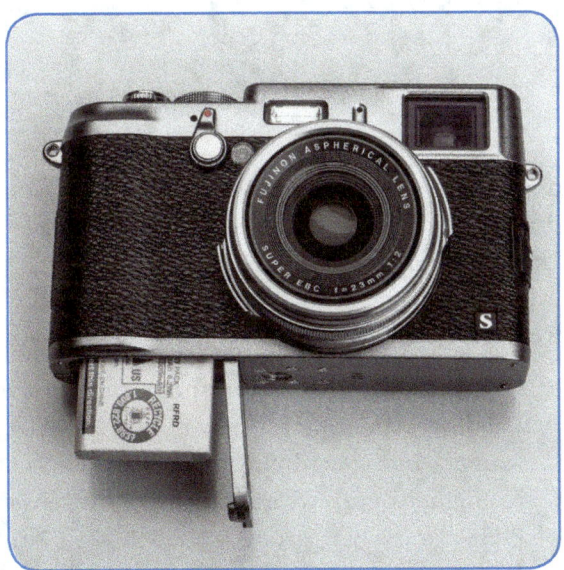

Figure 1-2. Battery Going into Camera

Once you have a charged battery, hold the camera upside down and slide the latch on the battery compartment door toward the "Open" label; the door will pop open. Here, again, you need to be careful about inserting the battery, because it is possible to insert it incorrectly. Make sure the three gold-colored contacts are facing down into the camera, as shown in FIGURE 1-2, and make sure the curved side of the battery is at the outside edge of the camera, next to the orange plastic latch. You may have to nudge the orange latch to one side to let the battery slide past it.

Once the battery is inserted, the latch should spring closed above the battery, holding it in place, as shown in FIGURE 1-3.

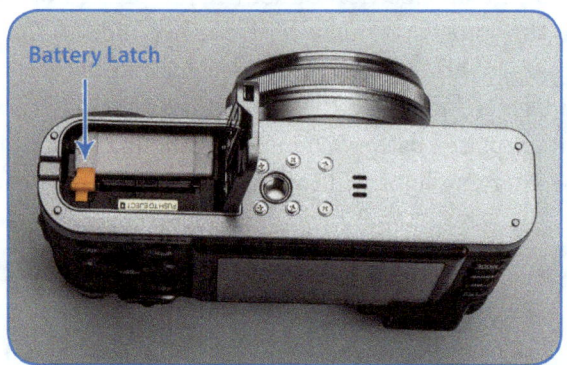

Figure 1-3. Battery Secured by Latch

Close and latch the battery compartment door, and you're done. (Or, if you're also going to insert a memory card, leave the door open for the next step.)

INSERTING THE MEMORY CARD

The X100S does not ship with any memory card included. With this camera, unlike some others, this is not a fatal omission, because the camera has some built-in memory that will let you take a few photographs even with no memory card inserted. The amount of built-in memory is not large—about 24 megabytes (MB)—which is pretty minuscule compared to the capacity of modern storage cards that can hold up to 256 gigabytes (GB), about 10,000 times greater capacity. But if you need to take a picture and don't have an available card, 24 MB might be enough in some cases. The internal memory can hold about 30 still photos of the smallest size at Normal (lowest) quality, but only 3 images shot at the largest size and highest quality in the JPEG format, and no images at all in the Raw format. You can store about 2 seconds of video in the internal memory. In practical terms, these figures mean you have to have a memory card in the camera to capture any meaningful amount of still images or videos.

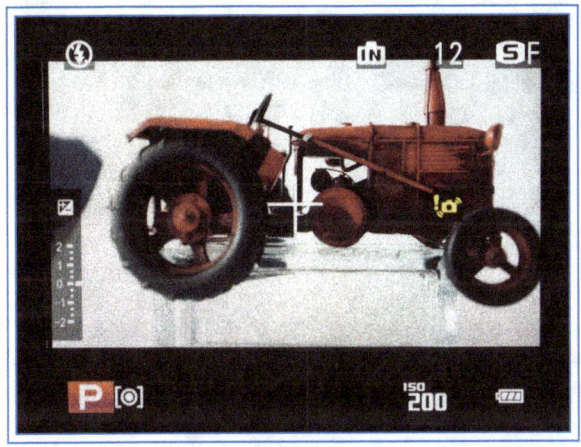

Figure 1-4. IN Indicator Meaning Internal Memory in Use

If you have no memory card inserted in the camera, the letters IN will display inside a white camera icon in the upper right half of the display (if one of the detailed display screens is selected), indicating that internal memory is being used, as shown in FIGURE 1-4.

If a memory card is inserted, the letters IN are not displayed, but you will usually notice a dramatic increase in the number in the upper right of the display, which represents the estimated number of remaining images that can be stored, as shown in FIGURE 1-5.

If you fill up the internal memory, you will see a message saying that the internal memory is full, and your shooting will come to a halt unless you delete some images from the internal memory or insert an SD card that has some free space on it.

Because of its very limited capacity, you shouldn't rely on the built-in memory if you don't have to, so you need to insert a memory card. The X100S uses SD cards, which are quite small, about the size of a large postage stamp. They come in several varieties, as shown in Figure 1-6.

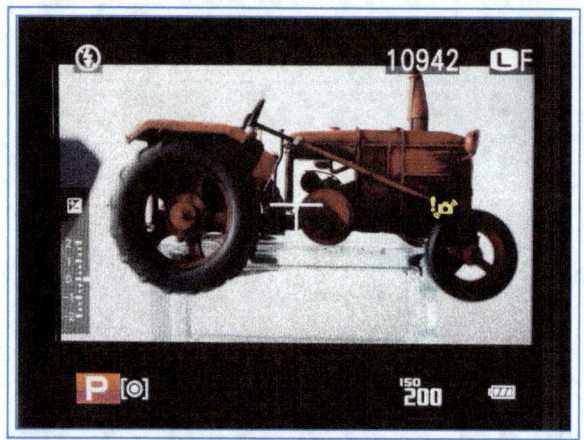

Figure 1-5. Images Remaining Indicator When Memory Card in Use

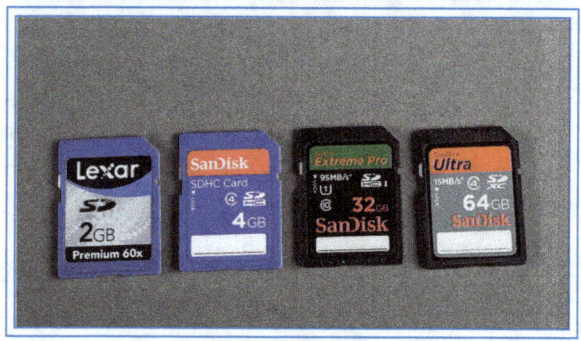

Figure 1-6. Card Types: SD 2GB, SDHC 4GB, SDHC 32GB, SDXC 64 GB

The standard card, called simply SD, comes in capacities from 8 MB to 2 GB. The next higher-capacity card, SDHC, comes in sizes from 4 GB to 32 GB. The newest, highest-capacity card, SDXC (for extended capacity) comes in sizes of 48 GB, 64 GB, and up; this version of the card can theoretically have a capacity up to 2 terabytes (TB) (one TB is equivalent to 1,000 GB), and SDXC cards have faster transfer speeds than the smaller-capacity cards. Note that the X100S cannot use another type of memory card called a MultiMediaCard (MMC), even though those cards are the same size as SD cards.

What card and size should you use? It depends on your needs and intentions. If you want to record a lot of high-definition (HD) video or large numbers of high-resolution stills, I recommend a 32 GB SDHC card, which will give you plenty of margin for extra storage. I often use a 32 GB SanDisk Extreme Pro, which offers plenty of capacity and speed, but there are many excellent options available.

There are several variables to take into account in computing how many images or videos you can store on a particular card, such as which aspect ratio you're using (3:2, 16:9, or 1:1), image size, and quality. Here are a few examples of what can be stored on a 16 GB SDHC card, which is a commonly used size these days: One of these cards can hold more than 450 photos shot in the Raw format, the largest size for stills; it can hold about 2400 of the largest JPEG images at the highest quality; or it can hold more than 20,000 still images at the lower, Normal quality and the smallest file size. A 16 GB card also can store about 52 minutes of HD video clips. (Each clip can last no more than 10 minutes, though.)

Of course, if you are going on an extended trip and want to limit the number of memory cards to keep track of, you can opt for one of the SDXC cards with tremendous capacity. As I write this, a card with a capacity of 256 GB is available, though it is quite expensive, at about $460.00 in the online listings I checked. With that card, you could store more than 7000 Raw images and correspondingly large amounts for other formats. However, because of the huge capacity of such a card, it can take extra time for the camera to get ready to shoot after you turn it on with an SDXC card installed. Personally, I have found a 32GB card to be sufficient for all practical purposes. However, I have used a Lexar Professional 128 GB SDXC card in the X100S with no problems. When I first inserted and formatted that card, with the camera set to take the smallest-sized images, the readout for images remaining in the upper right corner of the display screen read 99999, because the camera could not display a figure large enough to state the actual capacity of the card. When I switched the settings from small images to Raw images, the readout returned to a more standard value of 3906.

One other consideration is the speed of the card. If you plan to record video, you should get a card that is rated as Class 10 or higher for its speed. Although, as noted above, there are numerous options available, I have had excellent results with my 32 GB SanDisk Extreme Pro SDHC UHS-1 card, which is rated as reading and writing at 45 MB/second, and is in UHS speed class 1. (UHS, not surprisingly, stands for ultra-high speed.)

Finally, you need to realize if you have an older computer with a built-in card reader, or just an older external card reader, there is a chance it will not read the newer SDHC or SDXC cards. In that case, you would have to either get a new reader that will accept the latest cards, or transfer images from the camera to your computer using the USB cable. This problem has become less common over the past several years as computers and card readers have been upgraded to accommodate the SDHC and SDXC standards.

If you will have access to a wireless (Wi-Fi) network where you use your camera, you may want to consider getting an Eye-Fi card or one of its competitors.

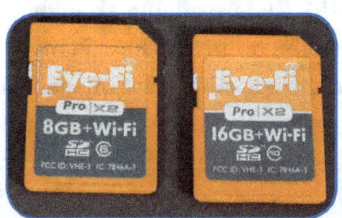

Figure 1-7. Eye-Fi Pro X2 SDHC Memory Cards

This special type of storage device, shown in FIGURE 1-7, looks very much like an ordinary SDHC card, but it includes a tiny transmitter that lets it connect to a wireless network and send your images to your computer over that network as soon as the images have been recorded by the camera.

I have tested both 8 GB and 16 GB Eye-Fi cards, the Pro X2 models, with the X100S, and both of these cards work well. Within seconds after I snap a picture with either card in the camera, a thumbnail image appears in the upper right corner of my computer's screen showing the progress of the upload. When all images and videos are uploaded, they are found in the Pictures/Eye-Fi folder or the Movies/Eye-Fi folder on my computer. The Pro X2 models can handle Raw files as well as the smaller JPEG files. (At this writing, the Pro X2 is the only variety of Eye-Fi card that can handle Raw files.) An Eye-Fi card is not a necessity, but I enjoy the convenience of having my images sent straight to my computer without having to put the card into a card reader or to connect the camera to the computer with a USB cable.

Other options include the ez Share Wi-Fi card, the Transcend Information Wi-Fi card, and the Toshiba FlashAir Wireless Memory Card. All of these cards are advertised as having capabilities similar to those of the Eye-Fi card, though I have not tried any of them myself.

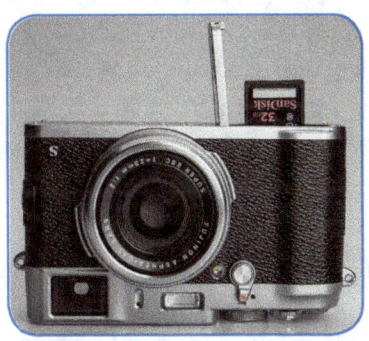

Figure 1-8. Memory Card Going into Camera

Whatever card you choose, open the same little door on the bottom of the camera that covers the battery compartment, and slide the card into the card slot until it catches, with the label facing the front of the camera, as shown in FIGURE 1-8.

Once you have pushed the card down until it catches, close the compartment door and push the exterior sliding latch back to the locking position. To remove the card, push down on it until it releases and springs up so you can grab it.

One note for when you're shooting continuous pictures with the camera: When the camera is writing images to the SD card, the indicator lamp at the upper right of the camera's back glows orange or blinks orange and green. When that lamp is displaying either of these signals, it's important not to turn off the camera or otherwise interrupt its functioning, such as by taking out the battery or disconnecting an AC power adapter. You need to let the card complete its recording process in peace.

Introduction to Main Controls

Before I discuss some of the basic options for setting up the camera using the menu system and controls, I will introduce the main controls that I need to talk about, so you'll have a better idea of which button or dial is which. I won't discuss these items in depth here; I will cover them in some detail in Chapter 5. For now, here is a series of images that show the major controls. For each item, I will briefly describe its main functions, leaving the details for Chapter 5 and other chapters that may discuss that control.

Top of Camera

On top of the camera are some of the more important controls and dials, shown in FIGURE 1-9. The shutter speed dial, directly to the right of the flash shoe, is used to set the camera's shutter speed when you are using either Shutter Priority or Manual exposure mode. If you set the dial to the red letter A, the camera will set the shutter speed automatically. The shutter button, next to the shutter speed dial, is the most important control on the camera. You press it halfway to lock exposure and focus, and all the way to take a picture or to start a movie recording. The power switch is the small lever on a ring that surrounds the shutter button.

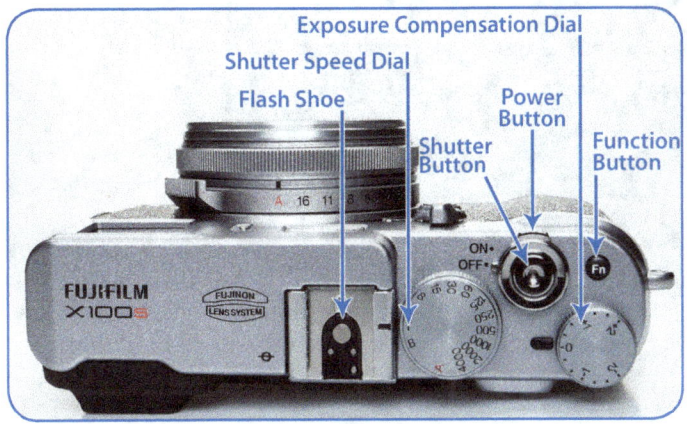

Figure 1-9. Controls on Top of Camera

Press the power button to the On or Off position to turn the camera on or off. The exposure compensation dial, in the right rear corner of the camera's top, is used to dial in positive or negative amounts of exposure compensation, to make the image brighter or darker as conditions may require. Finally, the Function button, at the right front of the camera's top, can be assigned to control any one of several settings, including the default value, ISO, among others, as discussed in Chapter 5.

BACK OF CAMERA–RIGHT SIDE

I have divided the controls on the camera's back into two categories to make it easier to identify them. First, I will discuss the dials and buttons on the right side of the camera's back, as shown in FIGURE 1-10.

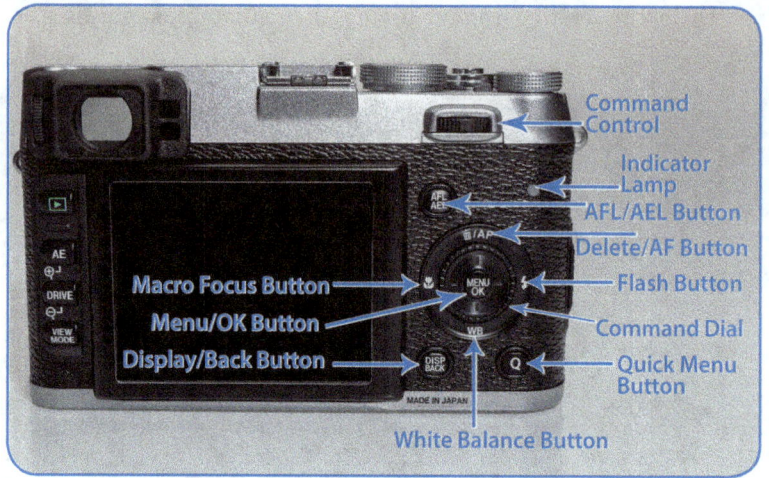

Figure 1-10. Controls on Right Side of Camera's Back

The first item at the top right is the Command Control, a versatile switch with several functions. As I will discuss in detail in Chapter 5, you can press this switch to the left or right, or press in on it, to adjust various settings, including aperture and Program Shift, or to duplicate the action of the Command Dial, discussed later. You also can press in on this switch to enlarge the focus area or an image being played on the screen. The AFL/AEL button is used to lock focus or exposure, and also can be used for autofocus when the camera is in manual focus mode.

The Command Dial is the ridged wheel in the center of the control area. The wheel itself rotates to make various selections and to navigate through menus. Each of the four edges of the wheel serves as a button (Left, Right, Up and Down buttons) that you press to activate the function indicated by an icon next to that edge: Autofocus area or Delete for the Up button; Flash for the Right button; White Balance for the Down button; and Macro autofocus for the Left button. The button in the center of the Command Dial, labeled Menu/OK, is used to activate the menu system and to confirm selections made in that system and on other settings screens, among other functions. The Display/Back button is used to switch the camera's display screens and to exit from menu screens.

The Q button, at the lower right of the control area, among other functions, is used to call up the Quick Menu, which lets you make many of the camera's most important settings from a single convenient screen. Finally, the indicator lamp, the small light at the upper right of this control area, glows orange, green, or red to indicate various conditions concerning focus, exposure, battery charging, and other items.

BACK OF CAMERA–LEFT SIDE

The controls on the left of the camera's back are shown in FIGURE 1-11.

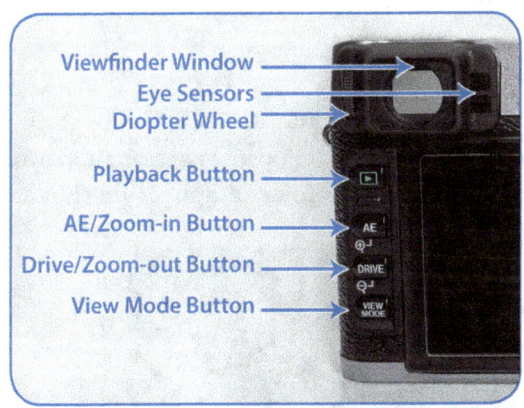

Figure 1-11. Controls on Left Side of Camera's Back

At the upper left of the camera's back is the viewfinder window, which you look into to compose the image and see shooting information that the camera overlays on the image. At the left of this window is the diopter adjustment wheel, which you can turn to adjust the viewfinder's focus to fit your eyesight. Two small eye sensors to the right of the viewfinder window sense when your eye approaches the viewfinder and cause the view to switch from the LCD screen to the viewfinder, if the View Mode button (discussed below) is set to enable automatic switching. At the top of the line of controls at the far left is the Playback button, marked by a green triangle. You press this button to start playback of your images and videos. Next in this line is the AE/Zoom-in button, which lets you control the area of the scene that is used by the camera's autoexposure metering system. In playback mode, it enlarges images. Below that control is the Drive/Zoom-out button, which lets you select among the camera's various options for continuous shooting, including burst modes, exposure bracketing, multiple exposures, panoramas, and shooting video sequences. In playback mode, this button reduces image size and calls up index screens. The last button at the bottom of the line is the View Mode button, which, as mentioned earlier, is used to switch the active display between the LCD screen and the viewfinder, or to set the camera so the eye sensors will switch the display as your head approaches or leaves the vicinity of the viewfinder window.

Focus Switch

The focus switch, shown in FIGURE 1-12, sits by itself on the left side of the X100S. It has three positions, from upper to lower, for manual focus, continuous autofocus, and single-shot autofocus.

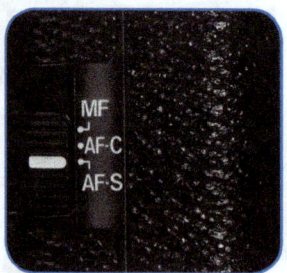

Figure 1-12. Focus Switch

Front of Camera

On the front of the camera, where the built-in flash unit sits, the only button or switch you can manipulate is the Viewfinder Selector, seen in FIGURE 1-13. This switch is used to select between the optical viewfinder and the electronic viewfinder.

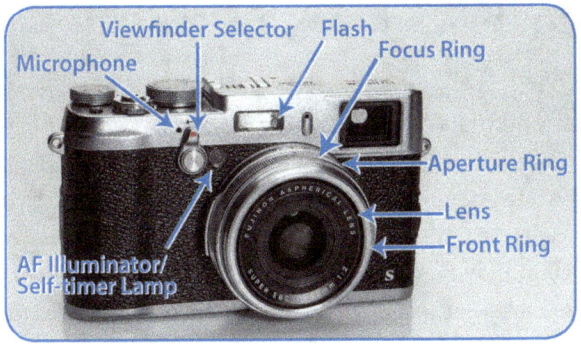

Figure 1-13. Items on Front of Camera

The other major items on the front of the camera are the lens, the aperture ring that surrounds the lens next to the camera's body, and the focus ring, with which you adjust focus when the manual focus mode is active. The camera's built-in flash unit sits just above the lens and the two microphone openings are on either side of the flash. A small lamp near the lens assists with autofocus and indicates use of the Self-timer.

BOTTOM OF CAMERA

On the bottom of the camera, as seen in FIGURE 1-14, are the tripod socket and the door that covers the compartment for the memory card and battery, as well as the speaker for movie audio and the camera's operational sounds.

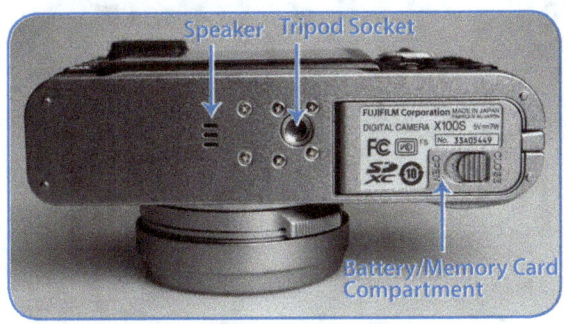

Figure 1-14. Items on Bottom of Camera

Setting the Language, Date, and Time

You need to make sure the date and time are set correctly in the camera before you start taking pictures, because the camera records that information (sometimes known as "metadata," meaning data beyond the information in the picture itself) invisibly with each image, and displays it later if you want. Someday you may be very glad to have the date (and even the time of day) correctly recorded with your archives of digital images.

Here is the procedure to set the date and time. Turn the power switch clockwise to turn the camera on, then press the Menu button in the center of the Command Dial to activate the menu system. Press the Left button, which is marked with a flower icon. When you press that button, the selection markers will move out of the menu screen to the left side of the display, highlighting one of the menu icons—a camera with a number from 1 to 5 for the Shooting menu, as shown in FIGURE 1-15, or a wrench with a number from 1 to 3 for the Setup menu, as shown in FIGURE 1-16.

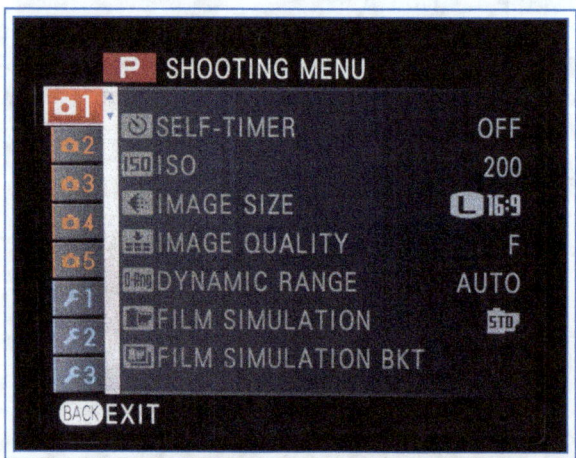

Figure 1-15. Left Menu Column Highlighted

Press the Down button, labeled WB, once or more until the wrench icon with the number 1 is highlighted, as shown in FIGURE 1-16.

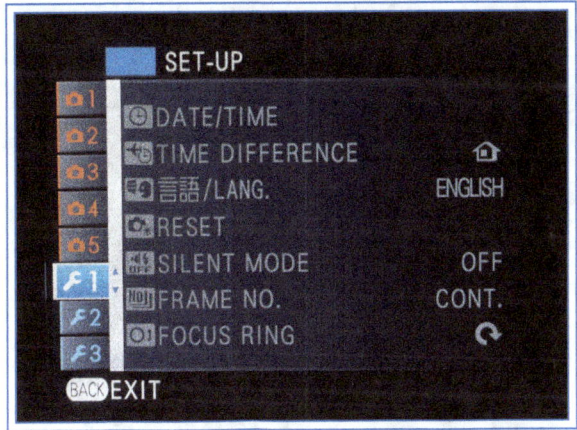

Figure 1-16. Wrench Icon for Setup Menu Highlighted

Then press the Right button, marked with a lightning bolt, to move the selection markers back into the menu list. The Date/Time item should be highlighted, as shown in FIGURE 1-17.

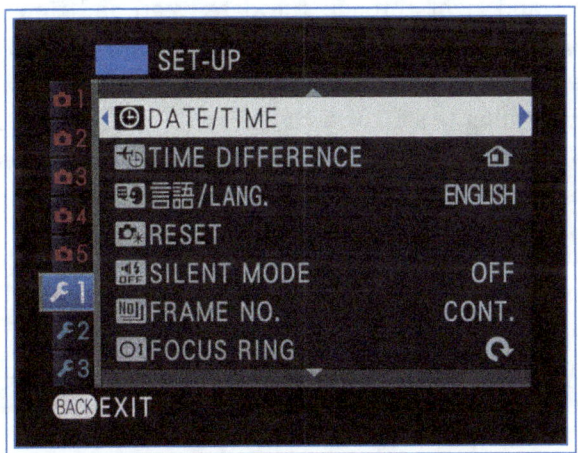

Figure 1-17. Date/Time Menu Option

If it is not, move the selection rectangle up and down through the menu items by pressing the Up and Down buttons or by turning the Command Dial, until the Date/Time item is highlighted.

Then, press the Menu/OK button or the Right button to activate the date and time settings, as shown in FIGURE 1-18.

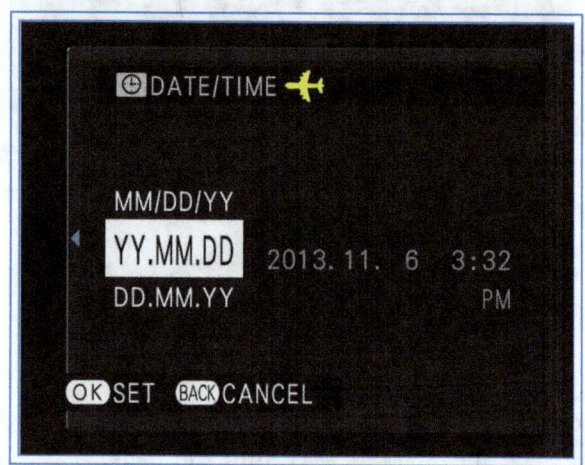

Figure 1-18. Date/Time Settings Screen

Move left and right through the date, year, and time settings by pressing the Left and Right buttons, and change the settings with the Up and Down buttons, or by turning the Command Dial. When everything is set correctly, press the Menu/OK button to confirm, and press the Display/Back button, to the lower left of the Command Dial, to exit the menu system.

If you need to change the language that the camera uses for the menus and other messages, navigate on Screen 1 of the Setup menu to the line that says Lang. for Language, and press the Menu/OK button or the Right button to move to the list of available languages, as shown in FIGURE 1-19.

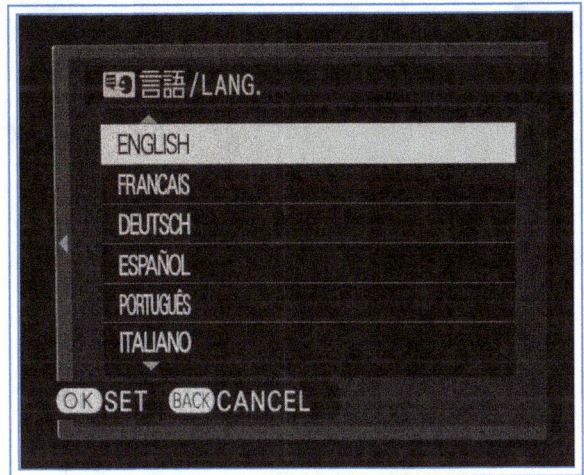

Figure 1-19. Language Menu Option

Then navigate with the Up and Down buttons to the language of your choice and press the Menu/OK button to select it. Press the Display/Back button to exit from the menu system.

CHAPTER 2:
Basic Operations

Taking Pictures

Now that the Fujifilm X100S has the correct time and date set and has a fully charged battery inserted along with a memory card, let's explore some scenarios for basic picture-taking. For now, I won't get into discussions of what the various options are and why you might choose one over another. I'll just describe a reasonable set of steps that will get you and your camera into action and will deposit a decent image on your memory card.

SOMEWHAT AUTOMATIC—PROGRAM MODE

As I noted in the Introduction, the X100S does not have an "Auto" mode, as many compact cameras, and even some entry-level and mid-range DSLRs, do. The X100S clearly was designed for the serious photographer who is willing to exert the effort to learn how to use the camera's controls and menus to produce the results he or she is looking for.

That does not mean that the camera requires you to handle every photographic decision manually, though; it will offer you a considerable amount of assistance, but there is no single setting that will turn over all decision-making to the camera.

Here are some steps to follow if you want to get started taking pictures with the X100S without having to go through a great deal of work with the controls and menus:

1. Remove the lens cap from the lens and put it in your pocket or some other safe place where it won't get lost; unfortunately, there is no way to attach it to the camera by a string or other mechanism. (See Appendix A for information about an automatic lens cap that addresses this problem.)

2. Turn on the power by moving the On/Off switch clockwise. The LCD screen will illuminate to show that the camera has turned on, unless you have the view mode switched to the viewfinder. If the LCD display does not light up, press the View Mode button located at the lower left of the camera's back until the display appears.

3. Find the shutter speed dial on top of the camera to the right of the flash shoe, marked with numbers up to 4000, and turn that dial until the red letter A is next to the black indicator line on the side of the flash shoe.

4. Locate the aperture dial surrounding the lens, right next to the camera's body, marked with numbers from 2 to 16. Turn that dial until its red letter A is next to the black indicator line on the lens.

The camera's dials should be set as shown in FIGURE 2-1. You should now see a white letter P on a red background at the lower left of the LCD display, as shown in FIGURE 2-2, indicating that the camera has been set to the Program shooting mode. (If you don't see the P, press the Drive button at the left of the camera's back, then navigate in the Drive menu with the direction buttons to select the top option, Still Image.)

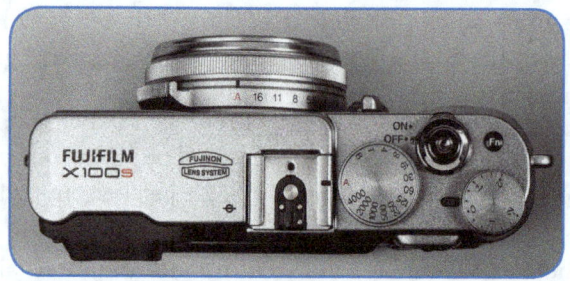

Figure 2-1. Aperture Ring and Shutter Speed Dial at A Positions

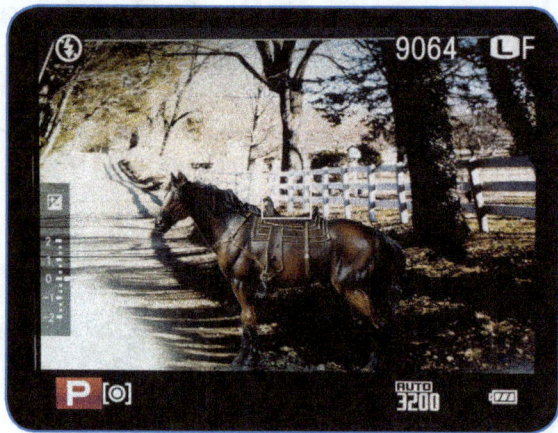

Figure 2-2. P Icon on Screen for Program Mode

5. Press the Menu button in the center of the Command Dial on the back of the camera. Press the Up and Down buttons (top and bottom edges of the Command Dial), or turn the Command Dial itself, to navigate to the menu entry for Image Quality, select that line with the OK button or the Right button, use the buttons or the dial to highlight the Fine setting, and press OK.

6. Navigate to the Image Size setting, select it, and choose L 3:2, meaning Large size, with an aspect ratio of 3:2. (Of course, you can choose other settings for both of these options if you wish, but the ones I have mentioned provide the highest quality that is available without getting involved with the Raw format, which I'll discuss later.) Press the Display/Back

button, at the lower left of the control area on the right of the camera's back, to exit from the menu screen back to the live shooting screen.

7. Look at the left side of the camera as you hold it to take a picture, and locate the sliding switch with three positions, marked MF, AF-C, and AF-S. Slide it, if necessary, so that the white indicator is pointing to the AF-S position, for autofocus-single shot (as opposed to manual focus or autofocus-continuous), as shown in FIGURE 2-3.

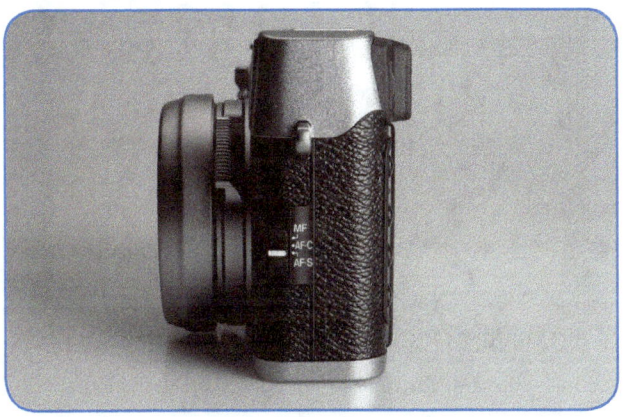

Figure 2-3. Focus Switch at AF-S Position

8. If you want to compose your image on the LCD screen on the back of the camera, no action should be needed. If you want to use the electronic viewfinder instead, find the View Mode button. Press that button twice, and the display will switch to the viewfinder, blacking out the LCD. You can then look inside the viewfinder to compose the shot and view the camera's settings. You can adjust the view for your eyesight by turning the diopter adjustment dial on the left side of the viewfinder's housing. Toggle between the LCD and the viewfinder whenever you want, using the View Mode button. (A third choice, discussed in Chapter 5, is to select Eye Sensor, in which case the view will switch to the viewfinder when your eye approaches the viewfinder.)

9. If you are indoors or otherwise in conditions that might
    call for the use of flash, press the Right button, marked
    with a lightning bolt, then quickly press it again or turn the
    Command Dial, until the Auto Flash setting appears on the
    screen, as shown in FIGURE 2-4. Press the OK button to select
    that setting. Later, in Chapters 5 and 9, I'll discuss the other
    flash options.

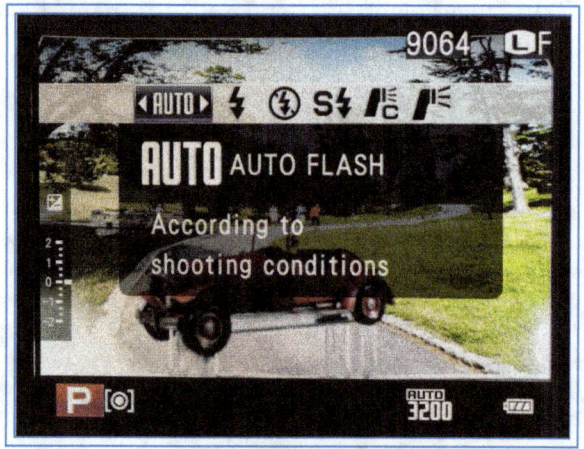

Figure 2-4. Auto Flash Highlighted on Flash Menu

10. Aim the camera toward the subject and look at the LCD screen
    (or into the viewfinder window, depending on your choice in
    Step 8) to compose the image as you want it. Once the picture
    is set up as you want, push the shutter button halfway. You
    should hear a beep and see a small green rectangle appear
    on the screen, indicating that the picture will be in focus,
    as shown in FIGURE 2-5. In addition, the indicator lamp at
    the top right of the camera's back should glow green. If the
    rectangle on the screen is red or the indicator lamp blinks
    green, that means the camera is having difficulty achieving
    focus. In that case, try moving the camera to a different
    angle or distance from the subject before pressing the shutter
    button halfway down again.

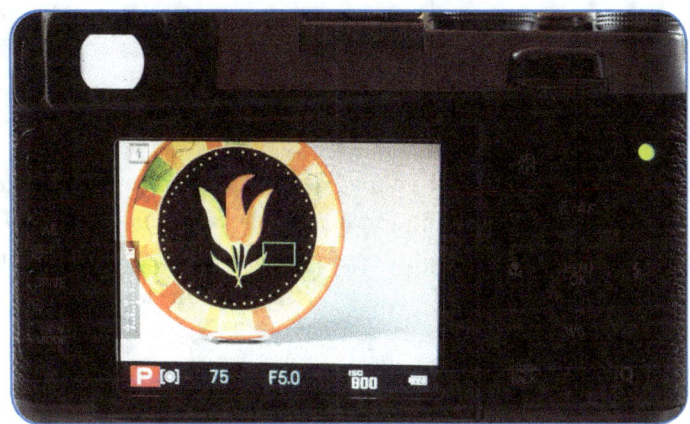

Figure 2-5. Focus Frame and Indicator Lamp Green for Good Focus

11. Push the shutter button all the way down to take the picture.

Basic Settings for Taking Still Pictures

At this point I won't discuss the various still-picture shooting modes, except to name them. Besides Program, which I just described, there are Shutter Priority, Aperture Priority, and Manual. I'll discuss all of those shooting modes later on, as well as motion picture shooting, panoramas, and other options. For now, I'm going to discuss a few of the most basic functions and features of the X100S that you can adjust to suit many of the picture-taking situations you may be faced with.

I'm not going to repeat the preliminary steps for taking a picture, because those were pretty basic. If you need a refresher on those items, see the list of 11 steps in the above discussion.

In Program mode, the X100S will determine the proper exposure, both the aperture (size of opening to let in light) and the shutter speed (how long the shutter is open to let in light). In this mode you don't need to make any decisions about those settings; you will need to make those decisions in other modes, which I'll discuss in Chapter 3. That still leaves lots of decisions you can make in this mode, though, so I will now discuss several of the major settings you can adjust in Program mode.

Focus

In the basic steps discussed above, we made sure the focus switch was set to the AF-S position for autofocus-single shot mode. With this setting, the camera will focus just once, when you press the shutter button halfway. This is a setting you are likely to use for many ordinary photo sessions.

There are several other focus-related options you can set using the Shooting and Setup menus, but for now I will discuss just one of them. Press the Menu button, then press the Up or Down button or turn the Command Dial until you reach the AF Mode menu item on the fourth screen of the Shooting menu, shown in FIGURE 2-6.

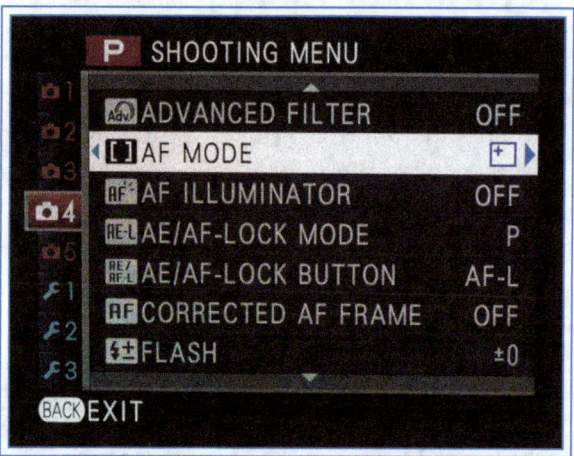

Figure 2-6. AF Mode Menu Item Highlighted

(You may find that it's quicker to move up in the menu items and wrap around to the bottom of the menu to reach this point, rather than just navigating down to this item.)

Once the AF Mode item is highlighted, press the OK button or the Right button to move to the next sub-menu screen, which provides two choices: Multi and Area, as seen in FIGURE 2-7.

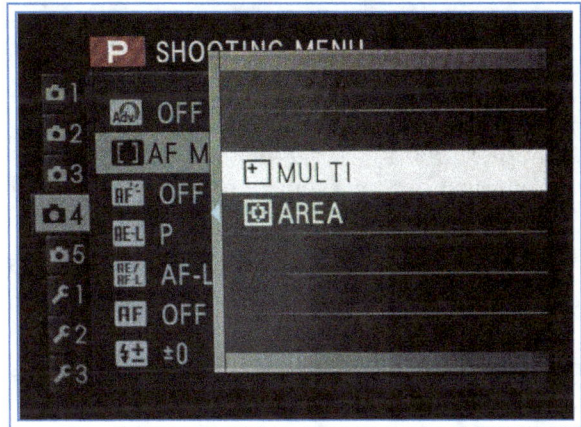

Figure 2-7. AF Mode Options Screen

If you choose Multi, the camera will decide which of 49 possible focus points in its display to use to set the focus for your image. (There are only 25 focus points available if you are using the optical viewfinder rather than the LCD or the electronic viewfinder.)

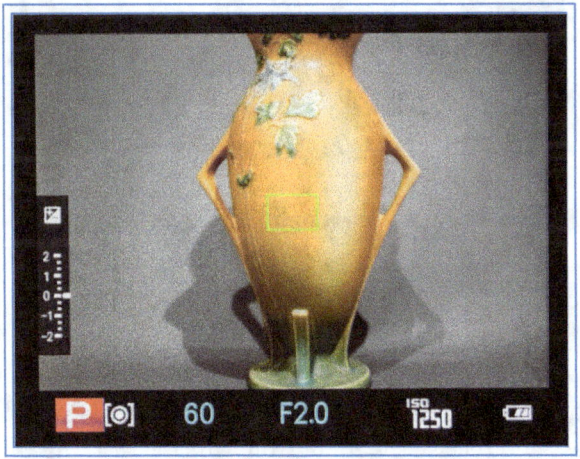

Figure 2-8. Multi Autofocus Frame - Green for Good Focus

The camera bases the selection of a focus point on determining which objects in the scene have the highest contrast, which could mean they are people or other likely subjects. With the Multi setting, the camera does not display any focus frame until you press the shutter button halfway down to lock in focus; at that point, the camera will display a single green rectangle at the location it has chosen for focus, as shown in FIGURE 2-8.

If you don't want the camera to make the choice of where to set the focus point, you can take control of this decision by choosing the other AF Mode option, which is Area. To make that choice, highlight the Area option on the menu screen and press the OK button to select it; then press the Display/Back button (to the right of the bottom of the LCD screen) to exit from the menu system. You will see a white rectangle in the center of the display, indicating the place where the camera will set its focus in the scene before it, as shown in FIGURE 2-9.

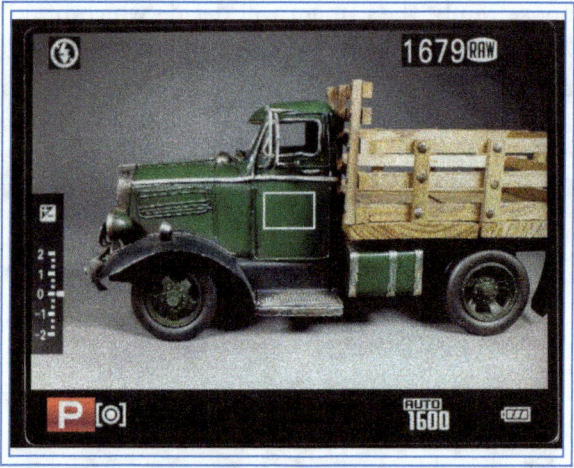

Figure 2-9. Area AF Frame - Before Moving

If you want to, you can now move the focus frame around the screen to any one of the 49 (or 25) focus points available. To do this, press and release the AF button, which is also the Up button, with a trashcan icon and the letters AF above it. The camera will display a screen with small crosses marking the available focus points, as shown in FIGURE 2-10.

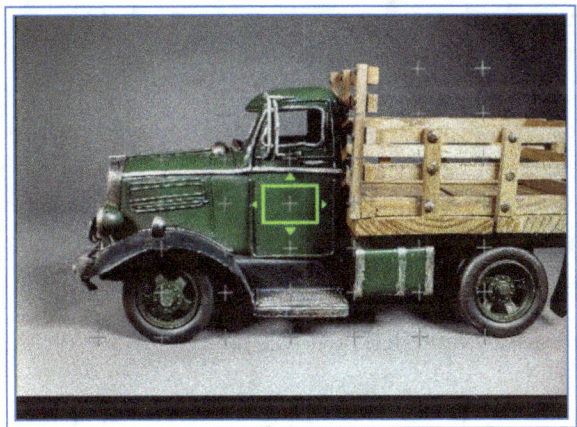

Figure 2-10. Area AF Frame - Ready to Move

You can now move the focus frame, which will have turned green, by pressing any of the four direction buttons on the Command Dial or by turning the Command Dial, until the frame is set at the point where you want it to stay. If you want to return the focus frame quickly to the center of the display, press the Display/Back button while the focus frame is activated for moving.

Then press the Menu/OK button, and you will see the focus frame, now turned white, at its new location, as shown in FIGURE 2-11.

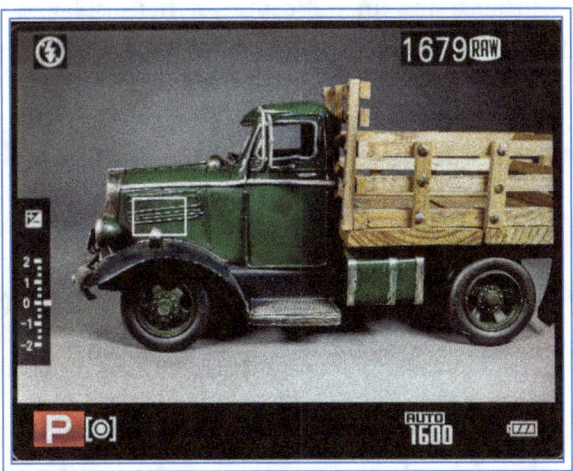

Figure 2-11. Area AF Frame - Moved to Front of Truck

Now, when you aim the camera at a subject, place the white focus frame over the most important object in the scene. Press the shutter button halfway so the camera will evaluate exposure and focus. You should hear a beep and the focus frame should turn green to confirm the focus. (If the frame turns red, that indicates a focusing problem; you may be too close to the subject or it may be difficult to focus on.) If everything looks okay to you, go ahead and press the shutter button all the way to take the picture.

If you want to change the size of the focus frame in Area mode, after pressing the AF button to activate the movable frame, press the Command Control to the left to make the frame smaller or to the right to make it larger. (The Command Control is the small black switch at the top right of the camera's back, below the shutter speed and exposure compensation dials.) To return the frame to its normal size, press in on the Command Control.

The Area autofocus option is useful when you need to focus on a person or object that is not located in the center of the frame, because you can easily move the focus frame to cover that subject. If you are faced with this type of scene and don't remember how to move the focus frame or don't have time to move it, there is another way to handle the focus situation. Aim the camera so that the white focus frame (in the center of the display) covers the most important subject, and press the shutter button halfway to lock in focus and exposure. Then, still holding the shutter button halfway down, move the camera to compose the scene the way you want it, with the subject off to one side. The focus will remain locked, and you can now press the shutter button all the way down to take the picture.

Finally, there is one more way to set the focus where you want it—by using the AFL/AEL button to lock focus. The use of this button, which is located to the upper left of the Command Dial and to the right of the top of the LCD screen, is determined by settings on the fourth screen of the Shooting menu, as discussed in Chapter 4. Depending on these settings, after pressing the shutter button halfway to focus, you can press and hold the AFL/AEL button (or press and release it) to lock focus on a particular subject, and then recompose the shot with that subject moved off-center. The focus will remain locked at the proper distance until the focus lock is released by pressing the button again or by releasing it, depending on the menu setting for the button's action.

Manual Focus

There are other autofocus settings, but I won't discuss those at this point. (See Chapters 5 and 9 for discussions of Macro focus and Chapters 4 and 7 for discussion of focus options on the Shooting and Setup menus.) Now I will talk about manual focus, the other major option for focusing. Why would you want to use manual focus when the camera will focus for you automatically? Many experienced photographers like the amount of control that comes from being able to set the focus exactly how they want it. And, in some situations, such as focusing in dark areas or on areas behind glass or through wire fences, taking extreme closeups, or when there are objects at various distances from the camera, it is important to be able to control exactly where the point of sharpest focus lies.

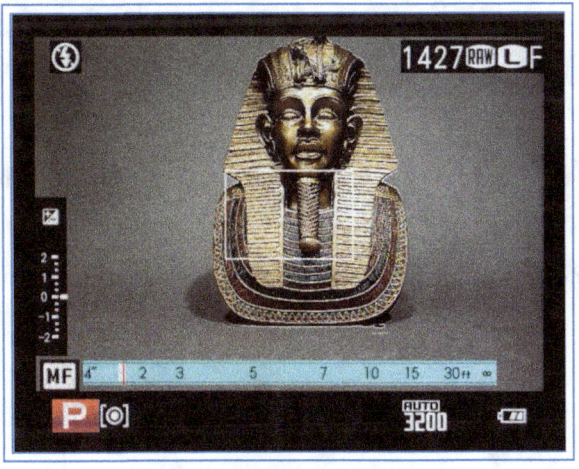

Figure 2-12. Manual Focus Scale

To activate manual focus, set the slide switch on the left side of the camera to its top position, marked with the letters MF. To adjust focus, turn the focus ring right or left. That ring is the ridged one with no numbers, farther from the camera's body than the aperture ring. As you move the focus point, you will see a red indicator bar move left and right along a scale at the bottom of the display, indicating the approximate focusing distance, as shown in FIGURE 2-12.

You may find it difficult to determine the sharpest focus using the normal view on the LCD screen or in the viewfinder. If so, you can press and release the center of the Command Control (the small switch above the AFL/AEL button) and the display area will be enlarged to help you focus on details in the subject. Press the Command Control again to return to the normal display. (If you need further focusing assistance, the MF Assist menu option on the third screen of the Shooting menu provides two other options, discussed in Chapter 4—Digital Split Image and Focus Peaking.)

Continue turning the focus ring until the focus is as sharp as you can get it, and then take the picture.

If you want the camera to provide autofocus assistance as you adjust manual focus by turning the focus ring, you can short-cut the process by pressing the AFL/AEL button, located to the right of the top of the LCD. When you press that button, the autofocus mechanism will take over and, if it can, pull the image into focus with a beep. Then you can continue to adjust the focus manually by turning the focus ring until the image is as sharp as you can get it.

Another suggestion for using manual focus (which applies for autofocus as well) is to use the electronic viewfinder rather than the LCD or the optical viewfinder. It often seems to be easier to achieve sharp focus using the electronic viewfinder.

EXPOSURE

Next, I will discuss some possibilities for controlling exposure, beyond just letting the camera make the decisions. The X100S's Program mode is very good at choosing the right exposure, but there will be some situations in which you want to override the camera's automation.

Exposure Compensation

First, let's take a look at the control for adjusting exposure to account for an unusual, or non-optimal, lighting situation. For example, consider FIGURE 2-13, in which the camera was aimed at a firefighter figurine against a white background. The figurine was fairly dark, but the large background area was bright white.

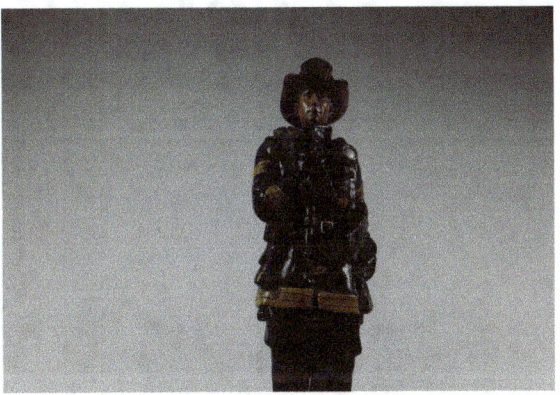

Figure 2-13. Image in Need of Exposure Compensation

In this image, the camera exposed for the brighter area, and, as it is programmed to do, it exposed the image to make the overall scene, including the background, appear moderately exposed, which resulted in the background being gray and the figurine appearing too dark.

One solution for this situation is to use the exposure compensation control. With many modern digital cameras, exposure compensation has to be adjusted by pressing a button and then manipulating a scale of adjustments on the camera's screen using a dial or buttons. With the X100S, the Fujifilm engineers have provided a refreshingly simple way to make this adjustment—by turning a dial that is dedicated to exposure compensation.

This dial is at the far right of the camera's top surface, and is of a generous size, with clear markings. To adjust exposure compensation, just turn the dial to a positive or negative value, up to two units in either direction.

As you do so, you will see a white pointer extend above or below the zero point on the scale at the far left side of the display, as shown in FIGURE 2-14.

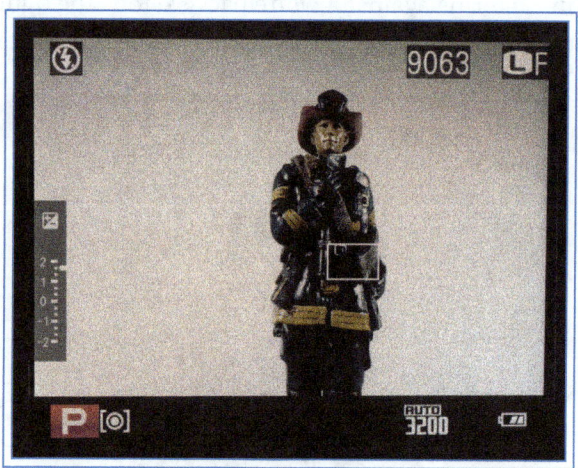

Figure 2-14. Exposure Compensation Scale on Screen

With a negative value, the image will be darker than it otherwise would; with a positive value, it will be brighter. If you are using the LCD display or the electronic viewfinder, the display will grow darker or brighter to indicate the effect of the adjustment. Exposure compensation has no effect when the camera is set to Manual exposure mode; if you turn the dial in that mode, you will see no change in the exposure scale.

With exposure compensation adjusted upward by 1.67 EV (exposure value), as shown in FIGURE 2-15, the figurine and the background both appear brighter and are no longer underexposed.

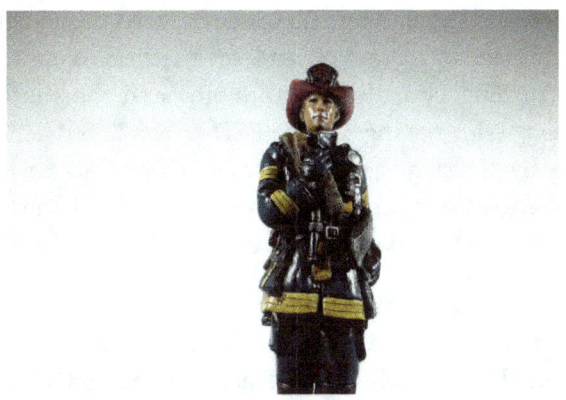

Figure 2-15. Final Image with Exposure Compensation Added

Once you've taken the picture, you should turn the exposure compensation dial back to the zero mark so you won't inadvertently change the exposure of later images that don't need the adjustment. I'll discuss exposure compensation further in Chapter 5.

FLASH

Later on, in Chapters 3 and 5, I'll discuss several other topics dealing with exposure, such as the Manual, Aperture Priority, and Shutter Priority shooting modes, exposure bracketing, and others. For now I'm going to discuss the basics of using the X100S's built-in flash unit, because that is something you may need to use on a regular basis. In Chapter 5, I'll discuss the use of the Flash button, in Chapter 9 I'll discuss other options for using the flash, such as controlling its output and preventing "red-eye," and in Appendix A, I'll discuss using other flash units.

The built-in flash on the X100S is not especially powerful, but it can provide enough illumination to let you take pictures in dark areas and to brighten up subjects that would otherwise be lost in shadows, even outdoors on a sunny day. As with several features of the X100S, the use of the flash is not as obvious or automatic as similar features on less advanced cameras. But, when you have used the flash once or twice, the procedure should become quite clear.

Let's explore a common scenario to see how the flash works. Make sure the camera is turned on and set to the Program shooting mode by turning both the aperture ring and the shutter speed dial to their red A settings. If the LCD screen is not active, select its display by pressing the View Mode button at the far left of the camera's back. Make sure the live view is displayed on the LCD. If it is not, press the Display/Back button until that view appears.

Now press the Flash button, and you will see a horizontal menu of flash options appear on the screen—Auto Flash, Forced Flash, Suppressed Flash, Slow Synchro, Flash Commander, and External Flash, as shown in FIGURE 2-16—if you're using the LCD screen or the electronic viewfinder.

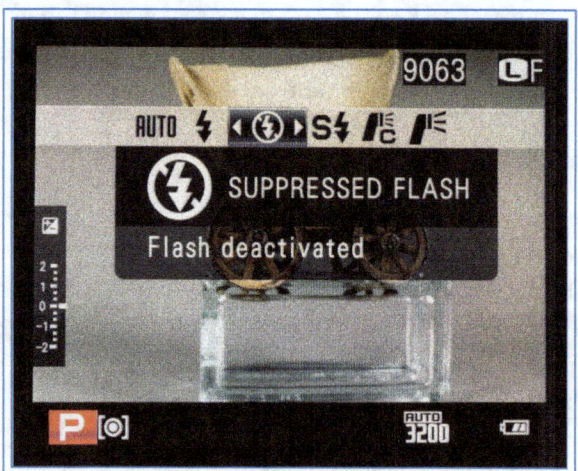

Figure 2-16. Flash Mode Menu

If you're using the optical viewfinder, you will see an individual flash mode icon in the upper left corner of the display; that icon will change as you cycle through the flash options. If you have Red Eye Removal turned on in the fifth screen of the Shooting menu, some of these flash options will include Red Eye in their names and will display an eye icon to indicate red-eye removal. The discussion here assumes that that option is turned off.

When the flash options appear, quickly press the Right or Left button, turn the Command Dial, or press the Command Control right or left, to cycle through the choices. (I prefer to just keep pressing the Right button, because that is also the Flash button, so you don't have to switch to another control.)

When Auto Flash is displayed, release the button or dial, and that option will be selected. You will not see any flash icon in the upper left corner of the screen for Auto Flash; for any of the other flash modes, you will see the appropriate icon displayed there.

With Auto Flash selected, aim the camera at your subject and press the shutter button halfway to evaluate exposure and focus. If the camera has determined that flash is needed, you will see a lightning bolt icon appear against a white background in the upper left corner of the screen, as shown in FIGURE 2-17, meaning that the camera will fire the flash when you press the shutter button to take the picture. If you don't see that icon, the flash will not fire.

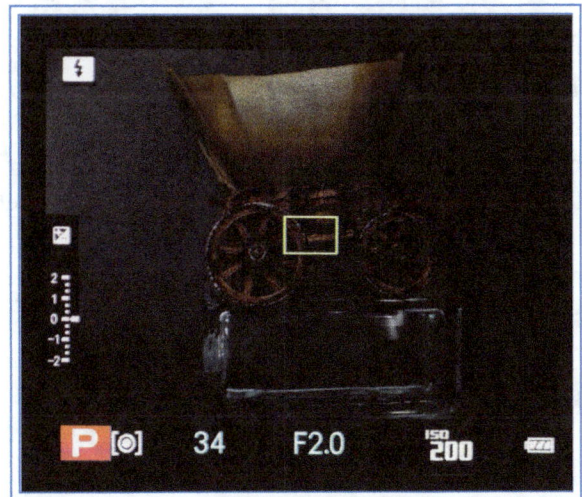

Figure 2-17. Icon Meaning Flash Will Be Fired

If, instead of Auto Flash, you choose Forced Flash, you will see the white lightning bolt icon on the screen at all times, as shown in FIGURE 2-18, and the flash will fire regardless of whether the camera's exposure system believes flash is needed.

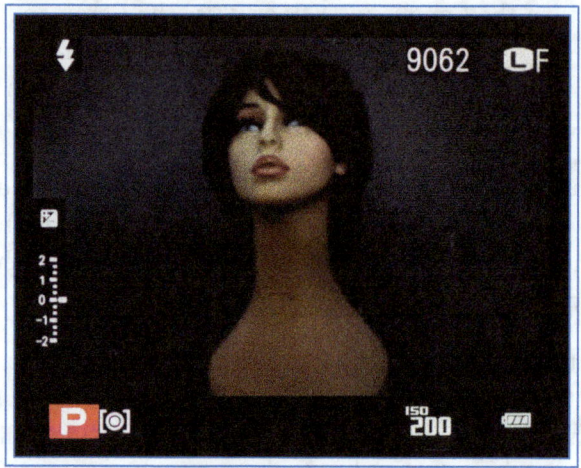

Figure 2-18. Forced Flash Icon

This setting, sometimes called "fill flash," can be of use in some outdoor settings, such as when you need to reduce the shadows on your subject's face. I will provide an example of the use of fill flash in Chapter 9.

If you choose Suppressed Flash, a no-flash icon will appear on the screen—that is, a lightning bolt inside the universal negative symbol of a circle with a diagonal line through it, as shown in FIGURE 2-19. With this setting, the flash will not fire under any circumstances. This option is useful if you are in a museum or other place where flash is not permitted, or if you just don't want any added light on your scene.

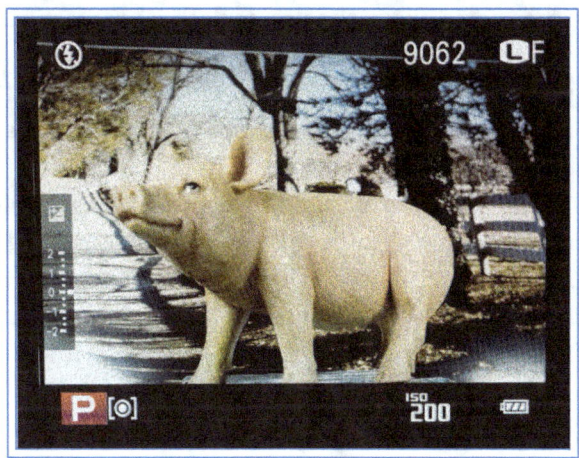

Figure 2-19. Suppressed Flash Icon

Finally, if you select Slow Synchro, indicated by an S next to the lightning bolt icon, as shown in FIGURE 2-20, the camera will try to select a slow shutter speed so the background will be illuminated by ambient light from the long exposure, while the flash lights the foreground subject.

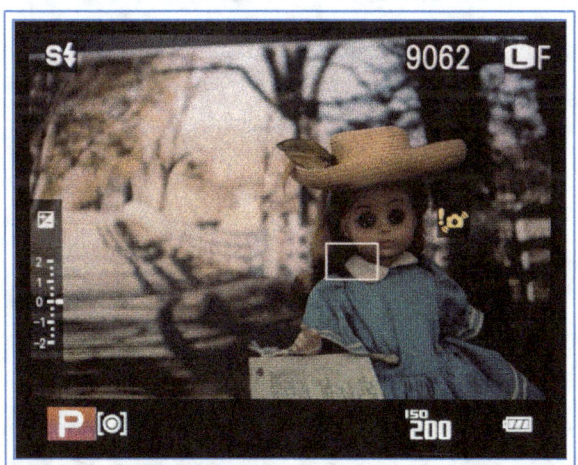

Figure 2-20. Slow Synchro Icon

I will discuss this mode and two others—Commander and External Flash—in Chapter 9.

Some further notes about the use of flash: If you activate Silent Mode by selecting the Silent Mode option on the first screen of the Setup menu or by holding down the Display/Back button, the camera suppresses all of its operational sounds, and the flash is deactivated and cannot be turned on. In this situation, if you try to select a flash mode the camera will display a message telling you to turn off Silent Mode, which you can do by pressing and holding the Display/Back button. The flash also cannot be activated if any of the burst-shooting options are activated using the Drive button. Those shooting options are discussed in Chapter 5.

Motion Picture Recording

Let's take a look at recording a short video sequence with the X100S. In Chapter 8, I'll discuss other options for video recording, but for now I will stick to the basics. Once the camera is turned on, press the Drive button, in the line of controls at the left of the camera's back. Scroll to the very bottom of the line of icons that appears at the left of the screen, until you have highlighted the Movie option, as shown in FIGURE 2-21.

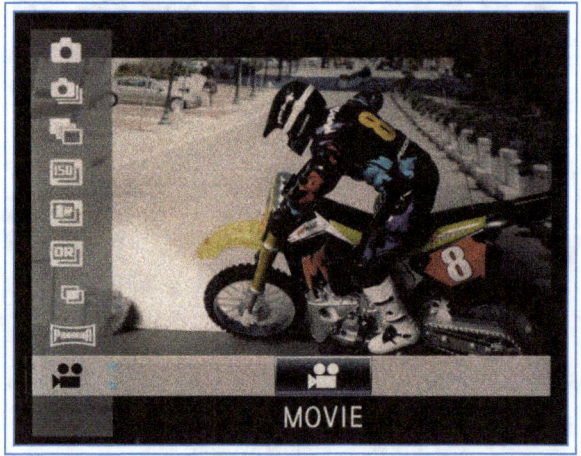

Figure 2-21. Movie Option Highlighted on Drive Menu

(It may be easiest to scroll up past the top of the list, and wrap around to the bottom of the list.)

Then set the aperture ring around the lens to its red A setting. (You can leave the shutter speed dial at any setting; it has no effect for video recording.) Slide the focus switch to the AF-C position. Next, press the Menu button to get access to the Shooting menu. You will notice that the menu is still called the Shooting menu, but the movie camera icon is displayed, and the options on the menu have changed, because the camera is set to record videos, not still images. There are only five options available on this menu, as shown in FIGURE 2-22—Movie Mode, Film Simulation, Mic Level Adjustment, Display Custom Setting, and Wide Conversion Lens.

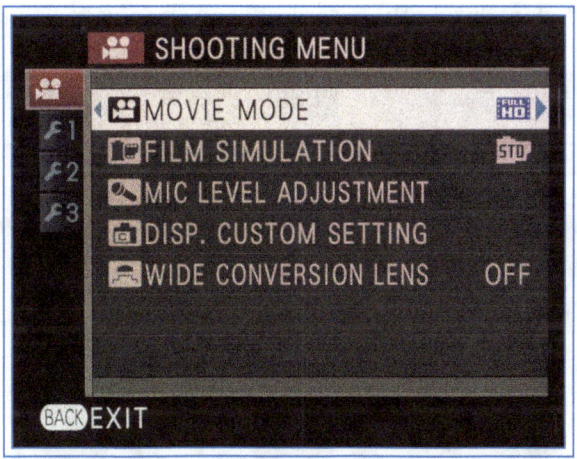

Figure 2-22. Shooting Menu Screen in Movie Mode

You can skip the Movie Mode setting for now; I'll discuss it in Chapter 8. Select whatever film setting you would like: Provia (standard), Velvia (vivid), Astia (soft), Pro Negative Hi or Standard, or one of the monochrome choices. (See Chapter 4 for a discussion of the Film Simulation options.) You can ignore the Display Custom Setting menu option for now; it provides choices for the information that appears on the screen while you're shooting movies. If you want, you can use the Mic Level Adjustment option to change the input volume of the recording, though the standard level of 3 is appropriate for most situations. The Wide Conversion Lens setting is needed only if you're using Fujifilm's optional add-on lens, which is discussed in Appendix A.

Finally, press the Down button, labeled WB, and select a White Balance setting from the menu. If you're unsure of which to choose, pick Auto for now. Otherwise, pick an appropriate preset value, such as Fine (for sunlight), Shade, Incandescent, or another, depending on the environment you'll be shooting your movie in.

That is all the preparation you need at this point. Now compose the shot the way you want it, and when you're ready, press the shutter button. You don't need to hold the button down; just press and let it go. The reddish indicator light on the camera's back will glow during the recording, and the screen will display a flashing red symbol, as well as a countdown of the minutes and seconds remaining for the recording, as shown in FIGURE 2-23.

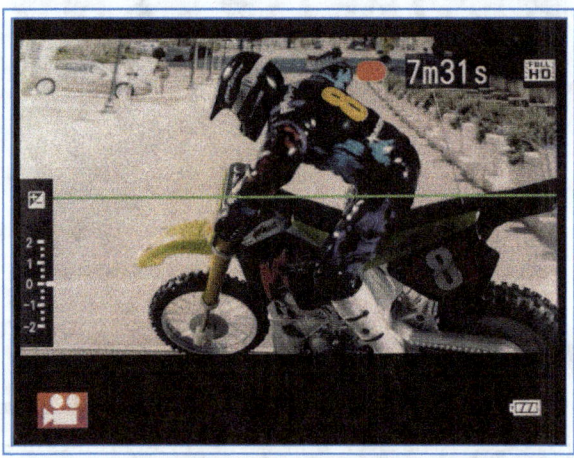

Figure 2-23. Shooting Screen While Recording Movie

The camera will keep shooting until it reaches a recording limit or you press the shutter button again to stop the recording. (You only have to press it halfway to stop the recording, although you have to press it fully to start the recording.)

The camera will automatically adjust exposure as lighting conditions change. Note that the time limit for any single recording is 10 minutes. After that time, the recording will stop, even if there is space remaining on the memory card. You can start a new recording as soon as the indicator light goes out, but you cannot record a single video sequence longer than 10 minutes.

One other point that's not specific to the X100S: Unless you have a good reason to do otherwise, try to hold the camera as steady as you can (using a tripod if possible), and don't move the camera except in very smooth, slow motions, such as a pan (side-to-side motion) to take in a wide scene gradually. Video from a jerkily moving camera can be very disconcerting to the viewer.

Those are the basics for recording video clips with the X100S. I'll discuss the movie options in more detail in Chapter 8.

Viewing Pictures

Before I delve into more advanced settings for taking still pictures and movies, as well as other matters of interest, I will discuss the basics of viewing your images in the camera.

REVIEW WHILE IN SHOOTING MODE

First, every time you take a still picture, the recorded image will appear on the display (LCD or EVF, depending on your choice) for a brief amount of time, if you have the Setup menu's Screen Set-up/Image Display option set to turn on this function. I'll discuss the details of that setting in Chapter 7. By default, your image will stay on the screen for about 0.5 second after you take a new picture. If you prefer, you can set that display to last for 1.5 seconds, to last until you press the OK button, or to be off altogether.

Reviewing Images in Playback Mode

If you are reviewing images that were taken previously, you enter playback mode by pressing the Playback button, marked with a small green triangle, to the left of the top edge of the LCD screen. You can then scroll through the recorded images using the Left and Right buttons or by turning the Command Dial. If you hold down the Left or Right button, the pictures will scroll rapidly.

You can enlarge any image by pressing the AE/Zoom-in button to the left of the LCD, and you can zoom back out using the Drive/ Zoom-out button. Repeated presses bring greater zoom levels. You can scroll around in an enlarged image using all four direction buttons.

If you have used the continuous-shooting feature of the camera, you will see some images that display a small inset image in the lower right, and that initially display a down-pointing triangle along with the message, PLAY CONTINUOUS SHOTS, as shown in Figure 2-24.

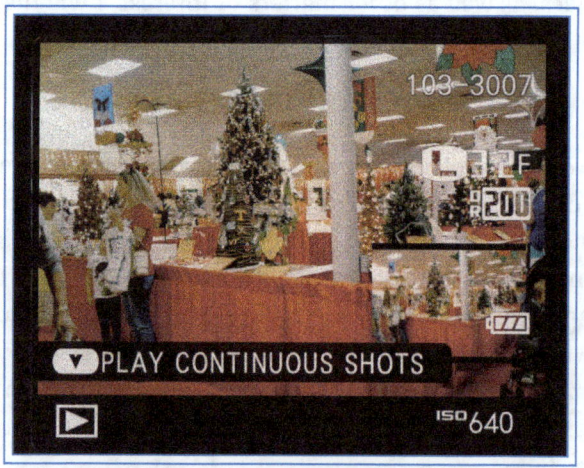

Figure 2-24. Message for Playing Continuous Shots

(That message disappears after about a second.) In that case, you can press the Down button to "open" a series of continuous shots, and then use the Left and Right buttons to move among the various individual shots in the series. To exit back to the main viewing screen so you can see other images and series of images, press the Display/Back button, as prompted by the camera's display. If you want to view only the first image in each series of images, just continue to scroll through the images normally without "opening" the sequence of continuous shots with the down button. (I'll discuss playback options in more detail in Chapter 6.)

PLAYING MOVIES

To play back movies, navigate through the recorded images by the methods described above until you find an image that is bordered by vertical columns of gray rounded rectangles, which represent the sprocket holes of movie film, as shown in FIGURE 2-25.

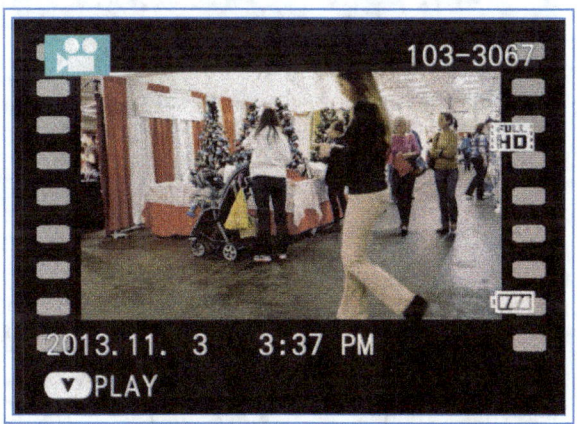

Figure 2-25. Movie Ready to Play Showing Gray Sprocket Holes

With the still frame from the motion picture displayed on the camera's display, press the Down button and the movie will start playing on the LCD, or in the electronic viewfinder if that display option is active instead of the LCD.

At the top of the display there will be a gray bar that moves across the screen to show the progress of the playback, as shown in FIGURE 2-26. You can pause and resume playback using the Down button and stop playback completely with the Up button. While the movie is paused, you can move through it one frame at a time using the Left and Right buttons. While it is playing, you can fast-forward at increasing speeds by pressing the Right button repeatedly, and you can rewind in the same way using the Left button. To adjust the volume of the sound, press the OK button in the center of the Command Dial to pause the playback, and then increase or decrease volume using the Up and Down buttons or by turning the Command Dial right or left.

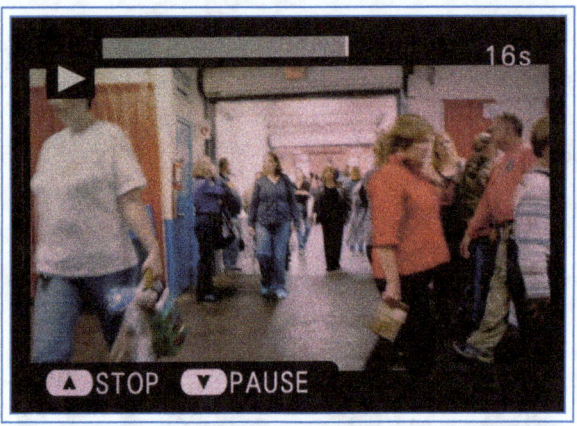

Figure 2-26. Progress Bar While Movie Playing

If you want to play the movies on a computer or edit them with video-editing software, they will import nicely into software such as iMovie for the Macintosh or any other program for Mac or Windows that can deal with video files with the extension .mov. This is the extension for Apple Computer's QuickTime video playback software; QuickTime itself can be downloaded from Apple's web site. For some Windows-based video-editing software, you may need to convert the X100S's movie files to the .avi format before importing them into the software. You can do so with a program such as mp4cam2avi, which can be found at http://sourceforge.net/projects/mp4cam2avi/.

CHAPTER 3:
The Shooting Modes

U p until now I have discussed the basics of setting up the X100S camera for stills and videos, relying on Program mode for capturing scenes with settings that depend largely on the camera's automation. As with other sophisticated digital cameras, though, with the X100S there is a wide range of options available for setting the camera, particularly for recording still images. One of the main goals of this book is to explain those options clearly and concisely. To do this, I need to turn my attention to several areas, including shooting modes, menu options, and the functions of the camera's physical controls. In this chapter, I will discuss the shooting modes and how to take advantage of the particular strengths of each one. In Chapters 4 and 5 I will cover the Shooting menu and the physical controls.

Whenever you set out to record still images, you need to select one of the available shooting modes: Program, Aperture Priority, Shutter Priority, or Manual exposure. So far, we have worked only with the Program mode, because it is the best one to start with when you want to take pictures with the camera without too much difficulty. Now it is time to discuss all four of these basic modes in some detail.

Before discussing these modes, though, it is worthwhile to point out one important characteristic of the X100S: This camera does not come equipped with any "automatic" or "scene" modes, which are a prominent feature on many compact cameras, even quite sophisticated ones like the Leica D-Lux 6 and the Sony DSC-RX100 II. Those modes, with names like Portrait, Beach, Sports, Fireworks, and Sunset, let the photographer make a single selection that sets the camera with what the manufacturer considers to be optimum settings for that particular type of shot. For example, with a Sunset mode, the camera probably will emphasize the reddish hues of a sky with a setting sun; with Sports, the camera likely will use a fast shutter speed and set itself for continuous shooting to capture quick-moving action. In addition, many compact cameras have a shooting mode called "Auto" or something similar, which essentially takes over all decision-making, including determining what kind of scene is being photographed, as well as what settings to use.

However, the X100S is by no means lacking in special features. In fact, it has many settings, available through its menus and controls, which let you, the photographer, exercise a great deal of control over virtually every aspect of your still photography, including simulating various film types, controlling color, sharpening, dynamic range, sharpness, noise reduction, highlights, and shadows, besides the standard items that most high-quality compact cameras offer control over, including White Balance, ISO, and image size and quality.

In other words, what the X100S lacks in "automatic" or "scene" modes, it more than makes up for in the sophistication of the control it provides to the photographer over all aspects of his or her shooting. It just takes some digging in to the details of the menus and controls to understand how to use that level of control to best advantage.

One last note on shooting modes with the X100S: If you have used other recent models of compact cameras, you may have become used to selecting a shooting mode using a control that is usually called a "mode dial." This is a selector knob on top of the camera that lets you select one of the "auto" or "scene" modes, as well as, usually, the standard four modes of Program,

Aperture Priority, Shutter Priority, and Manual exposure. (Not all cameras have all of these modes, of course.) These last four modes are sometimes designated as PASM. The X100S has the PASM modes, but no other modes for shooting stills, and it has no mode dial. The modes are all easily selected, but here, again, Fujifilm appears to be assuming that users of this camera will have no problem in learning how to make adjustments that require some understanding of basic photographic principles.

Program Mode

This is the only shooting mode I have discussed in any detail up to this point. Program mode provides more automation than any other mode on the X100S, but it still requires you to make sure several basic settings are adjusted the ways you want them or you risk ending up with results that are unexpected or even unusable.

To set this mode, turn the aperture ring (the large numbered ring around the lens, closest to the camera's body) so the red letter A is next to the indicator line, as shown in FIGURE 3-1.

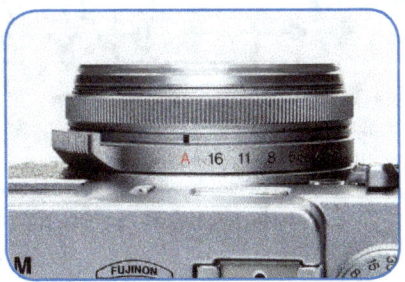

Figure 3-1. Aperture Ring at A Position

This setting tells the camera to set the aperture automatically. Then turn the shutter speed dial (the round knob on top of the camera next to the flash shoe) so that its red A is next to the similar indicator line, to make the shutter speed setting automatic as well, as shown in FIGURE 3-2.

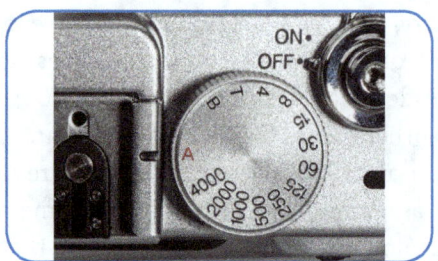

Figure 3-2. Shutter Speed Dial at A Setting

You will now see a large white P against a red background at the bottom left of the display, to indicate that Program mode is selected, as shown in FIGURE 3-3.

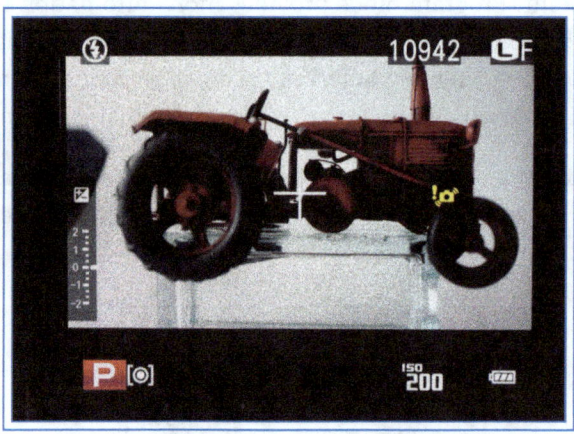

Figure 3-3. Program Mode Icon on Screen

(There will be no red background if you are using the optical viewfinder instead of the LCD or the electronic viewfinder, and there will be no P if you have selected certain other settings, such as the Panorama or Multiple Exposure setting on the Drive menu.)

Now, just aim at your subject, and the camera's autoexposure metering system will evaluate the available light and select both a shutter speed and an aperture that will result in a normal exposure, taking into account all of the settings that have been made, including metering mode, ISO, Dynamic Range, and others. The shutter speed will appear directly to the right of the P indicating Program mode, and the aperture will appear to the right of that value, as shown in FIGURE 3-4, where the values are 1/80 second and f/5.0.

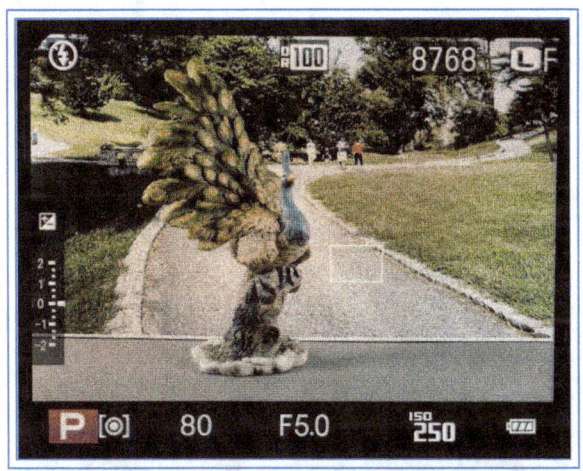

Figure 3-4. White Aperture and Shutter Speed Numbers in Program Mode

In some circumstances, the values selected by the camera for shutter speed and aperture will appear on the screen automatically, before you press the shutter button halfway to evaluate exposure, and in other cases the values will not appear until you press the button. This different behavior depends on the settings you make for two other menu options: ISO and Dynamic Range, both of which I will discuss in Chapter 4. ISO is a measure of the light sensitivity of the image sensor; with higher values, the camera needs less light to expose the image. Dynamic Range is a setting that can be increased to let the camera record better details from areas in shadows and bright highlights. If either of those two options is set to its Auto setting, then the camera will not display the shutter speed or aperture until you press the shutter button halfway. However, if you have set both ISO and Dynamic Range to specific numerical values (such as, for example, ISO 400 and Dynamic Range 200%), then the camera will display the shutter speed and aperture it has selected constantly, as the lighting conditions change. In addition, if the camera displays these values before you press the shutter button, it will display them in white, as shown in FIGURE 3-4; if it displays them only after you press the shutter button, it will display them in blue, as shown in FIGURE 3-5.

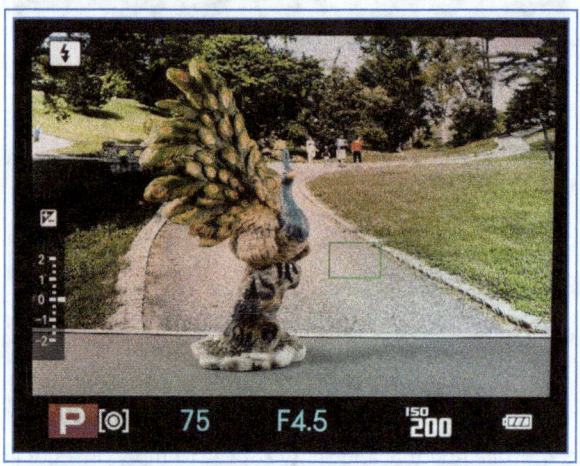

Figure 3-5. Blue Aperture and Shutter Speed Numbers in Program Mode

So, if you see white numbers on the display, that means you have both ISO and Dynamic Range set to specific values.

Program mode lets you control many of the settings available with the camera, except for the two that you have just set to be automatic—shutter speed and aperture. Even though you can't directly set those two values, though, you still can override the camera's automatic exposure to a fair extent by using exposure compensation, Program Shift, and exposure bracketing. I discussed exposure compensation in Chapter 2, and I'll discuss it further, along with exposure bracketing, in Chapter 5.

Program Shift is a feature that lets you adjust the pair of values the camera selects in Program mode for shutter speed and aperture. For example, if the camera selects, say, 1/80 second at f/3.4, the Program Shift feature will find equivalent combinations that result in the same exposure, such as 1/60 second at f/3.5,

1/50 second at f/4.0, or 1/40 second at 4.5. To use this option, when the camera is in Program mode, aim at your subject and let the camera's metering system evaluate the exposure. The selected shutter speed and f-stop (aperture setting) will appear to the right of the P for Program mode. Then, just turn the Command Dial right or left or press the Command Control right or left to find an equivalent set of shutter speed and aperture. When the camera is using one of these equivalent pairs of settings rather than the originally chosen setting, it displays those settings in yellow, as shown in FIGURE 3-6; the original settings selected by the camera will appear in white if you turn the control back to select them.

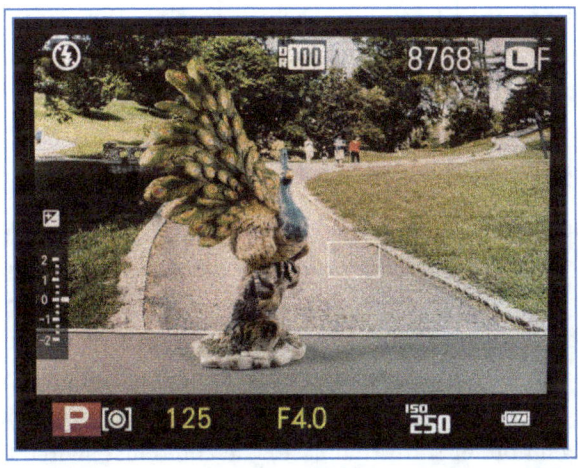

Figure 3-6. Yellow Aperture and Shutter Speed Numbers with Program Shift

Note that in some cases Program Shift is not available, and turning the Command Dial will not change the camera's settings of aperture and shutter speed. Those cases are when the flash is turned on to any setting when it might fire, including Auto Flash; when the Dynamic Range option on the Shooting menu is set to Auto; or when the ISO option on the Shooting menu is set to Auto. One way to tell whether or not Program Shift is available is to see whether, as discussed above, the camera displays both shutter speed and aperture automatically before you press the shutter button halfway, and displays them in white. If so, then Program Shift is available. Otherwise, it is not available.

Why would you use the Program Shift option? Does it make sense to let the camera make its best calculation of the proper exposure and then override it? It may, in some cases. For example, you may want to see what the camera calculates as the normal exposure, and then decide if you can use a somewhat wider aperture to achieve a blurred background, or a somewhat faster shutter speed to stop the action or prevent blur from camera motion. And, when you're experimenting with the camera to see what it is capable of, it can be very helpful to try various combinations of aperture and shutter speed to find out which combination gives you the best results in different situations. With a digital camera, there's no added cost for trying these different approaches, and Program Shift is one good way to experiment.

There is one limitation of Program mode that is worth remembering: With this mode, the slowest shutter speed that the camera will select is ¼ second. In all other modes, the camera can be set to shutter speeds as slow as 30 seconds, and in Manual exposure mode you can select the Bulb setting, which I will discuss later in this chapter. In Program mode, though, even if the lighting conditions would call for a speed of, say, 2 seconds, the camera will not set it. In that case, you could just switch to one of the other shooting modes and make the appropriate settings.

One final note: If the camera selects a shutter speed of 1/30 second or slower, it will display a yellow icon, as shown in FIGURE 3-7, which is a warning about the problem of blurred images from camera shake at such a slow speed. (This icon will not be displayed if you are using the optical viewfinder.)

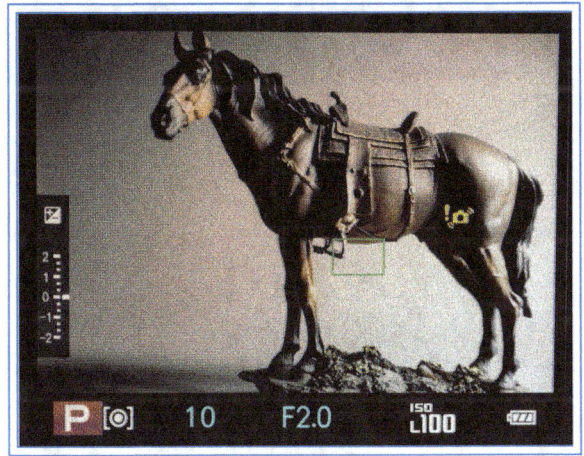

Figure 3-7. Yellow Icon for Slow Shutter Speed

Shutter Priority Mode

In Shutter Priority mode, you choose whatever shutter speed you want, and the camera will set the corresponding aperture in order to achieve a proper exposure of the image. In this mode, you can set the shutter to be open for a variety of intervals ranging from 30 full seconds to 1/4000 of a second in some circumstances. If you are photographing fast action, such as a baseball swing or a hurdles event at a track meet and you want to stop the action with a minimum of blur, you will want to select a fast shutter speed, such as 1/1000 of a second. In other cases, for creative purposes, you may want to select a slow shutter speed to achieve a certain effect, such as leaving the shutter open to capture a trail of automobiles' taillights at night.

Controlling shutter speed is a powerful tool for creative photography. Here are two examples, for which I used the shutter speed to achieve a certain effect. For FIGURE 3-8, I used a shutter speed of 1/1000 second to freeze a group of playing cards as they fell through the air, giving an appearance of an action from a magic trick.

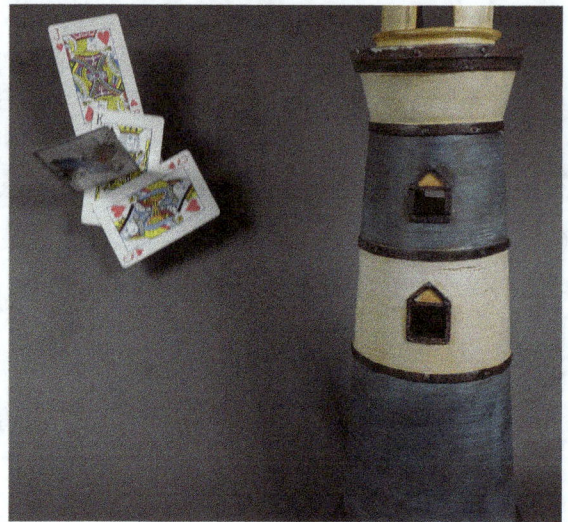

Figure 3-8. Action Stopped with Shutter Speed of 1/1000 Second

For FIGURE 3-9, I used a shutter speed of two full seconds to capture an image at a holiday craft show. The long shutter speed blurred the action and smeared the colorful display, giving it an impressionistic appearance.

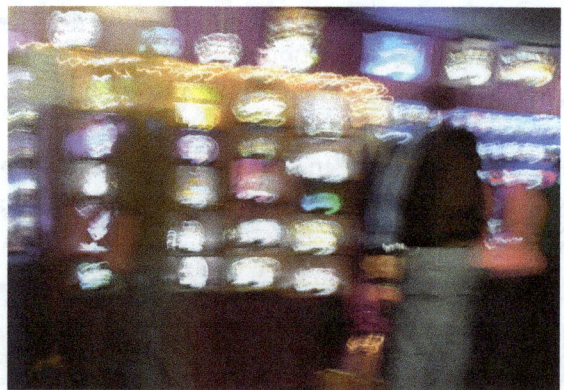

Figure 3-9. Image Blurred with Shutter Speed of Two Seconds

You select the Shutter Priority mode by setting the aperture dial around the lens to the red A that indicates the automatic setting for aperture, as shown in FIGURE 3-10.

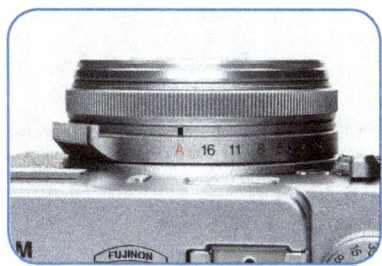

Figure 3-10. Aperture Ring at A Position

Then you select the shutter speed by turning the shutter speed dial. The LCD (or viewfinder, if selected) will display the selected shutter speed at the bottom left of the screen, to the right of the S indicating Shutter Priority mode, as shown in FIGURE 3-11.

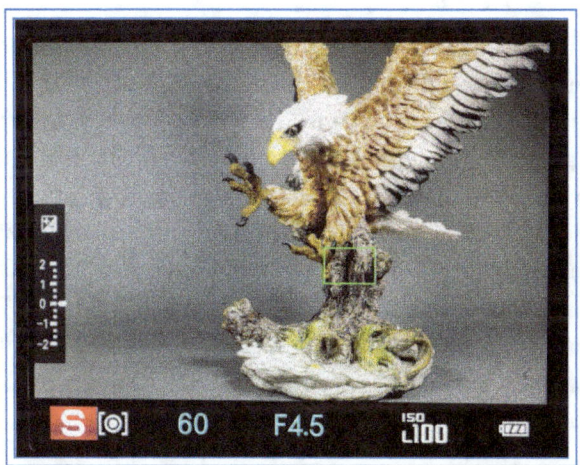

Figure 3-11. Aperture and Shutter Speed in Shutter Priority Mode

As you point the camera at scenes with varying lighting, the camera will select and display the appropriate aperture (such as f/4.5, for example, displayed as F4.5 on the screen in FIGURE 3-11) to achieve a proper exposure. In a way similar to how Program mode operates, the camera's behavior changes according to the settings for ISO and Dynamic Range. If you have specific values set for both ISO and Dynamic Range, the camera will display the selected aperture constantly and in white figures, even before you press the shutter button to evaluate exposure. If you have either ISO or Dynamic Range set to Auto, though, the camera will not display the chosen aperture until you press the shutter button halfway, and then will display it in blue figures.

Certain shutter speeds are not available directly from the dial on top of the camera, but can still be set. To select these less-common speeds, when the shutter speed dial is set to a particular number turn the Command Dial to set intermediate values. For example, if you set the shutter speed dial to the number 125, meaning 1/125 second, you can then turn the Command Dial and set the nearby speeds of 1/80, 1/100, 1/160, and 1/200 second. The next faster speed, 1/250, is a main selection, which is set on the shutter speed dial itself.

Also, although the camera's overall range of shutter speeds is from 1/4000 second to 30 seconds and Bulb, not all of these speeds are available in every situation. In particular, shutter speeds of 1/4000 and 1/3000 second are available only when the aperture is set to f/8.0 or higher (more narrow apertures); shutter speeds of 1/2000, 1/1600, and 1/1500 second are available only with apertures of f/4.0 or higher. Shutter speeds of 1/1000 second and slower are available with all aperture settings. (In Program mode, as noted earlier, the slowest shutter speed available is ¼ second.) If you select a shutter speed that is not available, it will be displayed in red numbers.

After you have selected a shutter speed and pushed the shutter button halfway down (or the camera has automatically displayed the aperture), you need to watch the aperture number on the display. If that number turns red, that means that proper exposure at the selected shutter speed is not possible at any available aperture, according to the camera's exposure metering system. For example, if you set the shutter speed to 2 seconds in a well-lighted room, the aperture (f-stop) number (which likely will be f/16.0, the most narrow setting available) may turn red, as shown in FIGURE 3-12, indicating that proper exposure is not possible.

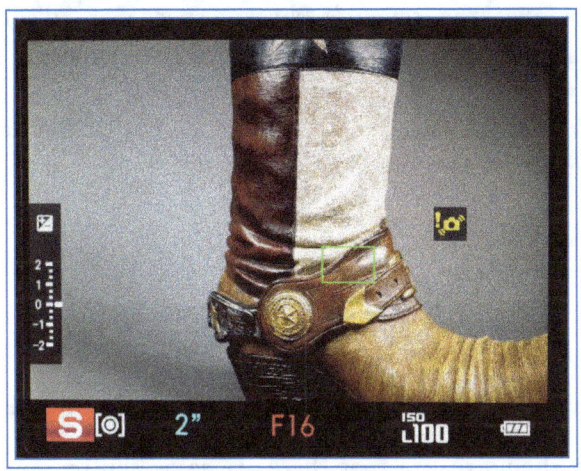

Figure 3-12. Aperture Number in Red Warning of Bad Exposure

One good thing in this situation is that the camera will still let you take the picture, despite having turned the number red to warn you. The camera is saying, in effect, "Look, you may not want to do this, but that's your business. If you want an overly bright picture for some reason, help yourself." (This situation is less likely to take place when you're using Aperture Priority mode, because in that mode, there is a wide range of shutter speeds for the camera to choose from—a range from 30 seconds to 1/4000 second in some situations, depending on various factors, as discussed later in this chapter.)

If you set the shutter speed to 1/30 second or slower, the camera will display the yellow icon that warns about the problem of camera shake at such a slow speed.

When setting the shutter speed, the faster values can be tricky to read, because only the denominator of the fractions is shown. For example, 1/500 second is shown as 500 and ½ second is shown as 2. The longer times may be easier to read; the camera displays them using quotation marks. So, for example, 2 seconds is displayed as 2", and 1.3 seconds is displayed as 1.3."

Also, some of the camera's shutter speeds are displayed as fractions whose denominators are decimal numbers, such as 1/1.3. I would have trouble understanding such numbers without doing some arithmetic, so here is a brief chart that converts these few values into terms that may be easier to comprehend:

Fractional Shutter Speeds:

1/2.5	0.4 or 2/5 second
1/1.6	0.625 or 5/8 second
1/1.3	0.77 or 10/13 second (rounded to 0.8 second)

You also should realize that there are some shutter speeds that the camera will set in Aperture Priority mode that you cannot set in Shutter Priority mode. For example, the camera may select a shutter speed of 1/2.8, 1/3.1, 1/3.5, 1/4.5, 1/5.3, and others. I have only seen it do this when either Dynamic Range or ISO is set to Auto, when you have to half-press the shutter button to get the camera to evaluate the exposure and display a shutter speed.

TIME EXPOSURES WITH THE T SETTING

As you can see by looking at the X100S's shutter speed dial, the slowest numerical shutter speed that can be set from that dial is represented by the number 4, meaning ¼ second. As noted above, you can also set the slower variations of that setting, 1/3 second, and 1/2.5 second (0.4 second) by turning the Command Dial to select the intermediate settings. If you want to set the shutter speed any slower than 1/2.5 second, you have to use the T setting, representing time exposures.

With the T setting, there is, of course, no numerical setting on the shutter speed dial itself that serves as the "main" setting, as there is for other settings. Therefore, once you have turned the dial to the T selection, you need to use the Command Dial to choose any actual shutter speed. The choices start with three numbers that appear in blue: 2, 1.6, and 1.3, representing ½ second, 1/1.6 second (0.625 second), and 1/1.3 second (0.77, rounded to 0.8 second). After that, all of the selections are followed by a double apostrophe, representing speeds of one second or slower: 1", 1.3", 1.5", 2", 2.5", 3", 4", 5", 6.5", 8", 10", 13", 15", 20", 25", and 30". This progression of speeds represents increments of 1/3 EV.

So, if you want to set an exposure for, say, 10 seconds, turn the shutter speed dial to T and turn the Command Dial until the 10" figure appears, as shown in FIGURE 3-13.

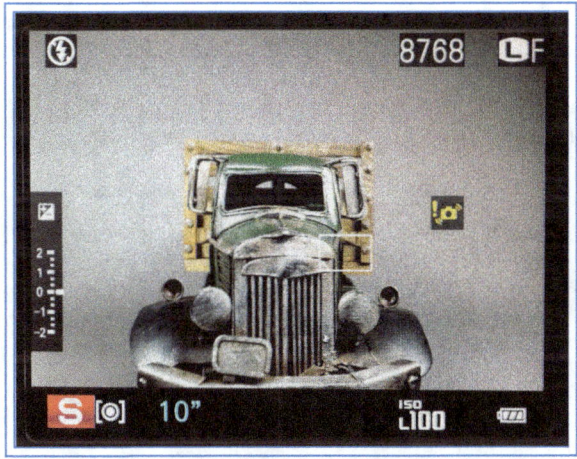

Figure 3-13. Shutter Speed Setting of Ten Seconds

When you select shutter speeds longer than one second, you should consider turning on the Long Exposure Noise Reduction option on the second screen of the Shooting menu, as discussed in Chapter 4. If you do, though, you will have to wait for the camera to process the image with noise reduction, which can take several seconds, even after waiting the several seconds for the exposure itself to take place.

Of course, you should use a tripod at these long shutter speeds, unless you are trying to create an image that includes streaks or patterns caused by camera movement during the exposure.

One last note on Shutter Priority mode: If you turn the shutter speed dial to the B setting, for Bulb exposure, the camera will automatically select a 30-second time exposure; for the B setting to have its full effect, the camera must be set to Manual exposure mode, as discussed later in this chapter.

Aperture Priority Mode

Aperture Priority mode is the inverse of Shutter Priority mode. You set this mode by turning the shutter speed dial on top of the camera to the A setting, as shown in FIGURE 3-14, meaning that the camera will set the shutter speed value automatically to expose the image properly for the aperture you set.

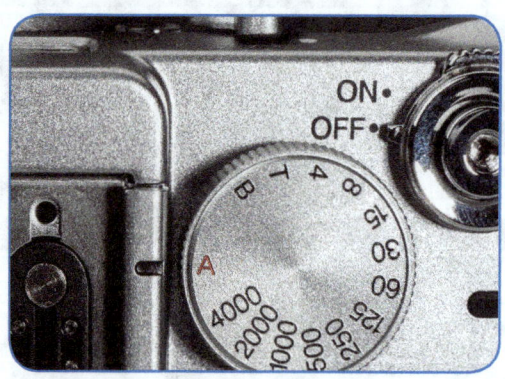

Figure 3-14. Shutter Speed Dial at A Setting

Before discussing the nuts and bolts of the settings for this mode, let's talk about what aperture is and why you would want to control it. The camera's aperture is a measure of the current width of its opening that lets in light to create the image. The aperture's width is measured numerically in f-stops. For the X100S, the range of f-stops is from f/2.0 (wide open) to f/16.0 (most narrow). The amount of light that is let into the camera to create an image on the camera's sensor is controlled by the combination of aperture (how wide open the lens is) and shutter speed (how long the shutter remains open to let in the light).

For some purposes, you may want to control the width of the aperture but still let the camera choose the corresponding shutter speed. Here is an example involving depth of field. Depth of field is a measure of how well a camera is able to keep multiple objects or subjects in focus at different distances (focal lengths). For example, say you have three of your friends lined up so you can see all of them, but they are standing at different distances—five, seven, and nine feet (1.5, 2.1, and 2.7 meters) from the camera. If the camera's depth of field is quite shallow at a particular focal length, such as five feet (1.5 meters), then, in this case, if you focus on the friend at that distance, the other two will be out of focus and blurry. But if the camera's depth of field when focused at five feet is broad, then it may be possible for all three friends to be in sharp focus in your photograph, even if the focus is set for the friend at five feet.

What does all of that have to do with aperture? One of the rules of photographic optics is that the wider open the camera's aperture is, the smaller its depth of field is at a given focal length. So in the example above, if you have the camera's aperture set to its widest opening, f/2.0, the depth of field will be relatively shallow, and it will be possible to keep fewer items in focus at varying distances from the camera. If the aperture is set to the narrowest opening, f/16.0, the depth of field will be considerably greater, and it will be possible to have more items in focus at varying distances.

The following images illustrate the effects of aperture settings on depth of field, using a small bell and an Egyptian figurine as subjects.

For FIGURE 3-15, I set the aperture of the X100S to f/2.0, the widest possible, and I focused on the bell in the foreground, using manual focus to get the image as sharp as possible. With this setting, much of the background is out of focus, because the depth of field at this aperture was quite shallow.

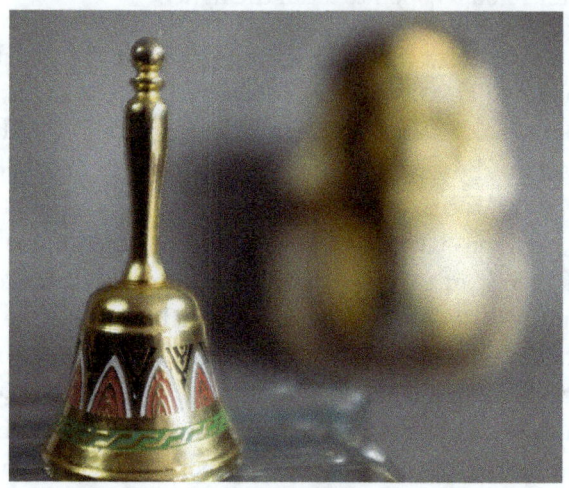

Figure 3-15. Blurred Background with Aperture Set to f/2.0

I took FIGURE 3-16 with the aperture set to f/16.0, the most narrow available with the X100S, and still focused on the bell. The result was a considerably broader depth of field, with more of the background in reasonably sharp focus.

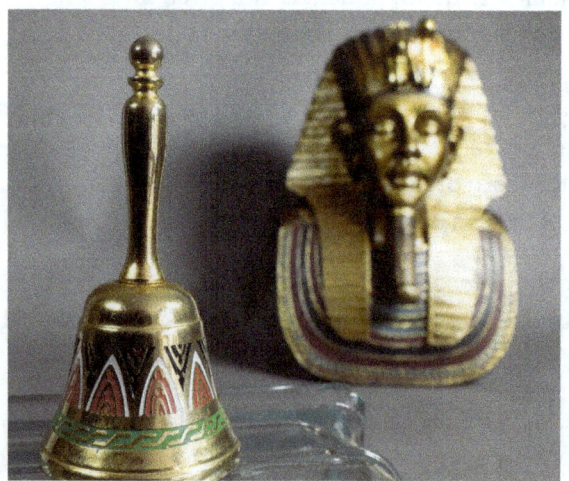

Figure 3-16. Sharper Background with Aperture Set to F/16.0

These images illustrate fairly clearly the advantage of "stopping down" to a narrow aperture such as f/16.0 when you want to enjoy a broad depth of field and keep as many subjects as possible in sharp focus.

In practical terms, if you want to have the sharpest picture possible, especially when you have subjects at varying distances from the lens and you want them to be in focus to the greatest extent possible, then you may want to control the aperture, and make sure it is set to the highest number (narrowest opening) possible.

On the other hand, there are occasions when photographers prize a shallow depth of field. This situation arises often in the case of outdoor portraits. For example, you may want to take a photo of a person standing outdoors with a background of trees and bushes, and possibly some other, more distracting objects, such as a swing set or a tool shed. If you can achieve a shallow depth of field, you can have the person's face in sharp focus, but leave the background quite blurry and indistinct. This effect is sometimes called "bokeh," a Japanese term describing an aesthetically pleasing blurriness of the background.

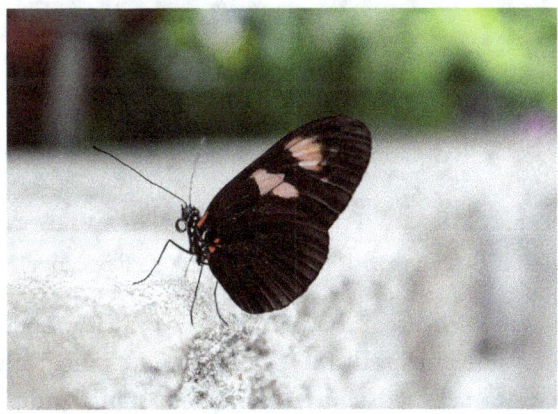

Figure 3-17. Example of Bokeh Effect (Blurred Background)

In such a situation, the blurriness of the background can be a great asset, reducing the distraction factor of unwanted objects and highlighting the sharply focused portrait of your subject.

For FIGURE 3-17, I set the X100S to a wide aperture of f/2.8, using a shutter speed of 1/60 second. With these settings, the result was an image that isolates the butterfly from its somewhat distracting surroundings, leaving the background quite blurry and indistinct.

Once you have decided what aperture you want for a particular shot, move the shutter speed dial on top of the camera to the A setting, then aim the camera at your subject and turn the aperture ring to set the aperture. The number of the f-stop will appear at the bottom center of the display, and the corresponding shutter speed chosen by the camera will appear on the display to the left of the aperture, as shown in FIGURE 3-18.

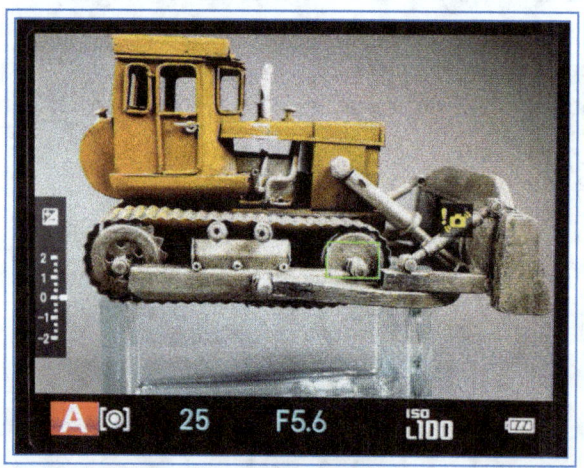

Figure 3-18. Aperture and Shutter Speed in Aperture Priority Mode

As is the case with Program and Shutter Priority modes, if you set specific values for both ISO and Dynamic Range, the camera will display its selected shutter speed constantly and in white numbers, even before you press the shutter button to evaluate exposure. If you have either ISO or Dynamic Range set to Auto, the camera will not display the shutter speed until you press the shutter button halfway, and then will display it in blue numbers, assuming the value will yield an appropriate exposure. If the exposure would not be adequate, the shutter speed number will be displayed in red.

You also have the ability to set intermediate aperture values, as with shutter speed. In this case, though, you use the Command Control (the black switch at the upper right of the camera's back) for the adjustments. Press that switch to the left or right to choose the other values. For example, when the aperture dial is set to f/5.6, you can press the Command Control to the left to select f/6.4 or f/7.1, or to the right to select f/5.0 or f/4.5.

There is one function of the X100S that is available only in Aperture Priority and Manual exposure mode, and only when the Function button (discussed in Chapters 4 and 5) is set to activate it. That is the Preview Depth of Field function. When you assign that option to the Function button, pressing that button sets the camera's aperture to the value that is selected, enabling you to see on the display screen what effect that aperture will have on the depth of field. For example, if you have set the aperture to f/8.0, while you are viewing the scene normally, the camera will not show how that setting will affect the depth of field. However, if you press the Function button, having assigned that option to the button, the display screen will "stop down" to this rather narrow aperture, becoming somewhat darker, and showing the background with greater depth of field than with the normal view.

There are some limitations on the settings that are available in Aperture Priority mode. In particular, as discussed above in connection with Shutter Priority mode, although you can set any aperture at any time, the camera will not select shutter speeds of 1/1500 second or faster unless the aperture is f/4.0 or narrower (higher numbers), and it will not select a shutter speed of 1/3000 second or faster unless the aperture is f/8.0 or narrower.

Also, when the camera is in Aperture Priority mode, the slowest shutter speed available is limited to ¼ second if the OVF Power Save Mode option is turned on in the second screen of the Setup menu. So, if you expect that the camera may need to select shutter speeds slower than that, make sure that setting is turned off.

Manual Exposure Mode

Finally, the X100S has a fully manual mode for control of exposure, which is a necessity for photographers who want to be able to choose the best settings for any given lighting situation. This is not the exposure mode you are likely to use when you are taking snapshots at a party or in any other situation in which you are photographing quickly unfolding events that won't be repeated. However, I have found myself using Manual mode more and more with various cameras in certain situations. For example, it can be beneficial to use Manual mode when I'm shooting indoors with artificial lighting with no time constraints. In this way, I can vary the shutter speed, the aperture, or both, to take shots with different levels of exposure, and choose the best one later, when editing them on my computer.

Also, in unusual lighting situations, such as taking long time exposures after sunset, Manual mode lets you experiment until you find the effect you are looking for. Here is one very specific illustration of the need to use Manual exposure mode. I have recently become interested in photographing water drops as they fall into a pan of water, and especially as two drops collide with each other, because of the beautiful patterns that often result. To accomplish these shots, I use a setup with a special device called the StopShot, made by Cognisys Systems, Inc. The equipment releases two drops in very rapid succession. As they fall toward the pan of water, their motion triggers an infrared sensor, which in turns fires a flash. The very quick burst of light from the flash illuminates the splash of the drops and freezes the action, as shown in FIGURE 3-19.

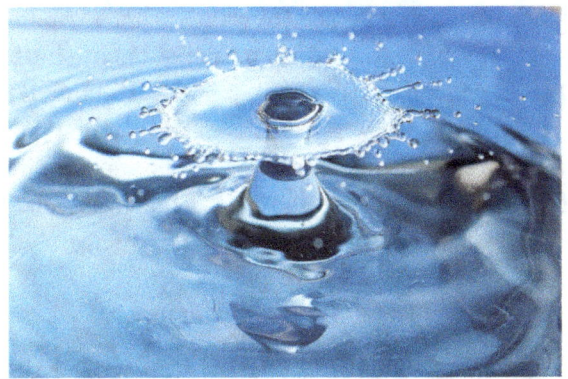

Figure 3-19. Water Drop Collision Image in Manual Exposure Mode

For this system to work, the room has to be dark, and the flash is not connected to the camera, so there is no way to use the camera's exposure metering. It is necessary to set the camera to Manual exposure mode, set the shutter speed to a value such as ¼ second, and use an aperture setting that provides a good depth of field so the area of the splash will be in clear focus. Then I turn on the Self-timer and press the shutter button. As soon as the timer finishes counting down, I trigger the water drops, and the flash should then fire just as the drops hit the water.

One other situation in which I find Manual mode to be very helpful is in creating HDR (high dynamic range) images, which combine multiple shots with different levels of brightness to end up with an image that exhibits a range of brightness values much greater than normal. When you create HDR images using software such as Photoshop, you need to take several shots of the same scene at different exposure levels, and then combine them in the software so the final image provides clear detail in both the shadowed and bright areas of the scene. One way some photographers create these images is by using autoexposure bracketing, which is a feature available with the X100S, as discussed in Chapter 4.

In my experience, though, a better way to create the component images for HDR done with software is to take multiple shots at different exposure levels using Manual exposure mode. In this way, you can, for example, set the camera on a tripod with the aperture set to, say, f/5.6, and then take shots at shutter speeds of, say, 1/500, 1/250, 1/125, 1/60, 1/30, 1/15, and 1/8 second. Some of these are likely to be considerably underexposed and some overexposed. When all of these shots are combined in the HDR software, the resulting composite image should have the characteristic super-realistic look of HDR images, as seen in FIGURE 3-20.

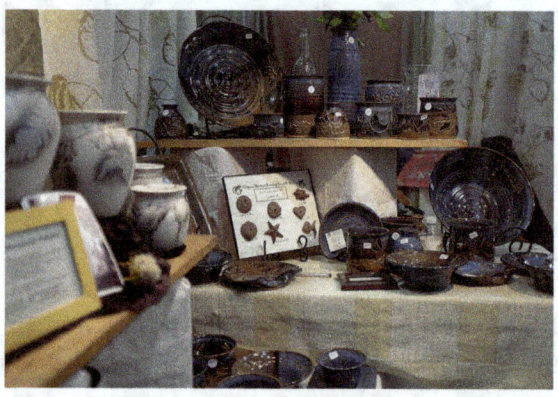

Figure 3-20. HDR Composite Image from Multiple Shots

Of course, there are other times when Manual exposure mode can be of great use, including situations in which you are looking for creative effects with underexposure or overexposure and you want to take several shots to decide which look is the best one. You also may want to use Manual mode in tricky lighting situations, when you're not sure the camera's metering system is giving the best possible exposure reading for the results you seek. And, you can use this mode to accomplish certain special effects, such as with light painting, when you use the Bulb shutter speed setting to leave the camera's shutter open for an extended period while you "paint" a subject with light from a flashlight in an otherwise dark room or outdoor setting.

The technique for using Manual exposure mode is not far removed from what I discussed in connection with Aperture Priority and

Shutter Priority modes. To control exposure manually, move both the aperture ring and the shutter speed dial away from their Automatic settings. In other words, don't set either control to the red letter A; instead, set a numerical value for each one, as shown in FIGURE 3-21.

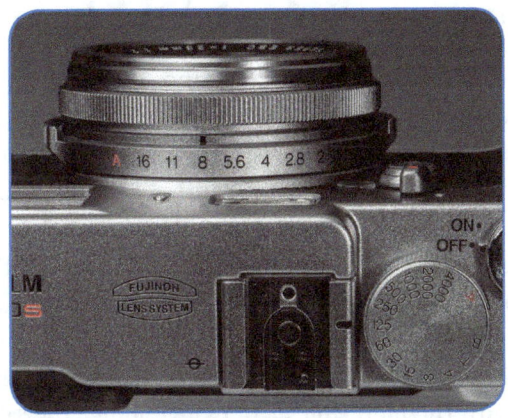

Figure 3-21. Manual Settings for Aperture and Shutter Speed

As with the other shooting modes, you will see a large letter, in this case M for Manual, at the lower left of the display, as shown in FIGURE 3-22.

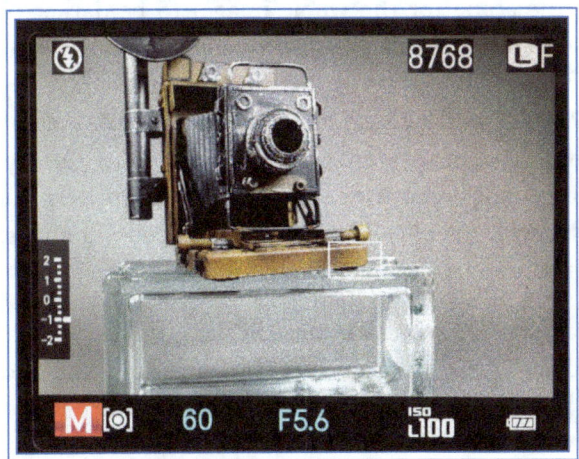

Figure 3-22. Manual Mode Settings on Screen

To the right of that letter will be the value for the shutter speed, and in the center of the display will be the aperture setting.

There also will be another change in the display. At the left of the screen is a scale with values from -2 to +2 and a pointer that appears to the right. In other shooting modes, that scale shows exposure compensation. In this mode, it has a different purpose.

As you adjust the values for aperture and shutter speed in Manual mode, watch the scale. If the pointer is at the zero mark, that means your current settings agree with the exposure setting measured by the camera. As you continue to adjust aperture or shutter speed, the pointer will move either up or down the scale. If it moves up, above the zero point, that means the current settings would result in an image that is overexposed, according to the metering system. If the pointer moves below the zero point, the resulting image would be too dark. If you want to select values that agree with the metering system, just adjust aperture, shutter speed, or both, until the pointer stops at the zero mark.

Of course, you don't have to make the white pointer meet the zero mark; that indicator exists only to give you an idea of how the camera would meter the scene. You very well may want parts of the scene (or the whole image) to be darker or lighter than the metering would indicate to be "correct." With Manual exposure mode, the settings for aperture and shutter speed are independent of each other. When you change one, the other one stays unchanged until you change it manually. The camera is leaving the creative decision about exposure entirely up to you, even if the resulting photograph would be washed out by excessive exposure or underexposed to the point of near-blackness.

Note that, just as with Aperture Priority mode, you can select intermediate aperture settings by pressing the Command Control to the right or left, and, as with Shutter Priority mode, you can select intermediate shutter speed settings by turning the Command Dial to the right or left.

As with the other shooting modes, if you set a shutter speed of 1/30 second or slower, the yellow camera-shake warning icon will appear on the LCD or electronic viewfinder display.

THE BULB EXPOSURE SETTING

Finally, there is one other aspect of Manual exposure mode that distinguishes it from all other shooting modes—the ability to make full use of the B setting on the shutter speed dial, for Bulb exposures. As I noted above, in Shutter Priority mode, you can set the dial to the B setting, but that setting will automatically produce a time exposure of 30 seconds in that mode. To get the full effect of the B setting, the camera has to be in Manual mode. In addition, the Drive mode must be set to Single-shot.

When you turn the shutter speed dial to the B setting, the word Bulb will appear at the lower left of the display, to the right of the M that indicates Manual exposure, as shown in FIGURE 3-23.

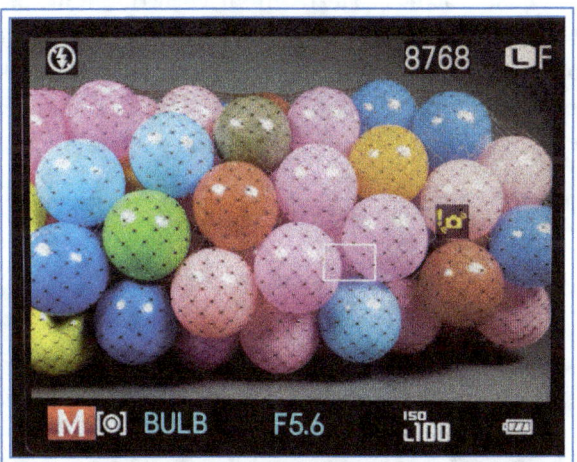

Figure 3-23. Bulb Setting for Shutter Speed

Now you have the ability to carry out a true Bulb exposure, which is named after the practice from the past when photographers pressed an air bulb to hold the shutter open for long periods of time. With the B setting, unlike other shutter speed settings, you have to hold the shutter button down to keep the shutter open, because there is no set time limit for the exposure. The shutter will remain open for as long as you hold it open by pressing the shutter button, up to a maximum of 60 minutes.

Of course, you are unlikely to want to hold your finger on the shutter button for periods longer than about a minute. Fortunately, the button on the X100S is threaded so it can accept a traditional cable release. You can press and hold down the plunger on the cable release, or, with some models of cable, you can lock the release in place and move away from the camera while the exposure takes its course, returning only when it is time to release the lock on the cable release. I discuss cable releases in Appendix A.

The Bulb setting opens up various possibilities for creative photography. For example, you can photograph star trails in the night sky; you can do light painting, as mentioned earlier, by shining a flashlight or other light source on objects in the dark, or by just tracing patterns in air with the light; or you can photograph trails of vehicles' lights, as shown in Figure 3-24. For that image, I attached a cable release to the X100S and used a Bulb exposure of 12 seconds to capture trails of taillights, some high up on a truck, which traced a pattern along the road at night.

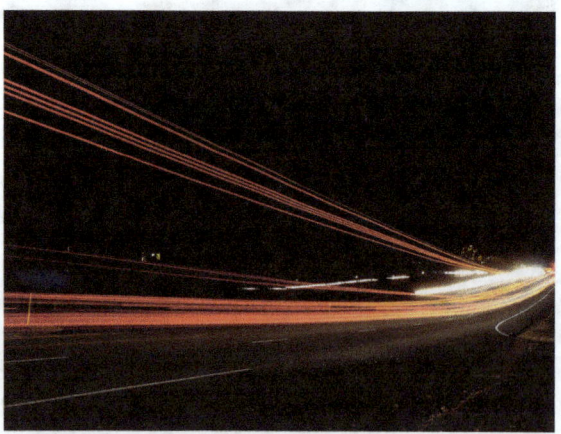

Figure 3-24. Bulb Exposure 12 Seconds, f/11, ISO 200

CHAPTER 4:
The Shooting Menu

Much of the power of the X100S lies in the many options included in the Shooting menu, which gives you considerable control over the appearance of your images and how they are captured. With the X100S, Fujifilm has also included the very useful Quick Menu system, discussed in Chapter 5, which gives you instant access to many basic settings such as the Self-timer, ISO, Image size, Image Quality, and White Balance without having to navigate in the regular menu system. However, there are several important settings, such as ND Filter, MF Assist, Advanced Filter, and AE/AF-Lock Mode, that are available only on the Shooting menu, and you may find it convenient to adjust other settings using the Shooting menu if you are used to using that menu system. So, it is important to become familiar with the options available on this menu.

The Shooting menu on the X100S is quite easy to use once you have played around with it a bit. To get access to this menu, press the Menu/OK button in the center of the Command Dial on the back of the camera, and the first of the menu's five screens will appear on the display, as shown in FIGURE 4-1. If you're using the optical viewfinder, the camera will automatically switch to the electronic viewfinder when you press the Menu button, so the menu screen can be displayed. (When you exit from the menu system in that case, the optical viewfinder will be reactivated to show the live view of the scene.)

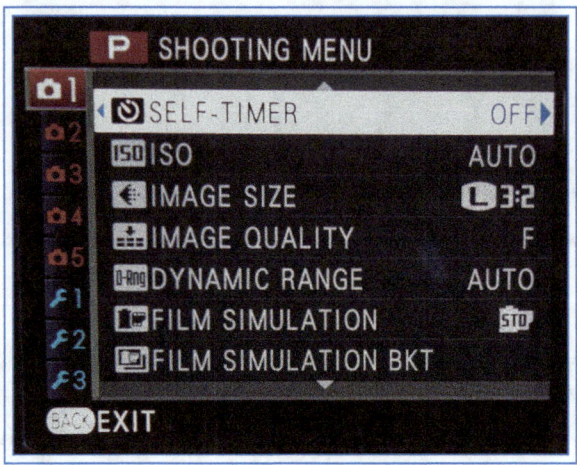

Figure 4-1. First Screen of Shooting Menu

To navigate through the items on the menus, turn the Command Dial or use the Up and Down buttons to move the selection bar from one item to the next. The menu will automatically advance to the next screen as you scroll down from the last item on a screen. You can wrap around from the bottom of the last screen to the top of the first screen, and from the top of the first screen to the bottom of the last screen. So, for example, if the selection bar is on the Flash item at the bottom of the fourth screen and you want to move to the Image Quality item on the first screen, the quickest way to do so is to scroll down through the last two screens, and then wrap around back to the Image Quality item on the first screen.

If you want to navigate through the menu by a whole screen at a time without having to scroll through each item on a screen, press the Left button to move the highlight to the far-left column, as shown in FIGURE 4-2. That column contains the numbers of the various Shooting menu screens, from 1 to 5. Once the highlight is in that column, you can move the highlight up and down through the list of numbered screens by turning the Command Dial or by pressing the Up and Down buttons. Once you have highlighted the number of the screen you want, just press the Right button to move the highlight back into the main body of that screen.

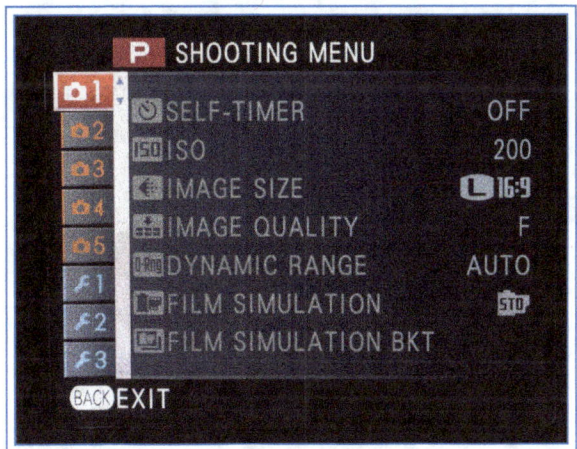

Figure 4-2. Left Menu Column Highlighted

In some situations, the available menu options will change depending on the camera's current settings. For example, as we saw in Chapter 2, if the Drive button has been used to set the camera for shooting movies, the Shooting menu options are very limited, as shown in FIGURE 4-3, because very few options are available for setting when movies are being shot.

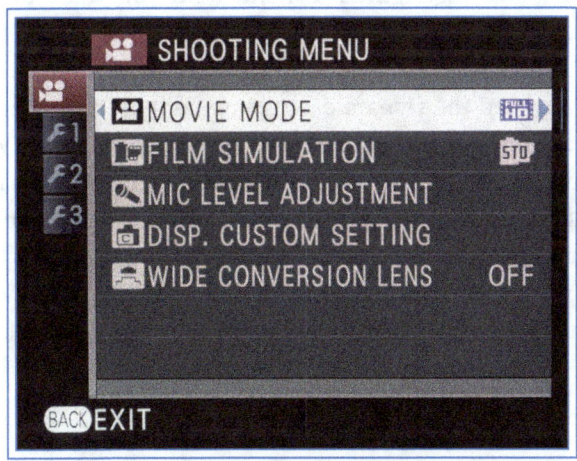

Figure 4-3. Shooting Menu Screen in Movie Mode

Also, if the Drive mode has been set to Panorama shooting, certain items, such as the Self-timer and Image Size, will appear dimmed on the menu screen, as shown in FIGURE 4-4, so you can still read them but cannot select them, because they are incompatible with the current setting.

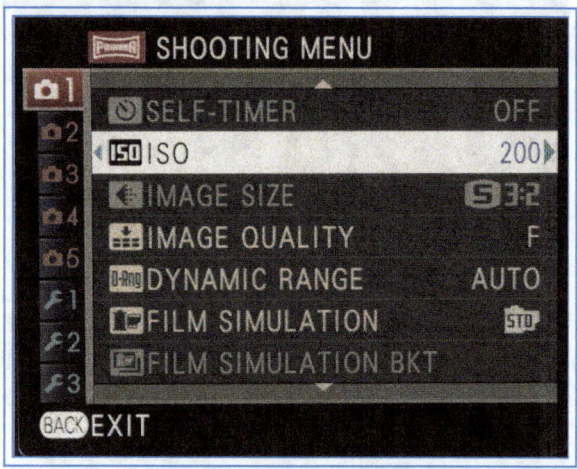

Figure 4-4. Dimmed Menu Items When Panorama Mode Set

When you have highlighted a menu item you want to control, press either the Right button or the Menu/OK button to move to the screen with choices for the setting. For example, once you have highlighted the Dynamic Range menu item, press the Menu/OK button or the Right button and you will see a screen with the four available choices: Auto, 100%, 200%, and 400%, as shown in FIGURE 4-5. (You may not see the Auto option, depending on other settings in effect.) Use the Up and Down buttons or turn the Command Dial to highlight the selection you want, and then press either the Left button or the OK button to confirm the selection.

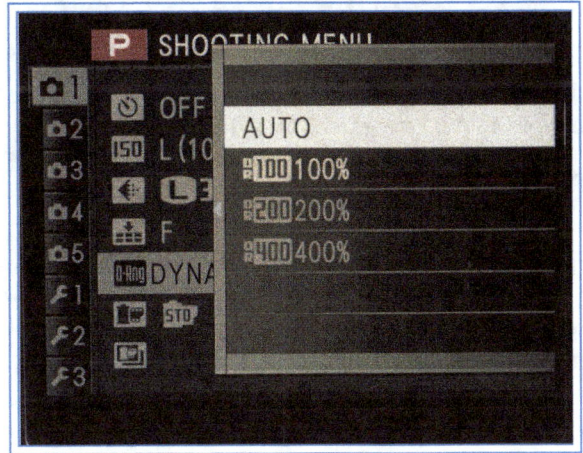

Figure 4-5. Dynamic Range Options Screen

Once you are done making your selection for a menu item, press the Display/Back button at the bottom left of the control area on the right side of the camera's back to exit the menu system. Or, if you prefer, you can press the shutter button halfway to return to the shooting screen.

Now it's time to discuss all of the options that are available through the Shooting menu. For the following discussion, I'm assuming you have the camera set to Still Image mode, rather than Movie mode or one of the other Drive mode options. To make sure of this, press the Drive button and make sure Still Image is the selected mode. If it is not, scroll up or down through the various options using the Command Dial or the Up and Down buttons until Still Image is selected, and press the OK button to confirm that selection.

One final note before discussing the Shooting menu options: In the menu system, when the camera is in shooting mode, besides the Shooting menu, whose screens are marked by red camera icons, there is the Setup menu, with three numbered screens each designated by a wrench, below the five Shooting menu icons at the left of the menu screen. When the camera is in playback mode, the two choices are the Playback and Setup menus. For now, I will discuss only the Shooting menu, which is designated at the upper left of the screen by a capital letter standing for the current shooting mode (P, S, A, or M) or by an icon representing the setting of Movie, Panorama, or Multiple Exposure mode.

On the Shooting menu, with Drive mode set to Still Image, you'll see a list of seven options on each of the first four screens and two options on the fifth screen. Each option (such as ISO) occupies one line, with its name on the left and its current setting (such as 800) on the right.

With Drive mode set to Still Image, you should have access to every option on the Shooting menu. If you have trouble getting to some menu options and can't figure out what setting is causing the problem, you can go the first screen of the Setup menu (whose screens are marked at the left by wrench icons) and scroll to the Reset option, the fourth option on that menu screen. Using that operation, you can reset all of the camera's basic shooting functions to their default values. In this way, you will undo whatever setting is causing a conflict with the setting you are trying to make.

Starting at the top line of the Shooting menu, I will discuss below each option, beginning with the first screen, shown earlier in FIGURE 4-1. For all of these options, I will discuss how to make the setting from the Shooting menu. As I will discuss later in this chapter and in Chapter 5, many of these settings also can be made using the Quick Menu or the Function button.

Self-timer

When you select this menu item and press the Right button or the OK button, the camera displays a menu of the three available choices for setting the Self-timer: 2 seconds, 10 seconds, and Off, as shown in FIGURE 4-6. If you set a delay of either 2 seconds or 10 seconds, the camera will wait for that length of time before taking the picture, after you press the shutter button. Choose 10 seconds if you need a substantial delay so you can include yourself in a group picture after pressing the shutter button; choose 2 seconds if you just need to avoid touching the camera during the exposure, so as to minimize the camera shake that can accompany a shutter press. You might need to use the 2-second delay when you're taking extreme closeups, because any camera motion can be magnified by the closeness to the subject. Or, the 2-second delay can help when you're shooting in dim light and a slow shutter speed is needed, because any camera motion during the long exposure is likely to blur the image.

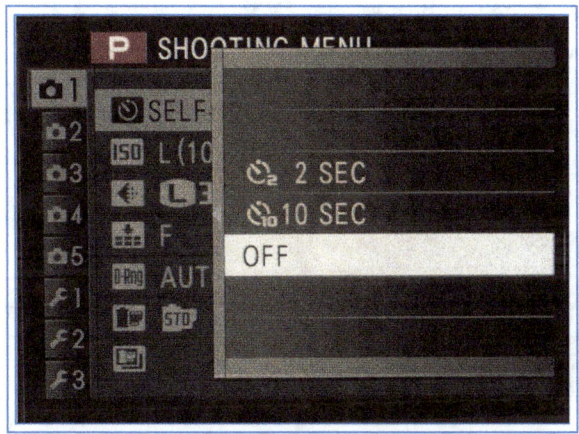

Figure 4-6. Self-timer Options Screen

Once you have selected a Self-timer setting, it will remain in effect until you cancel it using this menu option or until the camera is turned off. So, if you find there is an unusual delay after you press the shutter button, you may have turned on this option and forgotten to cancel it. Note also that the X100S's unusually bright lamp next to the lens blinks as the Self-timer counts down. (With the 10-second setting, the lamp glows steadily for a few seconds and blinks for the last few seconds.) If you want to avoid having this glaring light flash in your subject's eyes, you can disable it, along with the beeping that accompanies it, by pressing and holding the Display button to activate Silent Mode. (If you turn off the AF Illuminator option on the fourth screen of the Shooting menu, as discussed later in this chapter, that will disable the lamp for autofocus illumination only; it will not disable it from lighting up for the Self-timer countdown).

One excellent feature of the X100S is that you can use the Self-timer in conjunction with any of the Drive mode settings except Panorama and Movie shooting. Therefore, you can, for example, set the camera on a tripod with the Drive mode set for shooting continuously at six frames per second, turn on the Self-timer for a 10-second delay, and join a group, with the camera taking a rapid-fire series of shots after the delay, making it more likely that at least one image will be a keeper. When you use this approach, the camera will fire a group of five continuous shots, even though you have pressed the shutter release button only briefly. (When you're not using the Self-timer, you have to hold down the shutter release button to keep the continuous shooting going.)

ISO

The ISO acronym represents the International Organization for Standardization, which develops worldwide standards for many areas of industry, science, and other fields.

The original use of the ISO standard was to designate the "speed," or light sensitivity, of film. For example, a "slow" film might be rated at ISO 64, or even ISO 25, meaning it takes a large amount of exposure to light to create a usable image on the film. Slow films yield higher-quality, less-grainy images than faster films. There are "fast" films available, some black-and-white and some color, with ISO ratings of 400 or even higher, that are designed to yield usable images in lower light. Such films can often be used indoors without flash, for example.

With digital technology, the industry has retained the ISO concept to rate the light sensitivity of the camera's sensor. The ISO ratings for digital cameras are supposed to be essentially equivalent to the ISO ratings for films. So if your camera is set to

ISO 100, there will have to be a good deal of light to expose the image properly, but if the camera is set to ISO 1600, a reasonably good (but noisier or grainier) image can be made in very low light.

Generally speaking, you should shoot your images with the camera set to the lowest ISO possible that will allow the image to be exposed properly. (One exception to this rule is if you want, for creative purposes, the grainy look that comes from shooting at a high ISO value.) For example, if you are shooting indoors in low light, you may need to set the ISO to a high value (say, ISO 800) so you can expose the image with a reasonably fast shutter speed to stop action or with a narrow aperture to achieve a broad depth of field. Otherwise, if the camera uses a slow shutter speed, the resulting image would likely be blurry and possibly unusable.

Of course, it's important to realize that high ISO settings are not a cure-all for poor lighting conditions. It is true that the X100S, with its large, APS-C sensor, provides better low-light image quality than most cameras in its class. However, using the higher ISO settings is going to reduce image quality to a certain degree; the higher the ISO, the more such deterioration may be evident. However, with the X100S, Fujifilm has produced a camera that achieves a remarkably high-quality image, even at high ISO settings.

For example, FIGURE 4-7 includes two images of the same peacock figurine, taken with different ISO settings. I took the shot on the left with the X100S set to ISO 200, and the one on the right with a setting of ISO 25600. You may see a certain amount of degradation of the image on the right, but its quality is quite acceptable, at least in my opinion. It is only when the image is cropped to show a smaller portion at full size that the deterioration shows up more clearly. In FIGURE 4-8, a cropped version showing a smaller portion of the same image, you can see that the shot on the right, taken at ISO 25600, shows obvious signs of mottling or grain, especially in the peacock's tail.

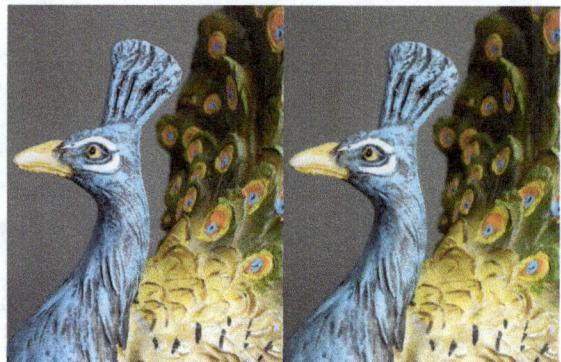

Figure 4-7. Left Image - ISO 200, Right Image - ISO 25600

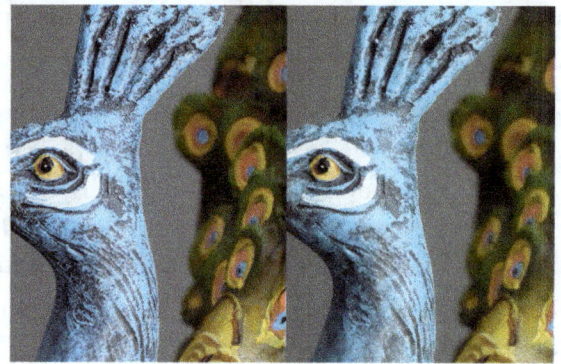

Figure 4-8. Left Image - ISO 200, Right Image - ISO 25600 - Cropped

To summarize: Shoot with low ISO settings (around 200) when possible; shoot with high ISO settings (800 or higher) when necessary to allow a fast shutter speed to stop action and avoid blurriness, to enable the use of a narrow aperture to achieve a broad depth of field, or when desired to achieve a creative effect with graininess.

With that background, here is how to set ISO on this camera. Press the Menu button and navigate to the ISO line, then press the Right button (or the OK button) to move to the screen that lets you select a value, which will range at least from 200 to 6400 in all cases, with the added values of 100 at the low end of the scale and 12800 and 25600 at the high end, in some situations.

The ISO on the X100S can be set as low as 100, but, as seen in FIGURE 4-9, that value is shown in parentheses on the menu screen.

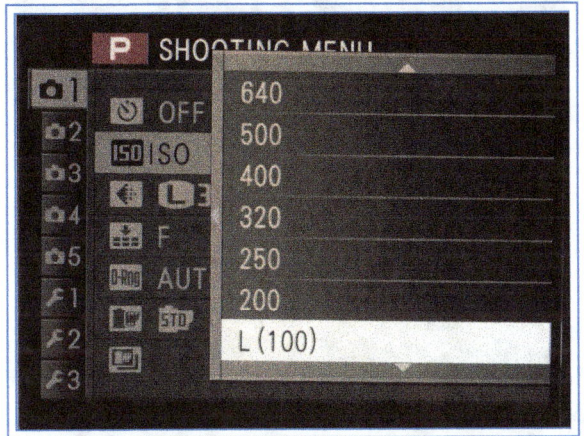

Figure 4-9. ISO Menu with ISO 100 Highlighted

The parentheses indicate that that setting is an extended one that is not naturally available with the camera's image sensor; with the 100 setting, your images will have reduced dynamic range. So, unless you need the 100 setting for a particular reason, such as to enable you to use a slow shutter speed or wide aperture for creative purposes, you should consider 200 to be the lowest setting for everyday purposes.

Similarly, ISO 12800 and ISO 25600, shown in FIGURE 4-10, are extended settings at the upper end of the scale, and ordinarily should not be used unless you really need them in order to let you use a fast shutter speed or for some other specific purpose. Neither ISO 100, ISO 12800, nor ISO 25600 is available for selection when shooting with Raw quality or with the Drive mode set to Panorama.

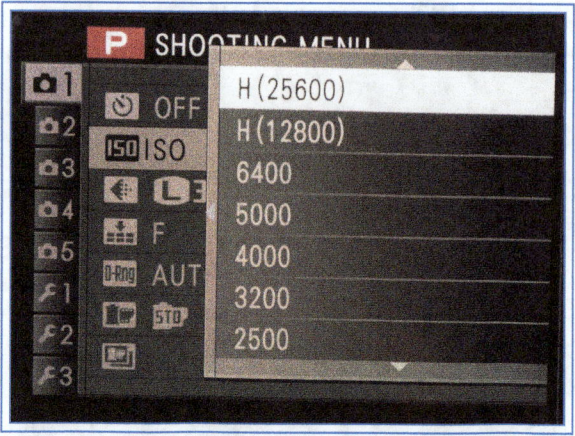

Figure 4-10. ISO Menu with ISO 25600 Highlighted

Of course, as with virtually all digital cameras, you do not have to choose a specific numerical setting for ISO. You have the option of setting ISO to Auto, in which case the camera will choose an appropriate setting based on the other settings in effect and the existing light conditions. The Auto ISO setting is found at the extreme end of the scale, just below the ISO 100 setting, as shown in FIGURE 4-11.

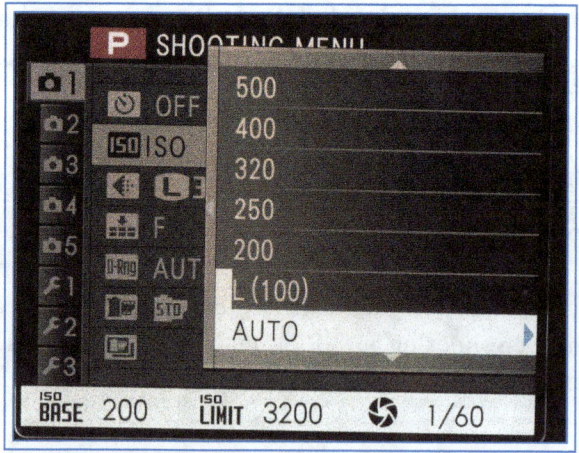

Figure 4-11. ISO Menu with Auto ISO Highlighted

If you select Auto for the ISO setting, then you have three other selections to make, as indicated by the right arrow that appears when the selection rectangle highlights this setting. If you press the Right button or the Menu/OK button when Auto is highlighted, the camera will display the screen shown in FIGURE 4-12, with the three settings that are related to Auto ISO: Default Sensitivity, Maximum Sensitivity, and Minimum Shutter Speed.

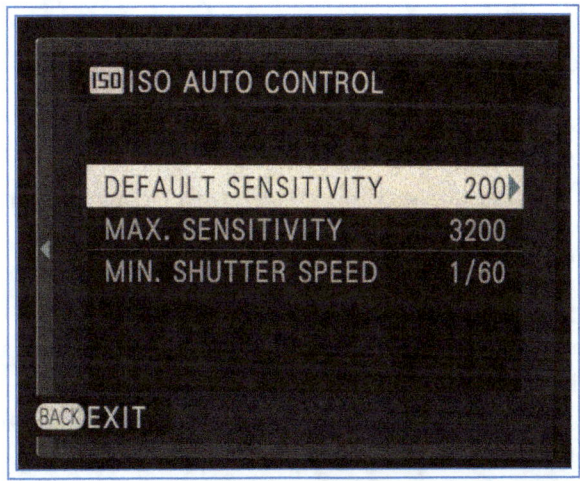

Figure 4-12. Sub-options for Auto ISO Menu Item

The first of these options, Default Sensitivity, can be set anywhere from ISO 200 to ISO 6400. The camera will use the Default Sensitivity setting as its base ISO value whenever Auto ISO is selected. The camera will not raise the ISO higher than this value unless it needs to do so in order to avoid using a slow shutter speed. It determines what shutter speed to use as the threshold level for this purpose from the setting you choose for Minimum Shutter Speed. Minimum Shutter Speed can be set to a value from ¼ second to 1/125 second. The camera will use the Maximum Sensitivity setting as the highest ISO level it will set. That level can be set from ISO 400 to ISO 6400.

With ISO set to Auto, the camera will attempt to expose the shot at the ISO value you have set for Default Sensitivity—

such as, for example, ISO 200. If it cannot do that, then it will automatically adjust the ISO setting, up to the maximum value selected for Maximum Sensitivity, such as, say, ISO 1600, if the current settings for aperture and shutter speed will not result in a proper exposure. The camera also will observe the Minimum Shutter Speed value if possible. However, if, after adjusting the ISO upward as high as the Maximum Sensitivity setting, the camera still cannot achieve a proper exposure, it will ignore the Minimum Shutter Speed setting and select a shutter speed as slow as necessary to expose the image properly.

For example, suppose you have the camera set to Aperture Priority mode with aperture set to f/2.8 in a room with average lighting, and the ISO setting at Auto, with Default Sensitivity set to 200, Maximum Sensitivity set to 1600, and Minimum Shutter Speed set to 1/60 second. When you press the shutter button halfway to evaluate the exposure, the camera may find that the image cannot be properly exposed at ISO 200, so it may increase the ISO level up to, say, 800, to produce a properly exposed image. The camera may set the shutter speed to 1/200 second, which is faster than the Minimum Shutter Speed setting, so it is an appropriate setting.

However, suppose you now set the aperture to f/8.0, a considerably more narrow setting. In our example, the camera may find that it cannot the expose the image properly at the Default Sensitivity setting of ISO 200, so it increases the ISO to 1600. However, even with that setting, the camera may find that the image will still be too dark, if it keeps the shutter speed within the range of the Minimum Shutter Speed setting of 1/60 second or faster. At this point, the camera is programmed to bypass the Minimum Shutter Speed setting, having tried its best to adjust the exposure using the ISO setting. In my example, the camera may now choose a shutter speed setting of 1/6 second, to achieve a normal exposure.

The Minimum Shutter Speed setting takes effect only in Aperture Priority and Program modes, when the shutter speed dial is set to the red A, meaning the shutter speed is set automatically by the camera. (This is natural because, if you have set the shutter speed yourself, it would not make sense for the camera to reset it to another value.)

If you are using Manual exposure mode, in which you select specific settings for both aperture and shutter speed, then, of course, the only adjustment the camera can make is to the ISO setting. In that case, if ISO is set to Auto, the camera will observe the default and maximum ISO settings, and will adjust the ISO only within those limits.

It should be noted that many cameras do not permit the use of an Auto ISO setting with Manual exposure mode, probably on the theory that the camera should not be making automatic adjustments in that mode. However, the Auto ISO setting can be very useful in Manual mode. For example, suppose you are taking photographs of a particular action, such as a person using a pottery wheel, and you are adjusting aperture and shutter speed for reasons other than exposure. That is, you may want a wide aperture to blur the background and a fast shutter speed to freeze the action. You can set the camera to use Auto ISO and let it determine the proper ISO setting to expose the image properly, while letting you set both aperture and shutter speed manually.

Of course, you don't have to use the Auto ISO setting at all, no matter what exposure mode you are using. You may well prefer to choose an ISO value on your own by setting a numerical value through the Shooting menu. However, Auto ISO can be quite useful if you would like to have this degree of automation available. Letting the camera lower the shutter speed and/or boost the ISO setting gives you some assurance of not having a poorly exposed image. Also, the Maximum Sensitivity setting lets you avoid having an image that is adversely affected by excessive visual noise that accompanies shots made at very high ISO levels.

Finally, the Minimum Shutter Speed setting gives you some assurance that the shutter speed will not be reduced to such a slow setting that your images will be affected by blur from camera motion. You also can use this setting to increase the likelihood that the camera will use a shutter speed fast enough to capture action, if you are shooting moving subjects.

Image Size

The next option on the Shooting menu, Image Size, works hand-in-hand with Image Quality, the option below it on the menu, to determine the overall resolution and quality of your images. This is one of the menu options that will be dimmed and unavailable for selection in some situations—namely, when you have selected Raw for Image Quality or Panorama for the Drive mode. (If the camera is set to Movie mode, this and many other menu options simply will not appear at all.)

With the X100S, Image Size actually has two components, which can be selected separately on some other cameras: resolution and aspect ratio. On the X100S, these two components are not named, but their numerical values are listed on the Image Size menu.

The resolution of the image is the number of pixels it has, given in a formula that contains the horizontal pixel count followed by the vertical pixel count. Therefore, the largest Image Size setting available on the X100S is 4896 x 3264, meaning the image has 4896 pixels horizontally and 3264 vertically. When you multiply these two numbers together, the result is about 16 million pixels, also written as 16 megapixels, or 16M. So, you will see the figure 16M at the bottom of the menu screen when you select this largest value for Image Size, as shown in FIGURE 4-13.

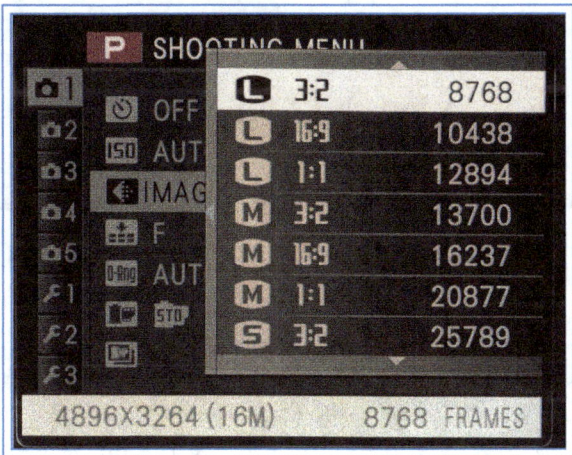

Figure 4-13. Image Size Menu Option with Largest Size Highlighted

Note that, when you select Image Size on the menu and move to the screen where you choose an image size, the number shown on the menu line is not related to the size of the image; rather, it is the number of images that can be taken with that setting. This can be confusing in some cases. For example, as I write this I have a 32 GB SDXC card in my camera—a card with a large capacity. On the Image Size menu, to the right of the first entry is the number 4267, which looks as if it might be the horizontal or vertical pixel count, but it actually means I can take 4267 more images with the current settings. The actual image size for each setting is shown at the bottom left of the menu screen. In this case, the actual size is shown as 4896 x 3264 (16M).

The sizes available for choice on the X100S become successively smaller, at 14M, 11M, 8M, 7M, 5M, 4M, and 3M. You can also determine the aspect ratio for each of these settings by examining the Image Size setting. For example, the 4896 x 3264 setting results in an image that is roughly 3 units wide for every 2 units tall, which means it has a 3:2 aspect ratio. That value is shown on the menu line. For example, as seen in FIGURE 4-13, the largest setting is listed as L 3:2, meaning Large, with an aspect ratio of 3:2. Three of the Image Size settings are in that ratio, which is a standard one for digital images, being the same shape as a frame of 35mm film. Three other settings are in the 16:9 aspect ratio, often known as "widescreen," which conforms to the shape of high-definition (HD) TV displays. The last three of the nine settings are in the 1:1 aspect ratio, which, of course, is a square shape. The 1:1 setting is becoming increasingly popular because of its usefulness for many sorts of subjects.

So, with the Image Size menu setting, you have two choices to make. First, you can choose your images' resolution, or number of pixels (megapixels). The larger the number of pixels, the larger you can make clear-looking enlargements on paper, and the more options you have for cropping the image to highlight particular details from the exposure. Second, you have the option of selecting an aspect ratio of 3:2, 16:9, or 1:1. Of course, you should bear in mind that you can always just decide to shoot with the maximum image size of 4896 x 3264 and then crop the image down later using software; in that way, you can create any aspect ratio you want, including 16:9, 1:1, 4:3, or any other. But, if you know you will soon be displaying your images on an HDTV set, for example, you can go ahead and select an image size with the 16:9 widescreen aspect ratio, and the desired result will come straight out of the camera. In addition, setting the aspect ratio when you are shooting lets you compose the image with that aspect ratio on the display screen, so you will know how much of the scene will be included in the final image.

For FIGURES 4-14 through 4-16, I took pictures of the same mural using the various aspect ratio settings, to illustrate how the various settings capture portions of an image. As you can see from FIGURE 4-14, with the 3:2 aspect ratio all possible pixels are captured. With the 16:9 aspect ratio used for FIGURE 4-15, some pixels are cropped away at the top and bottom. With the 1:1 aspect ratio, illustrated in FIGURE 4-16, some pixels are cropped away at the left and right.

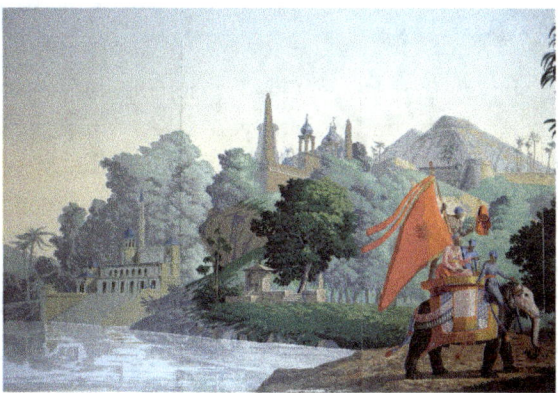

Figure 4-14. Aspect Ratio 3:2

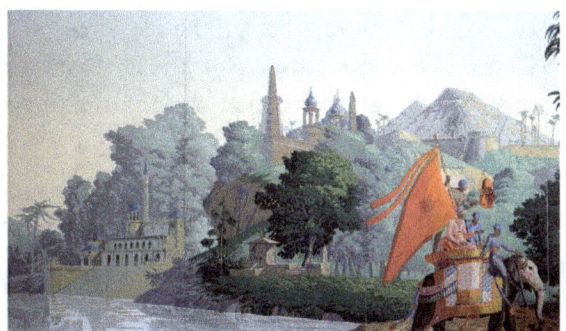

Figure 4-15. Aspect Ratio 16:9

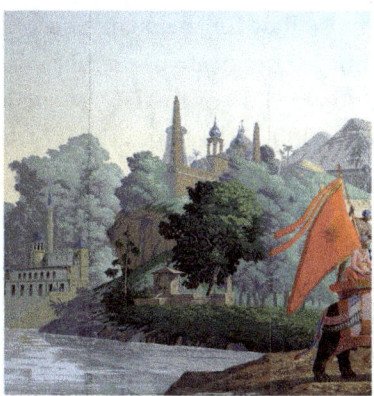

Figure 4-16. Aspect Ratio 1:1

Image Quality

As noted above, the Image Quality setting is closely related to Image Size. This option lets you select how much digital "compression," if any, the camera applies. That is, in some situations, the camera "compresses" data in image files by squeezing out a certain amount of information, preserving enough to recreate the image but reducing it so the file does not take up too much storage space. When image files are compressed in this way, they are known as JPEG files. (JPEG stands for Joint Photographic Experts Group, the body that develops industry-wide standards for digital image files.)

The five available options on the X100S are Fine, Normal, and Raw, as well as two combinations of those: Fine + Raw and Normal + Raw. The Fine and Normal options set the camera to record JPEG files. The Fine option uses less compression than the Normal option, resulting in higher quality for Fine files. With the Fine + Raw and Normal + Raw options, the camera records both a JPEG file and a Raw file for each captured image.

The Raw option, which leaves your files uncompressed, uses much more storage space than either of the JPEG options, and the Fine option uses substantially more storage space than Normal. For example, if you choose Raw for the quality setting, the camera can store about 230 images on an 8 GB memory card. If you choose Fine, it can store about 1200 of the largest images. If you choose Normal, it can store 1900 of the largest images. Of course, there is a trade-off of quality against storage space. If you are planning on making large prints, you should choose Fine or Raw.

You also may want to consider one of the combined selections, Fine + Raw or Normal + Raw. With those choices, the camera records two images—one Raw, uncompressed image at the largest size, and one image with whatever Image Size and Image Quality options you have selected. So, for example, you can choose Normal + Raw and set Image Size to the smallest choice of 1664 x 1664 pixels, or 3M. In that way, whenever you take a picture, the camera will record the full-size Raw file as well as a small, compressed image. This setup may be useful if you want to have the Raw files for later editing on your computer, but you want the much smaller files as proof copies that you can print out or view on a computer immediately without the processing that Raw files require. Also, some software may not be able to process Raw files at all, at least not until it is upgraded to a later version.

The Raw option is in a class by itself. As noted earlier, if you choose Raw for Image Quality, the menu option for Image Size becomes unavailable, because all Raw images are at the maximum size of 16 MP, and no other sizes can be selected. However, if you select the Fine + Raw or the Normal + Raw option, then you still can select an image size for the Fine or Normal component of the selection. The Raw format provides you with some very useful options for processing your images on the computer, which I will discuss in Chapter 9.

There is one other important point to note about the Raw setting. If you shoot using the Raw format, some menu options have no immediate, practical effect. For example, if you use Raw for Image Quality with Film Simulation set to Monochrome, the images will show up as black and white on the camera's display. However, when you look at them on a computer, they will appear in color, with all of the original information captured by the lens.

In other words, several of the camera's settings affect the appearance only of JPEG images—those shot with Fine or Normal quality. Of course, you have the option of shooting with Raw plus Fine or Normal, so you will have the benefit of the X100S's in-camera JPEG processing along with the ability to manipulate many of the image's parameters using the Raw file in your editing software. So, it is important to bear in mind during the discussion of the various settings for the X100S that not all of them have any immediate effect on Raw files. For those options, I will note that the setting affects only JPEG images.

Note, though, that I said such settings have no "immediate" effect on Raw files. The information is recorded in the Raw file, and, if you use the camera's Raw Conversion feature, discussed in Chapter 6, settings like Film Simulation will show up in a JPEG image that is converted from the Raw file.

Dynamic Range

This next menu option lets you choose the degree to which the X100S will apply its dynamic range processing to your images. Dynamic range, in general terms, is the range between the brightest and darkest parts of an image. If that range is too great, an ordinary digital image will not be able to show the details in both parts, because those details will either get lost in the shadows or be blown out by excessively bright highlights.

To deal with such situations, in recent years many photographers have made use of a technique known as high dynamic range (HDR) processing. With HDR, the photographer takes two or more shots of a scene that has a wide dynamic range, with some shots underexposed and others overexposed, and then merges them together using Photoshop or special HDR software to blend the best parts from all of the images. The end result is a composite HDR photo that can exhibit clear details throughout all portions of the image.

Because of the popularity of HDR, many camera makers have incorporated some degree of dynamic range processing into their cameras in an attempt to help the cameras even out areas of excessive brightness and darkness to preserve details. With the Fujifilm X100S, this feature takes the form of the Dynamic Range option on the Shooting menu.

There are four possible settings from the menu screen, as shown in FIGURE 4-17: Auto, 100%, 200%, and 400%. The Auto setting is available with the Program, Aperture Priority, and Shutter Priority shooting modes; it also is available with Manual exposure mode, despite a notation to the contrary on the chart at page 126 of the Fujifilm owner's manual. The Auto setting is not available when the Drive mode is set to Multiple Exposure, and no Dynamic Range settings are available with Movie mode.

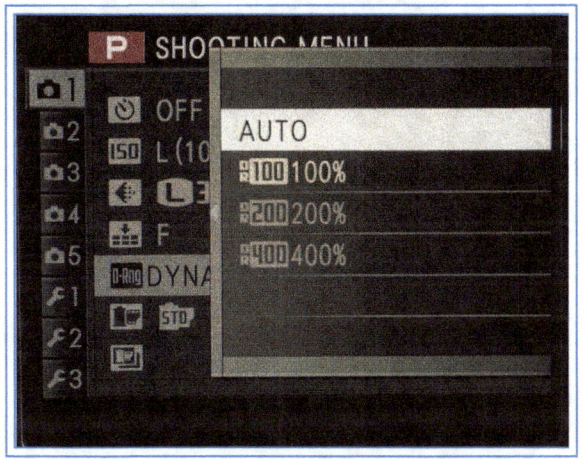

Figure 4-17. Dynamic Range Options Screen

When you choose Auto for Dynamic Range, the camera's metering system evaluates the scene and determines what level to use—100%, 200%, or 400%. The higher values are appropriate for use with scenes that exhibit increasingly stark contrast between light and dark, such as scenes that are partly in shadow and partly in bright sunlight. Essentially, what happens with this setting is that the camera underexposes the image somewhat to reduce excessive brightness in area of highlights. Then, to compensate, it boosts the details in shadowed areas. In order to accomplish these adjustments, the camera will boost the ISO setting if necessary.

To experiment with the Dynamic Range setting, I took a series of shots of a model truck that was partly in shadow, with a bright, sunlit area behind it. FIGURE 4-18 contains the three images, ranging from settings of DR 100% at the top to DR 400% at the bottom. As you can see, as the DR setting increased, the overexposure of the highlight areas decreased.

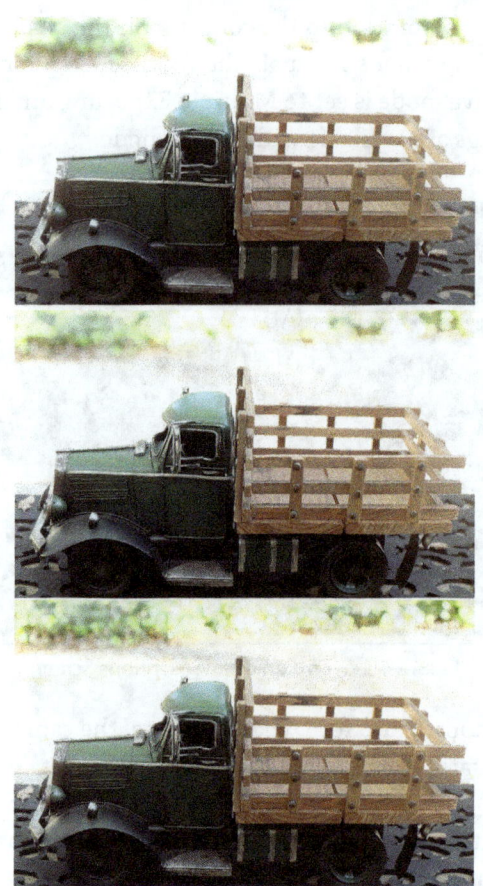

Figure 4-18. Top: DR 100 %, Middle: DR 200 %, Bottom: DR 400 %

I also tried a similar experiment using a mannequin head outdoors in a shaded area where some afternoon sunlight was illuminating the head, as shown in FIGURE 4-19. Again, the DR settings increase from the top image to the bottom image. In this case, where the scene did not have overexposed areas to begin with, the camera's DR processing had the effect of adding brightness to the shadowed areas.

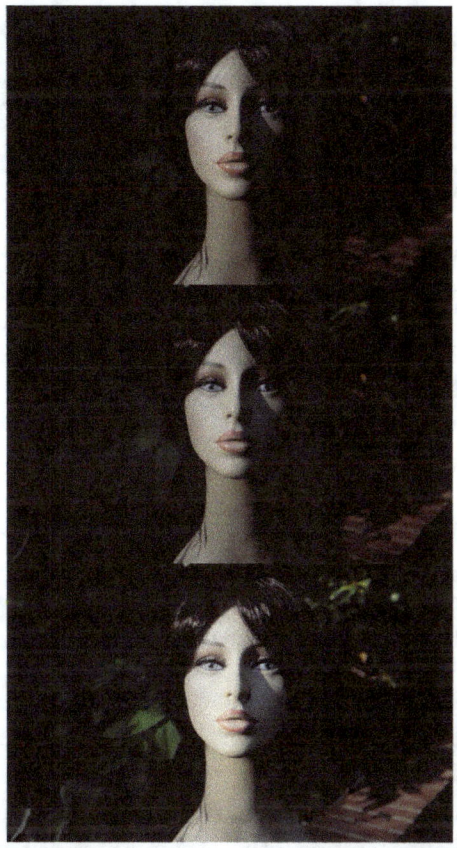

Figure 4-19. Top: DR 100 %, Middle: DR 200 %, Bottom: DR 400 %

For comparison, I also took six shots of the scene from FIGURE 4-18 using a wide range of exposure levels in Manual exposure mode. I merged those images together in Photomatix Pro HDR software, and tweaked the result until I got what seemed to be the optimal appearance of both the truck and the background. In my opinion, the HDR image done in software, shown in FIGURE 4-20, does a considerably better job of evening out the dynamic range of the scene than the internal Dynamic Range processing of the X100S.

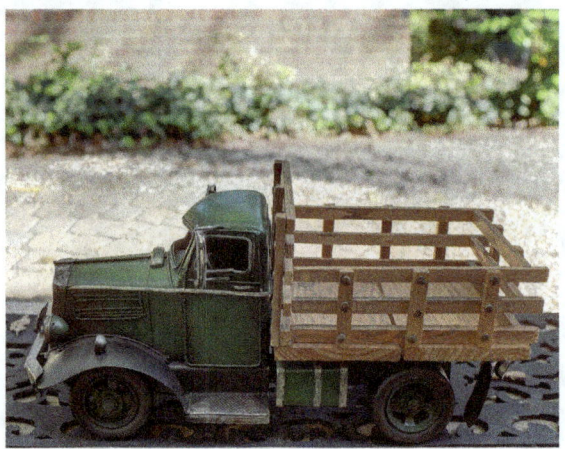

Figure 4-20. Composite HDR Image from Photomatix Pro Software

However, the Dynamic Range option can be of use when you need to take pictures that are partly shaded and partly brightly lit and you don't have the time or the inclination to take multiple pictures and then combine them with HDR software.

If you are using the Raw setting for Image Quality, you can always manipulate the image in your Raw-processing software to optimize the dynamic range. If you are shooting JPEG images (Fine or Normal), then you have to consider whether to use a Dynamic Range setting other than Auto. My practice is to always leave Dynamic Range set to Auto unless I am faced with a particularly challenging environment, such as one with both dark shadows and bright sunlight. In those cases, I may set Dynamic Range to 400%, but I also set Image Quality to Raw + Fine so I can take advantage of the post-processing capabilities of the Raw format to get the best possible quality in the final image.

Film Simulation

With the Film Simulation option, Fujifilm lets you set the camera to produce JPEG images with appearances modeled after various types of film, including several actual Fuji films: Provia, Velvia, Astia, Pro Negative High, and Pro Negative Standard.

Provia can be described as a normal-contrast color film that yields images with moderate levels of color saturation, or intensity. Velvia, on the other hand, produces high-contrast images with extra levels of color saturation. It can be used to heighten the dramatic appearance of a sunset, for example. Astia is designed to give you images with accurate color and a softer, lower-contrast appearance than either of the other two. Pro Negative High is designed for portraits taken outdoors; it emphasizes skin tones, and provides additional contrast compared to the Pro Negative Standard option, which is intended for in-studio portraits.

The X100S also offers five other film emulations: Monochrome; Monochrome with yellow, red, or green filter; and Sepia.

To select one of these options, just highlight it on the screen and press the OK button. The example images in FIGURE 4-21 illustrate the different looks that can be achieved with these settings, using the same scene so you can judge the differences.

As you can see, the differences among these settings are not all that dramatic. I generally use Provia (Standard) for color images, and then tweak them as needed in post-processing software. However, particularly if you are shooting JPEG images, you may find an advantage in exploring these settings and choosing the one that best suits your particular situation. If you are shooting Raw files, the Film Simulation setting will not affect the image, and you can just use your software to produce the result you are looking for.

When I am shooting JPEG images in black and white, particularly for street photography, I generally use the standard Monochrome setting. If I were to be trying for an antique look for an image, I might try using the Sepia setting.

The Film Simulation option is available when you are shooting movies with the X100S, so, for example, you can record a video sequence in black and white or with any of the other settings if you want to.

Film Simulation Comparison

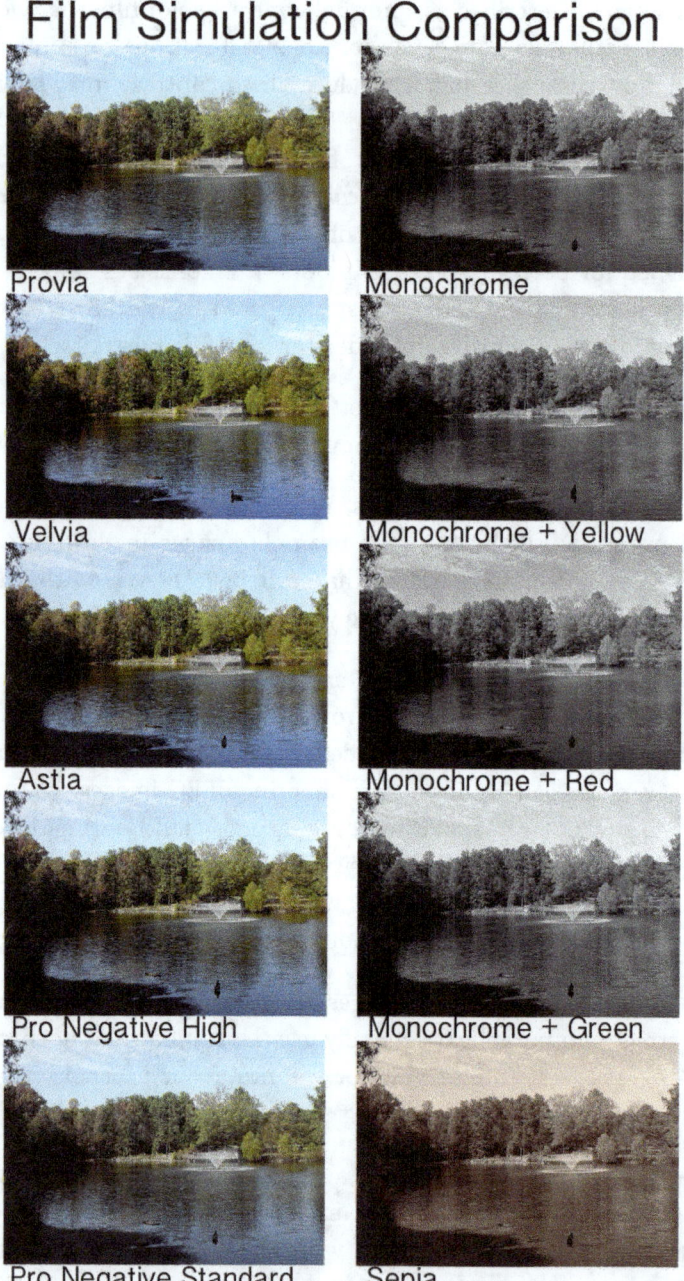

Provia

Monochrome

Velvia

Monochrome + Yellow

Astia

Monochrome + Red

Pro Negative High

Monochrome + Green

Pro Negative Standard

Sepia

Figure 4-21. Film Simulation Comparison Chart

Film Simulation Bracket

This next menu option works hand-in-hand with the Film Simulation Bracketing option on the Drive menu. As is discussed in Chapter 5, the Fujifilm X100S offers options for automatic bracketing with several settings, including exposure, ISO, Film Simulation, and Dynamic Range. When one of these bracketing options is turned on using the Drive button, the camera automatically takes three shots using slightly different settings for the option that is being bracketed. For example, if Film Simulation bracketing is turned on, then, when you press the shutter button, the camera will take three pictures in rapid succession, using three different settings for Film Simulation. With those results, you will have three images to compare so you can pick the best one for your present needs.

The Film Simulation Bracket menu option lets you specify which three Film Simulation settings the camera will use when you turn on Film Simulation bracketing with the Drive button. When you select this menu option and press either the Right or the OK button, the camera displays the screen shown in FIGURE 4-22, with three slots for selecting settings: Film 1, Film 2, and Film 3.

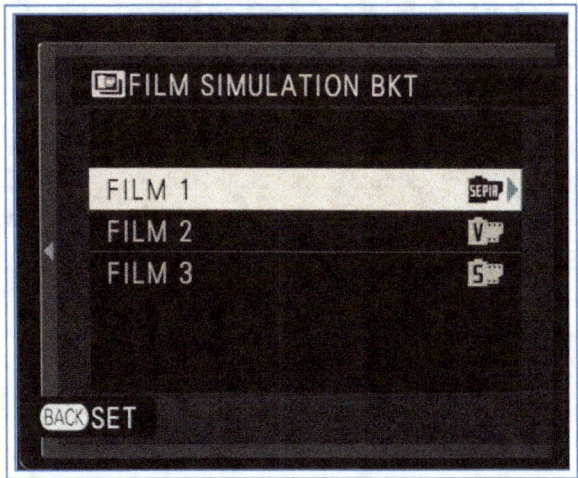

Figure 4-22. Film Simulation Bracket Menu Option

When you press the Right or OK button again to move to the next screen for any of those three settings, you will see the screen shown in FIGURE 4-23, which lets you select any one of the ten options for each slot.

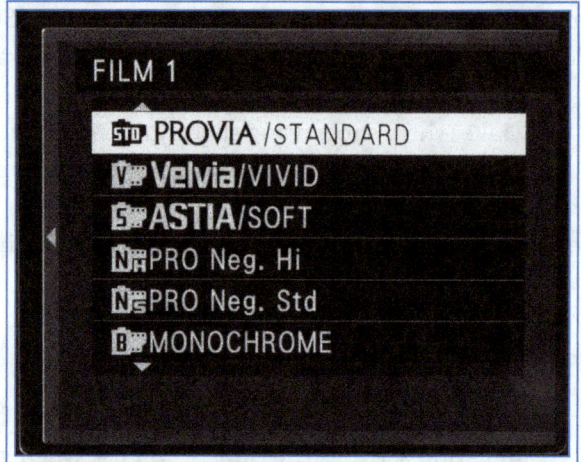

Figure 4-23. Film Simulation Bracket Menu Option

So, for example, you could set Film 1 to Velvia, Film 2 to Pro Negative Standard, and Film 3 to Monochrome with yellow filter. Then, when you select Film Simulation Bracketing from the Drive menu, the camera will take a series of three shots using those three settings, so you can choose the one that best accomplishes your purpose.

I will discuss other bracketing options in Chapter 5, in the discussion of the camera's physical controls, including the Drive button. For now, it should be noted that Film Simulation bracketing is not available when Image Quality is set to Raw. However, the Film Simulation Bracket menu option is available in that situation.

Now I will discuss the options that appear on the second screen of the Shooting menu, which is shown in FIGURE 4-24.

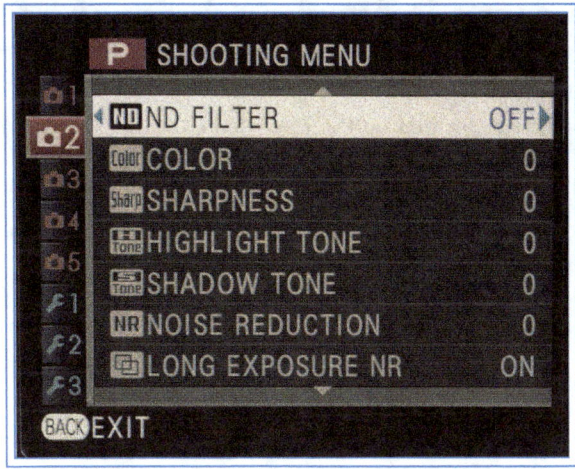

Figure 4-24. Second Screen of Shooting Menu

ND Filter

This first option on the menu's second screen provides you with a very useful tool for certain types of shots. When you turn the ND Filter option on, the camera electronically activates a virtual neutral density filter, which cuts down the light reaching the sensor just as if you had placed a glass ND filter over the lens. (A physical ND filter is a gray filter that does not change the color or quality of the image, but just cuts down on light transmission.)

The ND Filter option is of most use when you need to use a slow shutter speed or a wide aperture, but the lighting conditions are so bright that you cannot do so without overexposing the image. For example, you may want to take a picture of a waterfall using a shutter speed of ½ second so the water will appear as a continuous, smooth flow, rather than as a rough, choppy stream with droplets flying around. If the light is too intense, you may not be able to take a properly exposed shot at that slow shutter speed, even at the lowest available ISO setting and the narrowest aperture. If you activate the ND Filter option, the camera reduces the light by three full f-stops, which means the light is cut down to one-eighth the normal amount. (Each stop cuts the light in half, and cutting it in half three times equates to cutting it to one-eighth.) So, for example, if you were shooting at f/5.6 and 1/15 second, with the ND Filter turned on, you will be able to shoot at about ½ second, producing the effect you are looking for.

FIGURES 4-25 and 4-26 illustrate my efforts to use a slow shutter speed to smooth out the water in a downtown fountain.

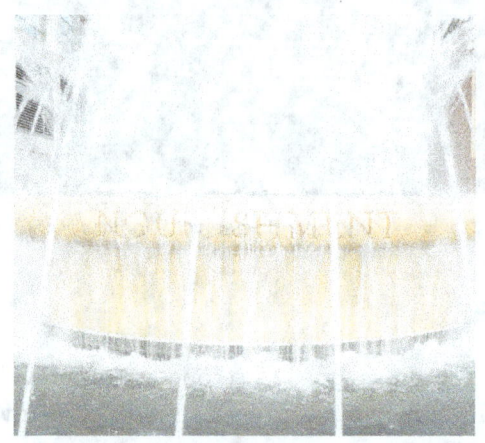

Figure 4-25. Image Taken Without ND Filter

In FIGURE 4-25, I set the camera to its narrowest aperture of f/16.0, and set ISO at a low setting of 200. When I used the slow shutter speed of 1/15 second to smooth out the flow of the fountain, the image was badly overexposed. I had no way to expose the image properly using this shutter speed, because the sunlight was too bright.

For the image in FIGURE 4-26, I activated the ND Filter by setting this option to On, and then, with the light reaching the sensor considerably reduced, I was able to take the picture with the same settings, and the result was a properly exposed image of the fountain, showing the smoothed-out flow of its streams of water.

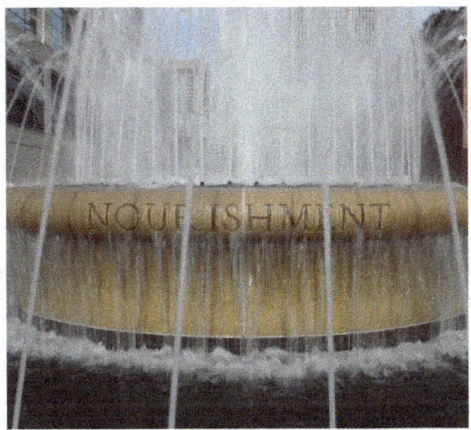

Figure 4-26. Image Taken Using ND Filter

Some photographers find the ND Filter option so useful that they program it as the feature that is activated by the Function button on top of the camera. Then, when they are confronted by a scene that is too bright to use the aperture or shutter speed they want, they just press the button and quickly put the virtual filter into place; afterwards they can just as quickly cancel its use. (Later in this chapter there is a discussion of how to assign a feature to the Function button.)

Note that the ND Filter option, unlike some of the other settings on the Shooting menu, affects Raw files just as it does JPEG images. Also note that, if you have ISO set to Auto, the camera may increase the ISO setting when you turn on the ND Filter, thereby defeating the purpose of using the filter. So, it's generally a good idea to set a specific numerical value for ISO when you are using the ND Filter. (You are likely to want to use ISO 100 or 200 anyway, to help force the use of a slow shutter speed or wide aperture.) Finally, be sure to turn off the ND Filter once you no longer need it; this feature is one that stays activated until you cancel it, even after the camera has been powered off and back on again.

Color

The Color option gives you one more tool to control the look of your JPEG images. This menu setting lets you adjust the color density of your images to one of five levels: High, Medium High, Mid, Medium Low, or Low, as shown in FIGURE 4-27.

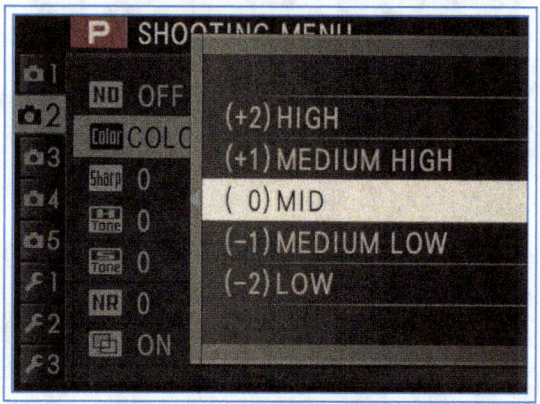

Figure 4-27. Color Menu Option

The default value is Mid. This setting, which increases the intensity, or saturation, of colors, is one way to fine-tune the appearance of your JPEG images in very precise ways. In the example shown in FIGURE 4-28, the image on the left was taken with Color set to Mid; the one on the right had Color set to High.

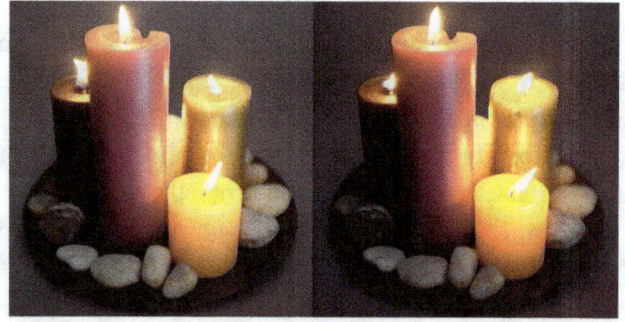

Figure 4-28. Left Image: Color Mid, Right Image: Color High

There is not a dramatic difference in the appearance of the two images, but there is added intensity in the colors of the candles in the right image, especially the candle farthest to the front.

You probably will not want to use this feature in isolation; if you adjust Color along with Sharpness, Highlight Tone, and the other parameters discussed below, you should be able to fine-tune your JPEG results to achieve the overall look you want for any particular image or group of images.

Sharpness

The next selection on the Shooting menu, Sharpness, is another tool to help you craft the particular appearance for your JPEG images. Like Color, this setting comes with five levels of adjustment, but with different names: Hard, Medium Hard, Standard, Medium Soft, and Soft, as shown in FIGURE 4-29.

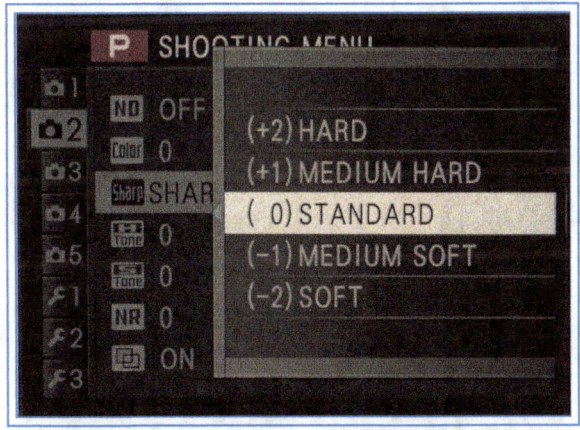

Figure 4-29. Sharpness Menu Option

This option varies the degree to which images have hard, crisp edges, as opposed to "softer," smoother lines and areas. The image on the left in FIGURE 4-30, showing an enlarged area of the feathers of an eagle figurine, had Sharpness set to Standard; the one on the right had it set to Hard. Here, again, the difference between the two results is not extreme, but, used with other available settings, Sharpness can help achieve a harder-edged look when you want to.

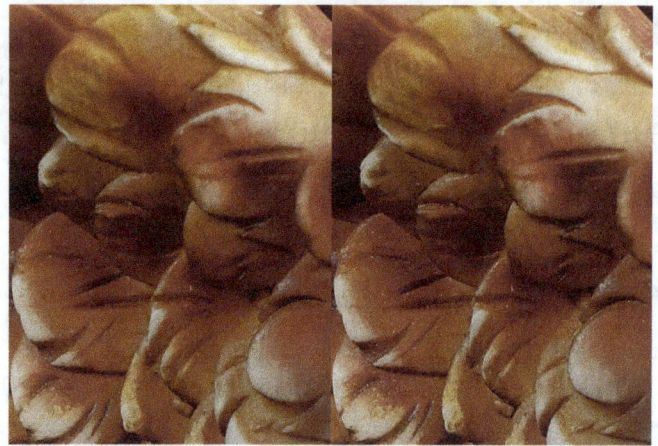

Figure 4-30. Left Image: Sharpness Standard, Right Image: Sharpness Hard

Highlight Tone

Highlight Tone is the next option for setting a distinctive look for your JPEG photos. In this case, changing the level alters the amount of contrast in the lighter parts (highlights) of images, using the same five options as for Sharpness: Hard, Medium Hard, Standard, Medium Soft, and Soft, as shown in FIGURE 4-31.

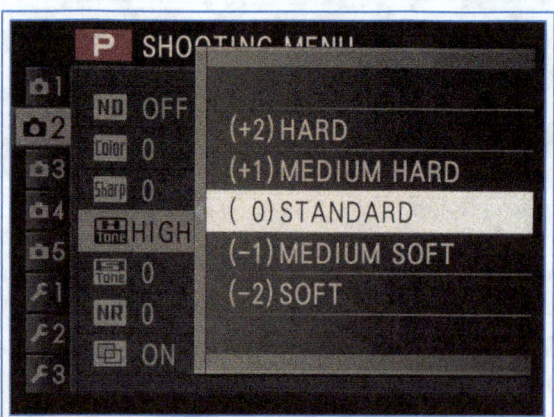

Figure 4-31. Highlight Tone Menu Option

This setting can produce fairly dramatic changes; on the left in
FIGURE 4-32, the setting was Standard; on the right, it was Hard,
resulting in brighter highlighted areas.

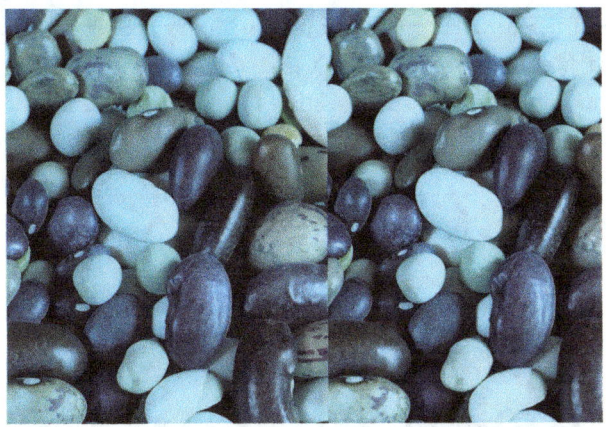

Figure 4-32. Left: Highlight Tone Standard; Right: Highlight Tone Hard

Shadow Tone

The Shadow Tone option lets you control the contrast in darker
portions of JPEG images, with the same five levels as for Highlight
Tone, above. Here again, as with Highlight Tone, you can achieve
fairly dramatic differences in the appearance of your images. If you
use a setting of Hard, as in the image on the right in FIGURE 4-33,
the dark areas are sharply emphasized; the image on the left, with
a setting of Standard, shows less emphasis in the shadow areas.

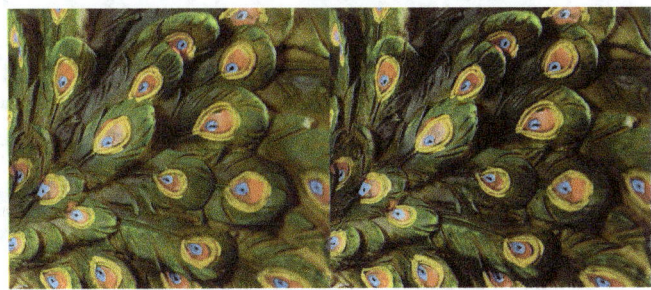

Figure 4-33. Left: Shadow Tone Standard, Right: Shadow Tone Hard

Finally, I have taken these four settings and used them together in one of many possible combinations, just as an example of how to create a particular look that may suit your taste. For FIGURE 4-34, in the bottom image I set Color to Medium High, Sharpness to Medium Hard, Highlight Tone to Medium Soft, and Shadow Tone to Medium Soft; the top image has normal settings. The result of using this group of settings would be good if you want a somewhat hard, realistic look for your JPEG images.

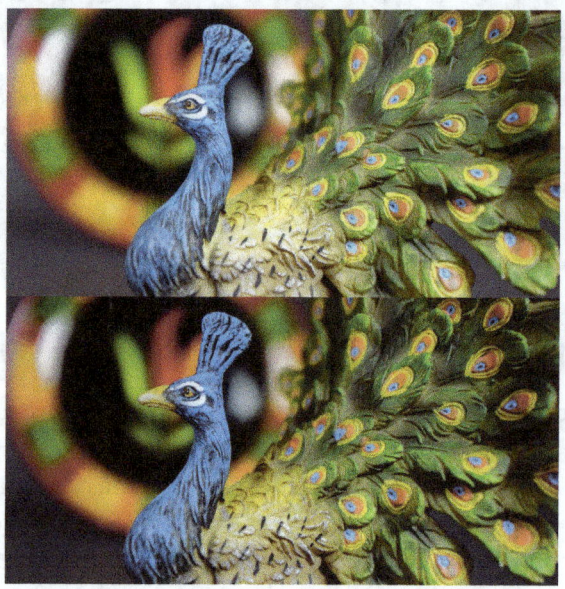

Figure 4-34. Top: Normal Settings, Bottom: Several Changes

There are, of course, hundreds of other combinations of those four settings that you can experiment with, and thousands if you combine them with other menu options, such as Noise Reduction, discussed below, Film Simulation, Dynamic Range, and others. One of the great features of the X100S is its many available adjustments for image processing, and you very well may want to take advantage of that capability to produce JPEG images with a custom-crafted appearance.

Noise Reduction

The next menu option, whose settings screen is shown in FIGURE 4-35, gives you the ability to control how much noise reduction the camera uses when processing your JPEG shots.

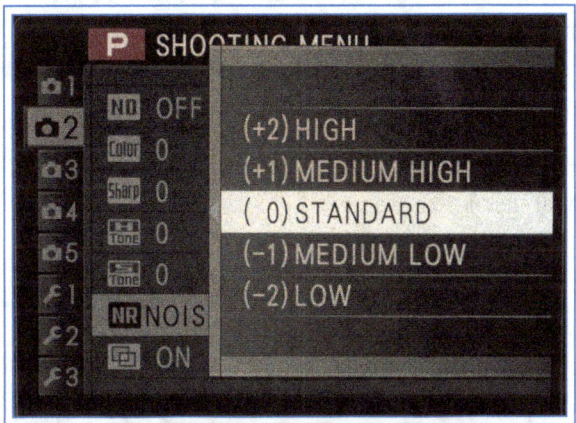

Figure 4-35. Noise Reduction Menu Option

This feature is of use when you are shooting with the higher ISO levels. The higher the ISO, the more chance that visual noise will be introduced into the image. With standard noise reduction, the camera's circuitry reduces the noise level, but in doing so it also reduces the details that are clearly visible in the image. If you would rather preserve the details and accept a certain amount of noise, or you would rather deal with noise using post-processing software, you can use this menu option to select one of the lower levels of noise reduction. This feature uses the same five levels as the Color option, discussed earlier.

Long Exposure Noise Reduction

This final option on the second screen of the menu can be set either On or Off. The default setting is On. If you leave it turned on, then, whenever you take a long exposure using the T (Time Exposure) or B (Bulb) setting (or if you are shooting in dim light and the camera chooses a long exposure), the camera will apply noise reduction in an effort to reduce visual noise in the image. Although the noise reduction has the helpful effect of reducing noise, it also can reduce the details in the image, and it can add significantly to the time it takes to process your images in the camera. So, if you don't want your shooting session to be held up by this sort of processing, you may want to turn off Long Exposure Noise Reduction. You can always deal with image noise later, using Photoshop or specialized noise-reduction software, among other options.

FIGURE 4-36 shows the third screen of options on the Shooting menu. I will discuss those next.

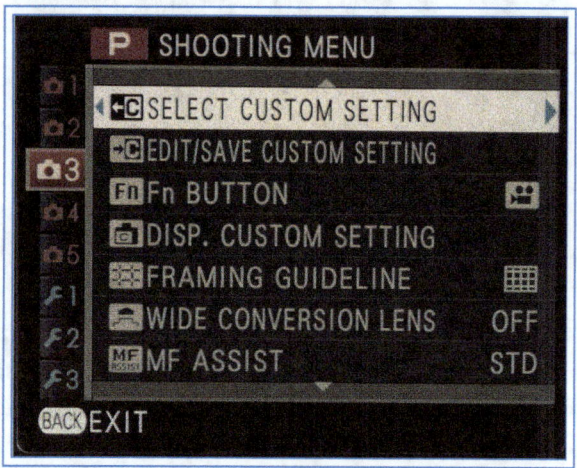

Figure 4-36. Third Screen of Shooting Menu

Select Custom Setting

The first option on the third menu screen, Select Custom Setting, works along with the one after it, Edit/Save Custom Setting. That second option, discussed below, gives you the ability to set up several parameters on the Shooting menu for a particular type of shooting session and then save them to one of the camera's three virtual banks of custom settings, called Custom 1, Custom 2, and

Custom 3, as shown in FIGURE 4-37. The Select Custom Setting menu option lets you choose one of those three banks of settings.

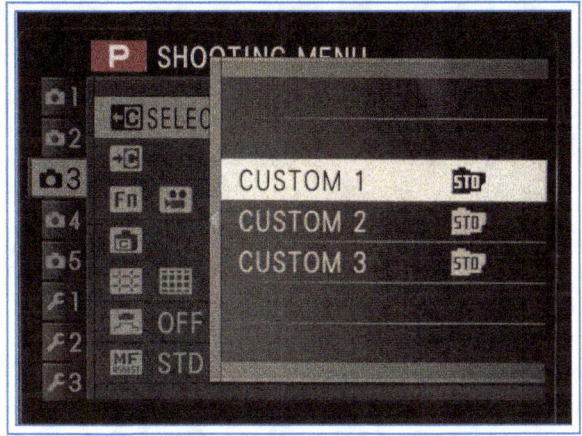

Figure 4-37. Three Slots for Saving Custom Setting

In other words, with the Edit/Save Custom Setting option, you can store your three favorite combinations of settings, and, with the Select Custom Setting option, you can instantly recall any one of those three sets at any time, just by using this menu item. To make the process of selecting a custom setting even faster, you can assign the Select Custom Setting menu item to the Function button, as described in Chapter 5. Then, you can just press that button, and you will quickly be able to select your chosen setting from the brief menu screen that appears.

This system is convenient because it lets you quickly set up the camera for a particular type of shooting without having to go into several menu items individually to change their settings. However, as I will discuss below, there is not a great variety of settings that can be stored, so this option is not as useful as it might be.

Edit/Save Custom Setting

As discussed above, this menu option works together with the Select Custom Setting option to let you store three sets of favorite settings that can be recalled quickly just by using the Select Custom Setting option to choose one of the three storage banks: Custom 1, Custom 2, or Custom 3.

As I noted above, one problem with this feature is that you cannot save a very wide variety of settings with the X100S. This situation arises partly because of the nature of the X100S's physical controls. It would not make sense to store in the camera's memory values that are set with dials or switches, such as shutter speed, aperture, and focus mode, because, when you recalled those values from memory, those recalled values might conflict with the values set by the physical controls, leading to considerable confusion.

Here is how this option works in practice. Select the Edit/Save Custom Setting option and press the Right button to go to the next screen, where you can highlight Custom 1, Custom 2, or Custom 3, using a screen similar to that in FIGURE 4-37, but with a right arrow at the right side, indicating that there is a further screen of options. Highlight the slot you want to set up by moving the selection rectangle with the Command Dial or the Up and Down buttons, and press the Right button again. You will now see a screen that is similar to the Shooting menu, but that contains only the options that you can save to a custom setting, as shown in FIGURE 4-38.

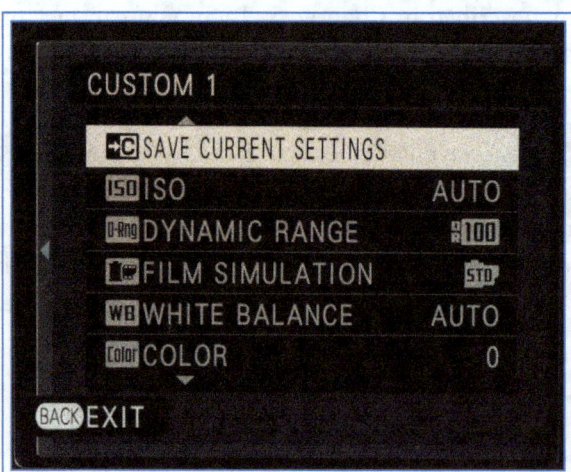

Figure 4-38. Settings Screen for Save Custom Setting

In addition, it includes White Balance, which does not appear on the Shooting menu; that setting is normally adjusted by pressing the WB button (Down button). At the top of the screen is the Save Current Settings option, which I will discuss below.

On this screen, move to each setting, such as ISO, Dynamic Range, and Film Simulation, and adjust it as you want. When you are done with all of the settings, press the Display/Back button to exit. You will see a screen like that in FIGURE 4-39, with a red bar at the top that says Save Custom Setting, and Custom 2 Set OK?

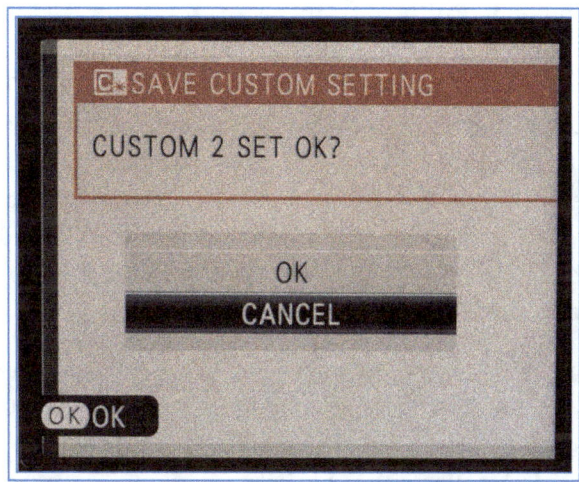

Figure 4-39. Confirmation Screen for Save Custom Setting

(The number after Custom will correspond to the Custom slot you selected in the first step.) At the bottom of that screen, highlight OK and press the OK button confirm, or highlight Cancel to cancel, then press the OK button to carry out the operation (or cancel it).

Note that the procedure in the preceding paragraph is the way to save the settings you have just made using the Edit/Save Custom Setting menu item. There is a possibly confusing aspect to this feature that you should be aware of. At the top of the screen for the Edit/Save Custom Setting option, there is an item called Save Current Settings. At first, I thought that item was what you use to confirm all the choices you made with this screen. That is not the case. In fact, if you select that item, you will reset all of the items on this screen to the values that are currently set in the camera.

In other words, that first option on this menu screen, as seen in FIGURE 4-38, Save Current Settings, lets you just go into this option and select that one item, rather than selecting a series of values from the menu screen. In that way, you can just save whatever settings you are already using in the camera.

The values you can store are almost all items that affect JPEG images, but not RAW. You can save settings for ISO, Dynamic Range, Film Simulation, White Balance, Color, Sharpness, Highlight Tone, Shadow Tone, and Noise Reduction. The only one of these that substantially affects your Raw images is ISO. If you are shooting Raw, it does not matter as much how you have these items set; you can adjust them after the fact in your Raw processing software. With ISO, though, you cannot make adjustments later in Raw software, so your ISO setting will have a real impact on your Raw shots.

Of course, it is desirable to get your settings adjusted the way you want them when you capture the image; for example, if you shoot with the correct White Balance, the image will be ready to use without any White Balance adjustments in software, so you will save time by having the settings correct from the outset, even for Raw images. And, you may well want to shoot your images in JPEG with the X100S because of the great array of features and adjustments it provides for in-camera processing of such images, such as Film Simulation, Color, Sharpness, Shadow Tone, and others. Personally, I have come to appreciate the convenience of being able to set up the camera for street photography when I go on a shooting session. I have my Custom 1 slot set up with the following values: ISO 1600 (to allow fast shutter speeds for stopping action and avoiding blur from camera motion); Dynamic Range 100; Film Simulation Monochrome; White Balance Fine (daylight); Sharpness Medium Soft; Noise Reduction Low. I leave Color, Highlight Tone, and Shadow Tone at their default settings.

Although it would be nice to have more settings available for memory and recall, the X100S offers a reasonable variety of choices, with three slots to store them in, so you can save settings for three types of shooting. You might, for example, have one set for street photography, one for snapshots, and one for portraits.

One final note: The X100S offers a shortcut for calling up the 3 slots for editing and saving settings. Just press and hold the Q button when the Quick menu is displayed, and the Edit/Save Custom Settings screen will appears, with the 3 slots displayed.

Function Button

With this menu option, you can choose what operation is assigned to the Function (Fn) button, which sits on top of the camera to the right of the shutter button. I will discuss the use of this button in Chapter 5. Essentially, when you press it, it immediately calls up whatever single setting you have assigned to it using this menu option. If, instead of giving it a quick press, you press and hold the Function button, it calls up this menu item from the Setup menu, so you can reassign the button's function.

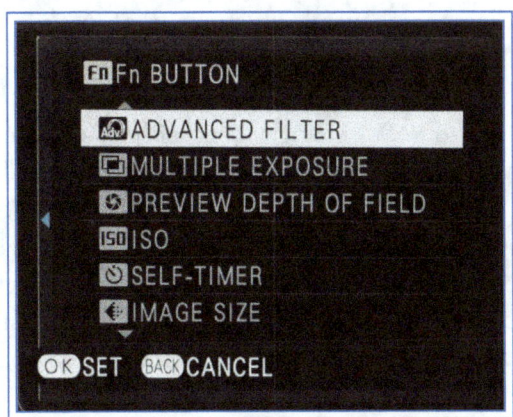

Figure 4-40. Menu of Settings for Function Button

To set the button's function, press the Right button or the OK button when this menu item is highlighted, or just press and hold the Function button when the camera's shooting screen is displayed. You will see a screen like that shown in FIGURE 4-40, displaying a list of the options that can be assigned to this button.

By default, the Function button gives you access to the ISO setting. Just press the button, and the camera lets you change your ISO value quickly without having to press the Menu button to get access to the ISO setting on the Shooting menu. If you prefer, you can set the Function button to control any one of several other values or operations: Advanced Filter; Multiple Exposure; Preview Depth of Field; Self-timer; Image Size; Image Quality; Dynamic Range; Film Simulation; ND Filter; AF Mode; Select Custom Setting; Movie recording; Raw/JPEG toggle; or Wide Conversion Lens.

Most of the choices for the Function button are self-explanatory, because pressing the button produces the menu screen that is associated with the item in question. For example, if you assign the Image Size option to the button, when you press the button, the screen for selecting an Image Size setting appears, and you can proceed to choose that setting just as if you had called up the menu by pressing the Menu button.

However, there are several functions that behave somewhat differently than normal when assigned to the Function button– Multiple Exposure, ND Filter, Movie, and Raw. Each of these options is an on-off setting; it is either activated or not. Therefore, when you press the Function button to call up any of those four options, the camera immediately turns it either on or off, depending on its current setting. The camera does not need to bring up a menu screen to let you make selections. As a consequence, each of these functions can be used even when you are using the optical viewfinder. (Ordinarily, when you are using the optical viewfinder and press the Function button, the camera switches to the electronic viewfinder so you can use the menu system to make a selection for the setting that was called up by the Function button.)

With the Raw option, the button acts as a switch to toggle between Raw and JPEG for the Image Quality setting. With this setting, if Raw is initially turned on, the camera switches to JPEG with Fine quality. If either Raw plus Fine or Raw plus Normal is initially selected, the camera switches to the JPEG setting (Fine or Normal) only; another press of the button switches back to Raw.

The ISO setting works a bit differently from the other settings just discussed. When ISO is assigned to the Function button and you are using the LCD or the electronic viewfinder, this feature works as expected. That is, with a quick press and release of the Function button, the ISO menu screen appears, either on the LCD or on the electronic viewfinder display.

However, when ISO selection is assigned to the Function button and you press that button while the optical viewfinder is in use, the display does not switch; instead, the optical viewfinder remains active, and the ISO value at the bottom right of the viewfinder display starts flashing. At that point, you can turn the Command Dial or press the Command Control right or left to change the ISO setting. That is, you do not have to use any menu screen; you can change the setting directly on the optical viewfinder's screen.

Finally, there is one item that you can assign to the Function button that is not available through the menu system: Preview Depth of Field. When that item is selected for the Function button, a press of the Function button does not call up any menu screen or other display. Rather, when the button is pressed, the camera stops down the lens to the current aperture setting so you can see the effect of that setting on the depth of field. This option is available only when the camera is set to Aperture Priority or Manual exposure mode, when you are setting a specific aperture.

This depth-of-field preview needs a bit of explanation. When you are viewing the live view using the LCD or the electronic viewfinder, the camera shows the scene using the wide-open aperture of f/2.0, to provide the brightest view; the lens is not actually stopped down to its shooting aperture until the picture is taken. The depth of field of your image increases as the lens is stopped down to smaller apertures, until it reaches its greatest depth of field at f/16, where it can keep the most subjects in clear focus at different distances from the lens.

By pressing the Function button when it is assigned to the Preview Depth of Field option, you cause the lens to stop down to the actual aperture, and, depending on the current settings, you may see the display grow slightly darker and sharper, indicating a greater depth of field. To accomplish this, you need to press and release the Function button quickly. You will hear a brief sound, and then an aperture icon will appear in the upper left of the screen, as shown in FIGURE 4-41, indicating that the lens has been stopped down.

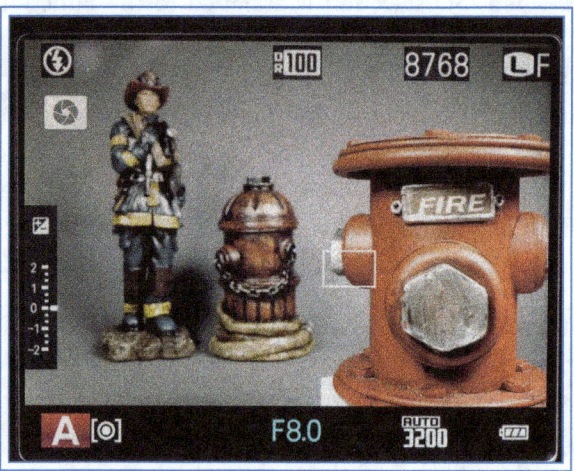

Figure 4-41. Preview Depth of Field Icon on Screen

When you have finished checking the preview, press the Function button again to cancel it. The preview function is available only with the LCD and the electronic viewfinder. If you are using the optical viewfinder, the display will switch automatically to the electronic viewfinder when you press the Function button to call up the depth-of-field preview.

Display Custom Setting

This next option on the Shooting menu lets you select what items of information are displayed in the optical viewfinder (OVF) as well as in the electronic viewfinder (EVF) and LCD displays when the camera is set to shooting mode. There is one important point to be aware of here: Even when items are selected with this menu option for viewing in either of the viewfinders or on the LCD, those items will not appear on the camera's display unless you have the Custom display option selected for the given display device.

To be more specific, both the OVF and the EVF have two different display modes or screens: the Standard display and the Custom display. The LCD has three different display modes: the Standard display, shown in FIGURE 4-42; the Custom display, shown in FIGURE 4-43; and the Detailed display, shown in FIGURE 4-44, which is labeled the Info Display on the shooting screen.

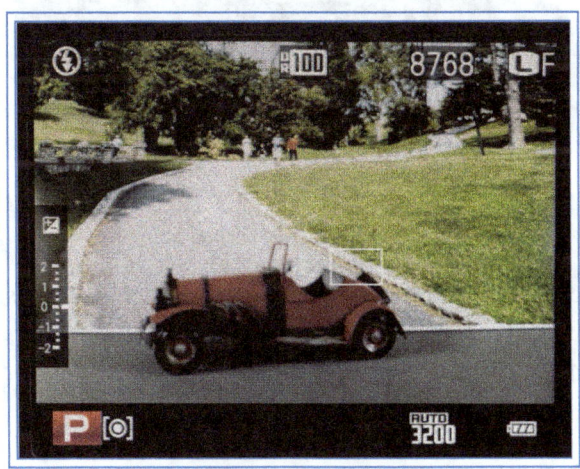

Figure 4-42. Standard Display Screen

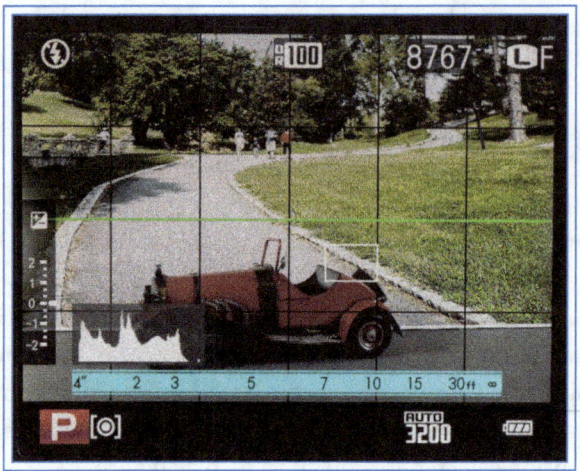

Figure 4-43. Custom Display Screen

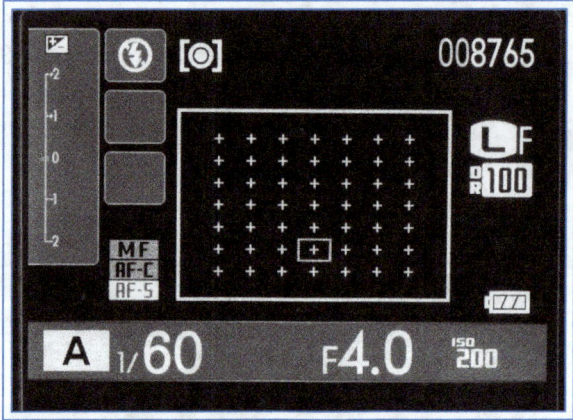

Figure 4-44. Detailed Display Screen

You alternate among these various displays by pressing the Display/Back button, at the bottom left of the control area on the right of the camera's back. The items that are selected for display using the Display Custom Setting menu item are being selected for the Custom display, and not necessarily for the Standard or Detailed display. So, if you have set up a particular item to be displayed in, say, the OVF, and you don't see it, such as the Framing Guideline, press the Display/Back button to select the

Custom display screen, and all of the items you have selected will now be visible.

This menu item is straightforward and easy to use. You just select this option and press the Right button to move to the screen shown in FIGURE 4-45, to choose either OVF (for the optical viewfinder) or EVF/LCD (for the electronic viewfinder and LCD screen).

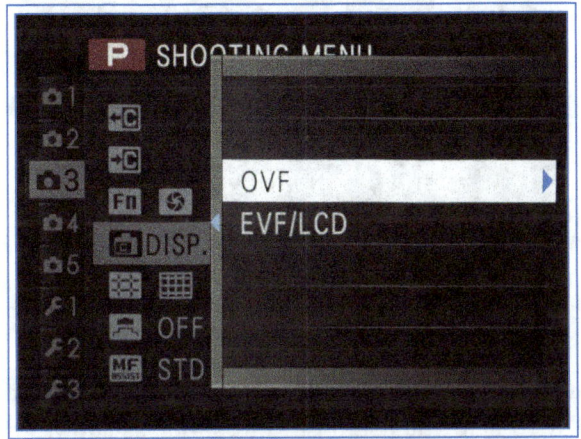

Figure 4-45. Display Custom Setting Options Screen

(The EVF and the LCD both display the same items of information, so this one choice affects them both.) Select the option you want to set up, and press the Right button again, which will take you to a screen like that in FIGURE 4-46, which lists all of the items that can be displayed. When the line you want to change is highlighted, press the OK button to either check or uncheck the box to the left of the listed item. All items with check marks will appear on the display in question, when the Custom option is chosen with the Display/Back button.

The items that can be displayed are: Framing Guideline; Electronic Level; Autofocus Distance Indicator; Manual Focus Distance Indicator; Histogram; Aperture, Shutter Speed and ISO; Exposure Compensation; Photometry; Flash; White Balance; Film Simulation; Dynamic Range; Frames Remaining; Image Size and

Quality; and Battery Level. Most of these are self-explanatory, but a few need some explanation.

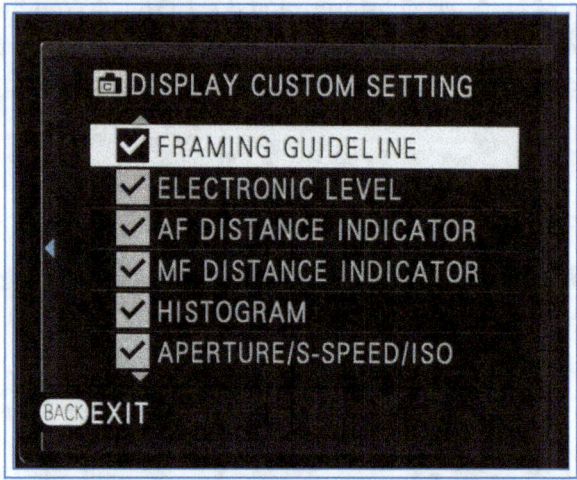

Figure 4-46. Display Custom Setting - Settings Screen

The Framing Guideline is a grid of lines that is superimposed on the display to help you compose your shots, as shown in FIGURE 4-47; you select the style of grid using the Framing Guideline option on the Shooting menu, discussed later in this chapter.

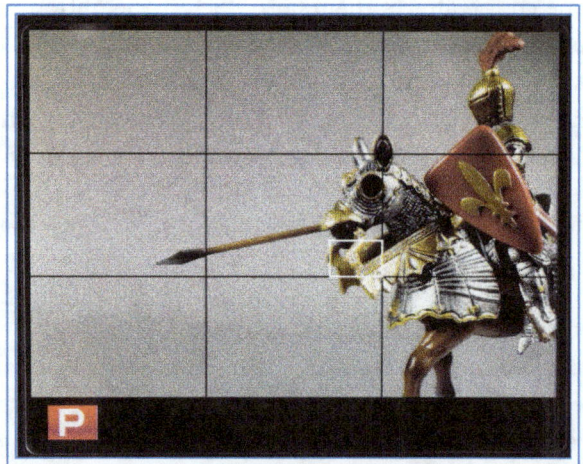

Figure 4-47. Framing Guideline in Use

The Electronic Level displays what Fujifilm calls a "virtual horizon." You will see a blue line that extends across the middle of the display and a white line of the same length that rolls up and down as the camera moves in and out of level status. When the blue line covers the white line, a single green line appears, indicating that the camera is level. FIGURE 4-48 shows the Electronic Level in the center of the display.

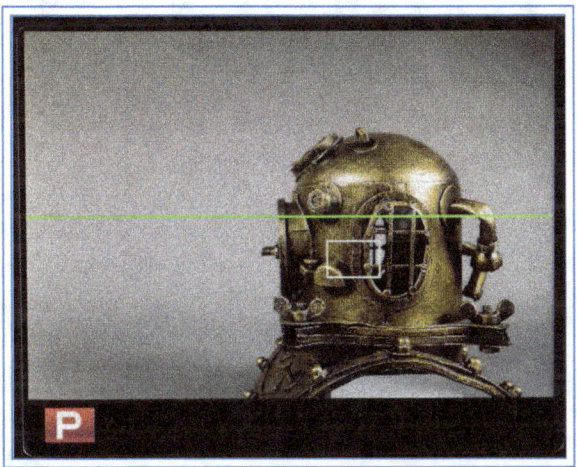

Figure 4-48. Electronic Level in Use

The Autofocus Distance Indicator, shown in FIGURE 4-49, consists of three parts: a light-blue scale at the bottom of the display that is marked in distance units (meters or feet, selectable through the Setup menu); a vertical red line that appears on the scale when autofocusing is accomplished, to show the approximate distance from the subject that the camera focused on; and a small white area surrounding the red line, which expands and contracts to indicate the depth of field at the current settings. The Manual Focus Distance Indicator displays similar features when manual focus is active.

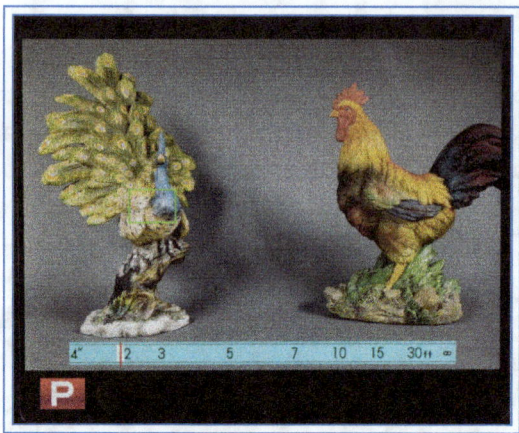

Figure 4-49. AF Distance Indicator on Screen

The Histogram is a chart of vertical white bars showing the distribution of dark and bright areas in the image. The darkest blacks are represented by vertical bars on the left, and the brightest whites by those on the right, with gradations in between. You should generally set the exposure so the Histogram looks roughly like a mountain that slopes up gradually from the left and right of the chart to a peak in the center. A Histogram that is skewed too far to the left or the right of the chart indicates likely underexposure or overexposure. The Histogram in FIGURE 4-50 is skewed somewhat to the left, indicating underexposure.

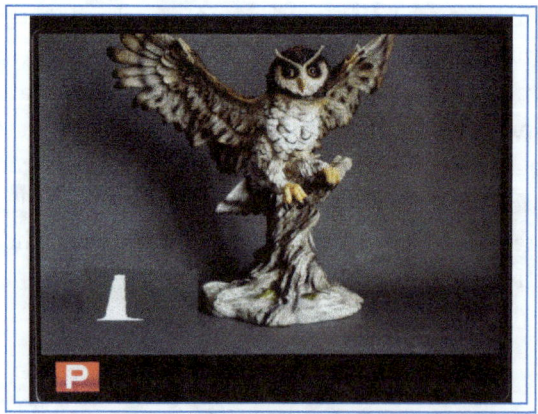

Figure 4-50. Histogram in Shooting Mode - Showing Underexposure

The way the Histogram works on the Fujifilm X100S can be a bit confusing, so I will go into a bit more detail. There are two different Histogram displays available with this camera—one for shooting mode, which is the one being discussed here, and another one that is available in playback mode, which I'll discuss in Chapter 6. These two Histograms work differently. The Histogram that is available in playback mode appears when you view the detailed display of a recorded image; press the Display button until you see the display of a thumbnail image with shooting information and the Histogram. That Histogram lets you know whether your image was underexposed, overexposed, or normally exposed.

The shooting-mode Histogram, however, can be misleading. It is of use only to show you how exposure compensation would change the exposure of your image. Even if the current settings would not result in a properly exposed image, this Histogram will not alert you to that fact. To gauge whether the image is going to be normally exposed, you need to check whether the aperture or shutter speed numbers turn red, or you can take a test image and check the playback Histogram. You cannot rely on the shooting-mode Histogram for this purpose.

Here is another point that can cause confusion if you're not aware of it. If you turn on OVF Power Save Mode in Screen 2 of the Setup menu, as discussed in Chapter 7, the Histogram will not display in the optical viewfinder, even if you have selected it with the Display Custom Setting option. You will see the white rectangle where the Histogram should appear, but the Histogram itself will not show up until you turn off that power-saving menu option. (It will still display in the EVF and on the LCD screen.)

The next item that needs some explanation, Photometry, is the term that Fujifilm uses for the light-metering method used by the X100S. There are three such methods—Multi, Spot, and Average, which I will discuss in Chapter 5 in discussing the AE button, which lets you select the metering mode. If you select Photometry for the Custom display, the camera will display an icon that represents the metering mode, to the right of the exposure mode icon in the bottom left corner of the display. For example, in FIGURE 4-51, the icon for the Multi setting is seen to the right of the A that stands for Aperture Priority mode.

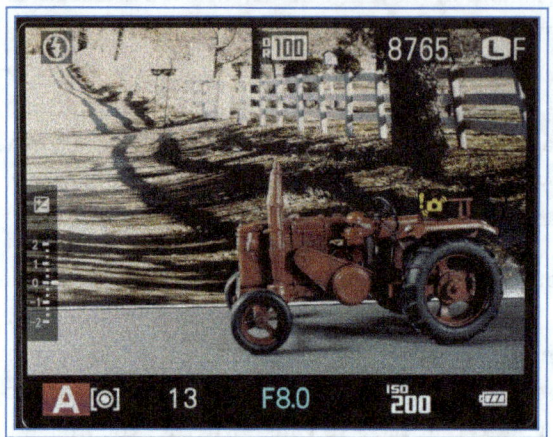

Figure 4-51. Multi Metering Mode Icon on Screen

Finally, the Flash item in the Display Custom Setting menu option is the Flash mode that is in effect, such as Forced Flash or Suppressed Flash, as seen in FIGURE 4-52, where the Suppressed Flash icon is seen in the upper left corner of the display.

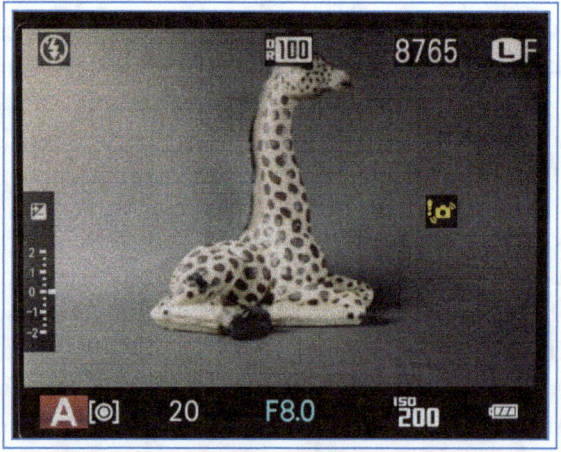

Figure 4-52. Suppressed Flash Icon on Screen

Framing Guideline

With this menu item, you can specify your choice of three options for the grid that can be superimposed on the camera's display to help you compose your images and videos. The choices, shown in FIGURE 4-53, are Grid 9, which sets up a pattern with nine blocks, as shown in FIGURE 4-54; Grid 24, a pattern with six blocks across the display and four going down the display, seen in FIGURE 4-55; and HD Framing, which puts only two lines on the display—one near the top and one near the bottom, resulting in a wide and narrow frame with the 16:9 aspect ratio of a widescreen (HD) image. That option is illustrated in FIGURE 4-56.

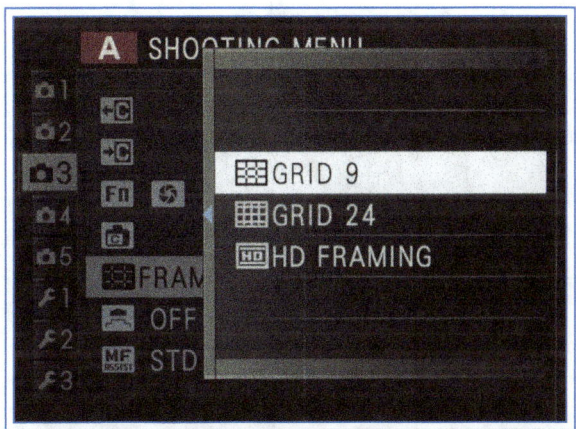

Figure 4-53. Framing Guideline Options Screen

Note that the Framing Guideline appears on only one display screen—the Custom display screen in shooting mode, which you can select using the Display button. As was discussed above in connection with the Custom Display Setting menu option, you can select what items appear in the Custom display, separately, for the LCD/electronic viewfinder and for the optical viewfinder. So, you can turn the Framing Guideline either on or off for either of those displays. The Framing Guideline menu option determines what format of grid will appear if you activate that option, but you don't have to activate it if you don't want it.

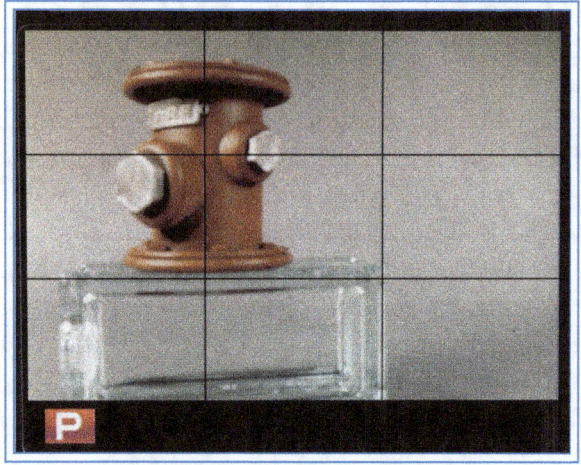

Figure 4-54. Grid 9 Option in Use

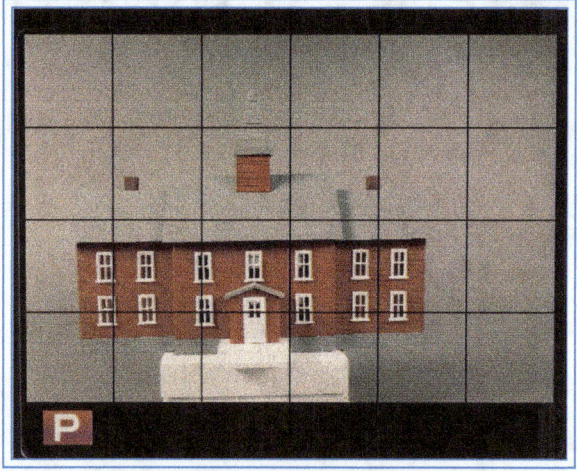

Figure 4-55. Grid 24 Option in Use

Personally, I like the nine-block grid in some situations, because it helps me compose images according to the Rule of Thirds. That rule suggests that you should place the most important subject at an intersection of the lines in this grid, which means it would be roughly one-third of the way from the edges of the image. It often seems to be aesthetically pleasing to have your subject off-center in this way.

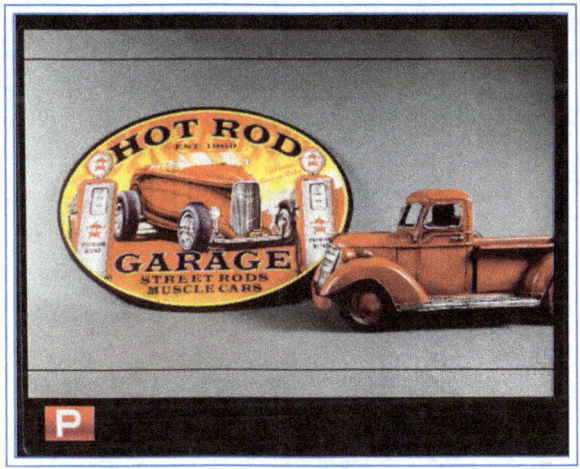

Figure 4-56. HD Framing Option in Use

Also, having the horizontal and vertical lines of the grid can be quite helpful in keeping your image perfectly level or straight. Of course, you also can have the Electronic Level available for that purpose if you want, but the unmoving grid lines can give you a somewhat different perspective than the moving line of the level.

Wide Conversion Lens

This menu option has only two settings – On or Off. You should turn it on when you are using Fujifilm's optional Wide Conversion Lens, model number WCL-X100, and leave it off when you are not using that lens. That lens, which I discuss in Appendix A, converts the effective focal length of the X100S's lens to 28mm rather than the normal 35mm. This menu option causes the camera to account for the different viewing angle when the lens is installed, so it can correct for distortion in JPEG images made while the lens is in use.

MF Assist

This final option on the third screen of the Shooting menu provides three extremely useful features to help you achieve sharp images when you are using manual focus. When you highlight this item and then press the Right or OK button, you will see the three options shown in FIGURE 4-57: Standard, Digital Split Image, and Focus Peak Highlight.

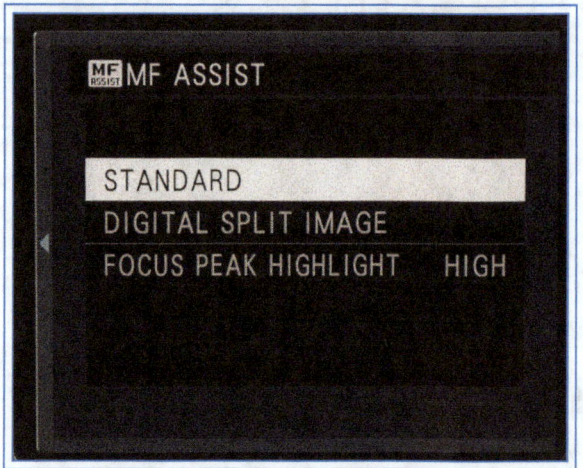

Figure 4-57. MF Assist Options Screen

If you choose Standard, then, when you are using manual focus, if you press in on the Command Control (the black switch at the upper right of the camera's back), the display will enlarge so you can see more clearly as you turn the focus ring to achieve sharp focus. You have to press in quickly on the control and release it; if you press it and hold it down, the camera will move to the next option on the MF Assist menu, and will display a white rectangle announcing which option is now in effect, as shown in FIGURE 4-58. To return the image to normal size, press and release the Command Control again.

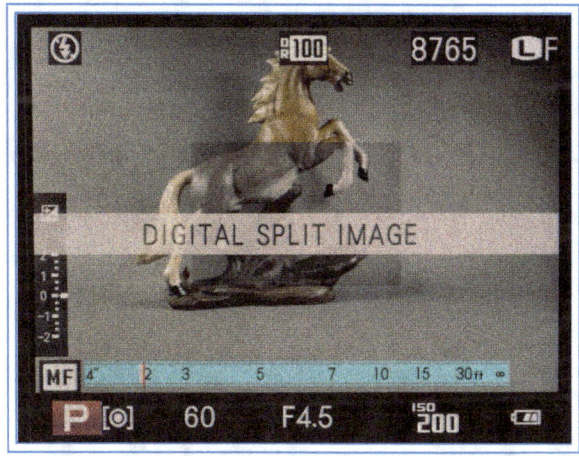

Figure 4-58. White Selection Bar for Next MF Assist Option

If you choose Digital Split Image, then the camera will place a shaded rectangle in the center of the screen, which emulates the functioning of a rangefinder camera's split-image focusing. With this option, the camera breaks up (splits) the image within that rectangle into three parts. When the image is in sharp focus, the three parts are lined up perfectly. As the image becomes further out of focus, the three parts are pulled apart, as shown in FIGURE 4-59.

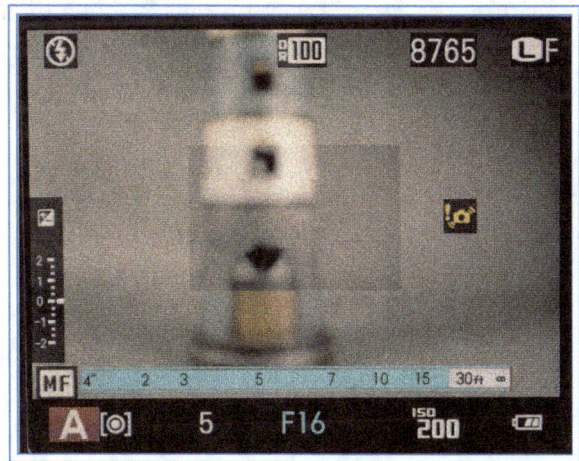

Figure 4-59. Digital Split Image Option in Use

With this system, particularly with subjects that have straight lines, it may be easier to tell when the subject is in or out of focus than with the plain, enlarged image of the Standard option.

If you choose the final option, Focus Peak Highlight, you then need to choose between the two settings for that option: Low or High, as shown in FIGURE 4-60.

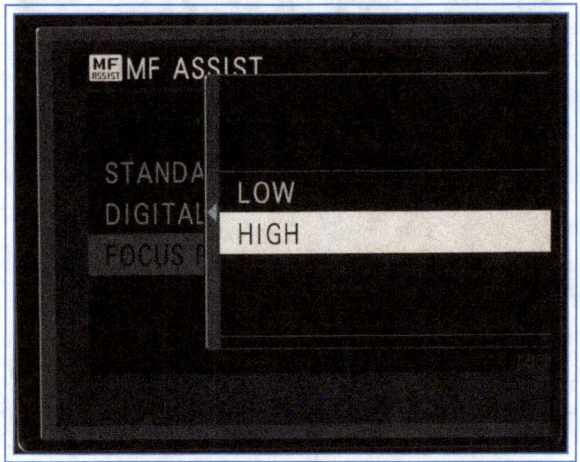

Figure 4-60. Focus Peak Options Screen

With this feature, the camera electronically places a highlight of bright pixels around the edges of areas that are in sharp focus. The sharper the focus, the brighter and more prominent the highlighting of the edges. FIGURE 4-61 illustrates the use of this option, set at the High level, showing the subject in sharp focus.

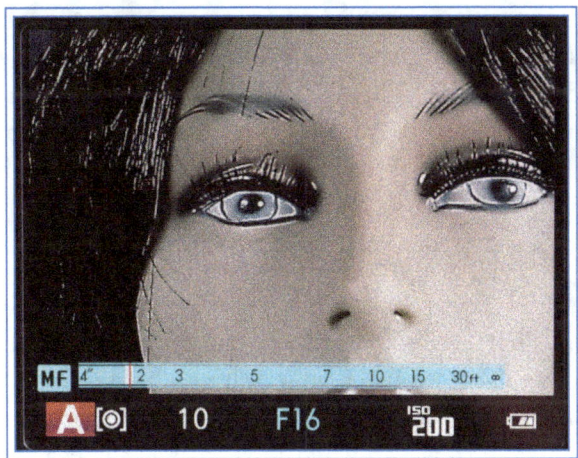

Figure 4-61. Focus Peak Highlight High in Use

It's important to understand how these manual focus aids work together, so I'll provide a brief summary. With Standard, the image will be enlarged when you press and release the Command Control; until you press that switch, no focusing aid will be in effect. With Digital Split Image, the image will be split when it is out of focus and united when it is in focus. There will be no enlargement unless you press and release the Command Control. With Focus Peak Highlight, the camera will place bright pixels on the screen at areas of sharp focus. Again, there will be no enlargement unless you press and release the Command Control.

However, for all three MF Assist settings, enlargement of the image will occur without pressing the Command Control if the Focus Check option, discussed immediately below, is turned on.

Focus Check, a menu option closely related to MF Assist, is found on screen 2 of the Setup menu. I will discuss it in Chapter 7. Briefly, that feature enlarges the display automatically as soon as you start to turn the focus ring when using manual focus. If that option is activated, you do not have to press in on the Command Control to enlarge the screen; the enlargement happens as soon as you move the focus ring in either direction.

With the features of the MF Assist menu option, it is easy to use manual focus effectively on the X100S. For general subjects, the Standard option may suffice. For subjects with prominent straight lines, you may want to use the Digital Split Image approach. For subjects in dark areas, it may be especially useful to use the Focus Peak Highlight option, so you can clearly see where the camera has detected the sharp edges of areas where focus is being achieved.

I have found Focus Peak Highlight especially helpful in two situations. First, when I was photographing the moon through a telescope, as discussed in Chapter 9, it was hard to focus because the moon does not have straight lines or other sharp features to enable focusing. However, when I used the Focus Peak Highlight feature, the camera placed a thick, white outline around the edge of the moon, making it much easier to focus. And, when I was photographing a mannequin head outdoors, as shown in FIGURE 4-61, I found I could focus on the eyes quite sharply, because the white highlights from the Focus Peak option were clearly visible against dark areas of the eye.

Next, I will discuss the options on the fourth screen of the Shooting menu, shown in FIGURE 4-62.

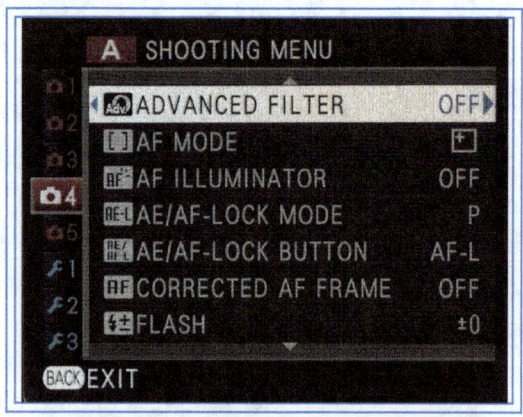

Figure 4-62. Fourth Screen of Shooting Menu

Advanced Filter

This first option on the fourth Shooting menu screen opens up a rich array of settings for capturing images with in-camera special effects. The Advanced Filter option lets you delve into various types of creative photo-making with considerable flexibility. Note, though, that the Advanced Filter settings do not work with Raw images. If you turn on one of these settings while Raw is selected for Image Quality, the camera will reset Image Quality to Fine until the Advanced Filter setting is turned off. You also will lose the ability to set several other menu options, including ISO, Dynamic Range, Film Simulation, Color, Sharpness, and others. However, this is understandable, because the camera will use its processing to manipulate several of these parameters to achieve a particular effect. Unfortunately, you also cannot use the Drive mode options, including Movie mode. This is too bad because some of these settings, especially the Miniature effect, could be used to good effect for making movies.

To use any of these settings, select the Advanced Filter menu option as shown in FIGURE 4-63 and scroll up and down through the choices at the right of the screen.

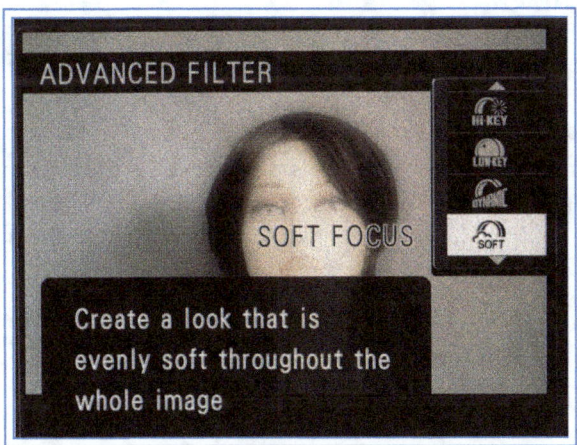

Figure 4-63. Advanced Filter Menu Option

There are 13 sub-options for Advanced Filter: Toy Camera, Miniature, Pop Color, High-key, Low-key, Dynamic Tone, Soft Focus, and six Partial Color options: Red, Orange, Yellow, Green, Blue, and Purple. A final option, Off, is used to turn off the Advanced Filter feature altogether. FIGURE 4-64 is a chart with one sample image taken with each effect, all showing the same scene—a red model car in front of a photographic background. (For Partial Color, I used only two of the 6 possible colors.) Along with the chart, I will discuss each option. For some of the effects, I will include an additional sample image of another scene to give a more realistic illustration of how the effect might be used.)

Following are some details about each of the settings.

OFF

Although Off is the final setting on the Advanced Filter menu, I will discuss it first, because of its importance. This setting is used to cancel all Advanced Filter settings. When you are engaged in ordinary picture-taking, you should make sure the Off setting is selected so that no unwanted special effects interfere with your images.

TOY CAMERA

The Toy Camera option, the first effect you can select at the top of the menu, gives you an alternative to using one of the popular models of "toy" film cameras such as the Holga, Diana, or Lomo, which are popular with hobbyists and artists who use them to take photos with grainy, low-resolution appearances. (There is a genre of photography called "Lomography," named for the Lomo camera.) With the Toy Camera setting, the X100S processes the image so it looks as if it were taken by a camera with a cheap lens; the image is dark at the corners and somewhat blurry.

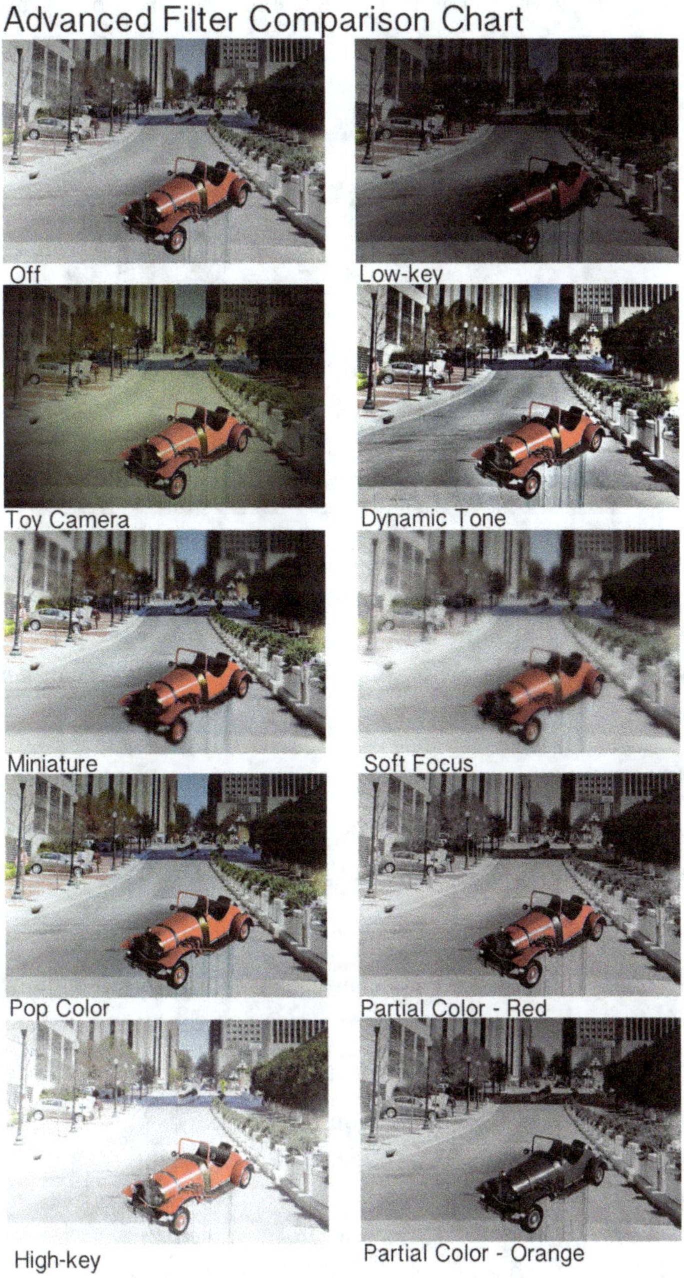

Advanced Filter Comparison Chart

Off

Low-key

Toy Camera

Dynamic Tone

Miniature

Soft Focus

Pop Color

Partial Color - Red

High-key

Partial Color - Orange

Figure 4-64. Advanced Filter Comparison Chart

FIGURE 4-65 shows a colorful playground structure photographed with the Toy Camera setting, giving the setting an appearance of unreality.

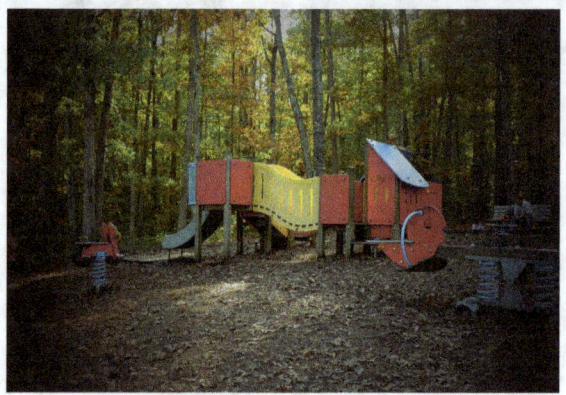

Figure 4-65. Toy Camera Example

Many people enjoy the stylized, purposely cheapened look of images taken with the Holga and similar cameras. The X100S comes with a built-in ability to let you experiment with this genre, so you might give it a try if you have any interest.

MINIATURE

The next Advanced Filter setting is called the Miniature effect. When you apply this option to an image, the camera adds blurring at the image's top and bottom, to simulate the appearance of a photograph of a tabletop model or miniature. Such images often appear blurred in one area, either because of the narrow depth of field of these closeup photos, or because of the use of a tilt-and-shift lens, which causes blurring at the edges.

For this feature to work well, you need to choose an appropriate subject. I have found that this effect looks interesting when applied to something like a street scene or a house, which might actually be reproduced in a tabletop model. For example, if you are able to get a high vantage point above a road intersection or a housing development, you may be able to use this processing to make it look as if you had photographed a high-quality tabletop diorama. You cannot adjust the size or location of the areas that the camera blurs at the top and bottom of the image, so you need to compose the image carefully, and try to frame in the center, vertically, the part of the scene that is to remain in sharp focus.

I used the X100S for an image of this sort in FIGURE 4-66, in which I photographed a canal, with the banks on either side in the blurred areas. The result is a scene that makes it look as if the canal is part of a tabletop layout.

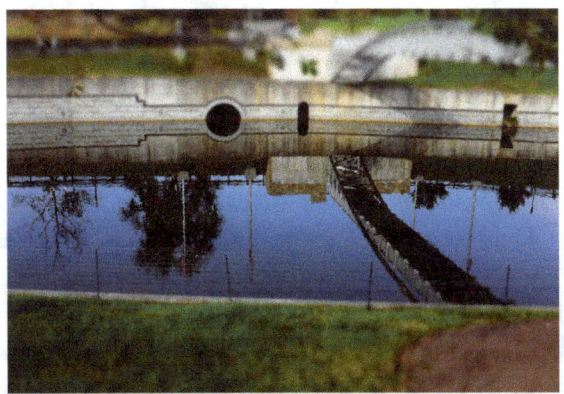

Figure 4-66. Miniature Effect Example

This effect can provide a lot of fun if you are willing to experiment with it; it can take some work to find the right subject and the best composition that will allow the sharp and blurry areas to achieve a satisfying result.

POP COLOR

This next setting, according to Fujifilm, is intended to give a "pop art" feel to your images through emphasis on bright colors with added saturation and contrast. As you can see in FIGURE 4-67, what you get with this setting is another way to add "punch" and intensity, along with added brightness, to your color images.

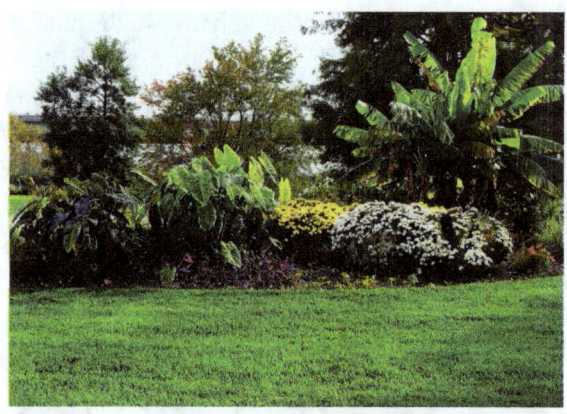

Figure 4-67. Pop Color Example

HIGH-KEY

The term "high key" refers to a technique with bright lighting throughout the scene, aiming for light colors and low contrast with few shadows. This technique often is used in fashion and advertising photography. On the X100S, this setting does not necessarily produce true high-key images, but their brightness and light tones provide a reasonable simulation of the effect. In FIGURE 4-68, I used this setting to emphasize the clean, white look of a new sink and fixtures, somewhat in the manner of an advertising image.

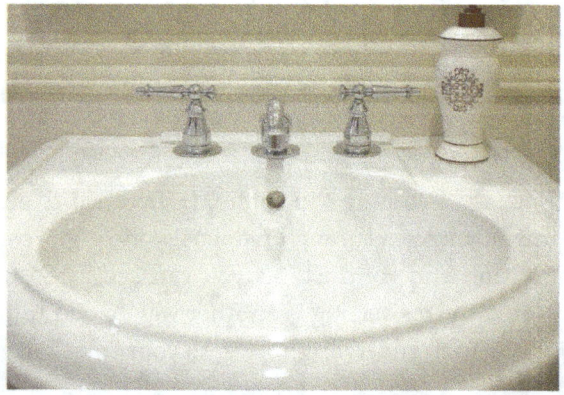

Figure 4-68. High-key Example

LOW-KEY

The next option, Low-key, is the opposite of High-key, emphasizing dark colors to produce a shadowy effect. In FIGURE 4-69, I used this option to try to convey a somewhat moody appearance for an area of old brick and heavy, dark wood trim above a fireplace.

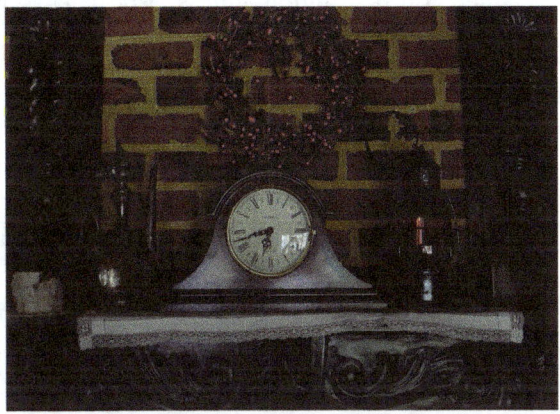

Figure 4-69. Low-key Example

DYNAMIC TONE

The Dynamic Tone setting can be looked on as the X100S's in-camera pseudo-HDR setting.

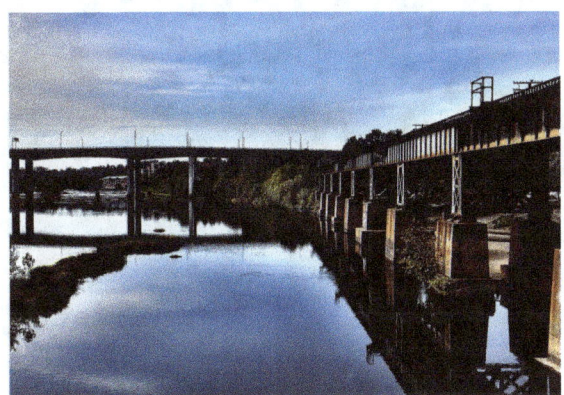

Figure 4-70. Dynamic Tone Example

Although the camera does not take multiple shots for this option, it uses special processing to enhance the dynamic range and contrast and to emphasize colors in a way that simulates the super-realistic appearance of some HDR composite images that are produced through software. The result is what Fujifilm calls a "fantasy" appearance for the image. In FIGURE 4-70, I used this setting to enhance a view of a railroad bridge on the James River. The camera added contrast and vividness, especially to the blues of the water and sky, and transformed the scene into a somewhat dramatic, super-realistic depiction of the setting.

SOFT FOCUS

With the Soft Focus setting, the X100S is programmed to purposely soften the focus throughout the image. With the right subject, this effect can help a scene appear quite peaceful and serene. In FIGURE 4-71, I used this setting to take a picture of some trees and bushes in a grassy area. The softness seemed to me to cast a dreamlike aura over the image.

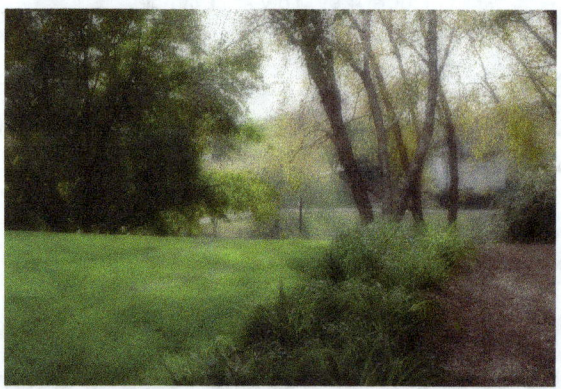

Figure 4-71. Soft Focus Example

PARTIAL COLOR

Finally, the camera provides six different versions of the Partial Color effect. This option lets you choose a single color to retain in an image; the camera then reduces the saturation of all other colors to monochrome, so that only objects of that single color remain in color in the image. I really enjoy this setting, which can be used to isolate a particular object with great dramatic effect.

The X100S has six sub-settings, each for a different color: Red, Orange, Yellow, Green, Blue, and Purple. In FIGURE 4-72, I used the Red setting to isolate a Stop sign from its surroundings. This setting can produce dramatic effects when there is only object in the image that retains its color, as in this case.

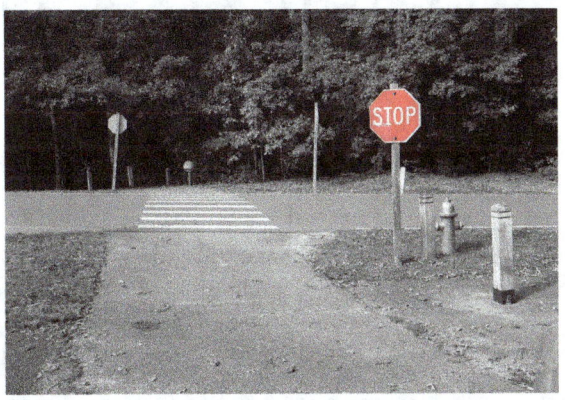

Figure 4-72. Partial Color Red Example

After you have chosen the color to be retained, aim the camera at your subject; you will see on the LCD display what objects will show up in color. There is no way to adjust the color tolerance of this setting, so you cannot, for example, set the camera to accept a broad range of reds to be retained in the image. By choosing a color that does not appear in the scene at all, you can take a straight monochrome photograph.

AF Mode

This option gives you two choices—Multi and Area—for setting up the way the camera chooses a location in the scene shown on the display as the point to focus on when you are using autofocus, as shown in FIGURE 4-73.

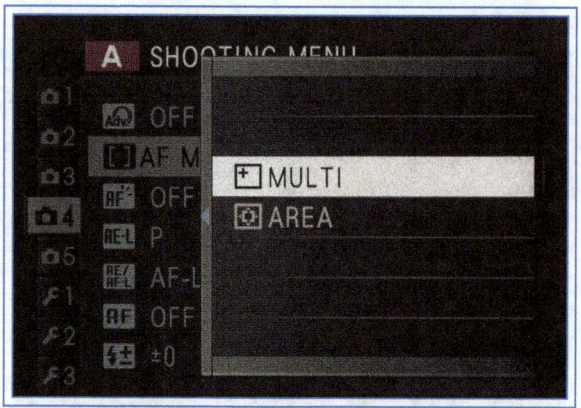

Figure 4-73. AF Mode Options Screen

There are 49 possible focus points when you are using the LCD screen or the electronic viewfinder, and 25 possible focus points when you are using the optical viewfinder. If you choose Multi for the AF Mode option, the camera will not initially place a focus frame on the display. Instead, it will use the whole screen as the focus area, and, when you press the shutter button halfway, it will attempt to focus using any one of its focus points, according to which subject in the scene appears to be the main subject. Once it has found a subject to focus on, it will display a green focus frame at that location, and the indicator lamp at the upper right of the camera's back will glow green, as shown in FIGURE 4-74.

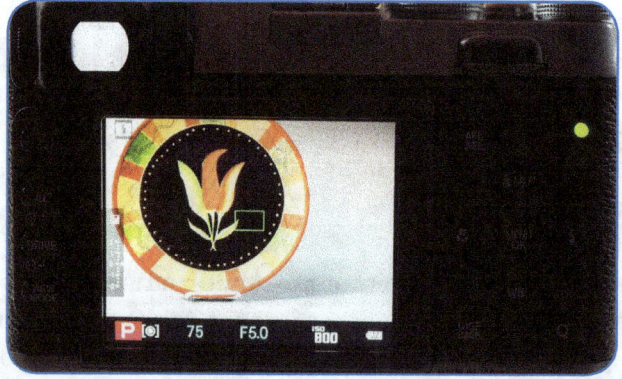

Figure 4-74. Focus Frame and Indicator Green for Good Focus

If, instead, you choose Area for the AF Mode, the camera will place a small white rectangular frame in the center of the image, as shown in FIGURE 4-75. The camera will focus only on a subject that falls within that frame.

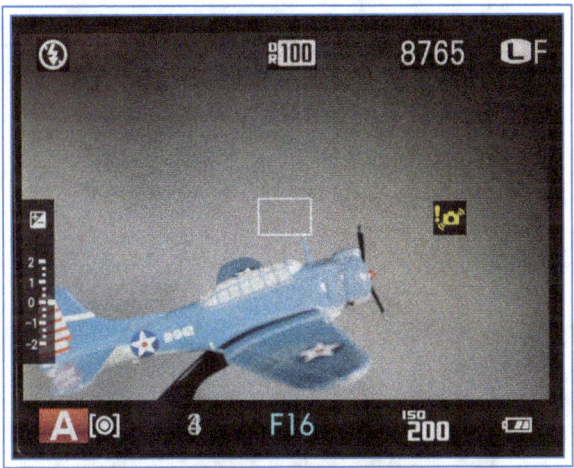

Figure 4-75. Area AF Mode Frame Before Moving

If you want to move the focus frame around the screen to any one of the possible 49 (or 25) focus points, press and release the AF button (Up button). The camera will display a screen with crosses marking the available focus points, as shown in FIGURE 4-76.

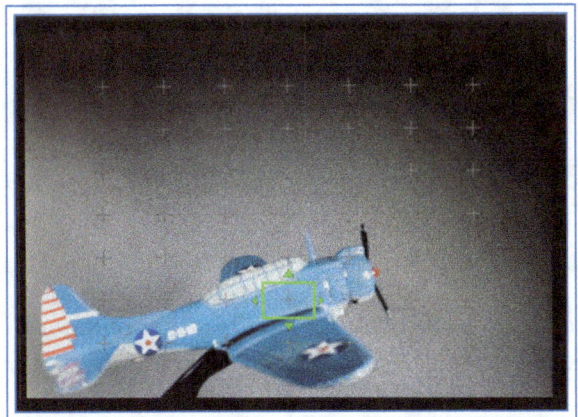

Figure 4-76. Area AF Mode Frame After Moving

You can move the focus frame, which will now be green, by pressing any of the four direction buttons or by turning the Command Dial until the focus frame is located where you want it. Then press the Menu/OK button, and you will see the focus frame, now turned white, at its new location, as shown in FIGURE 4-77.

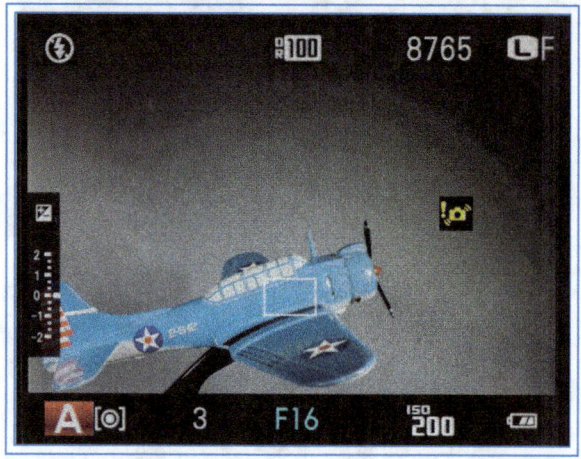

Figure 4-77. Area AF Mode Frame Ready to Focus After Moving

When you aim the camera, place the white frame over the most important object in the scene. Press the shutter button halfway so the camera will evaluate exposure and focus. You should hear a beep and the focus frame should turn green to confirm the focus. (If the frame turns red, you may be too close to the subject or it may be hard to focus on.) If everything looks acceptable to you, press the shutter button all the way to take the picture.

To change the size of the focus frame in Area mode, after pressing the AF button to activate the movable frame, press the Command Control to the left to make the frame smaller or to the right to make it larger. Press in on the switch to return it to normal size.

To return the frame immediately to the center of the screen, press the Display/Back button while the frame is activated for moving.

When the frame is fixed and ready to focus, you can press in on the Command Control to enlarge the area under the frame.

The Area option is useful when you need to focus on a person or object that is not in the center of the frame, because you can move the focus frame to cover the subject. If you don't remember how to move the focus frame, though, there is another way to handle this focus situation. Aim the camera so the white focus frame (in the center of the display) covers the most important subject, and press the shutter button halfway to lock in focus and exposure. Then, still holding the shutter button halfway down, move the camera back to compose the scene the way you want it, with the subject off to one side. The focus will remain locked, and you can now press the shutter button all the way down to take the picture.

You also can set the AFL/AEL button, located to the upper left of the Command Dial, to lock focus, as discussed in Chapter 5.

I personally prefer the Area setting for directing the location of the autofocus system, because I can move the frame directly over the subject that I want to be in sharpest focus, so I can be certain that the camera will focus on the right spot. However, if you are taking quick snapshots and won't have time to adjust the focus frame to the proper location, then you may want to choose the Multi option and let the camera determine where to set the focus point.

AF Illuminator

This menu option lets you turn on or off the white light beam that emanates from the AF Illuminator/Self-timer lamp on the front of the camera, just below the flash window. This beam comes on when the camera is trying to focus in a dark area; the light helps the autofocus mechanism find the patterns and shapes it needs to evaluate in order to achieve proper focus. You should usually leave this setting turned on, but you may want to turn it off when you're taking pictures in a place where the beam could be distracting or annoying to others, or where it might alert the subjects of your candid photography. (This light is remarkably bright, and you should not shine it in people's eyes if you can avoid doing so.)

The choices for this setting are On or Off. With On, which is the default setting, the lamp will fire when the camera's autofocus system determines that extra light is needed. With Off, the lamp will not illuminate to assist with autofocus. However, even with AF Illuminator turned off, the lamp will light to mark the countdown of the Self-timer. If you want to keep the lamp from lighting up at any time, you can set the camera to Silent Mode, either through the Setup menu or by pressing and holding the Display/Back button for two seconds. When the camera is in Silent Mode, the lamp will not light up for any purpose.

AE/AF Lock Mode

This option has a very specific function—to choose whether the AFL/AEL button has to be held down to do its work, or acts as a toggle switch that can be pressed and released. (You control the functions this button performs with the next menu item discussed below; this menu item controls only the physical behavior of the button itself.)

Select this menu item and choose either AE&AF On When Pressing, or AE&AF On/Off Switch, as shown in FIGURE 4-78.

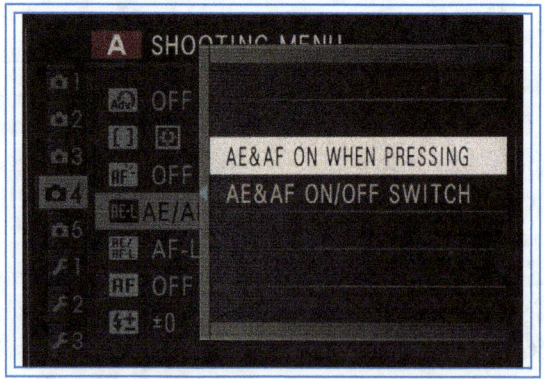

Figure 4-78. AE/AF Button Lock Mode Menu Option

If you choose the first option, the camera will display a P at the right side of the menu item, for Pressing; if you choose the second, the camera will display an S, for Switch. With the first option, you have to maintain pressure on the button to keep the exposure or focus, or both, locked. With the second option, the button becomes a toggle switch. In that case, you just press it and release it to lock or unlock the exposure and/or focus.

AE/AF Lock Button

The previous option lets you choose whether the AFL/AEL button has to be held down or acts as a toggle switch; this menu item gives the choice of what function the button performs when you hold it down or toggle it. The choices here, as shown in FIGURE 4-79, are AE Lock Only, AF Lock Only, and AE/AF Lock.

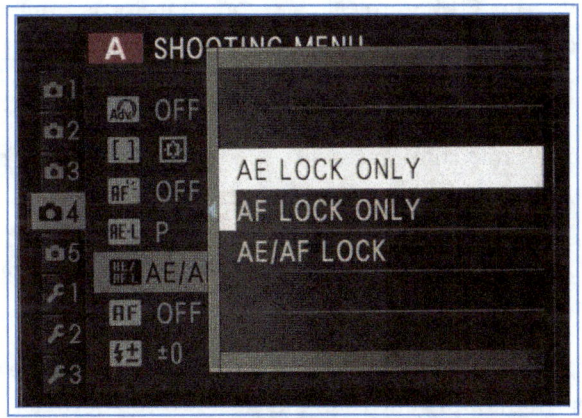

Figure 4-79. AE/AF Lock Button Menu Option

With the first choice, using this button locks only exposure; with the second, it locks only focus; with the third, it locks both. In Chapter 5, where I discuss the camera's physical controls, I will discuss scenarios for the use of this button.

Corrected AF Frame

This next entry on the Shooting menu adds a second autofocus frame to the display in the optical viewfinder in order to show you the effects of parallax on your view of the subject. When you use the optical viewfinder, you are looking through the camera's optical window, which is offset from the lens. When you use the LCD or the electronic viewfinder, you are seeing exactly what the lens sees. At long distances, this parallax effect is negligible. However, when you view an object fairly close to the camera using the optical viewfinder, you see a slightly different view than what will appear on the final image.

This option works only when you are using the optical viewfinder and you have set the AF Mode to Area in the Shooting menu. If you turn on the Corrected AF Frame option under these conditions, the X100S projects a second autofocus frame slightly to the right of and below the normal frame. Then, if you focus on an object fairly close to the camera and press the shutter button halfway, you will see three frames in the optical viewfinder: a solid white frame that represents the focus area at a far distance (infinity); a set of white focus brackets that represents the focus area at the closest non-macro focus distance, which is 1.6 feet (50 cm); and a green frame that represents the position of the AF frame at the current focus distance.

As you focus on objects farther and farther away from the camera, the green frame will get closer and closer to the normal AF frame for the far distance, indicating that the parallax error is becoming smaller and smaller. If you focus on an object about 1.6 feet (50 cm) from the camera, the green frame will coincide with the corrected AF frame, indicating that the parallax error is greatest at that distance. (Parallax error is not a factor at distances below that, because you then have to use Macro focus, and the optical viewfinder cannot be used with Macro focus, because the parallax error would be too great to correct.)

Personally, I prefer not to deal with multiple autofocus frames. I prefer just to use the electronic viewfinder or the LCD if I am dealing with a subject for which parallax error will be an important consideration. However, if you prefer using the optical viewfinder, then it is convenient to be able to turn on this option so you can see where your focus area will be placed when you are focusing with that viewfinder using the moveable focus frame.

Flash

This final option on the fourth Shooting menu screen, which is often called flash exposure compensation on other cameras, works in similar fashion to standard exposure compensation, discussed in Chapter 2. That is, you can dial in an amount of flash exposure compensation up to plus or minus 2/3 EV unit, in increments of 1/3 EV. (EV stands for exposure value, or f-stop, in this context.) When you do that, you are causing the camera to add or subtract the specified amount of flash power as compared to the normal setting, to brighten or darken the image by that amount.

To select this setting, go to its entry on the menu screen and press the OK button or the Right button to get to the adjustment screen, shown in FIGURE 4-80.

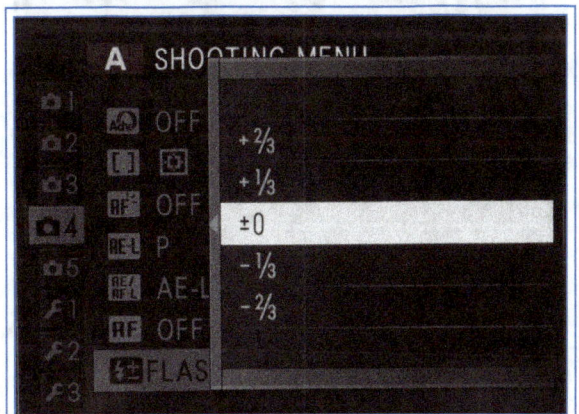

Figure 4-80. Flash Menu Item

At that screen, turn the Command Dial or use the Up and Down buttons to dial in as much as +2/3 EV or -2/3 EV, to make your flash exposures that much brighter or darker. Press the OK button to confirm your selection when the value you want to choose is highlighted by the selection rectangle. Any value you set for flash compensation will remain in effect even after the camera has been powered off and back on, so be sure to cancel it by setting it back to zero when you no longer need the adjustment. Note that the camera does not place any indication on the shooting screen that this setting is in effect, so you need to keep track of it yourself and make sure it is not set when you do not want it. This setting also works when you have a compatible external flash unit attached to the hot shoe.

Finally, I will discuss the two items on the fifth and final screen of the Shooting menu, shown in FIGURE 4-81.

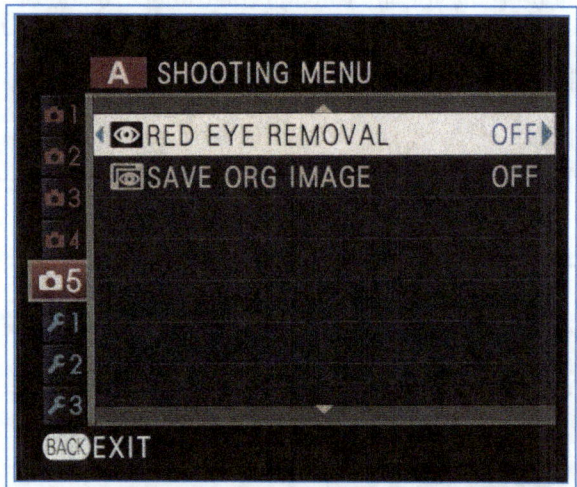

Figure 4-81. Fifth Screen of Shooting Menu

Red Eye Removal

This first option on the final Shooting menu screen lets you adjust the camera's approach to producing images that do not suffer from "red-eye"—the red cast to human eyes that results from on-camera flash that lights up the blood vessels on the retina. The first line of defense is to set the flash mode to Auto Flash, Forced Flash, or Slow Synchro with this Red Eye Removal menu option turned on. You will see an eyeball icon next to the flash mode's lightning bolt icon when Red Eye Removal is activated, as shown in FIGURE 4-82.

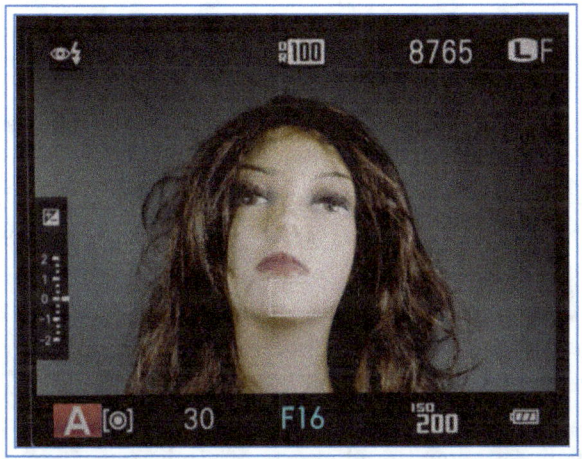

Figure 4-82. Red Eye Icon with Flash Mode Icon

With this option in effect, the camera fires its flash unit once before the image is taken with the actual flash shot; the "pre-flash" is intended to cause the subject's pupils to narrow, thereby reducing the ability of the later, full flash to enter them, bounce off the retinas, and produce the unwanted red glow in the eyes.

In addition to firing the pre-flash, when this menu option is turned on, the camera performs in-camera processing on the image itself if the camera detects a face in the image. This processing does a good job of eliminating or reducing red-eye in some cases, in my experience. This feature does not operate with Raw images, however.

My own preference is to leave this menu option turned off and to deal with red-eye effects by removing them with editing software, if necessary. However, if you will be taking flash photos at a party, you may want to use this menu option to minimize the occurrence of red-eye effects in the first place.

Note that the X100S also has a similar option in Playback mode, discussed in Chapter 6, which causes the camera to attempt to remove red-eye from images after they have been recorded by the camera.

Save Original Image

This final Shooting menu option lets you control whether or not the camera saves an unaltered copy of each image that is taken using the Red Eye Removal feature. As discussed above, when that menu option is activated, the camera not only fires the flash twice to reduce the red-eye effect, it also uses digital processing to try to remove the red spots in people's eyes. In doing this, it may affect an image in undesirable ways. Therefore, you may want to turn the Save Original Image option on, so you will have an unprocessed copy of the image. That copy may suffer from red-eye, but at least it will not show the ill effects of a misfired attempt at red-eye removal. Then, if the red-eye is bothersome, you can tackle it using your preferred photo editing software.

CHAPTER 5:
Physical Controls

One of the defining features of the Fujifilm X100S is that it has more physical control dials and buttons than many other compact cameras. With some cameras, you have to probe deeply into menu systems to adjust fairly basic settings such as White Balance, flash mode, or metering mode. With the X100S, although you still need to do a fair amount of work in the menu screens, there is a good assortment of controls that let you make quick adjustments to several of the most important settings. In this chapter, I will discuss the functions of each button and dial and explain how you can use them to achieve good images. I will not discuss items, such as the strap eyelets, microphone openings, flash, and viewfinder window, whose functions are obvious or are discussed in connection with other topics.

I will start with the control that occupies its own spot on the left side of the camera, as shown in FIGURE 5-1.

Focus Switch

This slide switch on the left side of the camera has three positions: MF for manual focus, AF-C for autofocus-continuous, and AF-S for autofocus-single. The operation of the switch is as simple as it gets: Just slide the switch to the position you want and leave it there. There are no menus to deal with, and no further choices to make. And, with the X100S, Fujifilm has tweaked the switch a bit from how it was set up on the X100. Now the two most often-used settings, MF and AF-S, are at the top and bottom positions, respectively. Because of this arrangement, you can easily set the switch by feel, without looking at it. Just slide it to the top for manual focus, or push it to the bottom for single-shot autofocus.

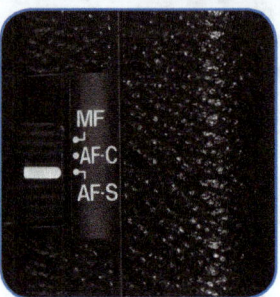

Figure 5-1. Focus Switch

There are some special considerations to be aware of, which I will discuss for each of the three options.

Manual Focus

If you select the MF position, the camera goes into manual focus mode. As I discussed briefly in Chapter 2, in order to focus manually, you just turn the focus ring to adjust the focus—to the left (as you stand behind the camera) to decrease the focus distance, and to the right to increase it. A red indicator bar will appear in the blue distance scale at the bottom of the display to show the approximate focus distance being set, as shown in FIGURE 5-2. If you look closely at that indicator you will see a small white area surrounding it, which gives an approximate idea of the depth of field at the current settings.

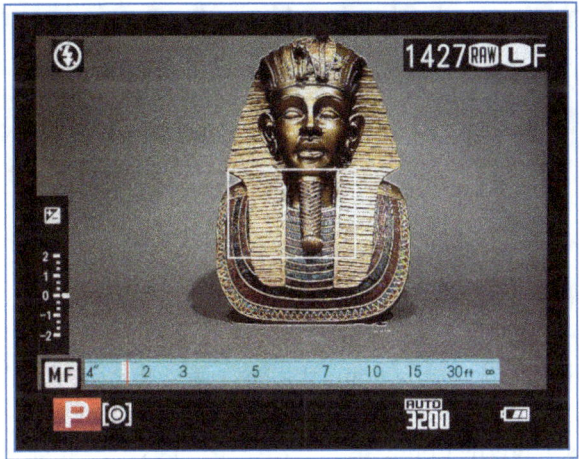

Figure 5-2. Manual Focus Scale on Display

If you have difficulty seeing the screen to judge the sharpness of the focus, you can enlarge the display. To do this, press in on the Command Control (the black switch at the top of the right side of the camera's back). For other purposes, you press this switch left or right, but in this case you press in on the center of the switch. You can then release the switch, and the display will stay magnified until you press the switch in again.

While the image is magnified, or while it is at normal size, you can at any time press the AFL/AEL button, which is just below the Command Control, to cause the camera to autofocus on the scene. In this way, even though you are using manual focus, you can get the benefit of the camera's autofocus system. If the camera is able to focus, it will beep to confirm the focus (if sounds are turned on), but the focus frame will not turn green as it does in autofocus-single-shot mode. Once the camera has used its autofocus, you can continue to adjust the focus manually until it is fine-tuned to your satisfaction.

If the enlargement of the focusing screen is not sufficient to let you focus clearly, you can use either the Digital Split Image or the Focus Peak Highlight option to add further enhancements. Those were both discussed in Chapter 4. You also can turn on the Focus Check option, found on the second screen of the Setup menu, discussed in Chapter 7, which causes the camera to enlarge the manual focus display as soon as you start turning the focus ring, without the need to press the Command Control.

You also should consider using the electronic viewfinder whenever possible for scenes that require critical focusing, because you are likely to find it easier to achieve sharp focus on that display than on the LCD. With the optical viewfinder, the scene is always in focus, so you cannot evaluate the manual focus using that view, other than by viewing the focus scale at the bottom of the display. However, if you press in on the Command Control to enlarge the image (or turn the focus ring with Focus Check turned on), the camera switches to the electronic viewfinder so you can evaluate the manual focus. You also can press the AFL button to cause the camera to use its autofocus, even when using the optical viewfinder.

Autofocus–Single Shot

When the focus switch is at the AF-S position, the X100S is placed into the autofocus mode for single shots. The camera does not try to focus until you press the shutter button. When you press the shutter button halfway to lock focus (and exposure), the autofocus system attempts to find a subject that it can focus on sharply.

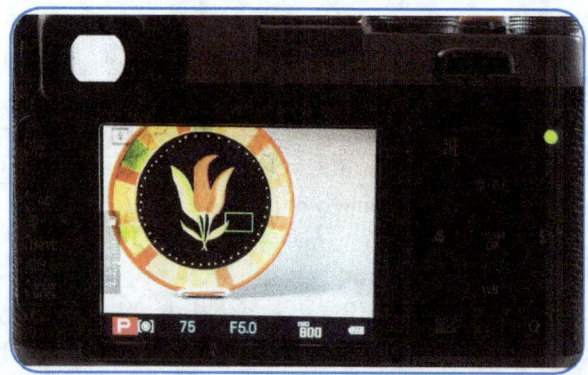

Figure 5-3. AF Frame and Indicator Lamp Green for Good Focus

If it is successful, you will hear a beep (unless beeps are turned off in the Setup menu), and you will see two indicators: a green focus frame will appear on the display, and the camera's indicator light, high on the right side of the camera's back, will glow green or blink green, as shown in FIGURE 5-3. If the light glows green steadily, focus is locked; if it blinks green, that means there may be an issue such as the risk of blur from a slow shutter speed, but the picture can be taken. Once the focus is set, it stays locked as long as you keep the shutter button pressed halfway down. If the subject moves, focus may be lost, because the camera will not adjust the focus distance to track the subject.

The area the camera focuses on is controlled by the AF Mode option on the fourth screen of the Shooting menu, discussed in Chapter 4. With the Multi setting, the camera selects the focus point; with Area, the camera uses the focus frame, which you can place where you want it. If you are using the Area setting and you want to enlarge the screen to get a better view, you can press in on the Command Control, in the same way as with manual focus. In this way, you can make sure the camera is focusing exactly where you want it to. Press the Command Control again to return the display to its normal size.

Autofocus–Continuous

If you slide the focus switch to the middle, AF-C position, the camera is placed into the autofocus mode for continuous focusing. When the camera is in this mode, you may hear continuous sounds from the camera as the autofocus mechanism adjusts to keep the subject in focus as the subject or the camera moves. You will see a white crosshair rather than a focus frame in the center of the image, as shown in FIGURE 5-4, and the camera will focus on whatever object is in the center of the image, under that crosshair. Then, when you press the shutter button halfway, the camera will lock focus and the continuous focusing will stop. When focus is confirmed, the crosshair will turn green, the indicator light will turn green, and the camera will beep.

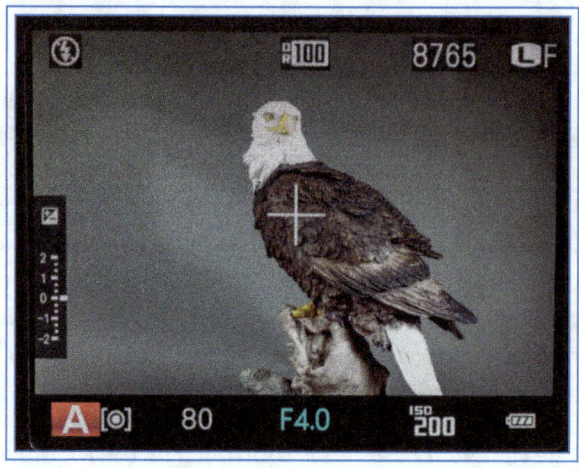

Figure 5-4. White Crosshair for Continuous AF Mode

The theoretical usefulness of the AF-C setting is to get the approximate focus set before you press the shutter button, so the final focusing will finish more quickly when it's time to take the picture, though it is not clear that focus times are much improved with this focus method. Also, this focus mode does not provide continuous focusing on a moving subject after the shutter button is pressed; in other words, there is no "tracking" autofocus as there is with some cameras. However, it may be that the AF-C mode provides more accurate focusing than the AF-S mode, particularly in low light and with low-contrast subjects, so it is worth trying. Of course, any sort of continuous autofocusing will drain your battery more quickly than normal, so be careful not to use it excessively if you are running low on battery power.

If you use the AFL/AEL button to lock focus while in AF-C mode, the crosshair will change into a green box, just as in AF-S mode.

When this focus mode is selected, the AF Mode menu option is dimmed and cannot be selected, because there is no focus frame that could be moved using the Area option for AF Mode.

Next, I will discuss the few items on the front of the camera, as shown in FIGURE 5-5.

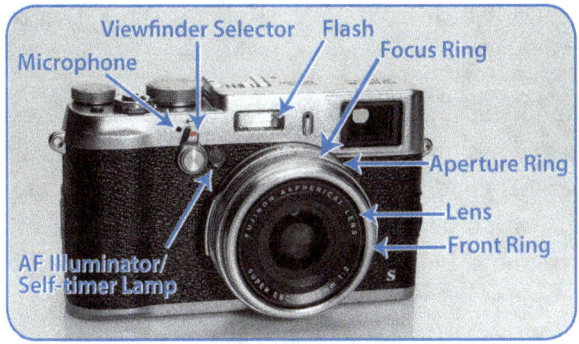

Figure 5-5. Items on Front of Camera

Lens Assembly

The X100S's lens and its associated items are among the most important items on the camera.

The lens itself is a high-quality Fujinon lens with an actual focal length of 23mm. Because the X100S has a sensor that is smaller than the size of a frame of 35mm film, the "35mm-equivalent" focal length of the lens is 35mm. In other words, the X100S's lens provides a field of view that is equivalent to that of a 35mm lens on a camera that uses 35mm film. That 35mm focal length is the hallmark of a wide-angle lens; a "normal" focal length is often thought of as about 50mm, and 35mm or lower is usually considered wide-angle. For this sort of camera, though, which is modeled to some extent after the rangefinder cameras of the past, it is quite normal to have a wide-angle lens of this sort, which is suitable for the wide views and broad depth of field that are useful for street photography and other sorts of picture-taking this type of camera often is used for.

The X100S's lens has a maximum aperture of f/2.0, which is considered a "fast" aperture for any lens. In other words, the lens gathers a good deal of light, making the camera useful for low-light photography. And, at the wide f/2.0 aperture, the lens has a shallow depth of field, which makes it possible for the X100S to capture images with blurred backgrounds, as discussed in Chapter 3.

While I'm discussing the lens, I will mention one issue that sometimes comes up about the X100S. Some potential purchasers of the camera wonder if they will be satisfied being limited to a single lens with a relatively wide-angle field of view. Personally, I have not found this "limitation" to be an issue. In fact, it can be liberating not to worry about zooming or choosing a focal length. For an excellent article about the joys of using the single focal length of the predecessor model, the X100, see the article by Steve Huff listed in Appendix C.

The ring around the lens that is closest to the camera's body is the aperture ring, whose only function is to set the camera's aperture. It turns easily and clicks into place on any full f-stop setting, from the widest setting at f/2.0 to the most narrow at f/16. If you set it to the red A, the camera will set the aperture automatically. As discussed in Chapter 3, you can set intermediate f-stops by pressing the Command Control to the left or right.

The ridged ring farther out from the camera's body is the focus ring. When the camera is in manual focus mode, you turn this ring to bring the image into sharp focus. There is no mechanical connection between the ring and the focus mechanism; rather, the camera uses an electronic system, which translates the motion of the ring into manual focusing. As discussed in Chapter 4, you can press the AFL/AEL button to shorten the process and have the camera provide an autofocus assist.

Finally, the outermost movable ring, called simply the "front ring" by Fujifilm, is a decorative item that is screwed on to the front of the lens. You have to remove this ring if you want to install the Wide Conversion Lens or the filter adapter for the camera, as discussed in Appendix A. This ring can be somewhat hard to remove; you have to grasp the camera firmly to get a grip on this thin ring, but it will screw off without difficulty once you get a good grip on it. Some users report that they have better success removing the ring if they leave the lens cap on, and grip the lens cap very firmly while twisting counter-clockwise; the front ring should be loosened by this action.

AF Illuminator/Self-timer Lamp

The lamp that sits just below the flash, near the lens, has two important functions. First, it serves as the AF Illuminator. In that capacity, the lamp sends out a beam in dim lighting conditions to assist with autofocus. The light cast by this lamp lets the autofocus mechanism "see" clearly enough to detect the contrasting edges it needs in order to evaluate the focus. Note that the use of the lamp can be controlled through the fourth screen of the Shooting menu. You can use the AF Illuminator menu item to turn the lamp off, in which case it will never illuminate for autofocus purposes. You can achieve the same effect by setting the Silent Mode menu item to On in the first screen of the Setup menu. That feature cancels the camera's beeps as well as all uses of the lamp and the flash. You can turn Silent Mode on or off quickly at any time by holding down the Display/Back button for about two seconds.

The other function of the lamp is as the indicator light when the Self-timer is operating. When the Self-timer is set for two seconds, the lamp blinks several times and then glows steadily as the countdown ends and the picture is taken. When the timer is set for ten seconds, the lamp glows steadily for several seconds and then finishes with a pattern similar to that for the two-second countdown.

You will notice that the lamp is quite bright and can be distracting or annoying to your subjects. And, of course, it can call attention to your camera (and you) if you are doing street photography in dim lighting, or if you are using the camera in any other location where you don't want to cause a disturbance. So, consider disabling it for one or both of its functions. Use the AF Illuminator menu option to cancel it for autofocus only, or the

Silent Mode option to cancel it for both autofocus and Self-timer purposes.

Viewfinder Selector

This switch with a red-marked handle sits just to the left of the AF Illuminator/Self-timer lamp as you face the camera. The little arrow above the handle reminds you of the direction in which to press the switch, whose only function is to select the optical viewfinder (OVF) or the electronic viewfinder (EVF). As you hold the camera for shooting, you pull the switch to your right and then let it go, to toggle between these two viewfinder modes.

Naturally enough, the switch is of use only when you have selected the viewfinder instead of the LCD using the View Mode button, or you have selected the Eye Sensor mode and you have your eye against the viewfinder, thereby activating it.

This switch is very convenient to use, and its presence adds considerably to the usefulness of the "hybrid viewfinder," one of the prime features of the X100S. When you are using the viewfinder, you can, with a flick of this switch, change from the OVF to the EVF. In this way, you can enjoy the best features of each viewfinder mode. With the OVF, you get an extremely bright view of the subject using natural light, seeing exactly what is in front of the camera through a bright optical "window." The image is always sharp, regardless of the actual focus, so you can see your subject clearly, and there is no display lag from electronic processing. In addition, the camera displays a good amount of shooting information in the OVF window. The OVF also includes helpful features such as the Histogram and the Electronic Level, if you have set up the display to include them using the Custom Display Setting option on the Shooting menu. (You can set what items are displayed in the OVF and, independently, what items are displayed in the EVF/LCD, using the Display Custom Setting option on the third screen of the Shooting menu.)

Finally, the OVF provides a field of view that is slightly larger than the image captured by the camera, so you can see the scene in a somewhat broader context than with the EVF or LCD.

However, when using the OVF, you are actually viewing the scene through a viewfinder window that is above and to the side of the lens. In other words, you are viewing through a window near the lens, and not through the lens itself. Therefore, there is a parallax effect, meaning the view you get through the OVF is offset somewhat from what the lens is actually aimed at, and from the view that will appear in the captured image. The parallax effect, naturally, is more of an issue as you get closer to your subject.

If you are shooting a landscape in the distance, the parallax effect will be negligible. Also, the X100S includes on the fourth screen of the Shooting menu an option called Corrected AF Frame, which helps you focus accurately through the OVF at moderate distances. But, if you are shooting a macro picture, the parallax effect is likely to be so significant as to make the view through the OVF practically useless. In fact, if Macro focus is activated, the camera will automatically switch to the EVF for this reason.

Also, the OVF view does not include all of the information provided in the EVF view, such as the icon showing that the Self-timer is turned on or that Silent Mode has been activated. It also does not show you the effects of various settings on matters such as focus, depth of field, White Balance, and exposure, as the EVF does.

So, to enjoy the advantages of electronic viewing, you can flick the viewfinder switch to change to the EVF view. With this view, you get a considerable amount of additional information, as noted above, but with a dimmer view, not the bright, crisp view provided by the OVF, and with some lag time for the display to refresh. The advantage, though, is that you are seeing exactly what the camera sees through the lens, so there is no parallax effect to worry about.

You could, of course, switch to the view on the LCD, which is identical to the view in the EVF. However, in bright sunlight it may not be possible to see the LCD. Also, you may prefer the traditional technique of holding the camera against your face to look through the viewfinder, which provides some extra stability for the camera, rather than holding the camera out in your arms so you can see the LCD.

Now it's time to discuss the top of the camera, where several important controls are found, as shown in FIGURE 5-6.

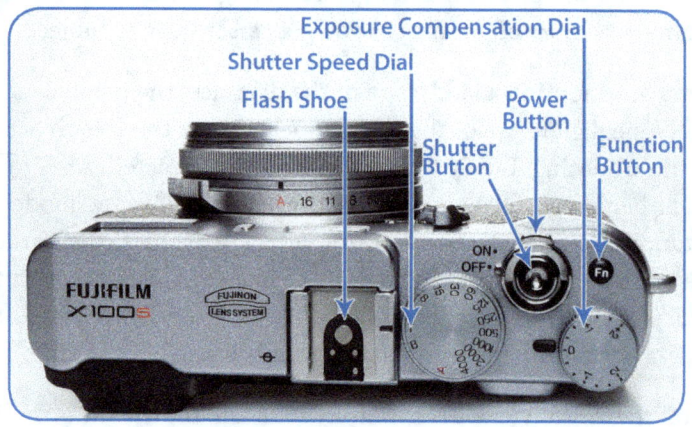

Figure 5-6. Controls on Top of Camera

Shutter Speed Dial

As discussed in Chapter 3, you use this dial to set the shutter speed when you are using the Shutter Priority or Manual exposure mode. When you are using Aperture Priority or Program mode, you turn this dial so its red letter A is lined up with the black indicator line, so that the shutter speed will be set automatically by the camera.

When you are setting the shutter speed, you are not limited to the values that appear on this dial. You can turn the Command Dial to set intermediate shutter speeds. For example, when the shutter speed dial is turned to the setting labeled 250, for 1/250 second, you can turn the Command Dial right or left to call up the intermediate settings of 1/160 second, 1/200 second, 1/320 second, and 1/400 second.

When the shutter speed dial is turned to the T setting, for time exposure, you can turn the Command Dial to call up the settings of ½ second, 1/1.6 second (5/8 second), 1/1.3 second (.8 second), 1 second, 1.3 seconds, 1.5 seconds, 2 seconds, and several other values up to 30 seconds. The values shorter than 1 second appear with no added symbol; those of 1 second or longer appear with a double apostrophe after the numeral, such as 2". (If the 2 were displayed with no apostrophes, the setting would be ½ second.)

When the shutter speed dial is set to the B setting, for Bulb exposure (named for the days when photographers used an air bulb to hold the shutter open), you press the shutter button and hold it down for as long as you want the exposure to last, up to 60 minutes. You can use a conventional cable release, screwed in to the shutter button, to trigger and hold the shutter down for long periods of time.

If the aperture dial is turned to the A setting, in which the aperture is set automatically, the B setting on the shutter speed dial sets the shutter speed to 30 seconds rather than Bulb. Also, if the Drive mode is set to continuous shooting or bracketing, the B setting will change to 30 seconds. The camera must be set for single shots in Manual exposure mode for the B setting to be fully available.

Shutter Release Button

The shutter release button is the single most important control on the camera. When you press it halfway, the camera evaluates exposure and focus (unless you're using manual focus). Once you are satisfied with the settings, you press the button all the way down to record the image. When the camera is set for continuous shooting, you hold this button down while the camera fires repeatedly. For movies, though, you just press this button and release it, and then press it again (either all the way or halfway) to stop recording.

The button also can be used to switch the camera back to shooting mode when you have been reviewing images in playback mode, and it can be pressed to bring the camera back to life when it has gone to sleep after a set period of time because of the Auto Power Off sub-option of the Power Management setting in the Setup menu. (To awaken the camera after this "sleep," you need to give the shutter button a fairly long press, not just a quick tap.)

Finally, Fujifilm has provided a useful feature that is in keeping with the "retro" styling of the X100S: The shutter button is threaded to accept a standard, mechanical cable release, which can be used to trigger the camera at any shutter speed to avoid camera shake that can be caused when you press the button with your finger. A cable release, particularly one with a locking mechanism, also can be of particular use when you are using the B setting for Bulb exposures; you can start the exposure by pressing the cable release and locking it, and end the exposure by unlocking the release. You also can screw in a "soft release," a small button that serves as a smoother surface for your finger to press when actuating the shutter. There is more discussion of cable releases and soft releases in Appendix A.

Power Button

The power button is a small ring with a handle, surrounding the shutter button. Its only function is to turn the camera on and off. When the Auto Power Off function is activated through the Power Management item on screen 2 of the Setup menu, the camera's power will turn off after the specified time, even if this switch is in the On position. In that situation, you can press the shutter button halfway to bring the camera back to operation, or you can turn the power button off and back on. As noted above, to wake the camera up with the shutter button, you need to give the button a fairly long press, not just a tap. You also can wake up the camera by pressing the Playback button, which will wake the camera up into playback mode.

Exposure Compensation Dial

This dial at the far right of the top of the camera is another aspect of the X100S's "retro" styling, as well as a welcome convenience for photographers. With some modern cameras, you have to find and press a tiny button and then turn a dial or press other buttons to adjust exposure compensation. With the X100S, all you have to do is turn this dial to your chosen setting, and you're done. The dial is marked with clear designations from -2 to +2 EV (exposure value) in increments of 1/3 stop. As you turn the dial, the setting appears on the vertical scale at the far left of the display, as shown in FIGURE 5-7, where a positive adjustment of 1.67 EV is shown.

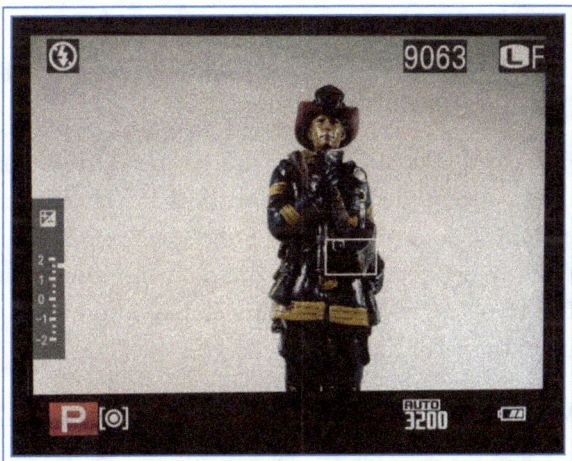

Figure 5-7. Exposure Compensation Scale on Screen

Exposure compensation is not available in Manual exposure mode. Turning the dial will have no effect in that mode. However, if you turn the dial while the camera is in Manual mode, any setting you have made will take effect when the camera is switched to Aperture Priority, Shutter Priority, or Program mode.

Function Button

This button, marked with the letters Fn for Function, is a very small control, just to the right of the shutter button. It is hard to see, but it sits in a perfect spot for your index finger to find it by sliding off of the shutter button. It performs the helpful task of giving you instant access to one operation of your choice, which can be selected through the Function Button option on the Shooting menu, as discussed in Chapter 4. As explained in that chapter, by default the button is assigned to control the ISO setting, but there are numerous other possibilities as well, including Preview Depth of Field, Toggle Raw/JPEG, and others. I personally find that the ND Filter setting is one of the most useful, because you can press this button to activate the ND filter immediately, without having to dig through a menu system to find it, and then select the On setting. If I don't expect to be faced with bright conditions that will require the use of the ND filter, I am usually content to leave the Function button set to its default setting of ISO, so I can get quick access to the ISO adjustment screen.

However, as I will discuss further in Chapter 8, if you expect to be recording video sequences on short notice it can be very useful to assign the Movie option to the Function button. Then, if you suddenly see an opportunity to record a movie, you can just press this button to place the camera immediately into Movie mode so you can start the recording.

The next location for controls is the left side of the back of the X100S, as seen in FIGURE 5-8.

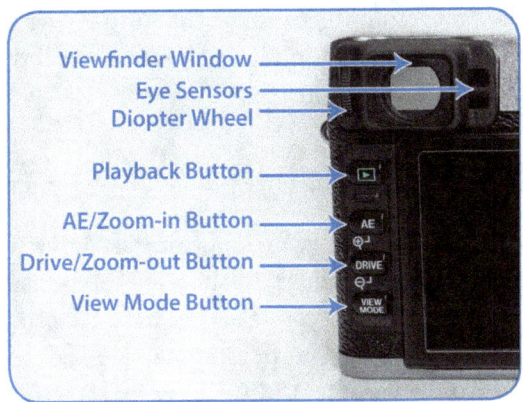

Figure 5-8. Controls on Left Side of Camera's Back

Diopter Adjustment Wheel

The small wheel on the left side of the viewfinder is used to dial in optical correction to the viewfinder so you can see a sharply focused image in the viewfinder window. Just press the View Mode button to activate the viewfinder display (either optical or electronic), and then turn this wheel in either direction until the image is at its clearest for your eyesight. In some cases, if you wear glasses, you may be able to dial in enough of an adjustment that you can take your glasses off and still see the image clearly through the viewfinder.

Playback Button

This button just below the viewfinder, marked with a small triangle, is used to put the camera into playback mode, which allows you to view your recorded images and videos on the LCD (or in the electronic viewfinder) and lets you get access to the Playback menu. If you press this button while the camera is in playback mode, the camera will switch to shooting mode. If you hold this button down while turning on the camera, the camera will start up in playback mode. Also, you can press this button and hold it for about one second to wake up the camera after it has automatically powered off because of the Auto Power Off setting. In that case, it will wake up in playback mode. I will discuss your options for playback in Chapter 6.

AE/Zoom-in Button

This control, just below the Playback button, has different functions in shooting and playback modes. In shooting mode, as the AE (for autoexposure) button, it lets you select the light metering system to be used by the camera for determining the proper exposure. Press the AE button and the camera will display its screen for selecting the metering method. If you are using the LCD or the electronic viewfinder, the camera will display the heading Photometry at the top of the screen, as shown in FIGURE 5-9.

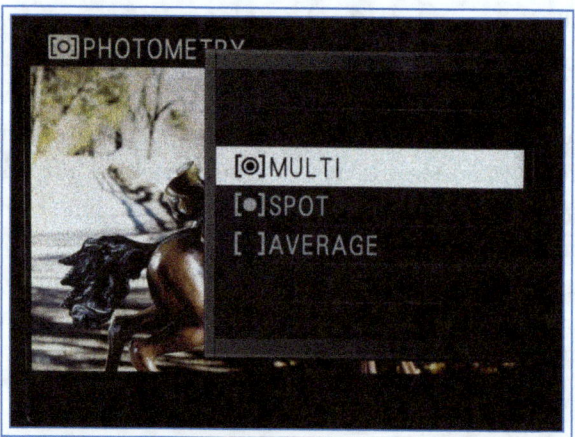

Figure 5-9. Photometry Options

If you are using the optical viewfinder, the camera will display only the icon for the currently selected metering method, in the top left corner of the screen. To select one of the choices, press the Up or Down button, turn the Command Dial, or move the Command Control switch to the left or right until your selection is highlighted. Press the OK button to confirm the selection and exit from this screen, and an icon representing the selected method will appear in the lower left corner of the display if the LCD or

EVF is in use, as shown in Figure 5-10. If the OVF is active, the icon will appear in the upper left corner.

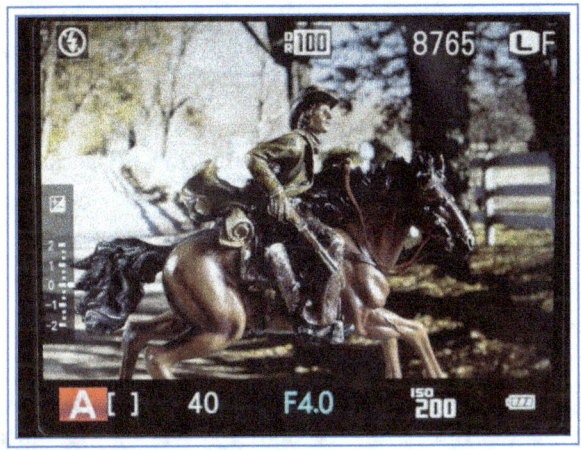

Figure 5-10. Metering Mode Icon for Average Mode

The three choices are Multi, Spot, and Average. With Multi, the recommended setting for general shooting, the camera evaluates brightness throughout the scene, but takes into account factors such as composition, colors, and how the brightness values are distributed throughout the scene. In other words, it tries to make an intelligent assessment of which part of the scene is most important and should be used to determine the correct exposure.

With Spot, the camera considers only the light inside the two percent of the scene in the very center of the display. (The camera does not display any frame or circle to mark the area used by the Spot setting.) When you set the metering method to Spot, you can see the effects of the exposure system quite dramatically by setting the camera to Program exposure mode and aiming the center portion of the screen at various points, some bright and some dark, and see how dramatically the brightness of the scene in the camera's display changes (if you are using the LCD or electronic viewfinder). If you try a similar experiment by moving the camera around to aim at differently lit areas in Multi or Average mode, you will still see changes, but more subtle and gradual ones.

Finally, with the Average setting, the camera measures the amount of light through all areas of the display and averages the results to obtain the value for the exposure setting. With this option, the camera does not attempt to determine what parts of the scene are most important. This method is useful for scenes that do not have great variations in lighting, such as landscapes.

ZOOM-IN BUTTON

In playback mode, the AE/Zoom-in button is used to zoom in on an image that is being viewed on the LCD or on the electronic viewfinder display. Once playback mode is in effect, press this button repeatedly to zoom to higher levels of magnification; a vertical scale will appear at the left of the display to show how high the magnification level is, and an inset image will appear at the right to show what part of the image is being displayed at the zoomed level. Also, if you have displayed index screens using the Zoom-out button, discussed later in this chapter, pressing the Zoom-in button will cycle through those screens until the normal display is reached again. Playback functions are discussed in more detail in Chapter 6.

Drive/Zoom-out Button

This next button down on the left side of the camera's back, like the first one, has different functions in shooting and playback modes. When the camera is in shooting mode, the Drive button gives you access to the multiple options for Drive mode, which are among the most important features of the camera.

The details for each of these Drive mode settings are discussed below. Before discussing them, though, I will provide a brief introduction to the concept of continuous shooting.

With film cameras, continuous shooting involves the use of a special motor to advance the film rapidly, and often the use of a special cassette to hold a large quantity of film. This sort of equipment is bulky and expensive, and, of course, shooting and developing large numbers of film exposures is quite expensive. With digital cameras like the X100S, expense is not a factor. Continuous shooting is literally available at your fingertips whenever you want to take advantage of it.

The usefulness of shooting rapid bursts of exposures is more obvious in some contexts than in others. For example, when you're shooting sports events, it's clearly worthwhile to fire off a swift sequence of shots in order to catch the instant when a baseball player tags a runner heading for home plate, or to catch a soccer ball as it bounces off a player's head toward the goal.

But continuous shooting also can be helpful in more ordinary shooting, such as when you're taking pictures of children at play. You have a better chance of capturing a fleeting smile, laugh, or cute gesture if you keep the exposures rolling. And, even when your subject is not moving noticeably at all, it can be advantageous to take multiple shots. For example, when you're taking a portrait, there may be subtle changes in the subject's expression, or in the way sunlight falls on a cheek, or in the subject's posture. Taking a series of shots gives you some insurance against coming away from the photo session with no winning images.

With that introduction, I will discuss the various continuous-shooting options the X100S provides. To get access to these options, press the Drive button, and a menu will pop up on the screen showing the menu of available settings, as shown in FIGURE 5-11. If you don't choose an option within about 3 seconds, the menu will disappear.

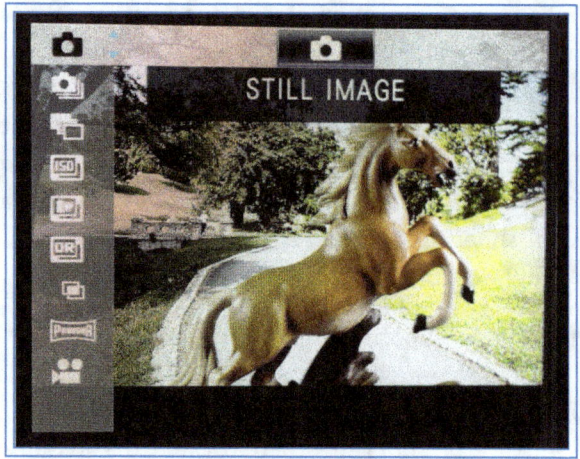

Figure 5-11. Still Image Selection

All of the settings (except the first one, for single shots) offer various ways to take multiple shots, including movies and panoramas, with a press (or press and hold) of the shutter button. For continuous shooting and panoramas, the exposure settings are fixed when the first image is taken, and they will not vary for later shots, even if the conditions would require different settings. You cannot use the flash for any of the multiple-shot settings, except Multiple Exposure. The two burst-shooting settings and the four bracketing options, discussed below, are available only with the four basic shooting modes: Program, Aperture Priority, Shutter Priority, and Manual. They cannot be used with the Motion Panorama option or the Multiple Exposure option.

STILL IMAGE

This option, shown in FIGURE 5-11, is the normal mode for shooting images. Select this option when you want to turn off all continuous shooting. Note that, in some cases, having one of the continuous Drive mode options will make it impossible to make other settings. For example, you cannot set the shutter speed to Bulb when continuous shooting is activated, and you cannot use the flash when any of the Drive mode options is in effect, other than Multiple Exposure. So, if you find that a setting, such as Flash, will not work, try setting the Drive mode to single shooting to see if that fixes the problem.

BURST SHOOTING

This second option on the drive mode menu is one of the most useful and powerful settings on the X100S, because it gives you the ability to shoot rapid-fire images as you hold down the shutter button. This capability is, of course, extremely useful in many contexts, from shooting an action sequence at a sports event to taking a series of shots of a portrait subject in order to capture his or her changing facial expressions.

When you scroll down to this line, you will see two speed choices in a gray bar extending across the display, as shown in FIGURE 5-12: 6.0 fps and 3.0 fps. These labels mean that you have the choice of setting the camera to shoot at either 6 frames per second or 3 frames per second.

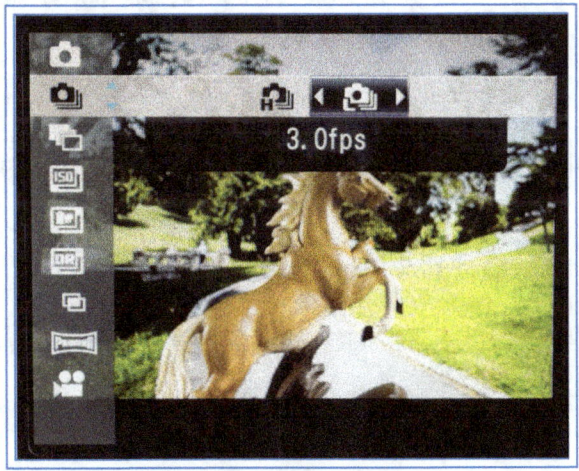

Figure 5-12. Burst Shooting Selection Menu

Using the Left and Right buttons, or pressing the Command Control left or right, highlight either 6.0 fps or 3.0 fps. That is the only selection you can make for this option. Once you have highlighted one of those choices, you can just let the selection screen disappear, which it will do quite quickly. (You have to move fast to get your selection made.)

The 6.0 fps and 3.0 fps rates are the maximum rates possible. In order to achieve the 6.0 fps rate, the camera needs to be using a shutter speed faster than 1/100 second; for the 3.0 fps rate, the camera has to be using a shutter speed faster than 1/10 second. If the shutter speed is slower than those values, the camera will still shoot continuously, but at a slower rate.

When the first image is taken, the camera locks in the focus and exposure and uses the same settings for all other shots in the same burst. The Fujifilm user's manual says that, with the 6.0 fps rate, you can take a burst of about 31 shots before the speed starts to slow down, and that, with the 3.0 fps rate, you can take a burst of 44 shots at the full speed. When I tested these burst modes using JPEG images with a shutter speed of 1/250 second, I found that the camera would produce closer to 50 shots before slowing down, using the faster setting. At the slower setting, it took about 100 shots at the expected speed.

When I did the same tests with Image Quality set to Raw plus Fine, I found that, with the faster burst setting, the camera took only 8 shots. With the slower burst setting, it took about 9 shots.

FIGURE 5-13 is a composite image showing a burst of shots of a bicycle rider that I took using the 6 fps setting. The sequence of shots goes from left to right, starting at the top. As you can see, the camera captured the rider quite clearly at this rapid shooting speed.

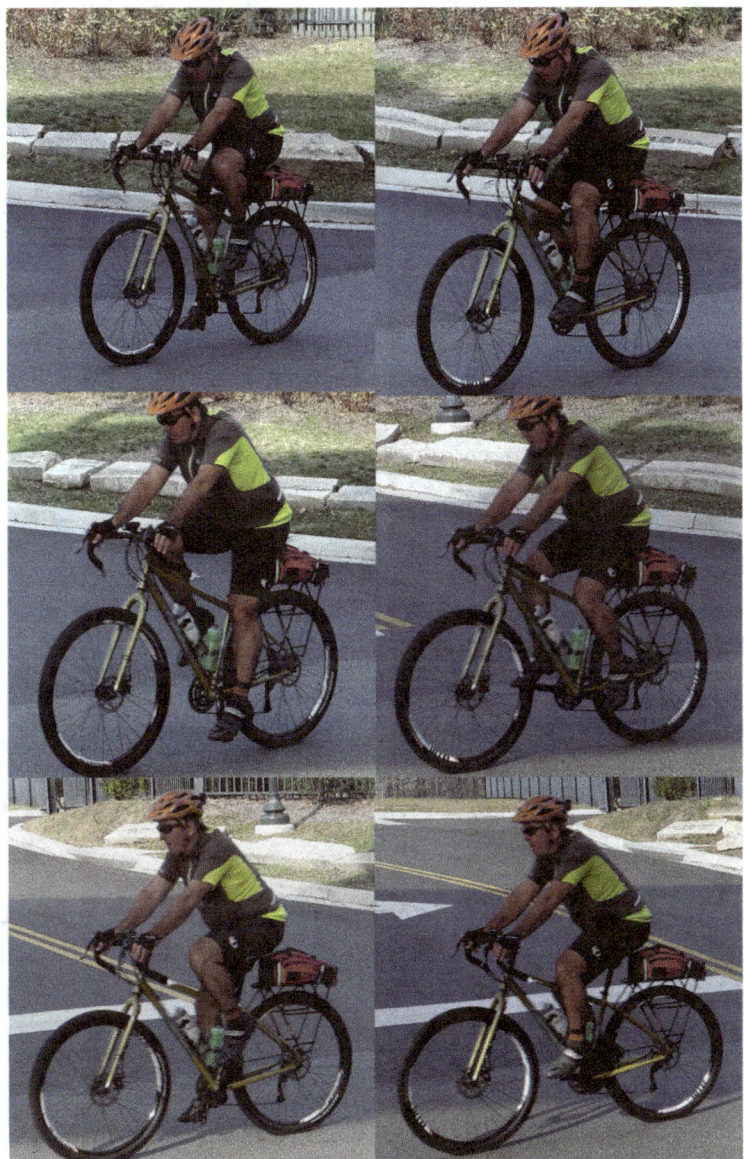

Figure 5-13. Burst Shooting Sequence at 6 FPS

Once you have finished shooting a burst of images, you will notice that it can take the camera quite a while to record them all to the memory card; you will see the indicator light blinking at the upper right of the camera's back. If you need to take a new picture during that time, you can do so, because the camera can keep storing the existing images while you take new ones. This is only possible if the indicator light is blinking green and orange; if it is glowing a steady orange, then you have to wait for the camera to finish its operation before you can take new images. You will not be able to play images in the camera while the camera is still recording the ones you just took.

One more note on burst shooting: With the Fujifilm X100S, unlike the situation with many other cameras, you can activate the Self-timer and it will trigger a burst of shots with the Drive settings. However, the burst is limited to 5 shots, no matter whether you are using the 6.0 or 3.0 fps speed, or whether you are using Raw or JPEG images. This feature gives you the ability to place the X100S on a tripod, activate both burst shooting and the Self-timer, and then join a group before the camera takes a string of 5 images of you and your group.

EXPOSURE BRACKETING

The third option on the Drive mode menu, exposure bracketing, is another very useful one. It lets you set up the camera to take three images continuously with one press of the shutter button, but with different exposure levels for each image, thereby giving you a greater chance of having one image that is perfectly exposed. You also can use this option to take a series of three exposures that can then be combined in software such as Photoshop or Photomatix Pro to create a composite HDR image.

Once you select this option, the camera will display a gray bar similar to the one for the continuous shooting option, as shown in FIGURE 5-14. In this case, there are three options to select using the Right and Left buttons, or by pressing the Command Control: intervals of 1, 2/3, and 1/3 stop. Highlight the option you want, which will set the amount by which the three bracketed exposures will differ in their exposure levels.

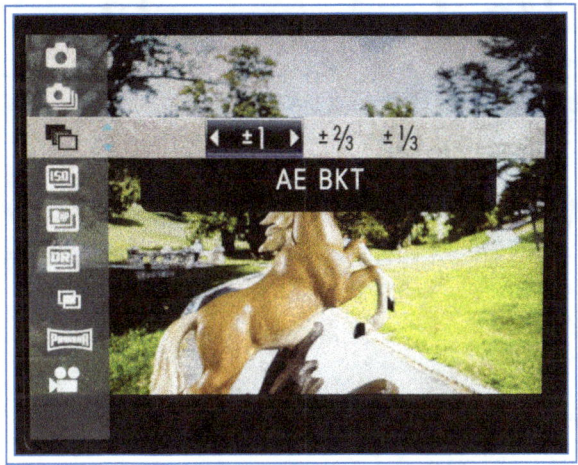

Figure 5-14. AE Bracket Selection Menu

Once you have set this option as you want it and composed your shot, press the shutter button and the camera will take three shots in rapid succession. In this case, unlike the situation with burst shooting, you do not have to hold down the shutter button, because the camera is programmed to make three exposures no matter how long the button is held down.

The first exposure will be taken at the metered value, the second one overexposed by the selected interval, and the third one underexposed to the same extent. If the camera is set to Aperture Priority mode, the shutter speed will be varied for the three exposures, and in Shutter Priority mode, the aperture will be varied. In Program mode, the camera may vary both values. In Manual mode, the camera will vary the shutter speed, even though the shutter speed dial is set to a specific value.

ISO Bracketing

ISO bracketing, the next option down on the Drive mode menu, as seen in Figure 5-15, works in the same way as exposure bracketing, except that, instead of varying the shutter speed or aperture, the camera varies the ISO setting for the three images.

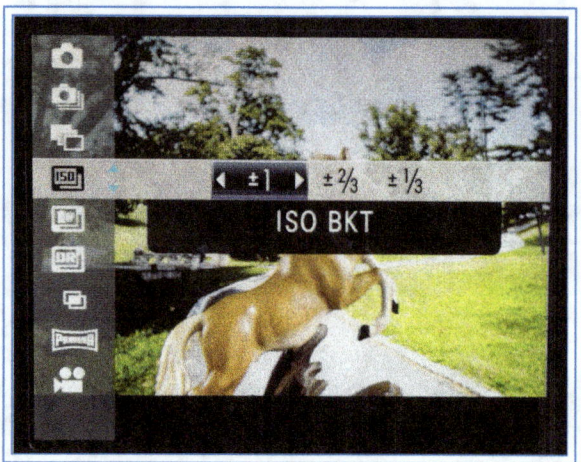

Figure 5-15. ISO Bracket Selection Menu

You have the same choices for the interval of stops between shots as with exposure bracketing. In this case, the camera actually takes just one shot and then internally creates two more shots, one with the ISO setting raised to produce overexposure and one with the setting lowered to produce underexposure. Therefore, you will hear the shutter operate only once. In other ways, the bracketing is just like exposure bracketing. The camera will not set ISO above 6400 or below 200 when using this feature. ISO Bracketing is not available with any Raw setting for Image Quality, and it does not even appear on the Drive mode menu when the Raw format is in use.

FILM SIMULATION BRACKETING

Next, with the Film Simulation bracketing option, shown in FIGURE 5-16, the X100S can produce a series of images using any three of the ten choices for color film simulation: Provia, Velvia, Astia, Pro Negative High, Pro Negative Standard, Monochrome, Monochrome with yellow filter, Monochrome with red filter, Monochrome with green filter, and Sepia.

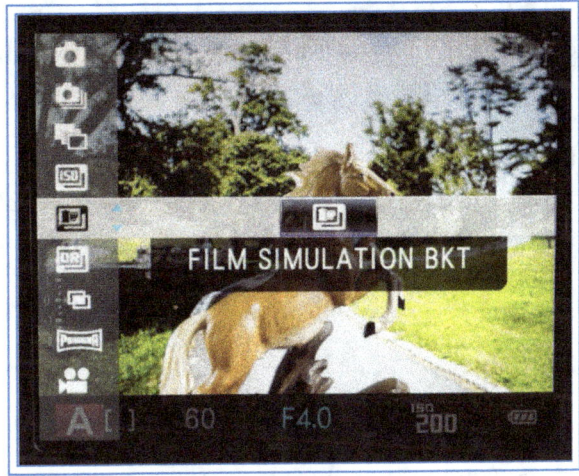

Figure 5-16. Film Simulation Bracket Selection Menu

With this option, you need to set up the three choices for the Film Simulation settings using the Film Simulation Bracket setting, which is the last option on the first screen of the Shooting menu. You can assign any one of the ten possible settings to each one of the three slots, which are labeled Film 1, Film 2, and Film 3. Then, when you activate this option on the Drive mode menu, there are no further settings for you to adjust—the camera takes one shot and then produces three images using the three Film Simulation settings you assigned to the 3 slots, to produce images using those three different film styles.

This feature gives you an excellent way to compare the results of using the various Film Simulation settings, so you can decide which one will give you the best results for a particular purpose. This option does not appear on the Drive mode menu when Image Quality is set to Raw or Raw plus Fine or Normal.

DYNAMIC RANGE BRACKETING

The last type of bracketing available with the X100S, whose setting screen is similar to that seen in FIGURE 5-16, lets you see the effects of three different dynamic range settings—100%,

200%, and 400%. As with Film Simulation bracketing, there are no adjustments for you to make on this screen. In this case, the camera takes three separate shots with the three different Dynamic Range settings. With this type of bracketing, the camera sets the ISO level to a minimum of 800 temporarily, and then sets it back to its previous value (if it was lower than 800) after the bracketing shots are done. This option, like the previous two, does not appear on the menu of Drive mode options when the Image Quality is set to Raw or Raw plus Fine or Normal.

Multiple Exposure

The next Drive mode option, Multiple Exposure, has no settings to make; this menu option appears in a gray band, as shown in Figure 5-17.

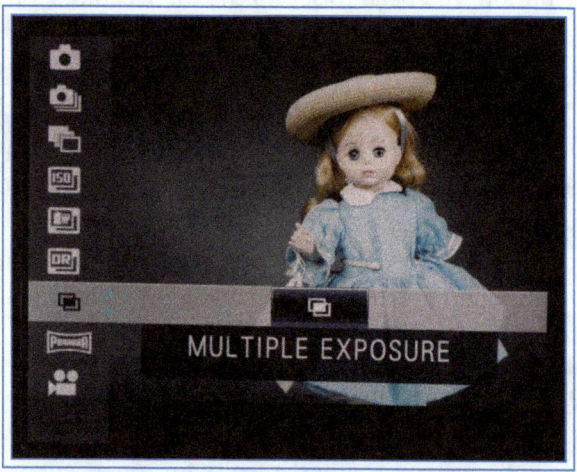

Figure 5-17. Multiple Exposure Option

When you select this menu item, the camera displays the shooting screen shown in Figure 5-18, with the Multiple Exposure icon, showing two overlapping image frames, displayed in the lower left corner of the screen over a red background.

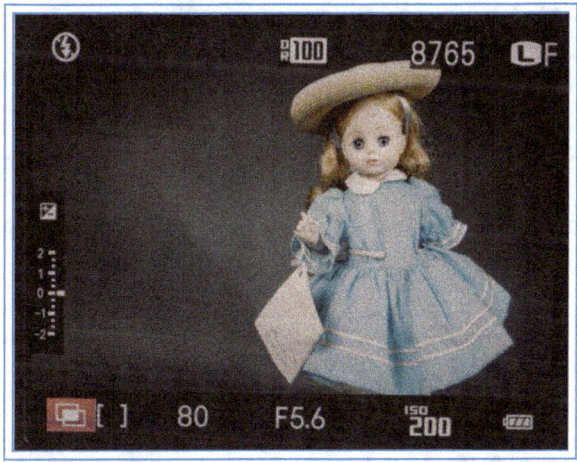

Figure 5-18. Multiple Exposure - Before First Shot

At this point, you can take the first shot for your multiple exposure composition, using any settings you wish, including flash, though you cannot use Raw for Image Quality. After you press the shutter button to take the first exposure, the camera will display a screen like that shown in FIGURE 5-19, giving you the options to press the Left button to retake the first shot; press the Display/Back button to cancel the whole operation; or press the OK button to accept the first shot and proceed to take the second shot.

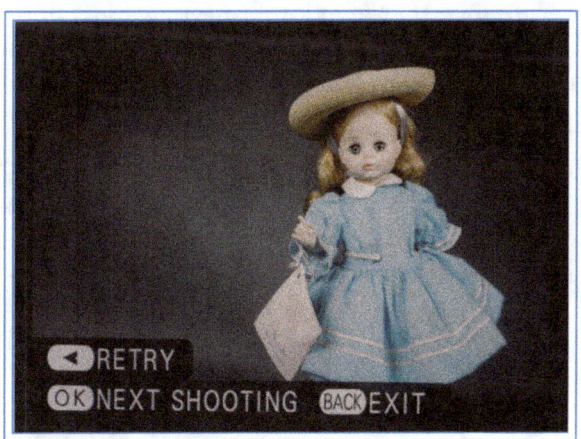

Figure 5-19. Multiple Exposure - After First Shot

The indicator lamp on the camera's back will blink green and orange until you press a button to move to the next shot, retake the shot, or cancel.

If you are satisfied with the appearance of the first image, press the OK button, and the camera will display a screen like that shown in FIGURE 5-20, which superimposes the image captured in the first shot over the live view of the scene.

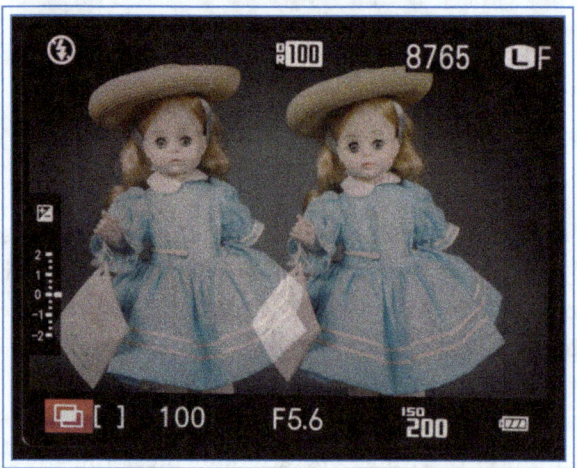

Figure 5-20. Multiple Exposure - Before Second Shot

Now you can move the camera to a new position, and see how the new image will interact with the one that was previously captured. Before taking the next shot, you can make any changes you want to the settings, such as exposure compensation, shutter speed, aperture, and even flash. When you have the new image aligned on the display as you want it and have made any needed adjustments to the settings, press the shutter button to capture the second image. The camera will then display the screen shown in FIGURE 5-21, giving you the options to retake the second image or to store the second image along with the first, as the complete multiple exposure.

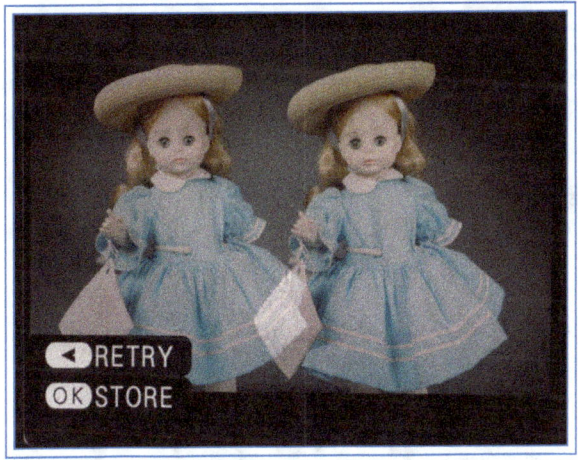

Figure 5-21. Multiple Exposure - After Second Shot

This is an excellent option for creative compositions, especially because you can make virtually any settings you want to for both images. FIGURE 5-22 shows the final result of using this option to photograph a ukulele in its case with the lid both open and closed. I adjusted the exposure compensation for both shots several times until I got a result that showed the case adequately while still revealing the ukulele inside it.

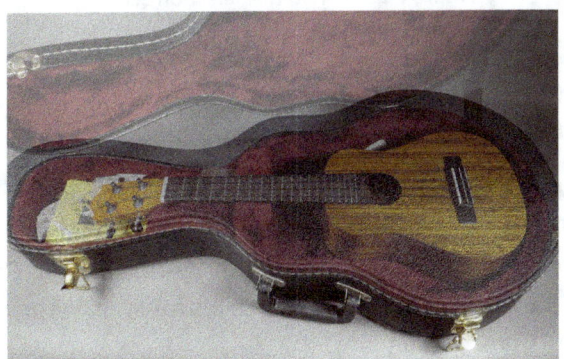

Figure 5-22. Multiple Exposure - Example of Final Image

As noted earlier, Multiple Exposure is the only Drive mode option that permits the use of the camera's flash.

MOTION PANORAMA

This next option on the Drive mode menu lets you shoot panoramic views made up of several exposures that are automatically stitched together in the camera. To use this shooting technique, press the Drive button and scroll down the list of icons to the Motion Panorama item, as shown in FIGURE 5-23.

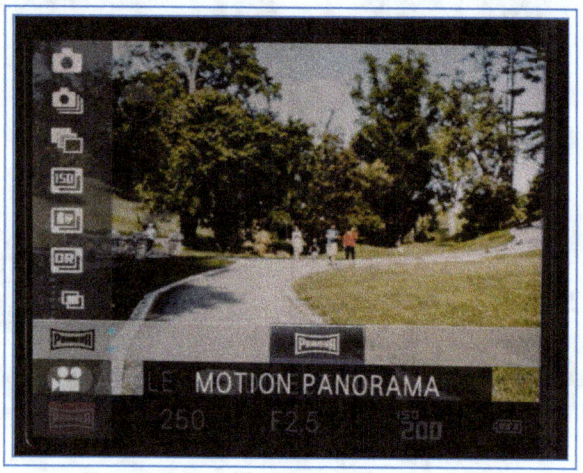

Figure 5-23. Panorama Selection Screen

Once this option is selected, you will see a screen prompting you to press the Left button to choose the angle for the panorama and the Right button to choose the direction.

If you press the Left button, you will see the screen shown in FIGURE 5-24. The only two choices for the angle are 120 degrees and 180 degrees. Make your selection by turning the Command Dial, by pressing the Left and Right buttons, or by pressing the Command Control right and left.

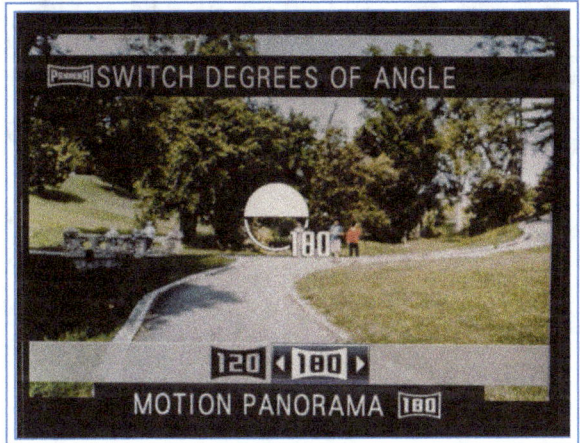

Figure 5-24. Panorama - Angle Selection Screen

Next, after the screen for selecting the angle automatically disappears, press the Right button to go to the screen for choosing the direction in which you will move the camera while shooting the panorama—right, left, up, or down, as shown in FIGURE 5-25. Use the same controls as for the angle to make this selection. This screen will disappear soon after you make your choice.

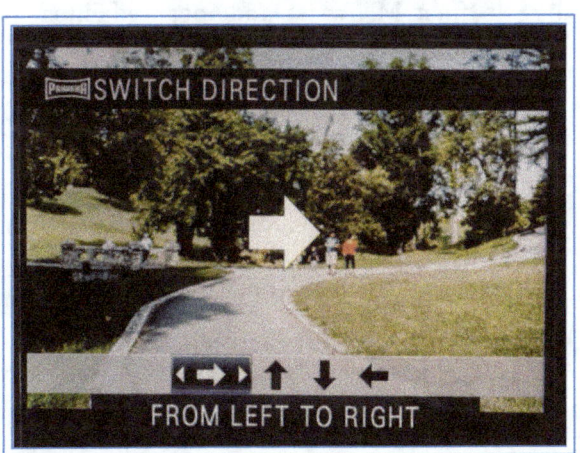

Figure 5-25. Panorama - Direction Selection Screen

Then, aim at the first part of your panoramic scene and keep the camera as level and steady as possible. You will get the best results using a tripod with a smoothly panning head (or a tilting one, for vertical panoramas). If you don't have a tripod available or prefer not to use one, you might try wrapping the camera's strap around your neck and holding the camera out from your body with the strap tight to stabilize it.

When you are ready, press and release the shutter button, and move the camera steadily through the full extent of your chosen angle in the direction you chose. When you have moved it through that angle, the camera will stop shooting. The exposure is set with the first frame, and it will not vary through the rest of the shots the camera takes to create the panorama.

If you press the shutter button all the way down while the panorama is in progress, the shooting will stop. When you choose a subject for a panorama, you should avoid including moving objects, such as people or cars, because they may show up at two or more different locations in the final image. Also, note that some settings are not available when the camera is set for panorama shooting, including flash, Raw for Image Quality, Photometry (metering mode), the expanded ISO settings (100, 12800, and 25600), the Self-timer, MF Assist, and Advanced Filter.

In Figures 5-26 and 5-27, I am including two sample panoramas taken with the X100S. The first one is a view of the James River, taken with a tripod and panning from left to right. The second one was taken indoors, handheld, also panning from left to right. In that panorama, which was taken at a crowded craft show, you can see that some of the people's bodies are distorted because they were captured in more than one of the multiple images that made up the panorama. Whenever there are people, vehicles, or other moving subjects in your panorama, there is a risk of multiple captures like the ones shown here.

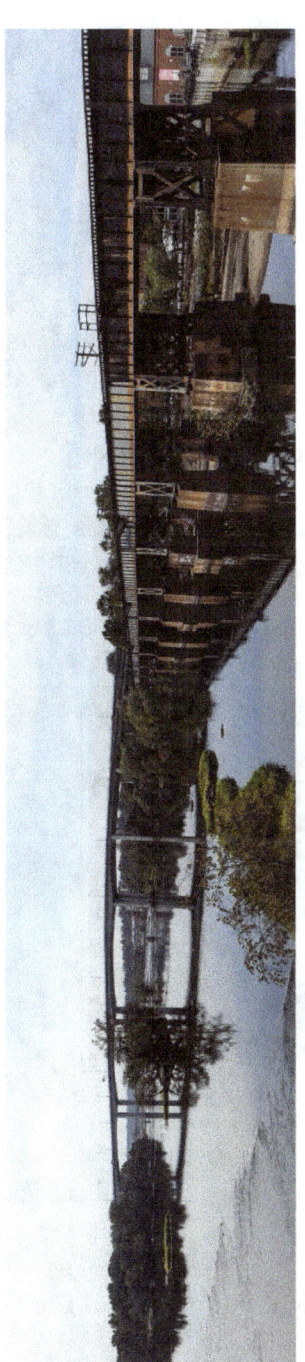

Figure 5-26. Sample Panorama - James River, Richmond, Virginia

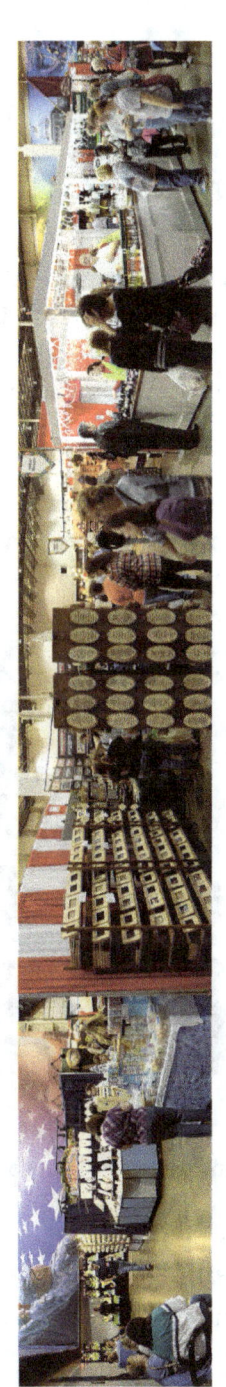

Figure 5-27. Sample Panorama - Crafts Show, Richmond, Virginia.

Movies

The final option on the continuous-shooting menu sets the camera to Movie mode, which I will discuss separately in Chapter 8.

Zoom-out Button

When the X100S is in playback mode, the Drive button functions as the Zoom-out button, as indicated by the magnifying glass icon with a minus sign, just below the button. In playback mode, if you have enlarged an image on the display by pressing the AE/Zoom-in button as discussed earlier, you can press the Zoom-out button to return it to normal size through decreasing degrees of magnification. Once the image is back to normal size, pressing this button again will call up an index screen that shows four images arranged in inset blocks on the screen, as shown in FIGURE 5-28.

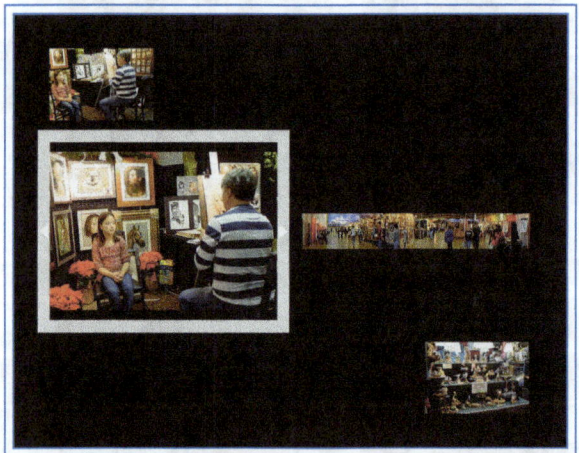

Figure 5-28. Playback Index Screen - 4 Images

Use the Command Dial or the Left and Right buttons to scroll through those images and on to other images stored on your memory card. Pressing the button again will bring up screens showing nine images, then 100. Move through these screens with the Command Dial or the Left and Right buttons. There is more information about playback functions in Chapter 6.

View Mode Button

The final button on the camera's left side has a straightforward function—to cycle through the three choices for viewing your display. The three choices are LCD, Viewfinder, and Eye Sensor. With LCD, the live view, menu screens, and playback of images all appear on the LCD screen on the back of the camera. If you press this button to select Viewfinder, the view is switched to the viewfinder. You then can choose between the electronic viewfinder (EVF) and the optical viewfinder (OVF) using the Viewfinder Selector, discussed earlier in this chapter. If you choose the EVF, then you will see everything in the viewfinder exactly as you did on the LCD, including menu screens and playback of images. However, if you choose the OVF, then you will see the live view along with shooting information in the viewfinder, but you will not see menu screens or playback of images there. If you call up a menu or playback screen while the OVF is active, it will appear on the EVF.

The third choice available with the View Mode button is the Eye Sensor mode. With that selection, the view will appear on the LCD unless your head (or some other object) is close to the viewfinder. When your head approaches the viewfinder, the two small sensors to the right of the viewfinder will detect the presence of your head and will automatically switch the view to the viewfinder. The view will switch back to the LCD once your head moves away from the viewfinder.

Which viewing mode you choose is a matter of personal preference, and it may depend on the current lighting conditions or other considerations, such as whether you want to hold the camera against your head to keep it extra steady, or you want to be able to hold out the LCD to study it at arm's length, for example.

Now I will discuss the controls on the right side of the camera, as shown in FIGURE 5-29.

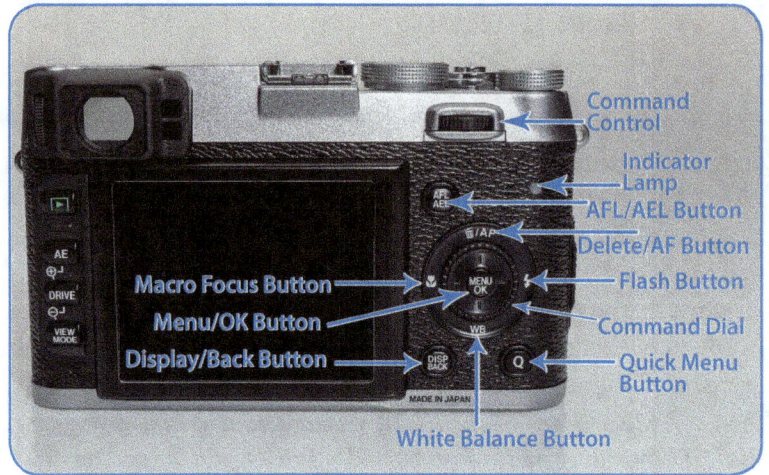

Figure 5-29. Controls on Right Side of Camera's Back

Command Control

Moving to the right side of the camera, the Command Control is the black rocker switch on the far right at the very top of the camera's back, just below and to the left of the exposure compensation dial. This versatile little switch has several functions, none of them very obvious. To operate it in most situations, just press it to the left or right quickly and release it; in a few other situations, you press in on it.

One function for this switch is to duplicate the actions of the Left and Right buttons on the Command Dial, but only in certain situations. For example, to choose a metering method you press the AE button and then use either the Command Dial or the Command Control to move up and down through the three options. When you have the Function button set to control ISO and you are using the optical viewfinder, after pressing the Function button, you can press the Command Control (or turn the Command Dial or press the Left and Right buttons) to change the ISO setting directly on the viewfinder display. When you are choosing a flash mode or choosing between Macro focus and normal autofocus after pressing the Macro focus button, the Command Control lets you move left and right among the available options.

The Command Control also comes into play when you are making exposure settings. When the camera is in Program exposure mode, you press the Command Control left or right to use the Program Shift feature, switching to new pairings of shutter speed and aperture that match the exposure provided by the pairing the camera selected initially using its autoexposure metering. (You also can use the Command Dial for this function.) When you are setting the aperture, in either Aperture Priority or Manual exposure mode, you use the Command Control to get access to intermediate aperture settings.

When you are using manual focus, pressing in on the Command Control will enlarge the screen so you can better evaluate the focus. In playback mode, you can press in on the Command Control to zoom in on the active focus point in the image being displayed. This function is very convenient for checking the sharpness of your recorded image. Press in again to zoom back out. (This function also works when you are reviewing images that appear on the screen right after being shot, in image review mode, but only if the Image Display item of the Screen Set-up item on the second screen of the Setup menu is set to Continuous.) Note that, if the image was taken with manual focus, a press of the button will zoom into the center of the image, because there is no active focus point as there is with images taken with autofocus.

When you are using autofocus and have set the AF Mode to Area, with a focus frame that can be moved around the screen and resized, you can press the Command Control left or right to resize the frame while the autofocus frame is activated for moving around the screen. If you press in on this switch when AF Mode is set to Area and you are viewing a scene, the focus area within the AF frame will be enlarged. Press in on the switch again to return the focus area to normal size.

Also, when an individual image is displayed on the screen in playback mode, you can press the Command Control to the left or right repeatedly to bring up other screens with detailed information about the image. I'll discuss that operation further in Chapter 6.

AFL/AEL Button

This first button at the top of the control area on the right side of the camera's back has two important functions. First, it lets you lock either exposure or focus, or both. You can choose which function or functions the button locks through the AE/AF-Lock Button item on the fourth screen of the Shooting menu, as discussed in Chapter 4. Depending on how you set that menu item, a press of the button will lock just focus, just exposure, or both focus and exposure. You also can use the AE/AF-Lock Mode item on that menu screen to determine whether you need to hold down the button to lock the setting(s), or whether the button acts as a toggle switch that you can press and release.

To use the button, aim the camera at your subject, and press and hold the AFL/AEL button, or press and release it, depending on how it is set up with the menu item, as discussed above. The focus and/or exposure value measured by the camera at that time will remain locked for as long as the button is held down (or until it is pressed again, if it is set up as a toggle switch).

For example, suppose you are at an historic site and you want to make sure your focus is set on an antique chest at one side of a display table. With the focus switch set to the AF-S position and the AFL/AEL button set as a toggle switch for locking focus only, aim the camera so that its focus frame focuses on the chest, press the shutter button halfway to focus, and press and release the AFL button. The camera will display a green frame showing that the focus is set at that point. With the focus still locked by the button, aim the camera back in the direction of the other items, with the chest off to the side. Now, when you press the shutter button down to take the picture, the focus will remain locked on the chest off to the side, even though the camera likely would have focused on some other point with the current composition.

The second job performed by the AFL/AEL button is to allow the quick use of autofocus when the camera is set to manual focus mode. As I discussed earlier in talking about manual focus, when the focus switch is on the MF setting, the normal way to focus is by turning the focus ring around the lens. But, if you want the camera to give you a head start on focusing, just press this button, and the camera will, if possible, focus automatically as well as it can. You can then continue the process by adjusting focus manually with the focus ring, if you want to.

Note that, because the AFL/AEL button always focuses the lens automatically when the camera is in manual focus mode, the button cannot be used to lock exposure when manual focus is in use.

Indicator Lamp

This small lamp, positioned to the right of the AFL/AEL button on the back of the camera, is hard to see until it lights up. It glows a bright green, orange, or red at various times to announce processes or problems. Some of the main signals to be aware of are a steady green when focus is locked; steady orange when images are being recorded; and blinking orange when the flash is charging. If the light is blinking green and orange, that means the camera is saving images to the memory card, but you can still take new pictures if you want to. (If the light is glowing steady orange, you cannot take additional pictures.)

The complete list of signals is at page 3 of the official Fujifilm user's manual for the X100S.

Command Dial and Buttons

The most prominent set of controls on the back of the camera is contained within the perimeter of the circular control pad, which includes the Command Dial, with a ridged rim, in the center. Turning the Command Dial serves multiple purposes, as discussed below. The four edges of the Command Dial function as the Up, Down, Right, and Left buttons; you press in on the ridged edge at the top, bottom, right, or left of the dial to activate those buttons. Each of the four buttons serves as a direction button to move through menus, images, settings, and other items in some contexts. Each of the buttons also has another purpose designated by a white icon or label next to the button. Finally, in the center of the Command Dial is the Menu/OK button. I will discuss each of these controls in turn.

COMMAND DIAL

The Command Dial is the ridged dial that surrounds the Menu/OK button. It serves various purposes when you place your finger on the raised edge and turn the dial left or right. When you are navigating through the camera's menu screens, turning the dial moves the selection rectangle from item to item. The dial also is used to select intermediate shutter speeds that lie between the main settings on the shutter speed dial when the camera is set to Shutter Priority or Manual exposure mode. When the camera is in Program shooting mode, turning the Command Dial carries out the "Program Shift" function of selecting an aperture-shutter speed pair that is equivalent to the settings initially selected by the camera's autoexposure system.

Turning the Command Dial left or right also selects items from the small menus that pop up on the display when you are using the camera's physical controls, such as the Flash, Macro focus, White Balance, or Drive mode button. When you have called up the ISO setting using the Function button while the optical viewfinder is in use, you can turn the Command Dial to change the ISO value.

In normal playback mode, you can turn the Command Dial left or right to scroll through your images in either direction.

Menu/OK Button

This button, one of the most-used controls on the camera, serves as a selection, confirmation, or "set" button when you choose certain options. For example, whenever you use the camera's menu system and highlight a desired menu option, you can press the OK button to confirm and set your selection.

You also press this button to get access to the menu system. Once a particular menu item is highlighted, you can press this button to get to the next screen, with that item's settings.

The Menu/OK button also has some more specific functions. You can use this button as a control lock to lock the Q button so it won't operate and to limit the functioning of the buttons on the Command Dial so they can't accidentally be pressed to activate the AF or Delete function, Flash mode, White Balance, or Macro focus. To do this, press and hold the OK button for about two seconds until a padlock icon appears on the screen. The four direction buttons on the Command Dial will still continue to work as navigation controls; they just won't perform their secondary functions. All of these controls will now remain locked until you hold the OK button down again to remove the lock.

In playback mode, you can press the OK button to pause the playback of a movie so you can adjust its volume. You also can press this button to end a slide show.

Direction Buttons

Each of the four edges—Up, Down, Left, and Right—on the Command Dial is also a "button" that you can press to get access to a setting or operation. This may not be immediately obvious, and sometimes it can be tricky to press them in exactly the right spot, but these four direction buttons are very important to your control of the camera. You use them to navigate through menus and through screens for settings, whether moving left and right or up and down.

You also use the direction buttons in playback mode to move through your images and, when you have enlarged an image using the AE/Zoom-in button, to scroll around within the magnified image.

In addition to these navigational duties, the direction buttons are used for several miscellaneous functions in connection with various operations. For example, the Down button is used to start playback of a movie, and the Up button is used to stop playback. The Down button also is used to "open up" a sequence of shots taken in continuous-shooting mode so the images in the sequence can be viewed individually. The Right button can be used to move to the next screen for a particular menu item to get access to the settings screen for that item, and the Left button can be used to move back to the prior menu screen. The Left button also is used to move the highlight to the far left column of the menu screen, so you can navigate up and down through the various screens of the menu system without having to scroll through all of the items on each screen.

Finally, each of the direction buttons also has its own separate identity, as indicated by the icon or label that appears next to each of the buttons, as discussed below.

Up Button: AF/Delete

When you are shooting, the AF button is used to let you alter the position of the autofocus frame, but only when the autofocus mode is set to AF-S (for single autofocus) and the AF Mode option on the Shooting menu is set to Area. When these settings are made, there will be a white rectangular focus frame in the center of the display. If these conditions are in place, press the

AF button, and the autofocus frame will turn green, with a small arrow on each side, as shown in FIGURE 5-30.

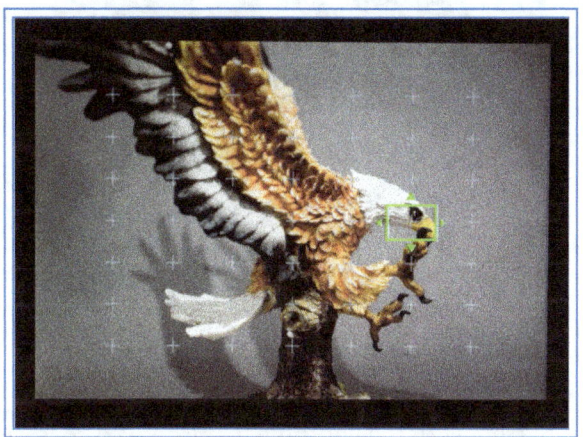

Figure 5-30. Moveable Autofocus Frame After Moving

You can then turn the Command Dial or press the direction buttons to move the focus frame wherever you want to place it on the display. When you have it placed where you want it, press the OK button or half-press the shutter button to lock it in place. To return the frame to the center of the screen while the frame is activated to move, press the Display/Back button. To resize the frame while it is activated to move, press the Command Control to the left or right. To return the frame to its normal size, press in on the Command Control.

When the camera is in playback mode, pressing the Up button while an image is on the display brings up a message asking if you want to erase that image, or multiple images, as shown in FIGURE 5-31. Press the OK button to proceed or the Back button to cancel, as prompted on the screen.

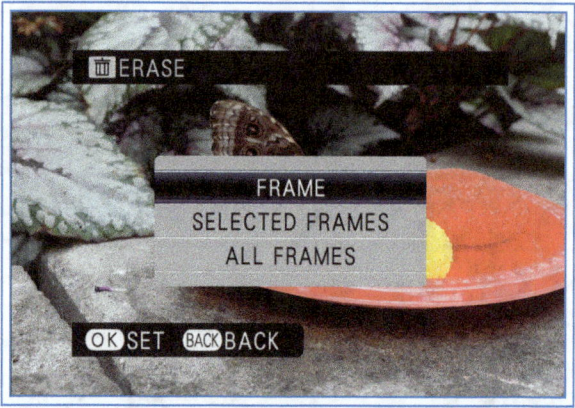

Figure 5-31. Screen from Pressing Delete Button in Playback Mode

Right Button: Flash

The Right button, with the lightning bolt icon next to it, also is the Flash button, the camera's control for changing the flash mode. When you press this button in shooting mode, a small menu pops up displaying the available options for the flash, with one of them selected, as shown in FIGURE 5-32.

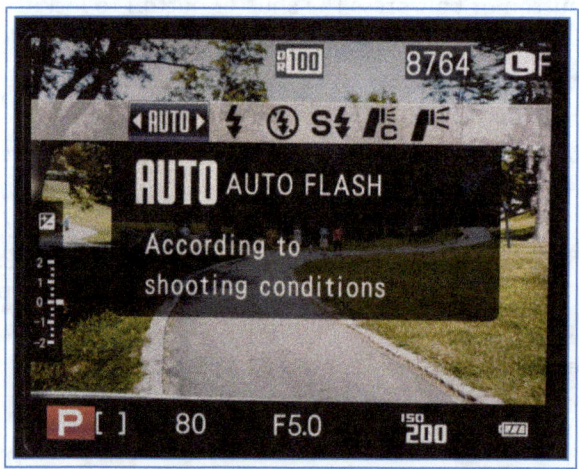

Figure 5-32. Flash Mode Menu

The available options will change depending on the current shooting mode. To select an option, you have to quickly move to your desired choice by using the Left and Right buttons, by pressing the Command Control right or left, or by turning the Command Dial. I find it easiest to keep pressing the Right button until the option I want is selected.

When the camera is set to Program mode, all options are available: Auto Flash, Forced Flash, Suppressed Flash, Slow Synchro, Commander, and External Flash. When the Red Eye Removal option is turned on in the fourth screen of the Shooting menu, the Auto Flash, Forced Flash, and Slow Synchro options change to include the red-eye removal icon—a small image of a human eye next to the flash icon, as shown in FIGURE 5-33.

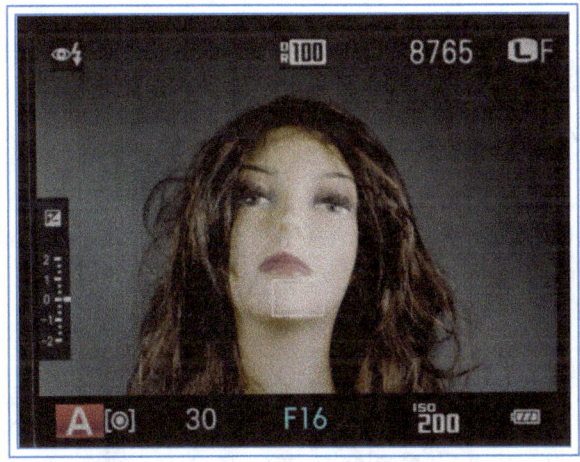

Figure 5-33. Red Eye Icon Next to Flash Icon

With the Red Eye Removal versions of these three Flash mode options, when you press the shutter button, the camera will fire a pre-flash before it fires the "actual" flash to take the picture. The idea is to force your subject's pupils to contract, so light cannot bounce off the retinas and produce the eerie glow of "red-eye."

In Aperture Priority mode, all flash modes are available except Auto Flash. In Shutter Priority and Manual modes, all are available except Auto Flash and Slow Synchro. Slow Synchro is not available in those modes because you are choosing the shutter speed, and for Slow Synchro to function, the camera has to choose the shutter speed. I'll discuss the Slow Synchro mode further in Chapter 9.

One more note about the use of flash: There are times when pressing the Flash button has no effect. One such situation is when the camera is set to one of the continuous shooting modes. The flash will not function with most of the Drive modes, including continuous shooting, bracketing, Panorama, and Movie. However, you can use the flash with the Multiple Exposure setting. If you have activated the camera's Silent Mode, either through the first screen of the Setup menu or by holding down the Display/Back button for a couple of seconds, the flash will not fire and pressing the Flash button will have no effect.

Down Button: White Balance

The Down button has the very important second function of letting you select the White Balance setting for the X100S. One issue that arises in all photography is that film, or a digital camera's sensor, reacts differently to colors than the human eye does. When you or I see a scene in daylight or indoors under various types of artificial lighting, we generally do not notice a difference in the hues of the things we see depending on the light source. However, the camera does not have this auto-correcting ability. The camera "sees" colors differently depending on the "color temperature" of the light that illuminates the object or scene in question. The color temperature of light is a numerical value that is expressed in a unit known as Kelvins (K). A light source with a lower Kelvin rating produces a "warmer" or more reddish light. A light source with a higher Kelvin rating produces a "cooler" or more bluish light. For example, candlelight is rated at about 1,800 K; indoor tungsten light (ordinary light bulb) is rated at about 3,000 K; outdoor sunlight and electronic flash are rated at about 5,500 K; and outdoor shade is rated at about 7,000 K.

If you are using a film camera, you may need a colored filter in front of the lens to "correct" for the color temperature of the light source. Any given color film is rated to expose colors correctly at a particular color temperature (or, to put it another way, with a particular light source). So if you are using color film rated for daylight use, you can use it outdoors without a filter. But if you happen to be using that film indoors, you will need a color filter to correct the color temperature; otherwise, the resulting picture will look excessively reddish because of the imbalance between the film and the color temperature of the light source.

With a modern digital camera, you do not need to worry about filters, because the camera can adjust its electronic circuitry to correct the "white balance," which is the term used in the context of digital photography for balancing color temperature.

The X100S, like most current digital cameras, has a setting for Auto White Balance, which lets the camera choose the proper color correction to account for any given light source, and it also has preset settings for the most common types of lighting situation, as well as a Custom setting and a Color Temperature selection that lets you specify the Kelvin value for your lighting source.

Here is how to set White Balance on the X100S. Press the Down (WB) button, and a menu will pop up on the right side of the screen listing all of the options, as shown in FIGURE 5-34.

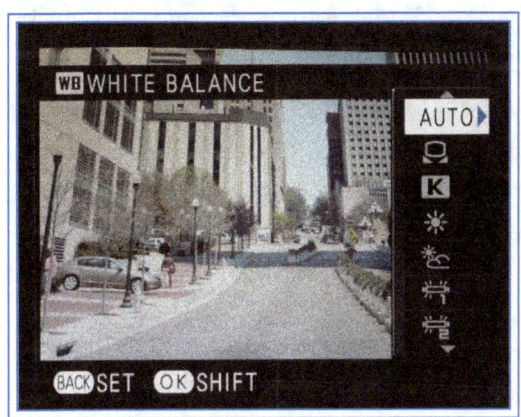

Figure 5-34. White Balance Menu

(Thankfully, this menu does not disappear quickly, as the Flash mode and some other menus do; it will stay on the screen as long as you need it.) By pressing the Down button, turning the Command Dial, or pressing the Command Control to the right, scroll down until the selection you want is highlighted. One helpful feature is that the image in the viewfinder or on the LCD changes to show the effect of each setting as you highlight it. All of the selections other than Auto, the first one, are represented by icons; as you highlight each one, a label for that setting appears to the left of the icon, superimposed on the display, as shown in FIGURE 5-35.

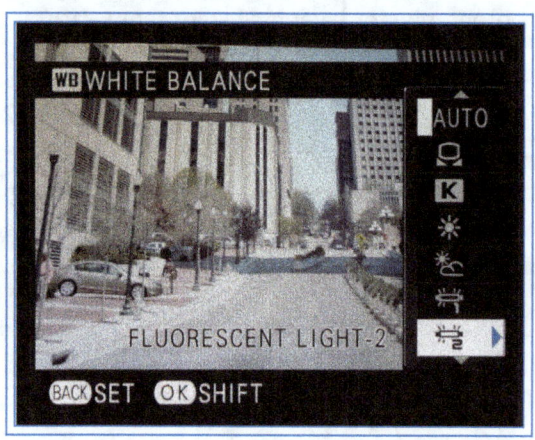

Figure 5-35. White Balance Selection with Label at Left

The choices for White Balance are Auto, Custom, Color Temperature, Fine, Shade, Fluorescent Light-1, Fluorescent Light-2, Fluorescent Light-3, Incandescent, and Underwater. They are largely self-explanatory except, perhaps, Fine, which is the term Fujifilm uses to mean direct daylight or sunlight. You do need to know a few details about how these settings work, though.

First, the three Fluorescent settings are provided for different varieties of these lamps: Number 1 is for "daylight" lamps; number 2 is for "warm white," and number 3 is for "cool white." You may see one of these labels on the lamp or on the packaging it came in.

If not, some test shots may be in order to figure out which setting is best for the particular fluorescent bulbs you are dealing with.

Next, if you select Custom, it is up to you to set the White Balance manually. Use this option when you are faced with mixed lighting from multiple sources, or from a reddish or otherwise unusual light source. To make this setting, highlight Custom, and then press the OK button or the Right button. The next screen, shown in FIGURE 5-36, will display a large white square along with messages advising you to press the shutter button to measure the White Balance, to press OK to adjust ("shift") the value, or to press the Display/Back button to cancel the operation.

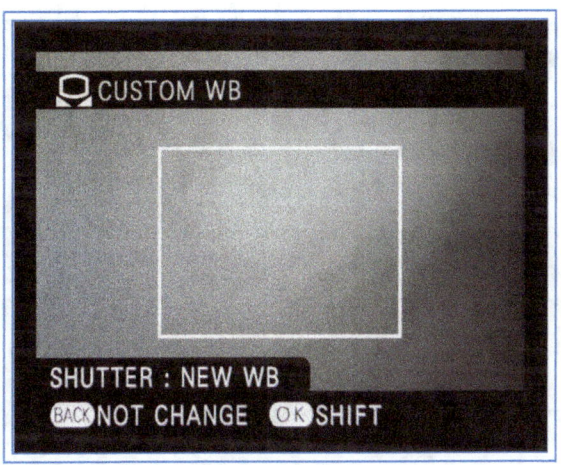

Figure 5-36. Custom White Balance Setting Screen

Now aim the lens at a uniformly white (or neutral gray) surface that fills the white square on the screen and press the shutter button. The camera will then display a message at the top of the display: either Completed!, Under, or Over. If Completed! is displayed, you have succeeded; press the OK button to set the new White Balance.

If you see Under or Over, that means the lighting was too bright or dim to register the White Balance properly; you can try again with exposure compensation adjusted for the lighting, or try with less or more light or in a different area. Once you are finally successful, the new setting will be available by choosing the Custom option for White Balance, even after the camera has been powered off and back on.

If you want to shift the Custom setting you have just saved, return to the measurement screen, but, instead of pressing the shutter button to measure the White Balance again, press the OK button, and the camera will display a screen like that shown in Figure 5-37, consisting of a grid with two axes, one moving horizontally, left to right, from cyan to red, and the other moving vertically, from bottom to top, from yellow to blue.

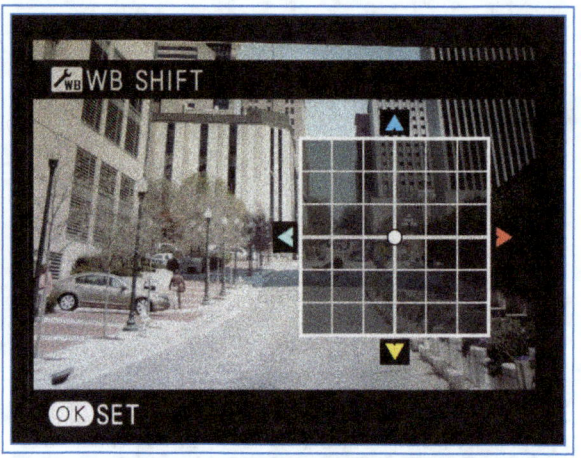

Figure 5-37. White Balance Shift Screen

Press the four direction buttons to adjust the colors as you want them by moving the white dot along either or both axes. Press the OK button to lock in the adjustment. There are nine levels of adjustment available, both positive and negative, so you can achieve a dramatically different color effect, depending on how much of an adjustment you dial in. In fact, if you want, you can use this feature for creative effects, such as imposing a distinctly reddish or bluish tint on an image.

This adjustment will stay in place for this particular White Balance setting even if the camera is powered off, so be sure to adjust the dot back to its neutral position if you no longer want the White Balance setting to be shifted.

You can take advantage of the Custom setting as a nice way to add a color tint to a scene for creative effect if you want. For example, you can set the White Balance manually using a red or orange surface for the measurement, which will result in a pronounced blue tint for any pictures taken under the same light source that you used when setting that White Balance value. Just be careful to turn the White Balance setting back to Auto or another suitable setting when you don't want that special effect for your images. (You also might want to recalibrate the Custom setting using a white or gray surface.)

The Color Temperature setting can be quite useful also. Once you highlight that selection and press the Right button to move to the next screen, the camera displays a menu listing all of the possible values, from 10,000 Kelvin at the top to 2500 Kelvin at the bottom. The middle portion of this scale is shown in FIGURE 5-38.

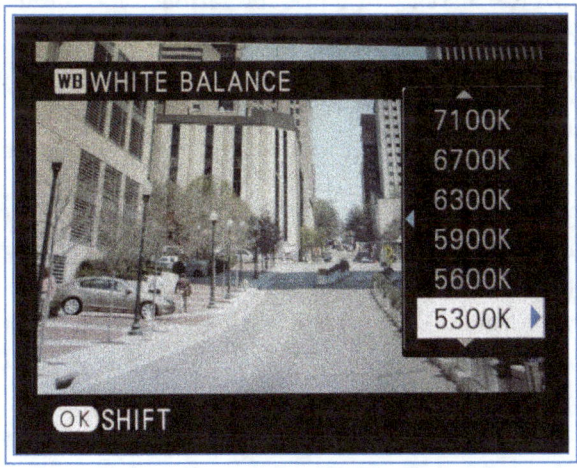

Figure 5-38. White Balance Color Temperature Setting Screen

If you have a meter to read the color temperature of your light source, you can use that value here. For example, the Sekonic Prodigi meter, shown in FIGURE 5-39, gives accurate readings of color temperature.

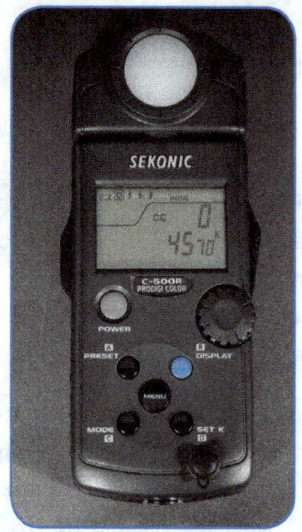

Figure 5-39. Prodigi Color Meter

Or, you can use a standard figure for various types of lighting, as set out at page 43 of the Fujifilm user's guide (candlelight at 2,000 K; sunlight at 5,000 K, for example). As you scroll through those values, the scene on the LCD display or in the viewfinder changes to show the effect of the setting on the colors of the image.

You also can use the Color Temperature option to achieve a particular look you want. For example, if you set the color temperature down in the 2500 K range, you will likely get a considerably "cooler" look than normal—that is, with more bluish tints, like a wintry scene. If you select a value closer to 10,000 K, the image likely will appear considerably "warmer" than normal, with reddish, sunset-like hues.

With any of the White Balance settings, including Auto White Balance, you can use the White Balance Shift feature, which I discussed above in connection with the Custom setting. To do that, when the particular setting, such as Shade or Incandescent, is highlighted on the menu, press the OK button or the Right button to move to the Shift screen. Then move the white dot to the appropriate position on the grid, and press OK to lock in the shifted setting for White Balance. Again, as with the Custom setting, this shift will remain in effect until you cancel it by moving the white dot back to the center of the grid.

The chart in FIGURE 5-40 shows how using different White Balance settings changes the appearance of your images. I shot the same scene multiple times under lighting balanced for daylight; the only thing that I changed for each shot was the White Balance setting on the X100S. For the Color Temperature setting, I took a reading with the Prodigi color meter, which resulted in a setting of 4800 K.

As you can see, several of the White Balance settings yielded acceptable results under these conditions. In my opinion, the Auto White Balance, Custom, Color Temperature, Fine, Fluorescent-2, and Underwater settings all yielded good results. The settings that most clearly were wrong were Incandescent and Fluorescent-3. With the Fujifilm X100S, I find that Auto White Balance gives acceptable results, but it is best to use the setting that most closely matches the lighting conditions when possible.

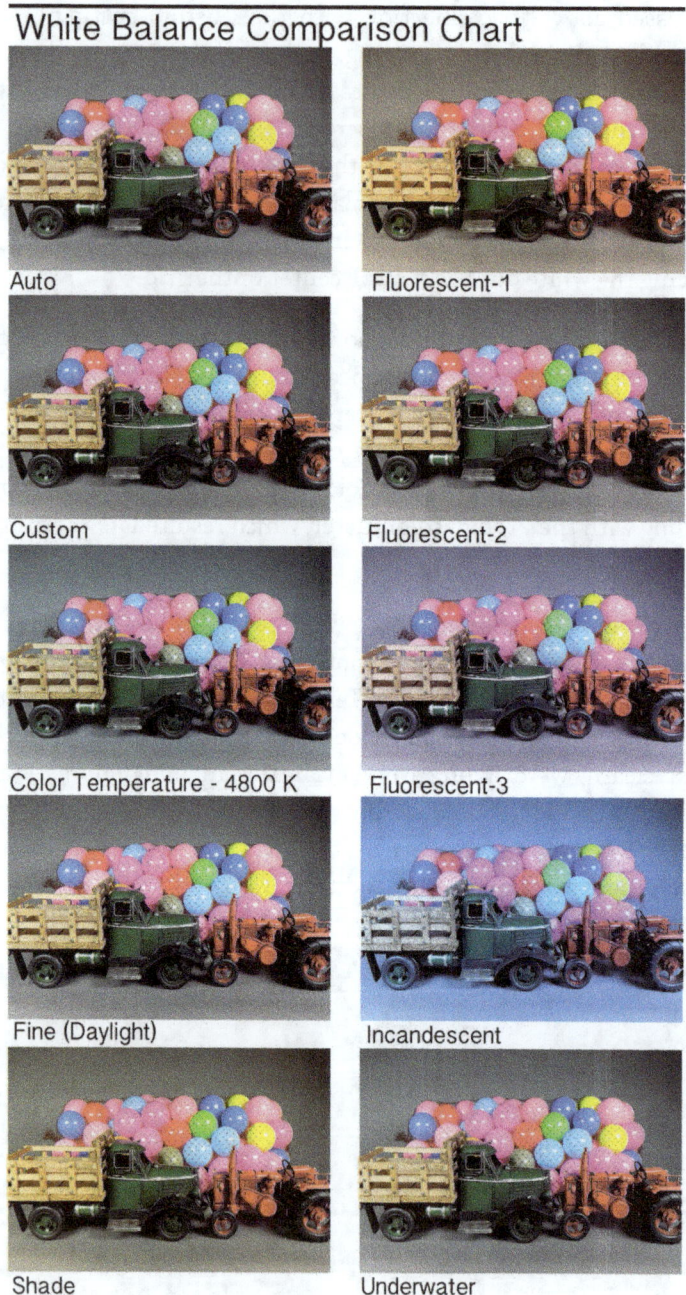

Figure 5-40. White Balance Comparison Chart

There is one more point about setting White Balance on the X100S that you need to be aware of. Somewhat oddly, there is no White Balance setting for Flash, as there is on many other cameras. The Fujifilm user's guide at page 42 says that the White Balance system adjusts for flash lighting only with the Auto and Underwater settings, and that you should turn the flash off in other cases. I have found that the Fine setting usually works quite well with the built-in flash, and you can also use the Color Temperature selection, setting it to about 5000 K and adjusting it from there as needed. However, given Fujifilm's admonition, it may be safer just to use the Auto White Balance setting when shooting with flash. Of course, if you shoot using the Raw image quality setting (or Raw plus JPEG), you can always adjust the White Balance later, in your Raw processing software.

Left Button: Macro Focus

This final button around the rim of the Command Dial is labeled with the flower icon that represents Macro, or closeup, focus. This button's only purpose (apart from its duties as the Left button) is to switch the X100S into Macro focus mode, so you can focus more quickly on subjects that are close to the camera.

The normal focus range of the X100S's lens is from 2.6 feet (80 cm) to infinity. In other words, if you're not using the Macro focus mode, the lens will readily focus on objects as close as 2.6 feet from the lens. If an object is closer than that, the camera's autofocus system may still achieve focus, but it will take longer, because its focus system is calibrated for the more distant objects. In some cases, I have found that the normal autofocus system will not focus at all on subjects within the Macro range.

If you press the Macro button to switch the camera into Macro focus mode, the focus range drops down so the camera will readily focus on objects between 3.9 inches (10 cm) and 6.6 feet (2.0 m). Using this much more limited range, the camera can more quickly zero in on close subjects, and it may be able to focus on subjects that are closer than the normal autofocus system can handle.

In order to activate Macro focus mode, press the Left button and then, as with the other buttons, quickly use the Left and Right buttons, the Command Dial, or the Command Control to move the selection block to the right to select the flower icon, as shown in FIGURE 5-41.

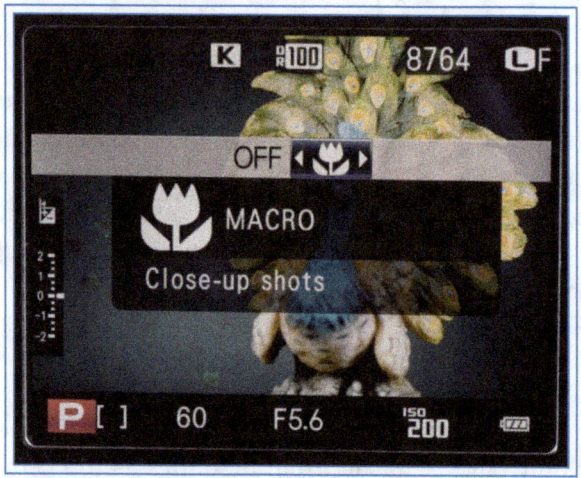

Figure 5-41. Macro Focus Selection Menu

(Your best bet is just to press the Left button twice quickly.) You will then see the flower icon appear on the left side of the display. If you are using the optical viewfinder, the camera will automatically switch to using the electronic viewfinder. This is because of the parallax effect—the optical viewfinder cannot provide an accurate view of a close object, because of the offset between what the lens sees and what the optical viewfinder sees.

You cannot select Macro focus when the camera is set for shooting panoramas or movies. When you use Macro focus, you should not use an aperture wider than f/4.0, because the lens was not designed to achieve sharp results at the widest apertures in Macro focus mode. I will discuss Macro shooting further in Chapter 9.

Display/Back Button

The button marked DISP/BACK, at the very bottom left of the area below the Command Dial, is used for several purposes.

DISPLAY BUTTON

First, this button can be used to switch among the various displays of information on the camera's LCD screen or in the viewfinder, in both shooting and playback modes.

In shooting mode, there are various displays available that are called up by successive presses of the Display button, depending on which display mode is in use. When you are using either the optical viewfinder or the electronic viewfinder, there are two different screens available—the Standard display, shown in FIGURE 5-42, and the Custom display, seen in FIGURE 5-43.

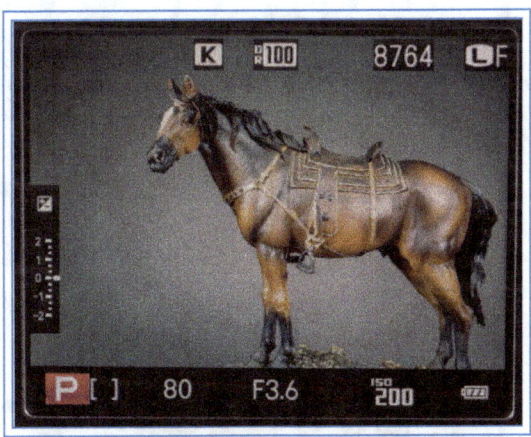

Figure 5-42. Shooting Mode Standard Display Screen

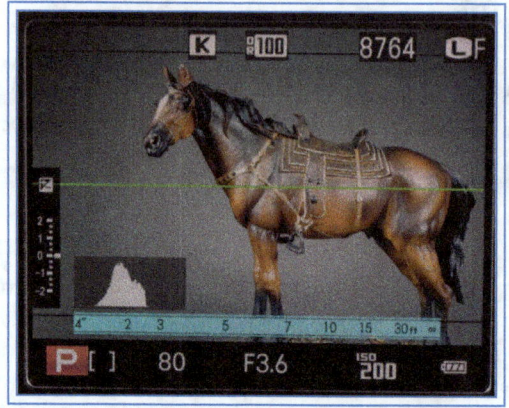

Figure 5-43. Shooting Mode Custom Display Screen

As was discussed in Chapter 4, the items that appear on the Custom display are selected using the Display Custom Setting option on the Shooting menu. The Standard display shows only basic shooting information, including aperture, shutter speed, ISO, exposure compensation, shooting mode, and focus distance.

When you are using the LCD display, there are three different screens available—the same Standard and Custom displays as with the viewfinder and, in addition, a screen called the Detailed display, shown in FIGURE 5-44.

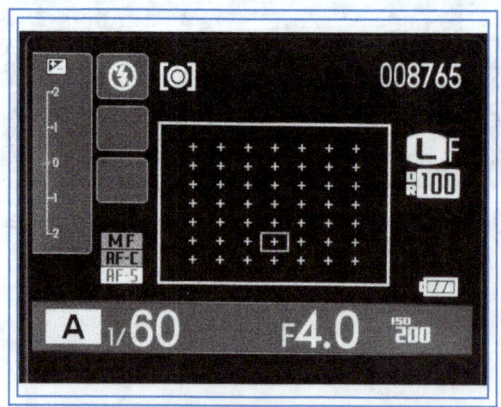

Figure 5-44. Shooting Mode Detailed Display Screen

That option does not present a live view of the scene, the Histogram, or the Electronic Level, but instead shows a black screen that provides basic information about exposure, image size, White Balance, and other items, plus a detailed representation of the focus area, showing which focus point is in use if one has been selected, whether chosen by the photographer (in Area AF mode) or by the camera (in Multi AF mode).

In playback mode, there are four screens available through presses of the Display button. All four screens are the same with either the electronic viewfinder or the LCD screen; there is no playback display in the optical viewfinder. The first option, shown in FIGURE 5-45, is a screen with general information, which shows the recorded image overlaid with icons and figures showing the date and time the picture was taken, its identification number, image quality and size, White Balance setting (if other than Auto), aperture, shutter speed, ISO, and Dynamic Range setting. The battery status icon also is shown.

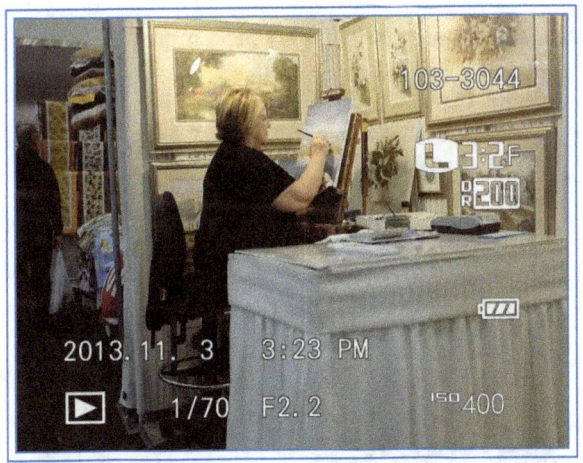

Figure 5-45. Playback Mode General Information Display Screen

The second view, not shown here, is of the image only, with no information overlaid on it.

The third view, seen in FIGURE 5-46, shows the Favorites screen, which includes only the image number, date and time, and your rating, along with a selection box for changing the image's rating (number of stars). I will discuss Favorites in Chapter 6.

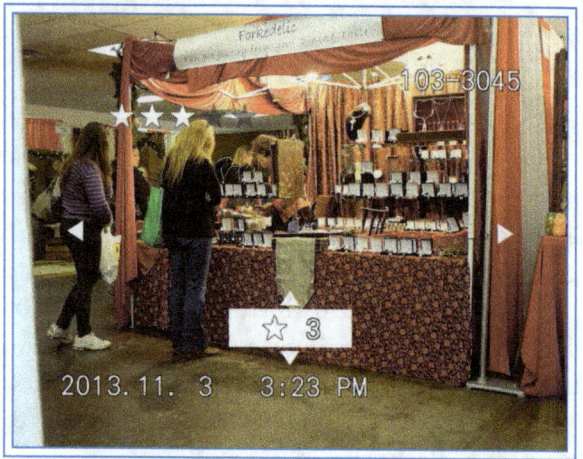

Figure 5-46. Playback Mode Favorites Screen

The fourth and final view in playback mode, shown in FIGURE 5-47, is the Detailed Information view.

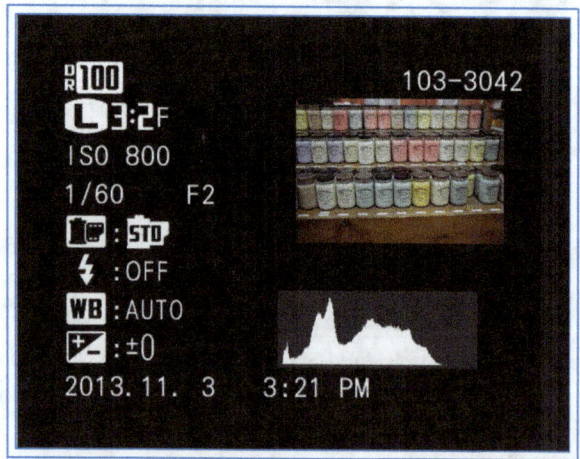

Figure 5-47. Playback Mode Detailed Information Screen

This screen includes a thumbnail version of the image, a Histogram below that, and, on the left side of the display, considerable details, including the Dynamic Range setting, image quality and size, ISO, shutter speed, aperture, Film Simulation mode, flash mode, White Balance setting, exposure compensation, and date and time the image was made.

No matter which of the four playback displays is selected, you also can call up a detailed series of information screens for any image by repeated presses of the Command Control switch to the right or left. I'll discuss that function further in Chapter 6.

BACK BUTTON

The Display/Back button also has a second identity as the Back button. In this capacity, the button serves to exit from menu screens or other selection screens. You will see a message on the display indicating that you can use the Back button to exit from a particular screen, as illustrated in FIGURE 5-48.

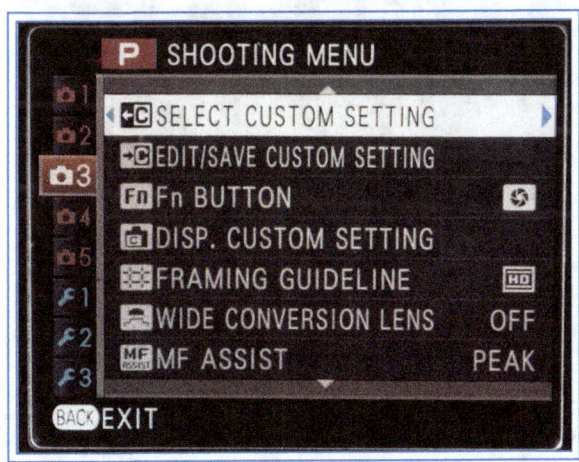

Figure 5-48. Example of Prompt to Press Back Button to Exit

The button also has a more specific duty when you are viewing the individual shots from a burst of continuous shots, in burst mode. To return to normal playback mode, in which you view just one shot from any burst, you press the Back button, as prompted by a message on the display. Also, if you have moved the autofocus frame around the screen when the AF Mode is set to Area, you can immediately return it to the center of the screen by pressing the Display/Back button while the frame is activated for moving.

Silent Mode

The very versatile Display/Back button has another function that is not obvious, but is quite important. If you press and hold the button for about two seconds, the camera enters Silent Mode, which also can be invoked through the first screen of the Setup menu, as discussed in Chapter 7. The camera will briefly display the message shown in FIGURE 5-49.

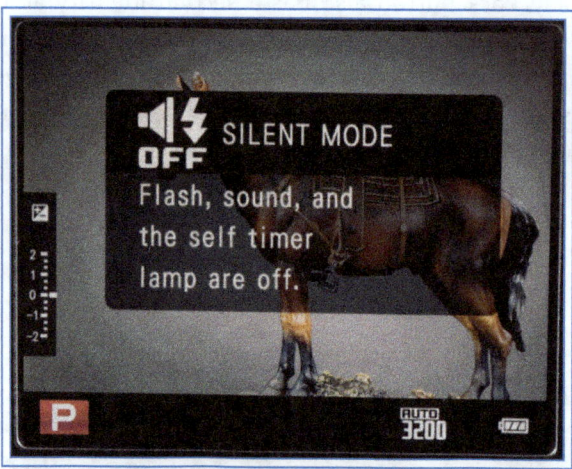

Figure 5-49. Message When Silent Mode is Activated

In Silent Mode, the camera not only suppresses all operational sounds, it also disables the AF Illuminator/Self-timer lamp and the flash, so there is little risk of attracting unwanted attention to yourself. Note that turning on Silent Mode is the only way to disable the lamp on the front of the camera for both of its functions, as the AF Illuminator lamp and as the Self-timer lamp. With the AF Illuminator menu option, discussed in Chapter 4, you can turn off the lamp's AF Illuminator function, but not its Self-timer function.

To cancel Silent Mode, press and hold the button again.

Checking and Updating Firmware

Finally, the Display/Back button has one more function that you won't need often, but that can be critically important. This button is used to check the firmware version that is installed in your X100S, and to update that version to a newer one when an updated version is made available by Fujifilm. Firmware is a term for something that is somewhat like both software and hardware; it is the programming for the camera's circuitry, which is electronically recorded into the camera either at the factory, or through your computer if you upgrade the firmware with an update provided by Fujifilm. A new version of the firmware can fix bugs and can even provide new features, so it's well worthwhile checking the Fujifilm web site periodically for updates. Instructions for installing an update are provided on the web site. Essentially, the process involves downloading a file to your computer, saving that file to an SD card formatted for the camera, then placing that card in the camera so the firmware can be installed.

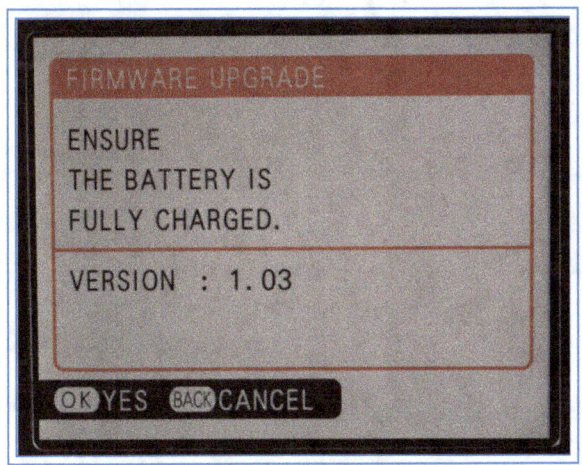

Figure 5-50. Firmware Version Screen

To check your firmware version, hold down the Display/Back button as you turn the camera on. The screen will show a message like that in FIGURE 5-50, stating the current version and telling you to press the OK button to upgrade to a newer version; you can press Display/Back again to cancel if you were just checking the current version of the firmware. As I write this, my camera has version 1.03. If you have any version with a number lower than that, you should look into downloading the latest version and upgrading. Fujifilm is quite good about providing useful updates. For example, it released an update for the firmware of the FinePix X100 camera in October 2013, even though that model was announced in September 2010, more than three years earlier, and had already been discontinued. As of this writing, you can check for firmware upgrades at the following website: http://www. fujifilm.com/support/digital_cameras/software/#firmware.

Q Button

This control, directly to the right of the Display/Back button, provides a very convenient feature of the X100S. In shooting mode, pressing this button immediately calls up the Quick menu, as shown in FIGURE 5-51.

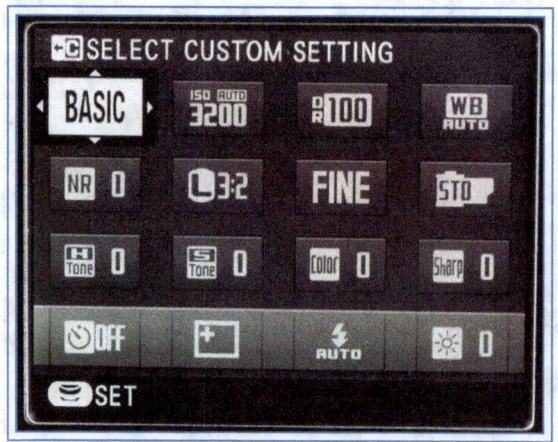

Figure 5-51. Quick Menu Screen

Using this screen, you have quick access to 16 of the camera's most important settings: Custom Settings, ISO, Dynamic Range, White Balance, Long Exposure Noise Reduction, Image Size, Image Quality, Film Simulation, Highlight Tone, Shadow Tone, Color, Sharpness, Self-timer, AF Area, Flash Mode, and LCD brightness.

To use this menu, navigate through the 16 settings by pressing the four direction buttons. When one of the 16 blocks is highlighted, change the setting for that item by turning the Command Dial or pressing the Command Control right or left. Exit from the menu by pressing the Q button or the OK button, or by half-pressing the shutter button.

While the Quick menu is displayed, you can press and hold the Q button again to call up the screen shown in FIGURE 5-52, which gives you access to the settings for the three banks of Custom settings.

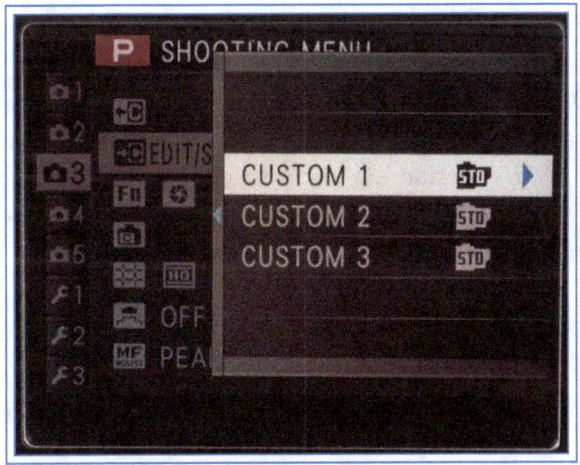

Figure 5-52. Custom Settings Screen from Holding Down Q Button

If you press and hold the Q button for about 2 seconds while the shooting screen is displayed, the camera will not display the Quick menu; instead, it will increase the brightness of the LCD screen (or the electronic viewfinder screen) to its maximum level, using what Fujifilm calls Outdoor Mode. Press and hold the button again to return the screen's brightness to normal.

When the camera is in playback mode, pressing the Q button has another special function not involving the Quick menu. If you press the button while a single Raw quality image is displayed, the camera calls up the Raw Conversion option from the Playback menu, which gives you a powerful set of options for converting that image to a JPEG version. With that process, you can alter the exposure, White Balance, Dynamic Range, and other settings for the image right inside the camera, and produce another version of it without affecting the original. I will discuss the details of this option in Chapter 6, in the discussion of the Playback menu. (If you press the Q button while a JPEG (non-RAW) image is displayed, nothing will happen; the button will not function.)

Because there is some danger that you could press this button unintentionally while in shooting mode and accidentally call up the Quick menu, interrupting your shooting, Fujifilm has included a way to lock out the use of the button. Just press and hold the Menu/OK button for about two seconds, and the use of this button, as well as the use of the four buttons on the Command Dial for their selection of Macro focus, AF/Delete, Flash Mode, and White Balance will be disabled until the Control Lock process is reversed by pressing and holding Menu/OK again.

CHAPTER 6:
Playback

I f you're like me, you take the images you've created and import them into your computer, where you manipulate them with software, then post them on the web, print them out, e-mail them, or do whatever else the occasion calls for. In other words, I don't spend a lot of time viewing my pictures in the camera. But that doesn't mean it's not a good thing to know about. Depending on your needs, there may be plenty of times when you take a picture and then need to examine it closely in the camera. Also, the camera can serve as a viewing device like an iPod or other gadget that is designed, at least in part, for storing and viewing photos. So it's worth taking a good look at the various playback functions of the X100S.

Normal Playback

I'll start with a brief summary of the basic playback techniques. First, when you take a new photo, your image may stay on the screen for a very short period for review, depending on the setting for the Image Display option of the Screen Set-up item on the second screen of the Setup menu, as discussed in Chapter 7. You can select either 0.5 second or 1.5 seconds, turn this function off, or set the camera so the image stays on the display until you dismiss it by pressing the OK button or pressing the shutter button halfway. If your major concern with viewing images in the camera is to check them right after they are taken, this feature is useful. However, you cannot do much with the image while it is displayed in this mode—you cannot display detailed information for it, delete it, or mark it as a Favorite. You can enlarge the image using the AE/Zoom-in button and shrink it back down with the Drive/Zoom-out button, but only if you have the Image Display option set to Continuous.

If you want more control over how your images are viewed, you need to use the settings that are available in playback mode.

To review your images in playback mode, press the Playback button, marked by a right-facing triangle at the upper left of the line of buttons on the camera's back. Once you press that button, the camera is in playback mode, and you will see the most recent image saved to the memory card that is in the camera (or, if no card is inserted, to the internal memory). To move back through older images, press the Left button or turn the Command Dial to the left. To move through the increasingly more recent images, use the Right button or turn the Command Dial to the right. To move rapidly backward or forward through the images, press and hold the Left or Right button.

Different Playback Screens

When you are viewing an image in single-image display mode, pressing the Display button repeatedly cycles through the four different screens that are available: just the full image with no information added, not shown here; the full image with basic information, including date and time it was taken, file name, image number, image size, and quality, as shown in FIGURE 6-1; a thumbnail image accompanied by detailed recording information, including aperture, shutter speed, ISO, recording mode, exposure compensation, and other data, plus a Histogram, as shown in FIGURE 6-2; and the Favorites screen, as shown in FIGURE 6-3.

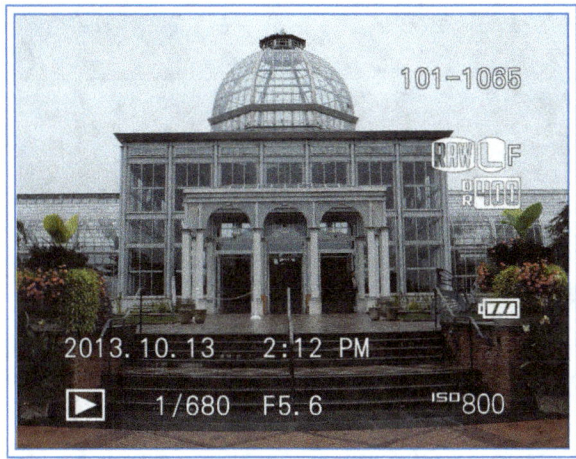

Figure 6-1. Playback Display - Basic Information

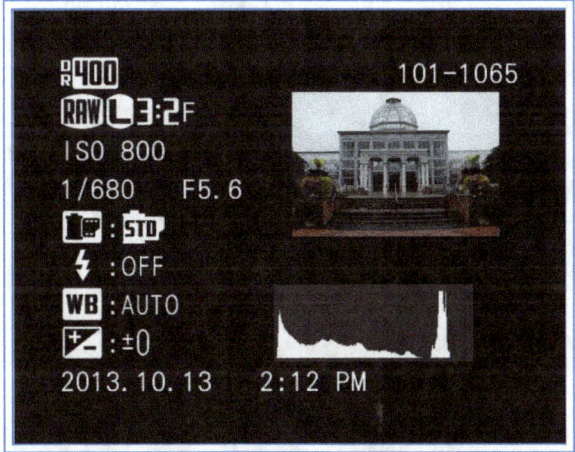

Figure 6-2. Playback Display - Detailed Information

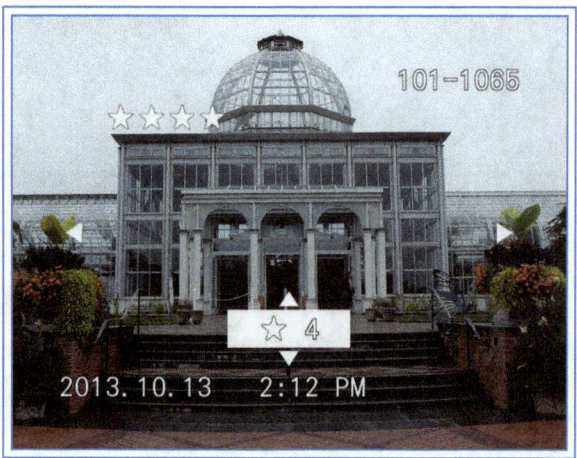

Figure 6-3. Playback Display - Favorites

At the bottom of the Favorites screen is a small white rectangle containing a star with a number from zero to five to its right. That number represents the rating of that image in the Favorites ranking. Now you can press the Up and Down buttons to change that rating. For example, you can press the Up button four times to give the image a rating of four stars.

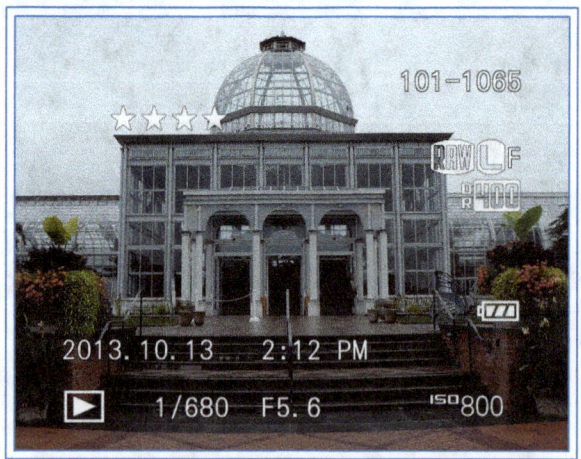

Figure 6-4. Image Marked as Favorite with 4 Stars

You can move to other images using the Command Dial or the Left and Right buttons, and change their ratings as you wish, also. Whenever you give an image a rating of at least one star, that number of stars appears in the upper left when it is displayed with the basic information display, as shown in FIGURE 6-4, or with the Favorites display. Later in this chapter I'll discuss how you can use the Favorites rankings to select and view images.

HISTOGRAM

As noted above, the most detailed playback information screen that is summoned by pressing the Display button includes a Histogram for the image being displayed. The Histogram is a graph, or chart, representing the distribution of dark and bright areas in the image in question. The darkest blacks are represented by vertical bars on the left, and the brightest whites by vertical bars on the right, with continuous gradations in between.

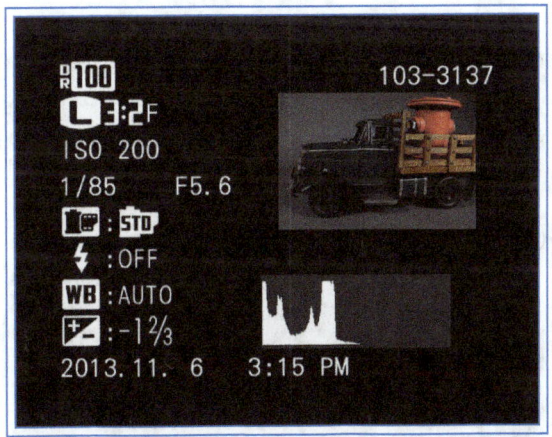

Figure 6-5. Playback Histogram for Underexposed Image

If you have a Histogram whose pattern includes an abundance of white peaks on the left side and few or none on the right, like that in FIGURE 6-5, that means there is an excessive amount of black and dark areas (high points on the left side of the Histogram), and very few bright and white areas (no high points on the right). A pattern that includes many white peaks bunched toward the right side of the screen would mean just the opposite—too many bright and white areas, as shown in FIGURE 6-6.

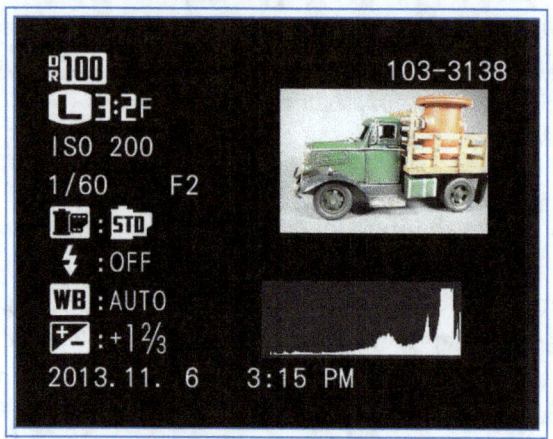

Figure 6-6. Playback Histogram for Overexposed Image

A Histogram that is "just right" would be one that includes a reasonable amount of white peaks in the middle, with tapering amounts toward the left and right sides of the chart. That pattern indicates a good balance of whites, blacks, and medium tones, as shown in FIGURE 6-7.

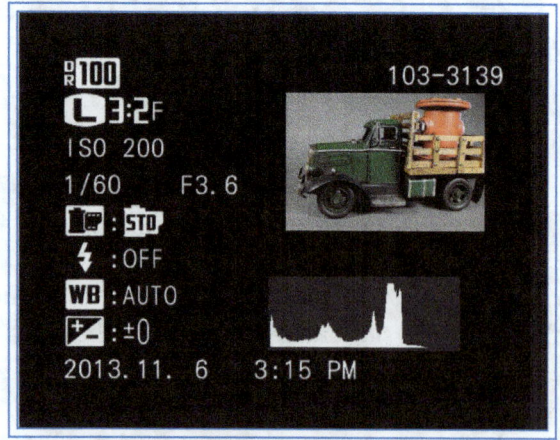

Figure 6-7. Playback Histogram for Normally Exposed Image

The Histogram is an approximation, and should not be relied on too heavily. It may be useful to give you some feedback as to how evenly exposed your image is, and whether you may need to re-take it with different exposure settings.

One additional note about the playback Histogram display on the X100S: If the image is overexposed, the overexposed highlight areas on the thumbnail image will blink, indicating that those parts of the image are excessively bright.

Index View and Enlarging Images

In playback mode, you can use the AE/Zoom-in and Drive/Zoom-out buttons to the left of the LCD screen to enlarge a single image or to view index screens of your images. When you are viewing an individual image, press the Drive/Zoom-out button once, and you will see a screen like that in Figure 6-8, showing four images, two large and two small, one of which is outlined by a light gray frame.

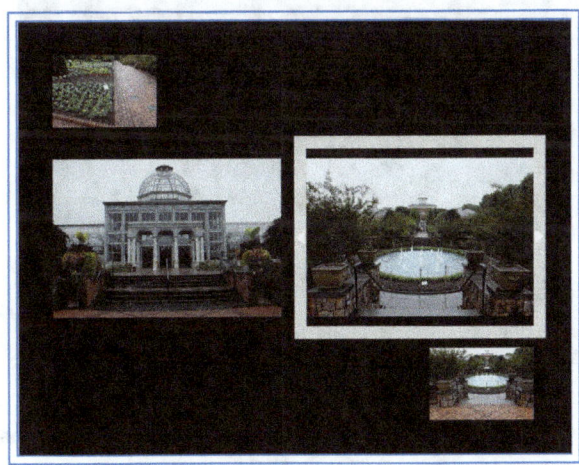

Figure 6-8. Playback Index Screen - 4 Images

In addition to that frame, which indicates which image is currently selected, the images on the screen may have either no frame, a green frame, or a dark gray frame. A green frame indicates a group of continuous shots and a dark gray frame indicates a movie. You can then press the OK button to bring up the outlined item (single image, group of continuous shots, or movie; I will refer to them all as images for simplicity, here) as the single item on the screen, or you can move through your images with the four-image index screen by pressing the Left and Right buttons or by turning the Command Dial. To return from the single image to the index screen, press the Drive/Zoom-out button again.

If you press the Drive/Zoom-out button once more, the camera will display an index screen with nine images, as shown in FIGURE 6-9, and a last press brings a 100-image index screen like that in FIGURE 6-10 (assuming in each case that you have that many images; if not, there will be blank spaces on the screen).

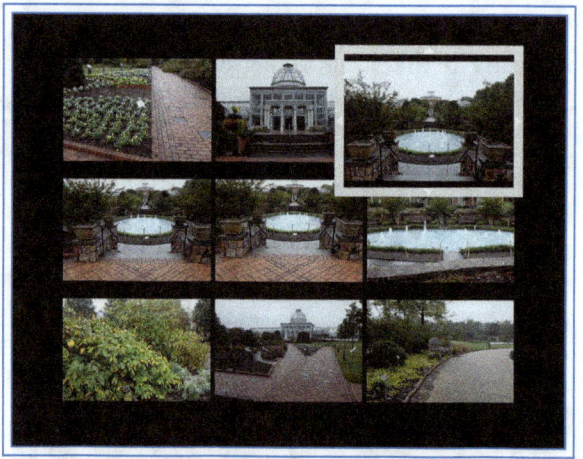

Figure 6-9. Playback Index Screen - 9 Images

You can maneuver through any of these screens to select a single image for viewing. If you want to reduce the number of images per screen, just press the AE/Zoom-in button repeatedly to reverse the progression of index screens. On any of the index screens other than the first one, you can navigate using all four direction buttons or by turning the Command Dial.

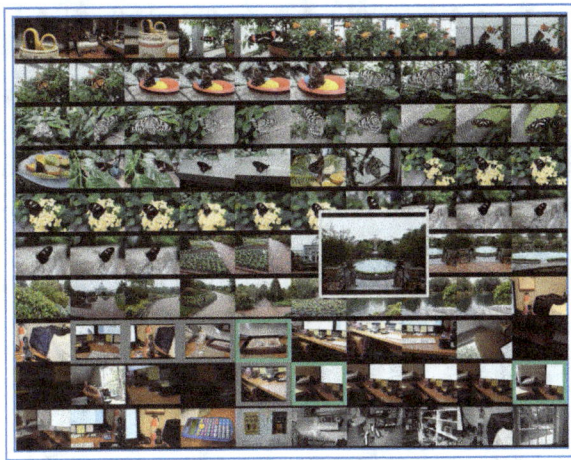

Figure 6-10. Playback Index Screen - 100 Images

When you are viewing a single image (not a movie or a series of continuous shots), a press of the AE/Zoom-in button enlarges your view of that image. You will then see a display in the lower right corner of the image like that shown in FIGURE 6-11, with a small version of the image that contains an inset gray rectangle that represents the portion of the image that is now filling the screen in enlarged view. A scale at the left shows the amount of enlargement.

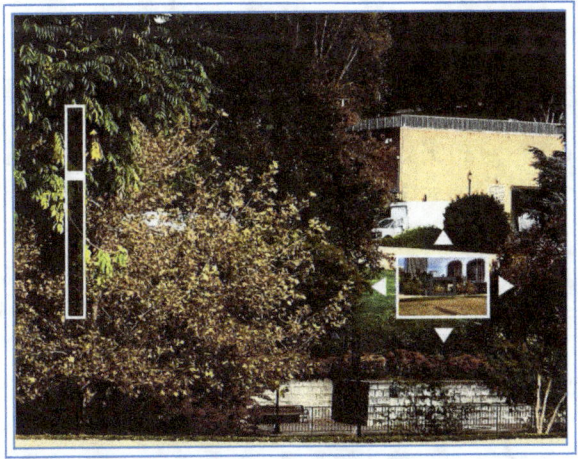

Figure 6-11. Enlarged Image with Inset Block

If you press the AE/Zoom-in button repeatedly, the image will be increasingly enlarged up to a maximum that depends on the Image Size setting. While the image is magnified, you can scroll around within it using the four direction buttons; you will see the inset gray rectangle move around within the white rectangle that represents the whole image. To reduce the image's size again, just press the Drive/Zoom-out button as many times as necessary. While the image is enlarged, you can turn the Command Dial to move to other images, at the same enlargement level.

Focus Point and Information Screens

There are some other things you can do when viewing a single image in playback mode. To zoom in on the focus point, press in on the center of the Command Control. The image will immediately be enlarged to its maximum size with the focus point centered on the display. To zoom back out to normal size, press in on the center of the Command Control again. If the image was taken with manual focus and there is no focus point, then the camera will zoom the image in to its center point. (If you used manual focus but pressed the AFL/AEL button to force the camera to use autofocus, the camera will zoom to the autofocus point, even though manual focus was in use.)

To see screens of additional information about an image, press the Command Control left or right one or more times. If you press it to the right, the first press will take you to the first of two black screens with detailed data about the image, as shown in FIGURE 6-12, including its settings for Dynamic Range, Color, Highlight Tone, Shadow Tone, and other items; the next press will produce a similar screen, shown in FIGURE 6-13, with data about color space, metering mode, and flash mode; and the third press will display a green crosshair that marks the focus point in the image, as shown in FIGURE 6-14. Once the first of these screens is displayed, you can also get to the next ones with the Down button.

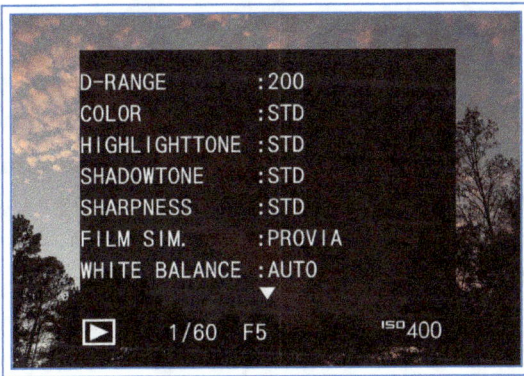

Figure 6-12. First Screen of Additional Information

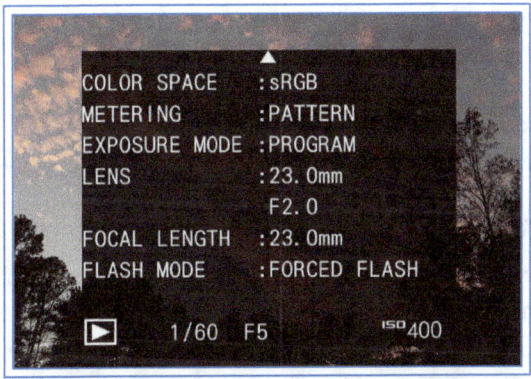

Figure 6-13. Second Screen of Additional Information

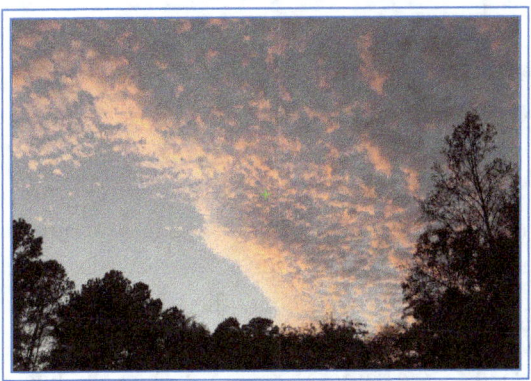

Figure 6-14. Third Screen, Showing Focus Point at Green Crosshair

RAW Conversion

Another operation you can carry out while an image is displayed in playback mode—if the image was captured with Raw image quality—is to convert the Raw image to a JPEG version using the X100S's set of built-in Raw processing tools. When a Raw image is shown on the display, press the Q button at the lower right of the camera's back and the camera will display the Raw Conversion screen from the Playback menu. I will discuss the details of how to use this feature later in this chapter, when I discuss the options on the Playback menu.

Viewing Shots Taken in a Burst

When you view a burst of continuous photos taken with the X100S, in normal playback mode the camera displays only the first shot of the burst. In other words, if you scroll through your shots, you will see only one image from this burst, even though there may have been eight or ten shots (or 100) in the burst. In order to see the individual images from the burst, you have to "open up" the sequence by pressing the Down button. You can then navigate through each of the shots in the burst, but you cannot advance beyond the burst. You will be "stuck" inside the same sequence of shots until you return to normal playback mode by pressing the Display/Back button.

I will use an example, which will make it easier to illustrate the way the X100S handles playback of bursts. Suppose you have selected continuous high-speed shooting by pressing the Drive mode button and selecting the 6.0 fps option from the list of choices. Now, when you aim the camera at your subject and hold down the shutter button for a few seconds, the camera will rapidly record a sequence of shots. The LCD display (or electronic viewfinder) will display a screen indicating that the images are being recorded to the camera's memory; then the live view of the scene will return.

When the camera has settled back to the live view, you can press the Playback button to start viewing your images. If everything worked as expected, there will be multiple images to view. However, when you press the Playback button, you will see only one image from this sequence. If you press any of the direction buttons or turn the Command Dial, you will move to an entirely different image or sequence of images, assuming one exists; you will not see the other images from this sequence.

Where did those other images go? Well, look at the display on the screen, which has a couple of unusual aspects. (I'm assuming you have the Standard information display active; if not, press the Display button and select the option with the "i" icon at the bottom.) For one thing, when the image is first displayed, for about a second you will see an icon with a triangle representing the Down button at the bottom of the screen, with a message indicating to press that button to "Play Continuous Shots," as shown in FIGURE 6-15.

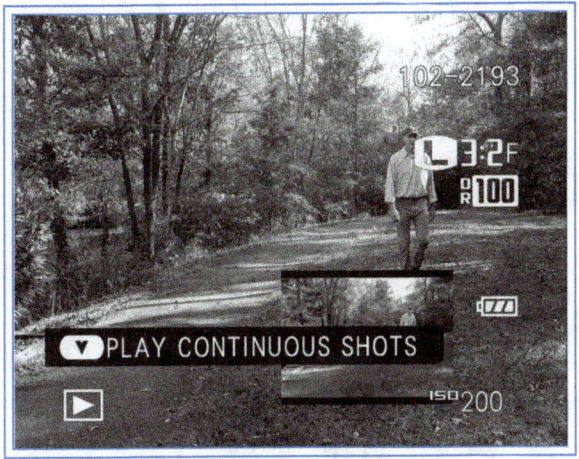

Figure 6-15. Message for Playing Continuous Shots

Also, no matter which display screen is active, in the lower right corner of the image you will see a small inset screen that contains views of the other images. That little square is almost like a movie, because it keeps cycling through all of the other shots from this particular burst. After the first second, that inset square is the only visible indication that you are viewing the first image from a burst of images.

In this normal playback mode, you can still perform operations such as deleting, rotating, copying, and protecting images. However, any such operation will affect all of the images in the burst. So, if you press the Delete button (Up button) while an image is displayed in this mode, and select the option to delete just this frame, all images in the burst will be deleted. You won't see any message warning you that all messages from the burst will be deleted, but, after you have selected OK to confirm the deletion, you may see a blank screen for a time while the camera goes through the process of deleting all of the images from the burst.

Now, go ahead and press the Down button to enter burst playback mode. You will see the same image as before, but the other information will change, as shown in FIGURE 6-16.

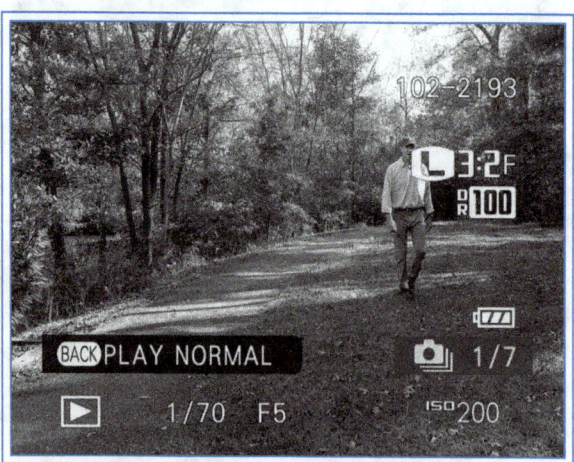

Figure 6-16. Message When Shots Displayed Individually

You will now see a message at the lower left indicating to press the Back button to return to normal playback. At the lower right you will see a continuous-shooting icon next to a set of numbers such as 1/7, indicating you are viewing the first of seven images in a burst.

You can now scroll through all of the individual shots from this burst by turning the Command Dial or pressing the Left and Right buttons. However, you will not be able to advance beyond these images—you will be "stuck" inside the burst until you press the Back button to return to single-image playback mode. You can magnify each individual image using the techniques described earlier. You also can perform any other operation on each image that is available using the camera's controls or the Playback menu, such as deleting, rotating, and the like. If you delete an image, the camera will move to the next image and ask whether you want to delete that one, and so on through all images in this burst.

The Playback Menu

I have discussed the options for basic review of images in normal playback mode as well as in burst mode, and I have covered other playback-related topics such as information screens, the Histogram, and enlarging images on the camera's display. Now it's time to discuss the numerous options that are available through the Playback menu.

For you to get access to this menu, the camera must be in playback mode, entered by pressing the Playback button and then pressing the Menu button to display the Playback menu. The triangle icon with the number 1 should be highlighted on the camera's display. You can now turn the Command Dial or press the Up and Down buttons to highlight the various entries on the three screens of the Playback menu. I'll go through the options on the menu one by one. The first screen of the menu is shown in FIGURE 6-17.

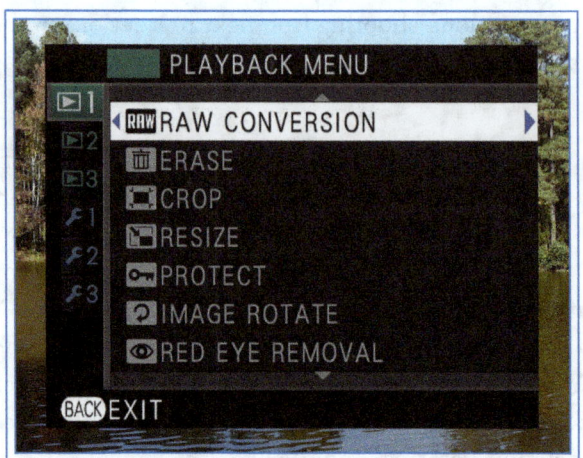

Figure 6-17. First Screen of Playback Menu

RAW CONVERSION

This first item on the Playback menu gives you a powerful set of tools for processing your Raw files right in the camera. As noted in Chapter 5 and earlier in this chapter, you can get access to these tools by pressing the Q button when a Raw image is displayed in Playback mode, but you also can select the Raw Conversion item from the Playback menu. In either case, this option works as follows.

First, note that this menu item will be dimmed on the menu screen and unavailable for selection unless the currently displayed image is a single Raw file, and not a JPEG file, a movie, or a burst of images. If you're not certain whether a given image was shot with Raw image quality, press the Display button until the Standard information screen appears; in the upper right corner, the Image Quality setting will be shown; the Raw label will appear next to the image size for all Raw shots, as shown in FIGURE 6-18.

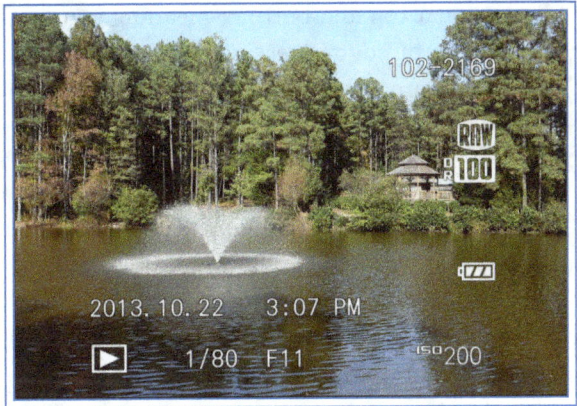

Figure 6-18. Image with Raw Icon

If you want to find all of your Raw shots so you can convert them, use the Image Search feature, discussed later in this chapter, and select the By Type of Data option for the search.

Once you have a single Raw image displayed on the screen in playback mode, press the Q button or select Raw Conversion from the Playback menu. In either case, the camera will display the Raw Conversion screen, as shown in FIGURE 6-19, with a thumbnail image at the left beside a large gray box that contains an impressive list of settings you can change.

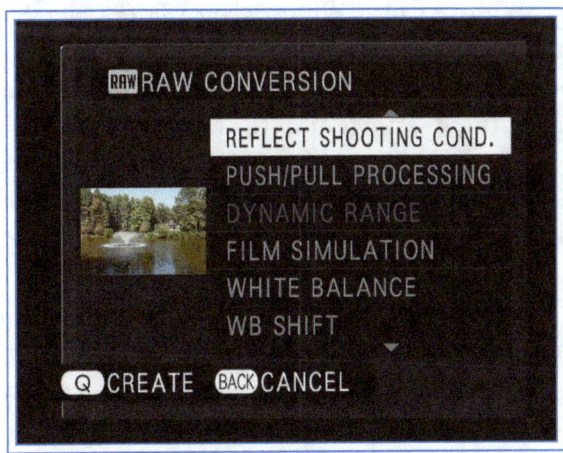

Figure 6-19. Raw Conversion Menu Screen

The box has arrows at top and bottom, meaning you can scroll up or down, wrapping around, by pressing the Up and Down buttons or by turning the Command Dial, to see all of the items in the list.

If you select the first item, Reflect Shooting Conditions, that will negate any changes you have made to the other items in the list. The camera will create a JPEG copy of the Raw file using the settings that were in effect when you took the picture. So, if the image was underexposed, had the wrong White Balance, and was shot using the Velvia Film Simulation setting, all of those settings will be preserved when you finish and create the JPEG copy of the image. This option is useful if you need to create a JPEG copy of your Raw file so you can send it by e-mail or edit it in a software program that cannot edit the Raw file, for example.

If, instead of creating a JPEG duplicate of the Raw image as shot, you want to change some of the settings, this is where the power of Raw images and the power of this menu option come into play. I won't attempt to discuss Raw processing in detail; there are many books, videos, and articles available that provide excellent information on that topic. Here are some general guidelines.

The parameters you can adjust using the Raw Conversion feature are the following: Push/Pull Processing, Dynamic Range, Film Simulation, White Balance, White Balance Shift, Color, Sharpness, Highlight Tone, Shadow Tone, Noise Reduction, and Color Space. What this means in practice is that you can, within some limits, change any of these settings after the fact, and fix mistakes in the settings you were using when you shot the picture. For example, if you accidentally turned the aperture dial to f/11.0 instead of f/5.6, resulting in an image two stops too dark, or you accidentally left the White Balance set for Incandescent when shooting in daylight, you can change both of those settings in the Raw processing, and make the image look just as if it had been shot with the correct settings. And, of course, you also can tweak the other settings, such as Dynamic Range, Sharpness, and Noise Reduction, to achieve a look that suits your taste.

To adjust one of these settings, highlight it on the menu screen and press the Right button to move to the adjustment screen. For example, the screen for Push/Pull Processing, shown in FIGURE 6-20, lets you adjust the exposure value (EV, or f-stops) of your image in increments of 1/3 stop in a range from -1 EV to +3 EV.

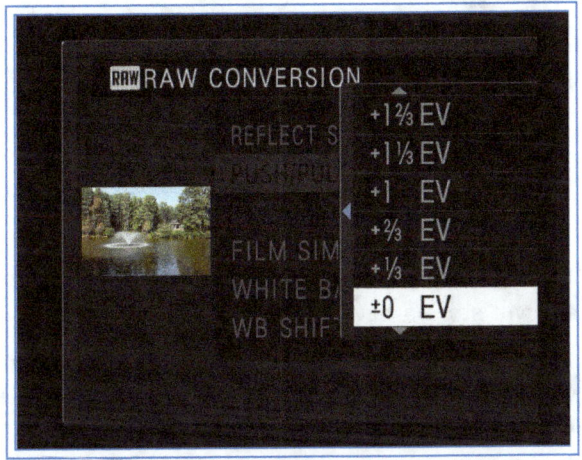

Figure 6-20. Push-Pull Processing Screen

Scroll through these values, highlight the one you want to use for the adjustment, and then press the OK button to confirm the adjustment. You will be returned to the list of parameters; you can continue to adjust any or all of them as you wish.

When you have finished making adjustments, press the Q button. Although the camera's screen indicates that you press the Q button to "Create" a new file, actually this action just produces a preview that you can still cancel out of. So, don't hesitate to press the Q button whenever you want to see the effects of any adjustments you have made to the various parameters. When you press the Q button, the camera will work for a while and then display a full-screen preview of the final product—a JPEG file that has had its settings altered from those in the Raw file, based on your Raw Conversion adjustments. An example is shown in FIGURE 6-21.

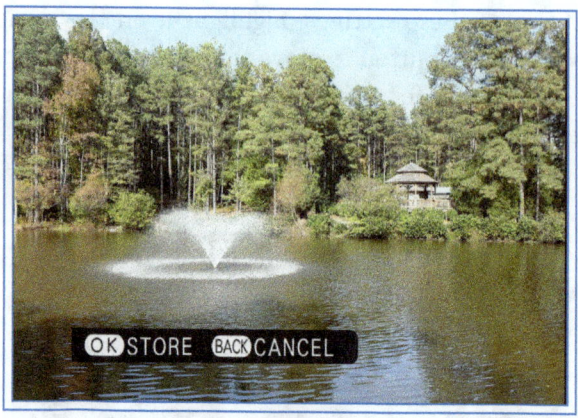

Figure 6-21. Preview of Altered Raw Image

If the preview image is acceptable, press the OK button and the camera will store a new JPEG version of the image with the altered settings; the original Raw file will be unaffected. If you want to keep making adjustments, press the Back button to cancel the conversion and keep working on the adjustments.

There are some limitations to this process, depending on the settings used for your images. For example, if an image was shot with ISO set to less than 800, the Dynamic Range setting will not be available for adjustment, because that value can be adjusted only when ISO is at least 800.

You can use this process any number of times for the same image, because the original Raw file is unaffected. For example, you can create one copy with increased exposure, one with decreased exposure, one with a different White Balance setting, and one with Film Simulation set to Monochrome. Also, note that this process can be used to see the effects of settings that do not alter the appearance of Raw images, such as Film Simulation. If you use the Reflect Shooting Conditions option, the converted JPEG image will show the effects of such settings, which, as noted earlier, are recorded in the Raw file's information, but do not become visible until the file is converted to JPEG.

ERASE

The second option on the Playback menu, Erase, is used for deleting multiple images or movies at one time. This is also one of the options that you can choose once you have selected a group of images using the Image Search menu option. The Erase feature works as follows.

If you are starting from the Erase item on the Playback menu, after you have highlighted that item on the menu screen, press the Right button or the OK button to move to the next screen, which gives you the choice of several options: Back, Frame, Selected Frames, or All Frames, as shown in FIGURE 6-22.

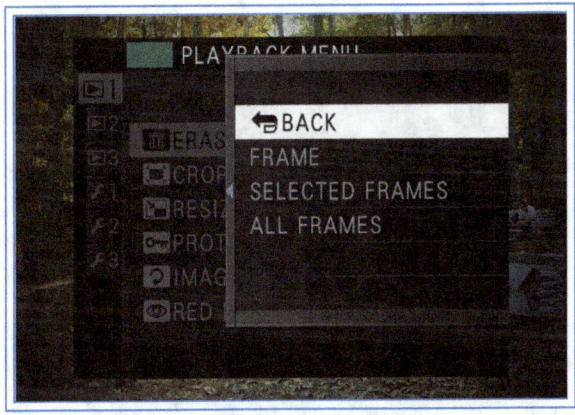

Figure 6-22. Erase Menu Option

You can choose Back to cancel; Frame to erase just the frame that was displayed on the screen; or All Frames to erase all images on the memory card. If you choose Selected Frames, you are presented with an index screen displaying nine thumbnail images at a time, as shown in FIGURE 6-23. Images that represent bursts of shots will be surrounded by green frames; those that represent movies will have gray frames. You can navigate through these thumbnails and mark (or unmark) them with the OK button. When you mark an image, a check mark will appear in the lower left corner of the image, as shown in FIGURE 6-24.

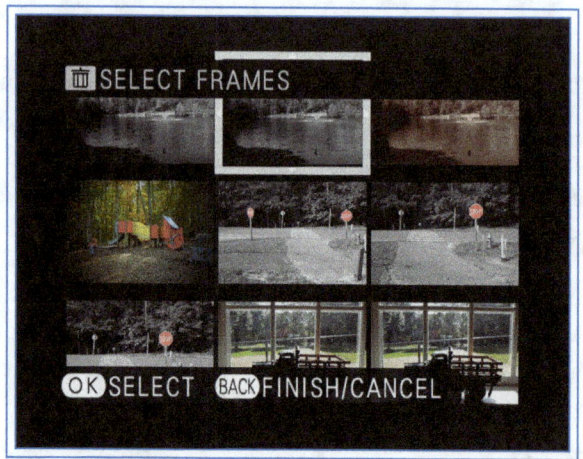

Figure 6-23. Erase Option - Screen to Select Images

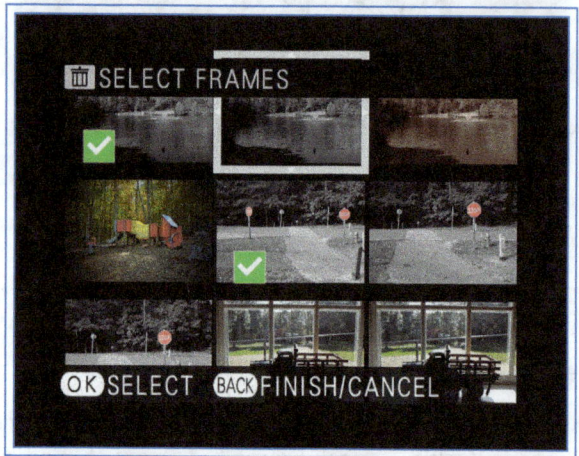

Figure 6-24. Check Marks for Selected Frames

When you have finished selecting images, press the Back button, and the camera will display a message asking you to confirm the deletion of the selected frames or cancel.

If you are starting from the Image Search item on the Playback menu (discussed later in this chapter) and move on to the Erase option after selecting images through a search, you will not see the Selected Frames option, because you already have selected frames. Therefore, the camera presents you with only three options: Back, Frame, and All Frames. That is, you can cancel the operation by choosing Back, erase just the image being displayed using Frame, or erase all images that were found with the Image Search option using All Frames.

You cannot erase images with this option if they have been protected with the Protect function, discussed later in this chapter. You need to remove protection before erasing them, or erase all data on the card using the Format command, discussed in Chapter 7.

CROP

This option for in-camera processing, which lets you save a cropped copy of any JPEG image, is quite user-friendly and it can be very useful. For example, you can crop an image of a group of people to create a closeup of a particular person's face, or you can enlarge a graphic to make it more readable if you are producing a quick presentation in your camera for a business meeting. Here is how to use this feature.

First, select the image that you want to crop. You can choose any single image that is large enough to be cropped, although it must be a JPEG image, not Raw. However, an image taken with the Raw + Fine or Raw + Normal setting can be cropped; the camera will crop the Fine or Normal (JPEG) image. If you want to crop a strictly Raw image, you can first use the Raw Conversion feature, discussed above, and convert the picture to JPEG using the Reflect Shooting Conditions option.

Once the chosen image is displayed on the screen, select this menu option and the crop scale will appear at the left of the display as shown in FIGURE 6-25, with the confirmation and cancel icons at the bottom. Now, enlarge the image using the AE/Zoom-in button until the portion you want to save in the cropped image appears centered in the display. Use the four direction buttons to move the image around as needed, and use the Drive/Zoom-out button to reduce the image's size if necessary.

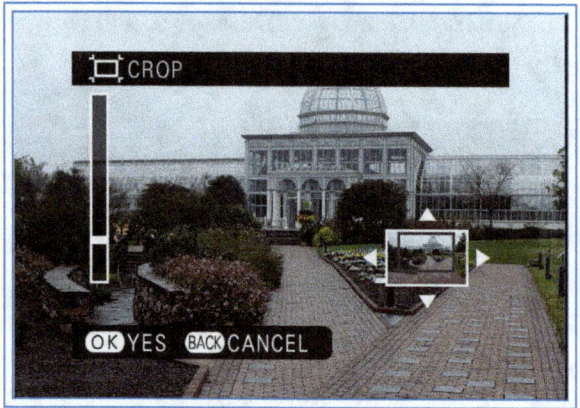

Figure 6-25. Crop Scale on Screen

Keep an eye on the confirmation and cancel icons; if they turn yellow, that means that the cropped image will be of a small size. Once you are satisfied with how the image looks on the display, press the OK button to make the copy, which is saved as a new file. The cropped image will be in the 3:2 aspect ratio, no matter what aspect ratio the original image was shot in.

RESIZE

This option provides you with another way to do a rudimentary form of in-camera editing. The Resize feature allows you to take any of your saved images and create a new version in a small file size that is suitable for sending by e-mail or posting on the internet. This function could come in handy if you need to take a quick photo and then e-mail it to a friend or colleague. If you don't have software available on your computer to edit the image down to a smaller size, you can let the camera take over this task. (Of course, you could take the image in the small size to begin with, but you might want to have a higher-resolution version available for later editing or printing, but still be able to create a small version for e-mailing after you have already recorded the original version.)

To use this feature, you first have to navigate to the image you want to alter. With this option, as with the Crop feature, any individual JPEG image can be used, as long as the image is not already too small to be resized. The camera will let you start the process with a Raw file, but it will end the operation with an error message indicating that Raw files cannot be resized in the camera.

Once the image to be resized is displayed, press the Menu button, then select the Resize option. On the next screen, as shown in FIGURE 6-26, you can choose from three progressively-smaller file-size options: M, S, and 640.

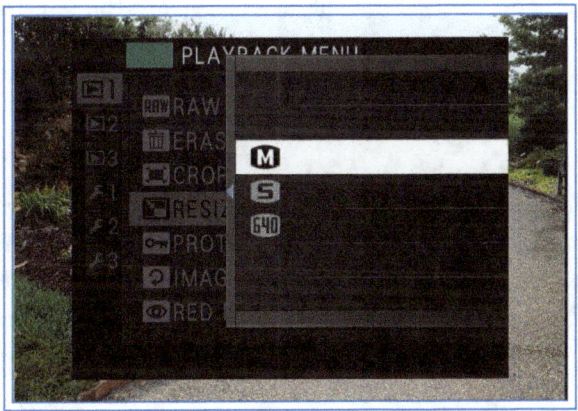

Figure 6-26. Resize Options Screen

Once you make your selection, the camera will ask you to confirm the operation on the next screen, as shown in FIGURE 6-27; if the original image is already too small for your selected option, the camera will tell you it cannot be done at that size.

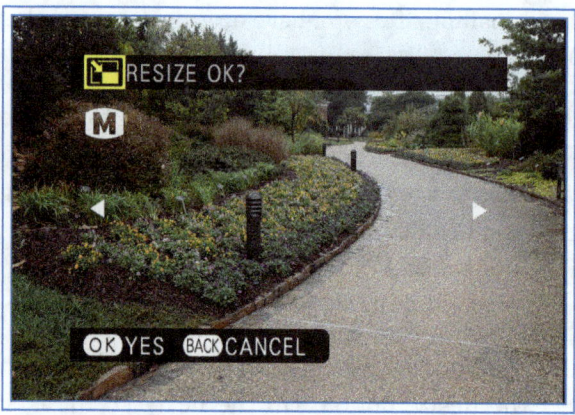

Figure 6-27. Resize Confirmation Screen

Once you have selected an acceptable size for the copy, press the OK button and the camera will make a copy of the selected image at your chosen size, and copy it to the end of the images on the memory card (or in internal memory).

PROTECT

With the Protect feature, you can "lock" selected images and videos so they cannot be erased with the normal erase functions, using the Delete button or the Erase command on the Playback menu. However, if you format the memory card using the Format command, all data will be erased, including protected images. Protected images also cannot be rotated using the Image Rotate option, discussed below.

To protect images using this menu option, first press the Right button or the OK button to get to the options screen, which gives you three choices: Frame, Set All, and Reset All, as shown in FIGURE 6-28. If you select Frame, you then navigate through your images and use the OK button to mark or unmark any images (including Raw images) and videos that you want to protect or unprotect. Then press the OK button to confirm.

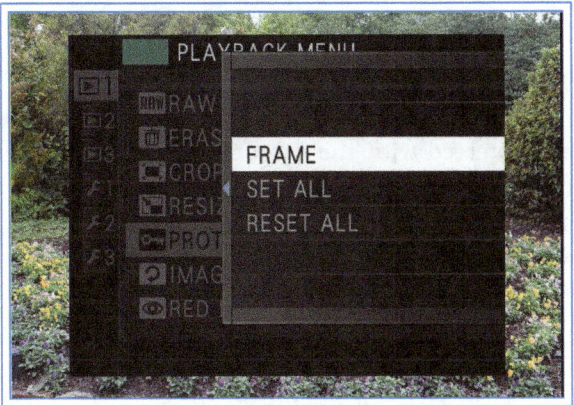

Figure 6-28. Protect Options Screen

An image that is protected will have a key icon in the upper left corner, as shown in FIGURE 6-29. That icon will be visible only when the image is viewed with the Standard information screen; the icon will not appear in the image-only view, in the Favorites-selection view, or in the Detailed view with the Histogram.

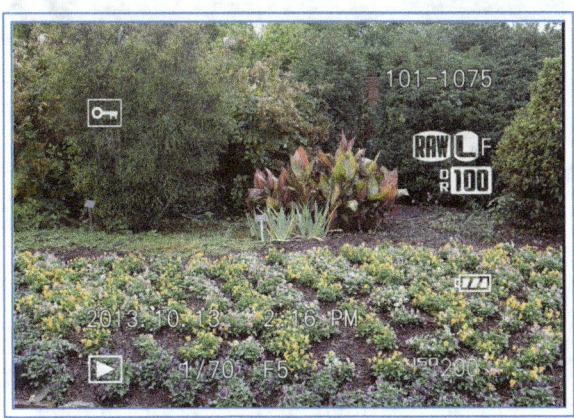

Figure 6-29. Protected Image with Key Icon

You can use the Set All option to protect all of the pictures on your memory card (or in the camera's internal memory), or Reset All to unprotect them all.

IMAGE ROTATE

Using this option, you can rotate your still photos 90 degrees clockwise or counter-clockwise. You cannot rotate images that have been protected with the Protect function, discussed above. However, you can rotate Raw images.

To use this feature, display the image to be rotated on the screen in playback mode, then select the Image Rotate option from the Playback menu. On the resulting screen, as shown in FIGURE 6-30, you will be prompted to use the Up or Down button to rotate the image counter-clockwise or clockwise. Press OK when it is rotated to the orientation you wish, or press the Back button to cancel the operation.

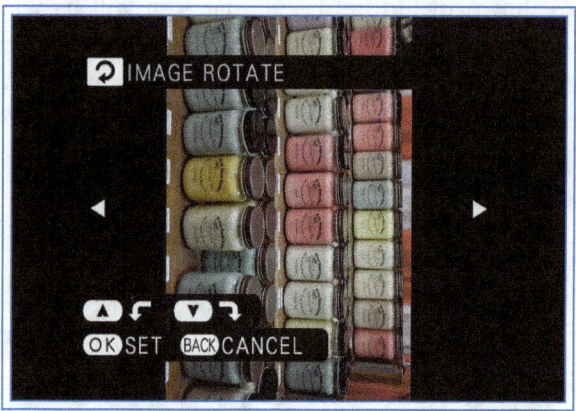

Figure 6-30. Image Rotate Screen

You don't have to use this function to rotate images that are taken with the camera held vertically; you can set up the camera to display those images in their natural orientation using the Autorotate Playback option of the Screen Set-up item on the second screen of the Setup menu, as discussed in Chapter 7.

RED EYE REMOVAL

This last option on the first screen of the Playback menu is another one that involves in-camera processing of your images. In this case, though, the camera will only work with JPEG files, not Raw images. If you select this menu item, the camera will examine the current image to see if it contains a face that may have "red-eye," the effect that can occur when on-camera flash bounces into the subject's dilated eyes and off the blood vessels in the retinas, giving an unpleasant reddish tinge to the person's eyes. If the camera believes this effect is present, it will display a message asking if it is all right with you to proceed with removal. If you confirm by pressing the OK button, the camera will process the image and save it with the red-eye corrected, to the extent correction succeeded.

I tested this process using a mannequin head with large red dots placed on the eyes to simulate the red-eye problem. FIGURE 6-31 shows the results in a pair of images, one with the simulated red-eye and the other after the Red Eye Removal option processed the image in playback mode. The camera did a good job of removing the red-eye effect in this case.

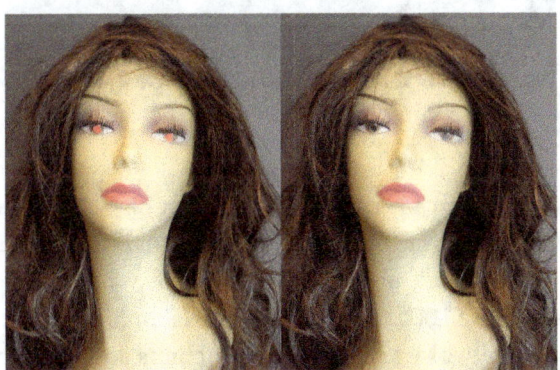

Figure 6-31. Red Eye Removal Before and After Images

I usually do not find much use for features of this sort, because it is easy to correct red-eye in software such as Photoshop and other editing programs. But, if you are in need of displaying a group of recent shots from a party and you want to clean up the shots that have red-eye, the X100S may be able to help you out. This option could be especially useful if, for example, you have just taken a group of flash photos at a gathering and you want to put together a quick slide show. You can fix up the unsightly red-eye effects quite quickly and easily, without having to transfer the images to a computer for editing.

Next, I will discuss the options on the second screen of the Playback menu, shown in FIGURE 6-32.

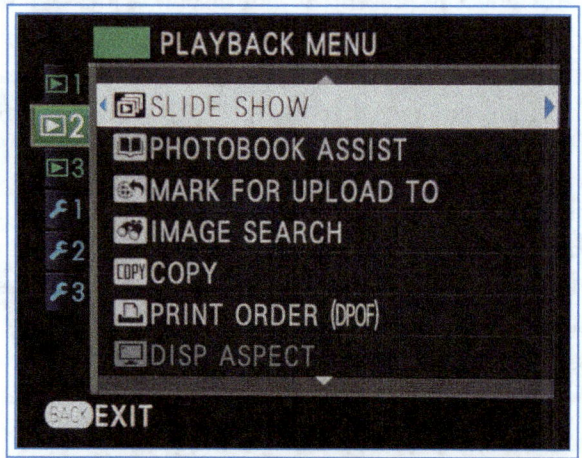

Figure 6-32. Second Screen of Playback Menu

SLIDE SHOW

Like most modern cameras, the X100S can display the images on your memory card (or in the camera's internal memory) in a slide show that plays back on the camera's display or on a connected HDTV set. The X100S does not offer elaborate options such as music or a variety of transitions; your pictures are played back with straight cuts or fades between them, and in silence. There are some choices you can make for your shows, though. Here are the details.

The first decision you should make is whether to use the Slide Show menu option as opposed to the Image Search option to launch your show. If you want to show all of the images and movies on the memory card in one continuous show, then the Slide Show option will work just fine. If, however, you want to show just a subset of your images, then you should use the Image

Search menu item, which is discussed later in this chapter. Once you have searched for and selected the images to show using that menu item, you can proceed directly from there to the Slide Show option by pressing the Menu button and selecting Slide Show.

Whichever way you get there, the Slide Show option works in the same way. Once Slide Show is highlighted on the menu screen, press the Right button to go to the screen with the options for the slide show: Normal (Face Icon), Normal, Fade-In (Face Icon), Fade-In, and Multiple, as shown in FIGURE 6-33.

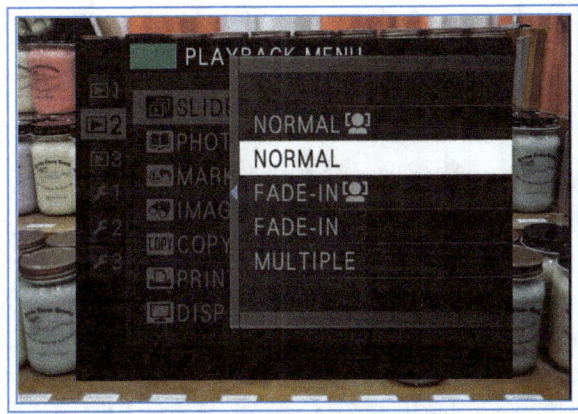

Figure 6-33. Slide Show Options Screen

If you choose Normal, the images and movies will display one after another with an interval of about three seconds in between. (Each movie, of course, will play fully before the next image or movie is shown.) If you choose Fade-In, the only difference will be that the images dissolve into one another. If you choose one of the menu items with the face icon added, the camera will zoom in on any faces it detects in the images (not the movies). If you choose Multiple, the camera will display several pictures on the screen at the same time, in different sizes. I find this display scheme to be distracting when I'm trying to view my images; I believe it could be useful if you want to have a background display running while people are paying attention to other things, at a conference or other event.

If you want to skip ahead or go back one image (or movie) during the show, press the Right or Left button. (This function is not available with the Multiple option.) To stop the slide show, press the OK button.

PHOTOBOOK ASSIST

This second option on the second screen of the Playback menu gives you a simple way to organize your JPEG images into PhotoBooks, the term Fujifilm uses for a collection or album of up to 300 photos that you select and save to the memory card with its own name. This can be a convenient option if you accumulate a lot of photos while on a trip and you want to display them on a TV set connected to the camera. You can group your images into different PhotoBooks by theme, by persons who are in them, by locations, or by any criteria you choose. Here is how to work with this feature.

First, select this option by highlighting it on the Playback menu, then press the Right button to move to the next screen, which has a list of books, all called New Book unless there already are some saved PhotoBooks. Navigate to a New Book line on the screen and press the Right button again to move to the next screen, where you can choose either Select From All or Select By Image Search, as shown in FIGURE 6-34.

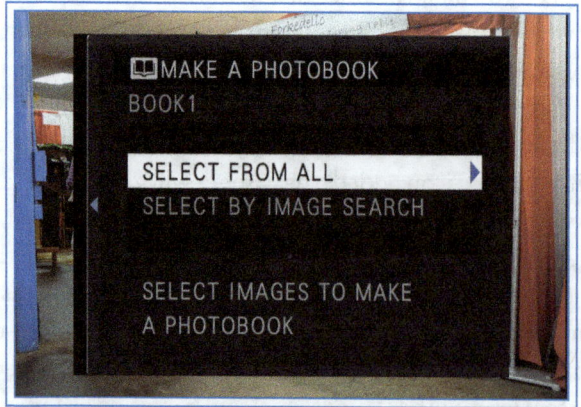

Figure 6-34. Image Selection Screen for PhotoBook Assist

If you choose Select By Image Search, you will move to a screen that lets you pre-screen your images through a search by date, face, Favorites, type of data, or upload mark. I will discuss those options later, in connection with Image Search, an option found further down on the Playback menu. For now, I will discuss the Select From All option.

Highlight Select From All, and the camera will take you to a screen displaying one of the images on the memory card, as shown in Figure 6-35, with a message prompting you to start selecting images for the PhotoBook.

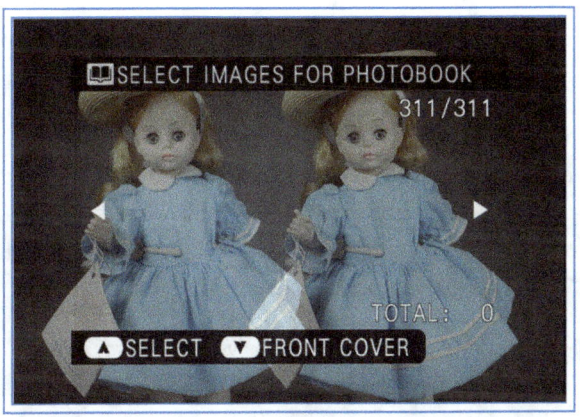

Figure 6-35. PhotoBook Assist - Selection Screen

At this point, you can scroll through your images and press the Up button to mark each image you want to include in the new book. An item that cannot be selected, such as a video, a Raw image, or a small-sized image, will have a message displayed saying it cannot be selected.

You can keep moving through all of the images in this way, pressing the Up button for each image to include. As you do this, a book icon will appear in the upper left corner of the screen, as shown in Figure 6-36.

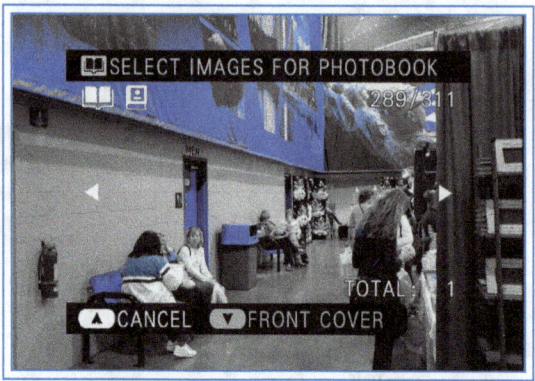

Figure 6-36. PhotoBook Assist - Selected Image with Book Icon

To remove an image from the selection, press the Up button again, and the book icon will disappear.

When the book is complete, the first image you selected will be the "cover" image, which appears along with the book's name on the PhotoBook Assist menu screen. If you want to use a different image for the cover image, press the Down button while that image is highlighted during the selection process.

When you have finished selecting your images, press the OK button. You will then see a screen with two choices: Select All and Complete PhotoBook, as shown in FIGURE 6-37.

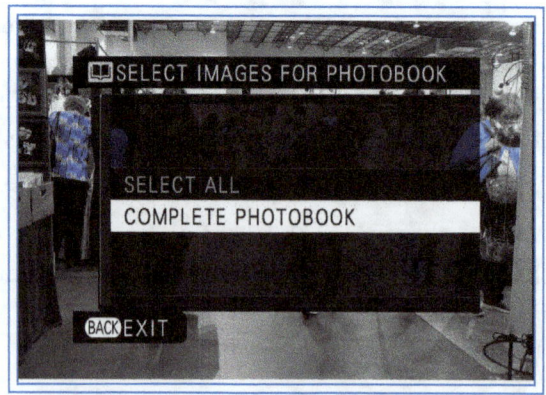

Figure 6-37. Screen to Complete PhotoBook

Highlight your choice and press OK to confirm. If you choose Complete PhotoBook, the camera will use the images you have marked and you will see a new entry in the list of PhotoBooks, such as BOOK1, BOOK2, etc. If you choose Select All, the camera will attempt to create a PhotoBook using all of the images on the memory card. It may not succeed, because a PhotoBook can hold only 300 images. Also, certain items, such as very small images, as well as movies and Raw images, cannot be included in PhotoBooks.

If, instead of Select From All, you choose Select By Image Search when creating the PhotoBook, you need to use the Image Search procedures, which are discussed below in connection with the Image Search menu item.

Once the PhotoBook is complete, you can view it at any time. Just go to the PhotoBook Assist menu item, press the Right button to go to the book selection screen, and select that book by name from the list that appears, as shown in FIGURE 6-38.

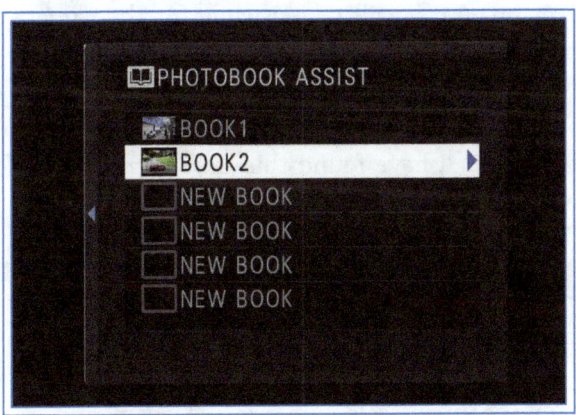

Figure 6-38. Screen to Select Completed PhotoBook

You can then use the Command Dial or the Left and Right buttons to scroll through the images, which are displayed with a nice-looking white border that simulates the page of a photo album, as shown in FIGURE 6-39. You cannot enlarge or delete images, or perform other operations on them, when viewing them in a PhotoBook.

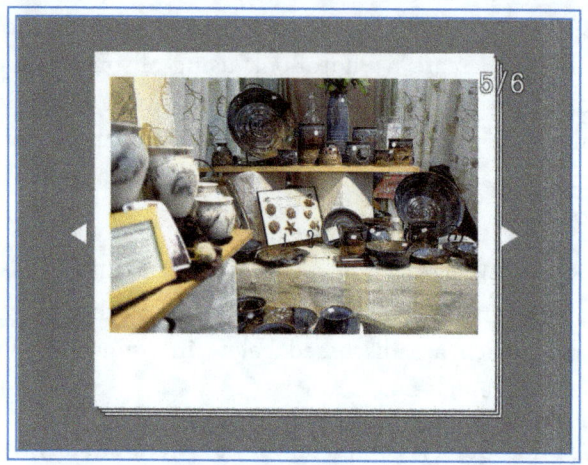

Figure 6-39. Page from Completed PhotoBook

A few other notes about PhotoBooks: If you have one or more PhotoBooks saved to your memory card that contain large numbers of images, it will take a while for the camera to enter playback mode after you press the Playback button; you will likely see a pattern of dots as the camera gathers the images into the PhotoBooks again. This performance might improve with a faster memory card, but I have found this slowdown to be a reason to avoid having large PhotoBooks.

If you want to change or delete a PhotoBook, here is the procedure. View the PhotoBook, display an image from it on the screen, and press the OK button. You will be given the choice to Edit or Erase the PhotoBook. If you choose Edit, you can go through the image-selection process again and change the images in the book. If you choose Erase, the camera will ask you to confirm, and then it will erase the entire book, renaming it as New Book, thereby freeing up a slot for you to add a book. You can have only six PhotoBooks on any one memory card.

MARK FOR UPLOAD TO

With this option, you can go through your images and videos and mark them for upload to YouTube, Facebook, or Fujifilm's own site, MyFinePix.com. The actual uploading of the files is done later using Fujifilm's MyFinePix Studio software for Windows. (Macintosh users are out of luck in this area.)

Once you select this menu option, a press of the Right button takes you to a screen with four choices, as shown in FIGURE 6-40: YouTube, Facebook, MyFinePix.com, and Reset All.

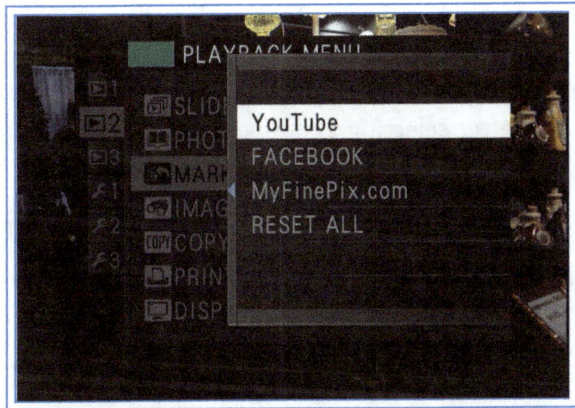

Figure 6-40. Mark for Upload Menu Option

If you choose Reset All, the camera will de-select all images from the three uploading queues. This process can take quite a while, even if you have not selected any images at all; to cancel, press the Display/Back button.

If you choose YouTube and press the OK button, the camera will display the first image or video; press the OK button to mark it for upload. The camera will then display the message, "Upload to YouTube OK?" as shown in FIGURE 6-41, and let you confirm with the OK button or cancel with the Back button. When you have finished selecting files to upload, press the Display/Back button to exit from the selection process.

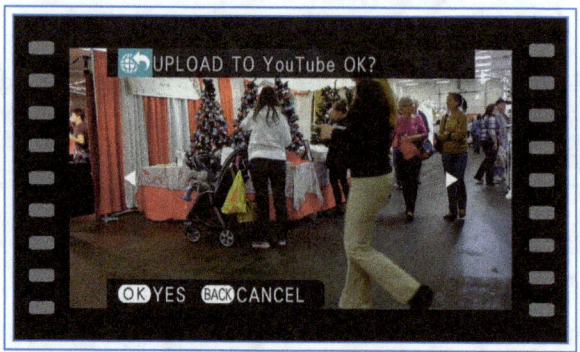

Figure 6-41. YouTube Upload Confirmation Screen

Note, though, that with YouTube, naturally enough, you can upload only movies, not still images. Somewhat oddly, Fujifilm has programmed the camera to let you scroll through all of your images, even after selecting YouTube for the upload destination; for every still image, you will see the message Cannot Execute, meaning that image cannot be marked for upload to YouTube. So, if you are marking movies for YouTube, you should first use the Image Search menu option, which lets you find all movies on the memory card using the By Type of Data search feature.

If you select Facebook for the destination, the process is the same as for YouTube, except that, this time, the Cannot Execute message appears for Raw files. That is, you can upload JPEG files and movies, but not Raw images. When you are done marking the files, exit the process with the Display/Back button.

If you select MyFinePix.com, you can select JPEG images, but not movies or Raw images.

Once you have the images marked for upload, you need to use the MyFinePix Studio software to accomplish the actual uploading. As noted above, that software is available for Windows-based computers only.

IMAGE SEARCH

The Image Search option lets you select a group of your images using one of several useful criteria: By Date, By Face, By Favorites, By Type of Data, or By Upload Mark. Highlight Image Search on the Playback menu, then press the Right button or the OK button to move to the next screen, shown in FIGURE 6-42.

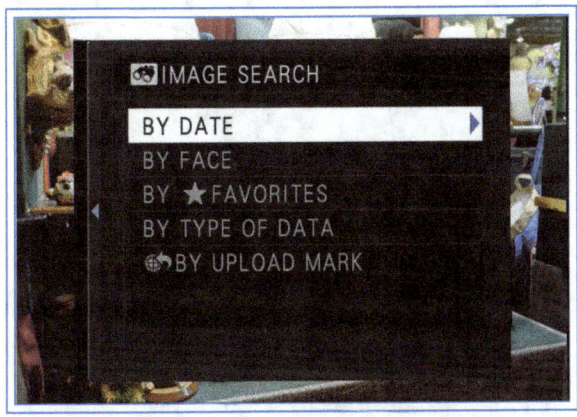

Figure 6-42. Image Search Options Screen

From that screen, highlight your choice of one of these criteria and press the Right or OK button again to move to the actual selection process. I will discuss below how to use each of the selection criteria. For all of these discussions, I am assuming that you have a reasonably large number of images on your memory card, with several for the criteria being discussed. For example, if you have images from only one date, some of the following discussion will not be applicable.

By Date

If you select By Date, press the Right button and move to the next screen, which will show a date at the left along with thumbnails on that side of the screen, and another series of thumbnails along the bottom of the display, as shown in FIGURE 6-43. A large image will appear in the middle of the screen. The thumbnails at the bottom represent the images taken on the date that is currently highlighted at the left. The large image corresponds to the thumbnail on the bottom of the screen that is currently highlighted with a frame.

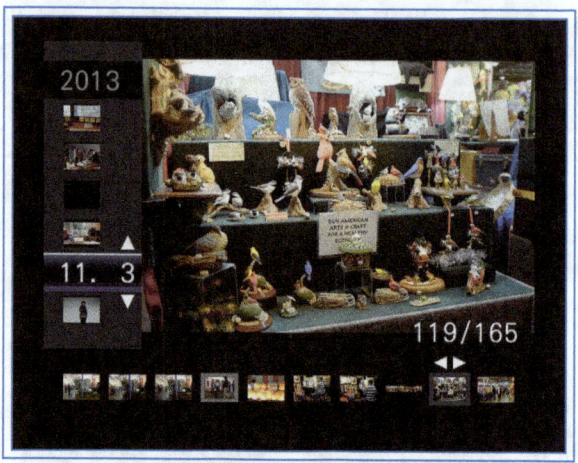

Figure 6-43. By Date Selection Screen

Use the Up and Down buttons to scroll through the various dates; the earliest date is at the top of the column on the left, and the latest is at the bottom. As you reach the last date, the selection will wrap around to the top, and vice-versa. For example, right now my earliest date is 10/30. As I scroll down I reach the latest date, which is 11/17. If I press the Down button one more time to scroll down, I scroll past 11/17, and 10/30 is displayed again. I can then press the Up button to move back to 11/17 if I want.

Once you have highlighted a date, turn the Command Dial or use the Left and Right buttons to scroll through the thumbnails at the bottom of the screen until you find the image you want from that date. Or, if you want to work with all images from that date, press the Menu/OK button to move to a screen that will display that date along with one image, as shown in FIGURE 6-44. Then press the Menu/OK button again, and the camera will display a screen with four options: Erase, Protect, Slide Show, and Exit Search. I discussed the Erase, Protect, and Slide Show options earlier in this chapter. If you select one of these options, the selected option will apply only to the images you have selected by date.

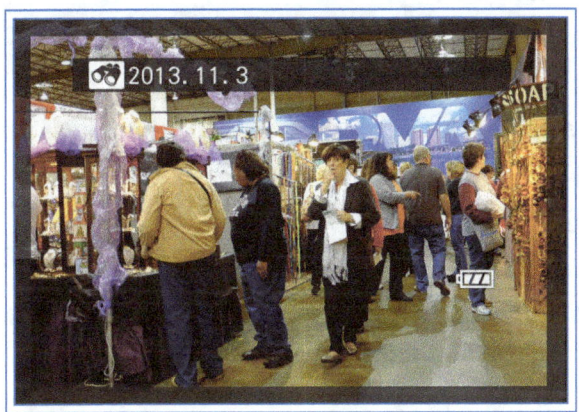

Figure 6-44. Screen to Select All from Date

By Face

With the next option, the camera will search for all photos that contain what seem to be people. Once you select this option, you will see that it is not limited to faces that fill the screen; there are several sub-categories, as shown in FIGURE 6-45: All Image, Closeup, Couple, and Group.

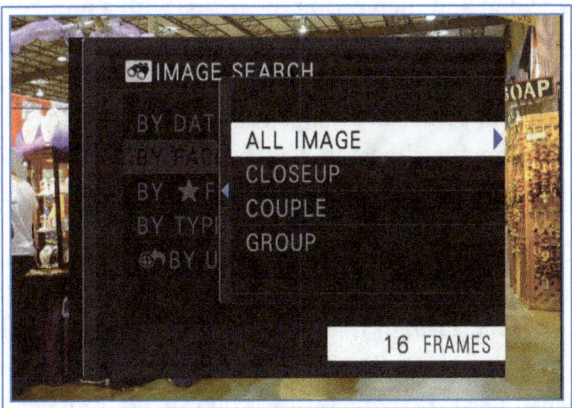

Figure 6-45. By Face Options Screen

You can choose All Image, which includes every shot that fits within any of these classifications, or you can pick any one of the individual categories.

This system, as you might expect, is not infallible, but the camera does a fairly good job of figuring out which of your images include people, either in closeup or otherwise. Depending on what sorts of images you have on your card, you may very well end up with some that have nothing that resembles a human or a face—to a human. There probably is some pattern that matches the camera's programming in an unexpected way. But using this option can be an excellent way to get a first rough cut at your collection for a new PhotoBook, or just for general viewing.

Once you have selected the category you want, press the OK button, and the camera will present you with the screen for choosing Erase, Protect, Slide Show, or Exit Search, so you can process the resulting group of images or cancel the operation.

By Favorites

This is one of the most straightforward options on the menu. As I discussed earlier, you can mark any image as a Favorite when it is displayed on the screen by using the Display button to select the Favorites screen and then rating the image with a number of stars, from one to five. Then, when you select By Favorites from the Image Search menu item, you will see a screen like that in FIGURE 6-46, which lets you select images according to their ratings. The selection screen for choosing a rating lets you know how many images there are on the memory card for each rating level.

One issue I find with this system is that you cannot select all images above a certain rating; you have to select just those with a specific, exact rating. That is, you cannot choose all images rated at two or more stars. The solution to this situation, in my experience at least, is make sure you rate your images in a way that makes sense for the selection process later on. For example, if you know you will later be choosing the images you want to put in a slide show, just make sure you rate them all with the same number of stars, so you can select them all at once.

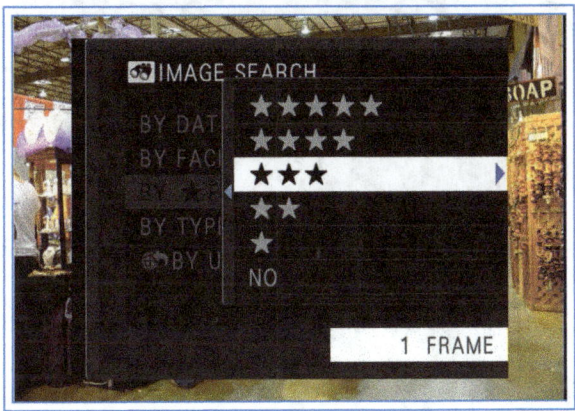

Figure 6-46. By Favorites Selection Screen

Finally, don't let the "Favorites" label limit your use of the ratings system. You can use this method to categorize images into any five classes. That is, if you are on a tour of a large city and you want to classify all your images of monuments in one class and those of museums in another, you could assign, say, three stars to monuments and four stars to museums so you can easily retrieve both categories later. Once you have made your selection of a number of stars, the camera will give you the standard options for processing the group of images.

By Type of Data

This is another straightforward way to categorize images, though this one is of a more technical nature. In this case, the four categories available for selection are Still, Movie, Continuous (unfortunately misspelled on the menu screen), and Raw, as shown in FIGURE 6-47. In this context, "still" means images that were taken in single-shot mode, not in continuous (burst) mode.

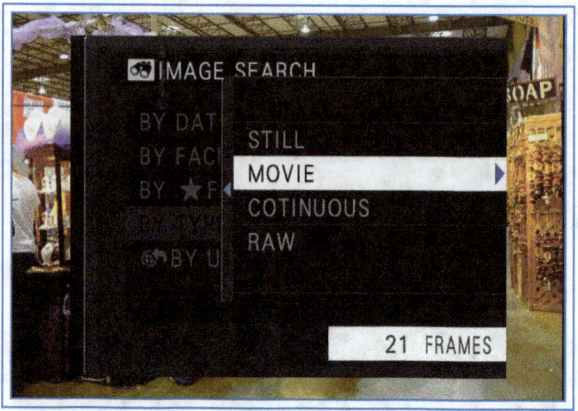

Figure 6-47. By Type of Data Options Screen

This feature actually can be quite useful. In particular, it can be useful for finding movies, which you might want to upload to YouTube or display on a television set rather than just on the camera's display. Using Image Search, you can quickly jump to all of the movies on your memory card and find those that you want to display in a slide show. Also, you may want to isolate all of your Raw images so you can use the Raw Conversion option on the Playback menu to make altered copies of them.

By Upload Mark

Finally, you can select images according to whether they have been marked for upload to YouTube (movies only), Facebook, or MyFinePix.com. This, again, is a straightforward option; you mark images or movies for upload to either of those internet services using the Mark for Upload To option on the Playback menu, discussed above.

COPY

The Copy option lets you copy your images from the camera's internal memory to the currently installed memory card, or from the memory card to the internal memory. When you choose this menu option, the camera first displays a screen with these two choices clearly labeled, as shown in FIGURE 6-48.

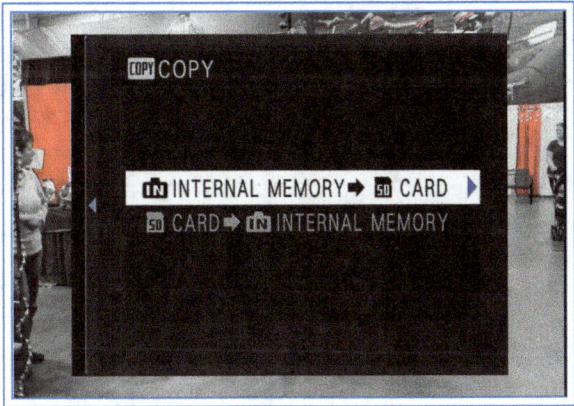

Figure 6-48. Copy Options Screen

Highlight one of those options and press the OK button or the Right button to move to the next screen. The camera will then give you the choice of copying all of your images ("All Frames") or just selected ones ("Frame"). If you choose the latter, the camera will display the first image and ask you to confirm the copy by pressing the OK button. Then press OK, and the camera will ask you once more to confirm the operation. The camera will then move on to other images with a similar procedure. If you choose to copy all images, the camera will ask you to confirm that operation as well.

If you regularly copy your images to a computer, you probably won't have much need for this option, but, like many of the options on the Playback menu, it can serve as a handy procedure when a computer is not available. Also, if you have taken a few images with the internal memory, it can be quite convenient to copy them to a memory card so you can save them, and then reformat the internal memory for future use.

Copying from an SD card to the internal memory is not likely to be a function you need often, but it could be useful if you're at an event with another photographer who got some great shots with another camera (even if it's not an X100S) that you need copies of. You could copy a few shots from his or her SD card to your internal memory (and from there to your SD card) to take home with you.

PRINT ORDER (DPOF)

If you want to select multiple images before sending them to the printer, use the DPOF (Digital Print Order Format) function, which is built into the camera. The DPOF system lets you mark various images on your memory card to be added to a print list, which can then be sent to your own printer. Or, you can take the memory card to a commercial printer to print out the selected images.

To add images to the DPOF print list, select the Print Order option from the Playback menu, then choose the With Date or Without Date option from the next screen, shown in FIGURE 6-49, to specify whether or not the pictures will be printed with the dates they were taken.

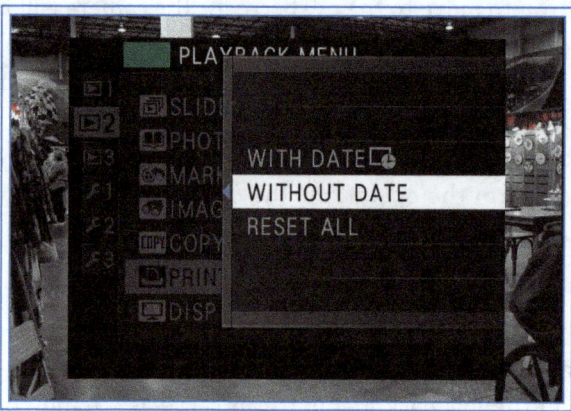

Figure 6-49. Print Order Options Screen

The camera will then display the first of your images, with a block showing 00 "sheets" specified, meaning no copies have been ordered yet. Turn the Command Dial or press the Left and Right buttons to move through the images. When one you want to have printed is displayed, press the Up button to mark it for printing; press the button repeatedly to increase the number of copies up to 99. Press the Down button to decrease the number of copies or to unmark the image by reducing the number of copies to zero. You can then keep browsing through your images and adding (or subtracting) them from the print list. As you add various numbers of copies for different images, a DPOF counter in the upper left corner of the display will give a cumulative total of the number of copies ordered for all images, as shown in FIGURE 6-50.

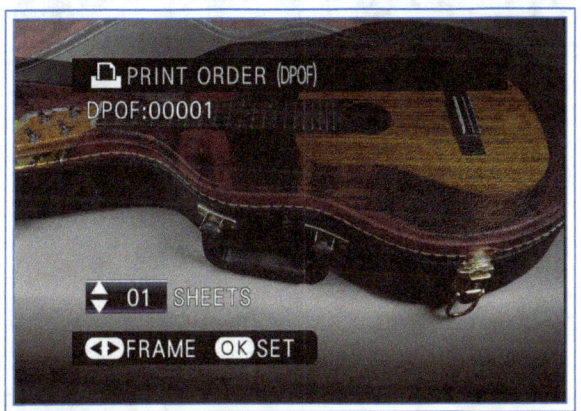

Figure 6-50. Print Order Selection Screen with Counter

When you have finished selecting images to be printed, press the OK button to confirm your choices and exit from the selection screen. Confirm the Completed message on the screen by pressing the OK button. You can then take the memory card to a service that prints photos using the DPOF system, or you can connect the camera to a PictBridge compatible printer to print the selected images. You can use the Reset All option on the first screen of this menu option if you want to unmark all images and remove them from the DPOF queue.

DISPLAY ASPECT

This final option on the second screen of the Playback menu, shown in FIGURE 6-51, is available for selection only when the camera is connected to an HDTV set with an HDMI cable.

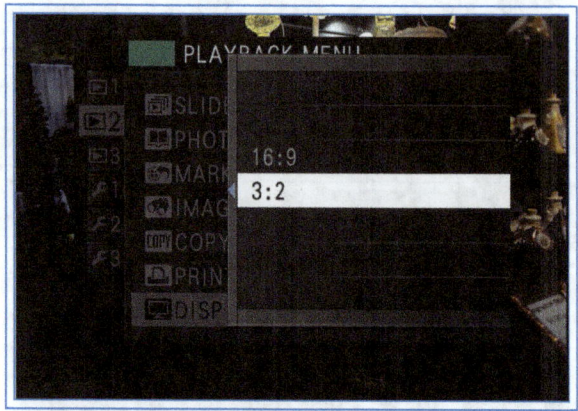

Figure 6-51. Display Aspect Options Screen

The purpose of this option is to specify how images that were taken in the 3:2 or 1:1 aspect ratio (non-widescreen) should be displayed on the HDTV. If you select 16:9, images in those two aspect ratios are cropped at the top and bottom to fit in the 16:9 format of the widescreen TV, filling the whole screen, as shown in FIGURE 6-52; if you choose 3:2, the images are shown uncropped, with black bands at the sides, as shown in FIGURE 6-53. Note that this option applies to images taken in the 1:1 aspect ratio as well as to those taken in the 3:2 aspect ratio, although the 1:1 aspect ratio is not mentioned on the menu screen or in the Fujifilm user's manual.

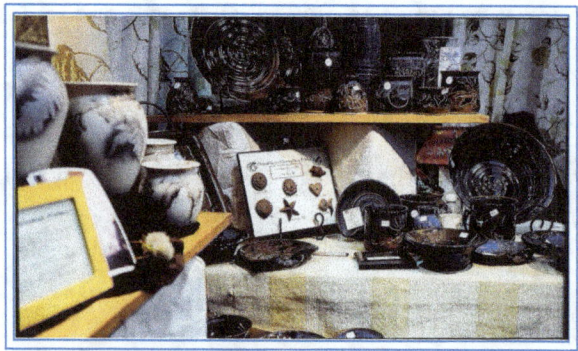

Figure 6-52. Image Displayed with 16:9 Setting

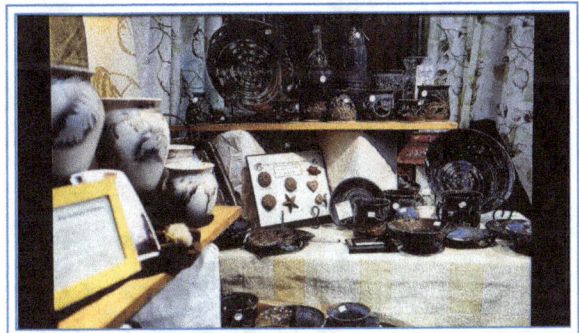

Figure 6-53. Image Displayed with 3:2 Setting

PLAYBACK VOLUME

This is the only item on the third and final screen of the Playback menu, as shown in FIGURE 6-54. When you select this item and press the Right or OK button, the camera will display the screen shown in FIGURE 6-55, which lets you control the initial volume of movies when you play them back in the camera. There are 11 values available, from zero to ten. The default value is seven.

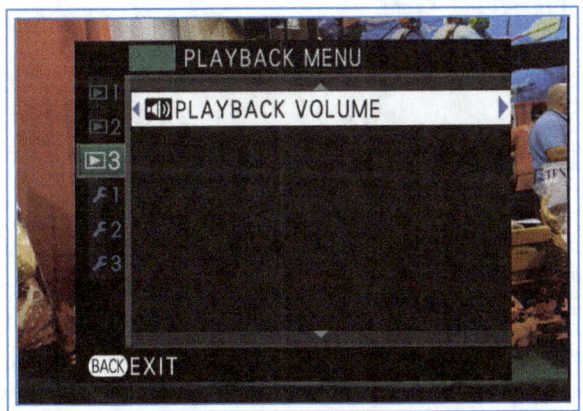

Figure 6-54. Third Screen of Playback Menu

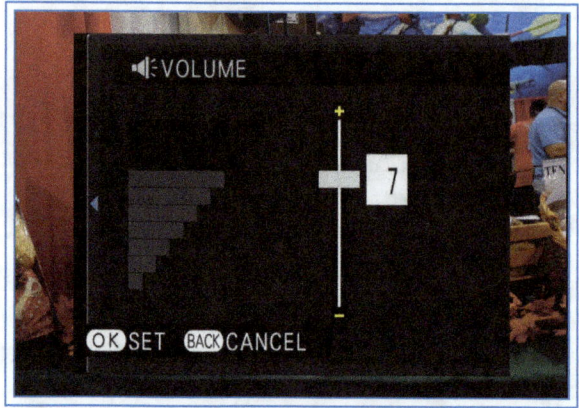

Figure 6-55. Playback Volume Setting Screen

You can also adjust the playback volume while a movie is playing. To do so, press the OK button to pause the movie, and then use the Up and Down buttons to adjust the volume along the vertical scale that appears along the left of the screen. Press the OK button again to resume playback with the new volume setting.

Printing Images

There is a great deal of variation among photographers with respect to how often they print their photographs on a printer. Some people are content to view their images on the camera's screen; many save them to a computer and share them on sites such as Flickr and Facebook; others send them to friends by e-mail.

If you want to produce copies of digital photographs on paper, there are various approaches to getting that done. You can import the photographs into a program such as Adobe Photoshop or Photoshop Elements, or use the software supplied by Fujifilm with the X100S, or any of many other programs that are available for photo editing. Once you have edited the images to your satisfaction, you can print the finished products from that software.

However, in some cases you may not be willing or able to spend the time to manipulate the pictures in software before printing them out. You may have access to a printer that will connect directly to the camera, and you may need or want to print out copies on photo paper without going through the time-consuming process of transferring the images to a computer first. Or, you may want to try a service that will take your memory card and produce high-quality prints directly from that card. The following discussion will cover the basic points of these procedures.

Printing Directly from the Camera

The X100S uses the PictBridge printing protocol, which lets the camera communicate directly with a wide variety of printers. The procedure is quite simple: Just plug the black USB cable that came with the camera into the micro-USB port inside the door on the right side of the camera. (This is the upper of the two ports in that location.) Then plug the other end of the cable into the USB port of a PictBridge-compatible printer. (This USB port is different from the one for the cable that connects the printer to a computer; this one is rectangular; the port for the cable to the computer has more of a square shape.) The printer does not have to be made by any particular company; I plugged the camera directly into my HP Photosmart C6180 printer, and the two devices communicated with no problems.

Once the connection is made and the printer is turned on, the camera should turn on automatically and display a special screen that appears only when it's connected to a PictBridge printer, as shown in Figure 6-56.

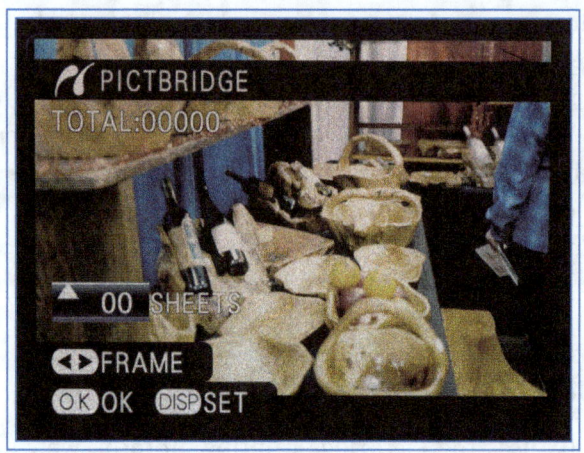

Figure 6-56. PictBridge Screen When Camera Connected to Printer

To print an individual image, navigate to the image you want to print and press the OK button; the camera will prompt you for the number of prints and the paper size. To print multiple images, when the print display screen initially displays, press the Menu button to bring up the Print menu, from which you can select images to print, print all images, or use the DPOF selection of images, as discussed earlier in this chapter. For further details about these procedures, see the Fujifilm X100S user guide at pages 99-103.

Once you have the settings as you want them, press the OK button on the camera to print out your photographs.

You cannot set Raw images to print using the DPOF process, only JPEG files.

Images Taken with Other Cameras

Finally, you should be aware that the X100S is set up to display a special symbol that indicates when an image on a memory card was taken with another camera. This symbol looks like a package wrapped up as a gift, as shown in FIGURE 6-57, which was taken with a Panasonic Lumix LX7 camera and then displayed on the X100S; Fujifilm labels such image as "gift" images.

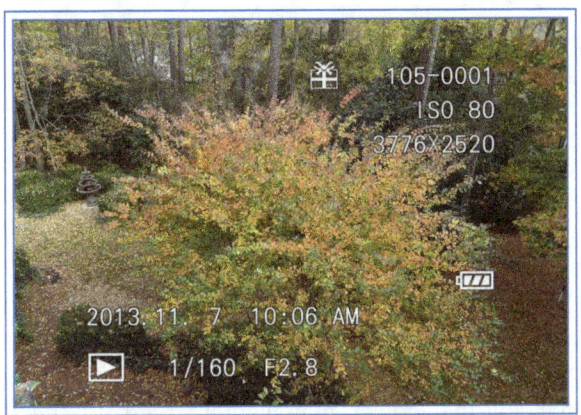

Figure 6-57. Gift Icon on Image from Another Camera

These images may or not display properly in the X100S. Even if they do display properly, some options will be unavailable for them, such as the Crop and Resize options on the Playback menu.

CHAPTER 7:
The Setup Menu

The last menu system to discuss is the Setup menu, which includes a variety of options for matters other than the appearance of your images, such as screen brightness, operational sounds, power management, setting the date and time, and the crucial operation of formatting a memory card.

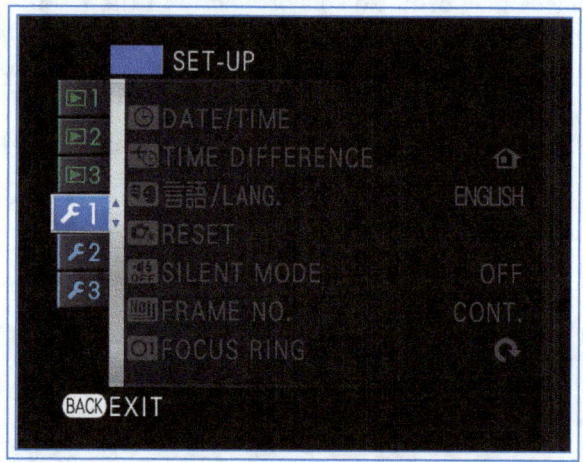

Figure 7-1. Wrench Icon Highlighted in Left Menu Column

As a reminder, you enter the menu system by pressing the Menu button. The available menus change depending on whether the camera is set to shooting mode or playback mode. However, in either case, you can enter into the Setup menu. After you first press the Menu button, use the Left button to highlight the top icon at the far left of the menu screen, which will be a camera icon if the camera is in shooting mode or a triangle if the camera is in playback mode. Once that icon is highlighted, use the Down button or the Command Dial to move the highlight to the top of the group of wrench icons further down in the left column, as shown in FIGURE 7-1; those icons, accompanied by numbers from 1 to 3, represent the three screens of the Setup menu. If you prefer, when the top camera or triangle icon is highlighted, you can press the Up button to wrap the highlight around so it highlights the bottom wrench icon in the left column; you can then navigate back up to the other two Setup menu screens.

Once one of the wrench icons is highlighted, use the Right button to move the selection block back into the list of menu items, and use the Command Dial or the Up and Down buttons to navigate through the various options on the Setup menu's screens.

If you need to get access to the Setup menu often, here is a tip that can speed things up. If you put the camera into playback mode, then the menu will have only three Playback menu screens that you need to navigate through to get to the Setup menu, as shown in FIGURE 7-1. You may find it quicker to reach Setup menu items if you don't have to plow down through the five screens of the Shooting menu to reach the wrench icons for the Setup menu. Also, you can hold down the Playback button while turning the camera on, to make the camera start up in Playback mode, making it easier to get to the Setup menu.

I will discuss all of the Setup menu choices in turn, starting with the first screen of the menu, shown in FIGURE 7-2.

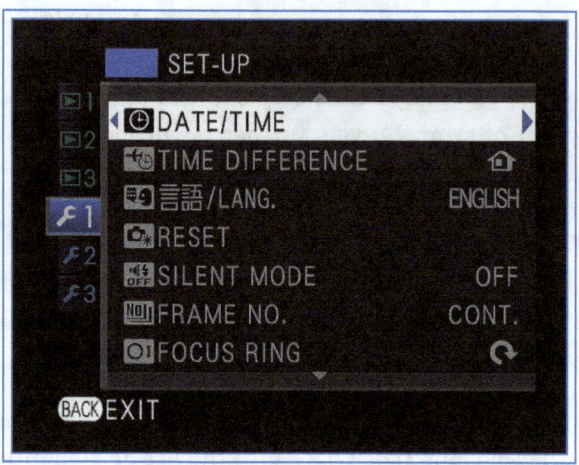

Figure 7-2. First Screen of Setup Menu

Date and Time

Chances are you set the date, time, and time zone when you first set up the camera. If you haven't done so or need to change the settings, use this menu option to set the date and time. Once the Date/Time menu option is highlighted, press the Right or OK button to move to the settings screen, shown in FIGURE 7-3.

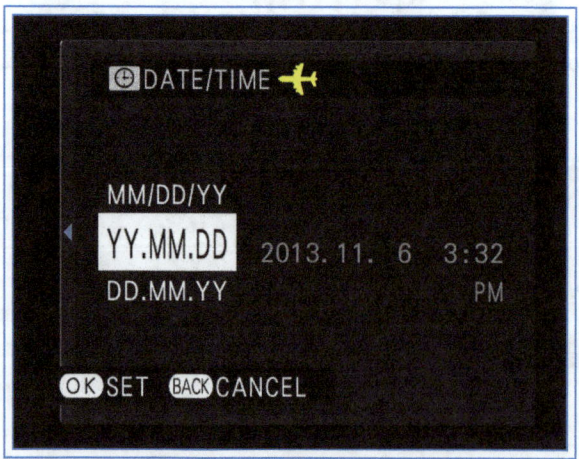

Figure 7-3. Date/Time Settings Screen

Then navigate through the various selections using the Left and Right buttons; change the values by turning the Command Dial or by pressing the Up and Down buttons.

It's important to have these settings correct, because the date and time information is recorded invisibly with every picture or video you capture with the camera. That information can be printed out or retrieved through your software, and you can search for your images by date, so you need to be sure these values are set properly from the outset. If you live in an area where the time changes in certain seasons (for example, Daylight Saving Time causes time changes in most parts of the United States), you will have to remember to reset the time yourself when the time changes; the camera does not have an option for doing that automatically. (If you don't ever travel, you can use the Time Difference option, discussed below, to set a separate "time zone" for Daylight Saving Time.)

Time Difference

The Time Difference option lets you set up one other time zone, called "Local," with a different time than the one you initially set in the camera, which is called your "Home" time. In this way, when you are travelling in a different time zone, you can set the camera quickly to the "Local" setting so that images recorded during the trip will reflect the correct time and date when they are taken.

To use this option, select it and choose Local on the second screen, shown in FIGURE 7-4. Using the direction buttons, highlight the large plus sign or minus sign, depending on whether the Local time is later (plus) or earlier (minus) than your Home time. Then go to the next two blocks and use the Command Dial or the Up and Down buttons to enter the hours and minutes of the time difference, as shown in FIGURE 7-5; press the OK button to confirm.

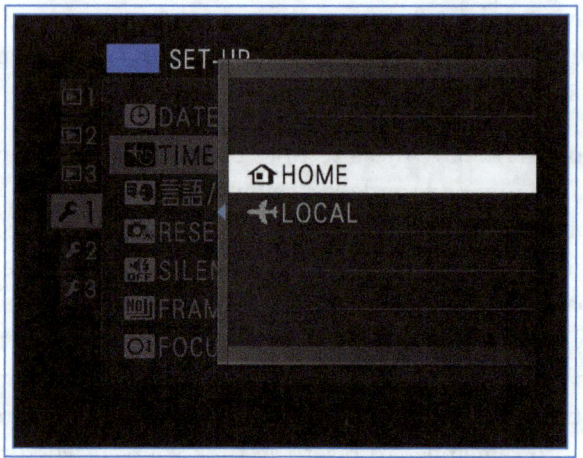

Figure 7-4. Time Difference Options Screen

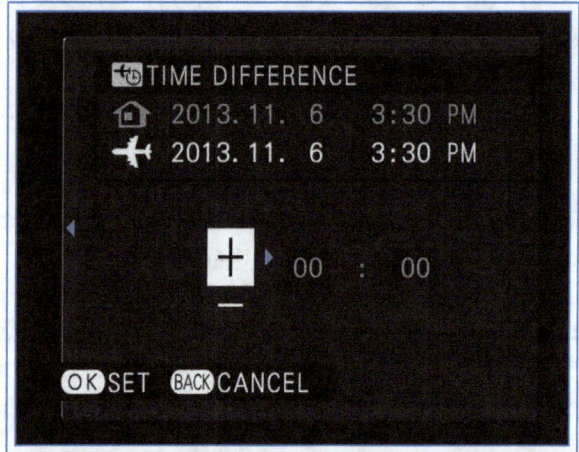

Figure 7-5. Time Difference Settings Screen

When you arrive at your destination, go back to this menu item and make sure that Local is highlighted. When you return home, use the menu option once more to select the Home option, so that your normal time zone will be in effect. (You don't actually ever select your normal time zone; when you set the date and time, those settings determine what time zone you are in for purposes of the Local setting.)

Language

This option gives you your choice of 35 languages for the display of commands and information on the camera's display.

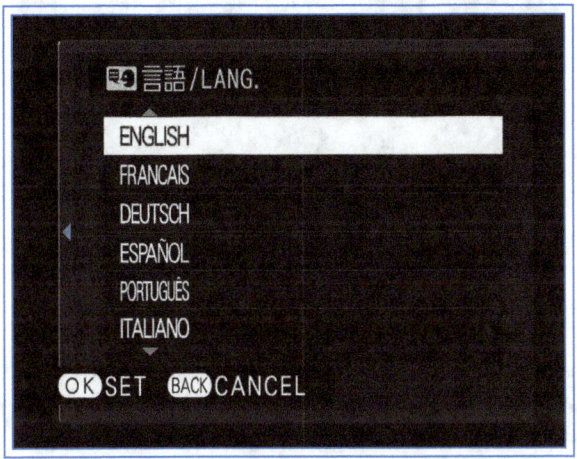

Figure 7-6. Language Menu Option

Once you have selected this menu item, navigate to the selection screen, shown in FIGURE 7-6, and scroll through the language choices using the Command Dial or the Up and Down buttons; press the OK button when your chosen language is highlighted.

Reset

Choose this menu option when you want to reset all of the camera's settings back to their original (default) values. This action can be useful if you have been experimenting with various settings and you find that something is not working as expected. It will give you a fresh start with known values for all of the major settings on the Shooting menu and the Setup menu. When you select this menu item and move to the next screen, you will see the two options shown in FIGURE 7-7, which give you a choice between resetting items on the Shooting menu and resetting items on the Setup menu.

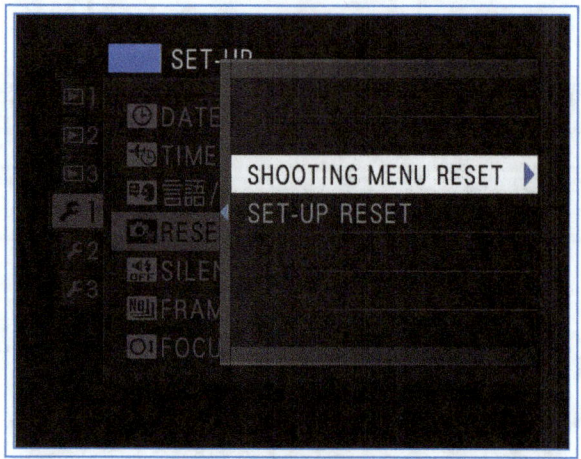

Figure 7-7. Reset Options Screen

If you select one of these choices and move to the next screen, the camera will display a confirmation screen like that shown in FIGURE 7-8, giving you one more chance to change your mind.

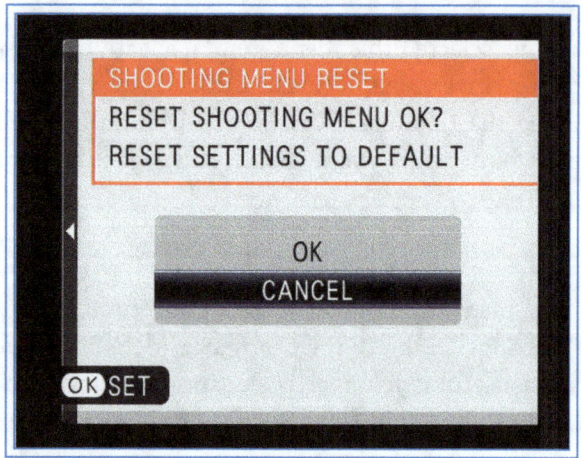

Figure 7-8. Reset Confirmation Screen

There are a few settings that will not be reset, including date and time, time difference, and background color.

Silent Mode

This next option is one of the more important settings on the Setup menu, at least for some photographers. One of the great attributes of the X100S is its ability to operate silently and unobtrusively. With its classic slim shape, mostly black color, and lack of a protruding lens or large grip, the camera can easily disappear into a photographer's hands. For street photography and other forms of candid photography, it is extremely helpful to supplement this cloak of invisibility with a cone of silence.

When you invoke Silent Mode from the Setup menu, the camera suppresses the operational sound made by the shutter as well as any beeps made to confirm focus or to announce errors. In addition, the camera goes beyond the "silent" label by turning off the AF Illuminator/Self-timer lamp and disabling the flash.

In this mode, the camera can be fairly hard to detect. However, one item that is left to alert a passerby is the indicator lamp on the back of the camera, just below the exposure compensation dial. This lamp emits a rather bright glow when the camera is recording images to the memory card or internal memory. Silent Mode does not dim this lamp, but you can, with a small piece of black tape. That step is recommended for the photographer who seeks near-perfect invisibility on the streets.

In addition, you may want to avoid having the live view and newly recorded images appear on the LCD to call attention to the camera. To do so, you can use the View Mode button to switch to use of the viewfinder. If you just want to dim the LCD display, you can use the EVF/LCD Brightness feature of the Screen Set-up menu option, discussed below, to reduce the screen's brightness. As an alternative approach, you can use the Display button to switch to use of the Detailed display in shooting mode, which uses a mostly black screen that does not include the live view. Along with that step, you probably would want to use the Image Display option of the Screen Set-up menu item to turn off the display of images immediately after they are captured.

One of the best things about Silent Mode is that you do not have to dig into the menu system to activate or deactivate it. Fujifilm has helpfully programmed the X100S so that you can press and hold the Display/Back button to toggle Silent Mode on and off. A press for about two seconds is all it takes. The camera displays a sound icon on the screen to confirm the change.

Frame Number

This next menu option, shown in FIGURE 7-9, gives you control over the way in which the camera assigns numbers to your images and videos.

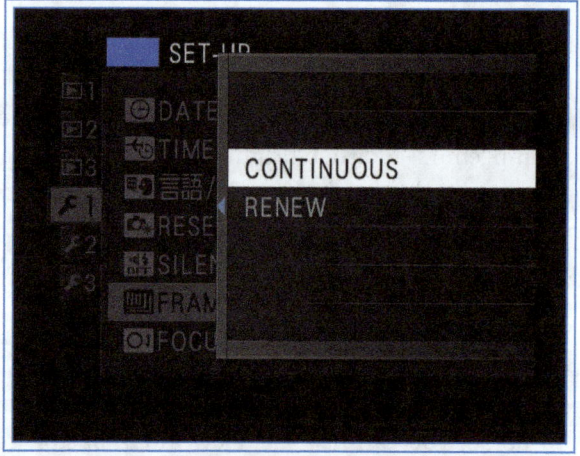

Figure 7-9. Frame Number Options Screen

There are two choices: Continuous and Renew. If you choose Continuous, then the camera continues numbering where it left off, even if you put a new memory card in the camera. For example, if you have shot 112 images on your first memory card, the last image likely will be numbered 100-0112, for the folder number (100, the first folder number available), and the image number (112). If you then switch to a brand new memory card with no images on it, the first image on that card will be numbered 100-0113, because the numbering scheme continues in the same sequence. If you choose Renew instead, the first image on the new card will be numbered 100-0001, because the camera resets the numbering back to the first number.

My own preference is to use the default option, Continuous. I like to keep a general idea of how many images I have taken, and this option gives me an idea of the cumulative number. Also, with this option I am less likely to have duplicate image numbers when I copy them to my computer from the memory card.

Focus Ring

With this final item on the first screen of the Setup menu, whose selection screen is shown in FIGURE 7-10, you can change the direction in which the focus ring is turned to increase the focal distance in manual focus mode.

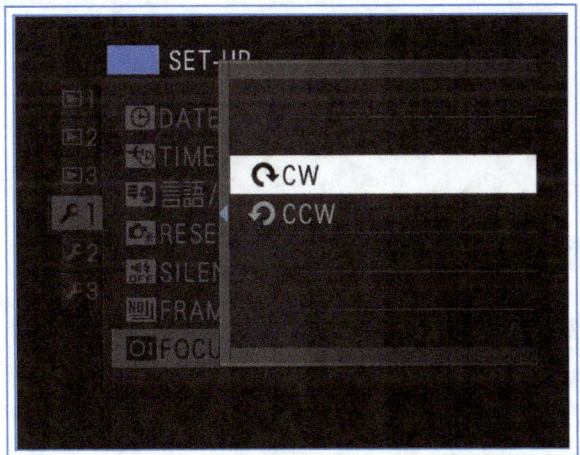

Figure 7-10. Focus Ring Options Screen

By default, you turn the ring clockwise (as you stand behind the camera) to increase the distance and counter-clockwise to decrease it. This menu option lets you reverse that situation. I don't know why you would want to do that, but if you are more comfortable turning the ring in the other direction, this is the perfect solution.

Next, I will discuss the items on the second screen of the Setup menu, shown in FIGURE 7-11.

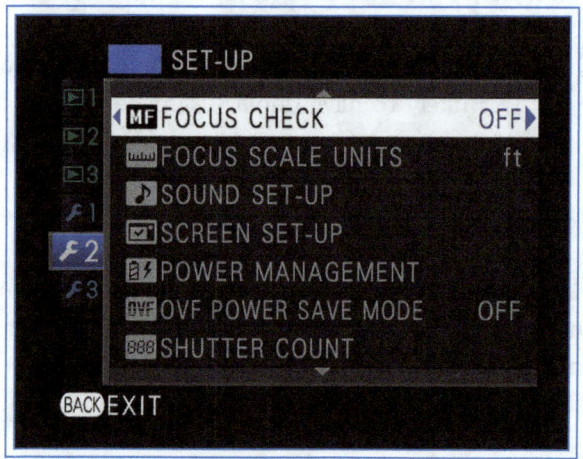

Figure 7-11. Second Screen of Setup Menu

Focus Check

This first option on the second Setup menu screen controls whether the image on the camera's display is automatically enlarged when you turn the focus ring to focus the image in manual focus mode. When this option is turned on and the camera is in manual focus mode, as soon as you start to turn the focus ring the center of the image enlarges to fill the display, making it easier to judge whether the scene is in focus. If you want to enlarge a part of the image other than the center, press the AF button (Up button), and the camera will display a screen for moving the enlargement area, as shown in FIGURE 7-12.

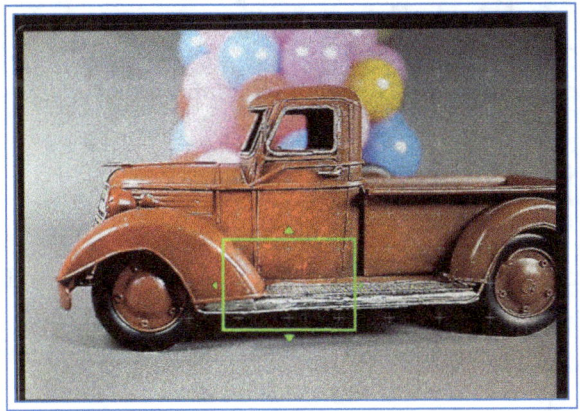

Figure 7-12. Screen for Moving Area for Focus Check

This screen is similar to the screen for moving the autofocus area when you are using the Area option for AF Mode, but the frame for the manual focus enlargement area is larger than the Area AF frame. Turn the Command Dial or use the four direction buttons to move the enlargement-area frame where you want it, and press the OK button to lock it in place. Then you can turn the focus ring again, and the camera will display an enlarged view of the area inside the frame at its new location.

Note that Focus Check is not the only option available for assisting with manual focus. As discussed in Chapter 4, you also can use the features provided by the MF Assist option on the third screen of the Shooting menu. One of those options, the Standard setting for MF Assist, is always available; with that option, you can press in on the Command Control in manual focus mode to enlarge the display. That feature is identical in operation to the Focus Check option, except that, with Focus Check, you do not have to press in on the Command Control; you just start turning the focus ring to achieve the enlargement. So, the only reason to use the Focus Check option is if you want to have the enlarging feature available immediately upon turning the focus ring, rather than having to press in on the Command Control to cause the display to be enlarged. I find the Standard setting for MF Assist to be sufficient, but you might prefer the instant action of the Focus Check option. My preference is to leave Focus Check turned off, so the enlargement doesn't occur when I don't want it.

Focus Scale Units

You can use this menu item to choose whether to use meters or feet as the unit of measurement on the focus scale. The blue focus scale, as shown in FIGURE 7-13, appears at the bottom of various display screens for manual focus and autofocus, depending on the options you select with the Display Custom Setting item on the Shooting menu.

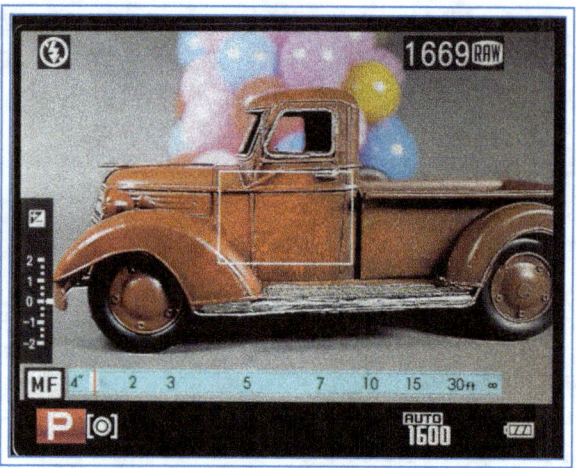

Figure 7-13. Manual Focus Scale on Screen

A red line appears on the scale to show the approximate point of focus, whether from your manual focusing with the focus ring or from the camera's autofocus system. In addition, a white area, which is somewhat hard to see, extends out from the red line in both directions to indicate the approximate depth of field of your shot with the current settings. When you select meters or feet with this option, that choice applies for both the autofocus and manual focus versions of the scale.

Sound Set-up

This next option on the Setup menu provides three sub-options for controlling the sounds made by your camera, apart from playback volume for movies. The three options, shown in FIGURE 7-14, concern volume for general camera operations, as well as shutter volume and sounds.

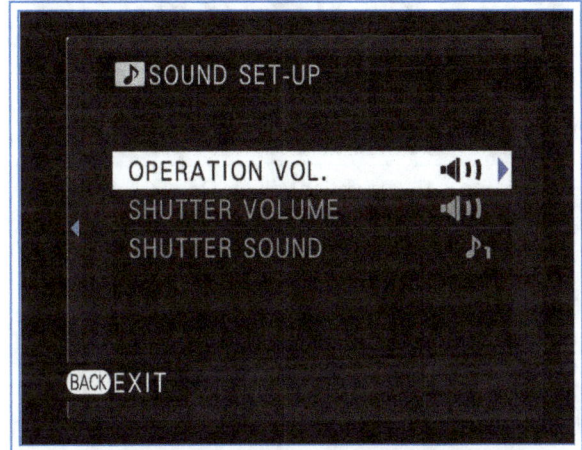

Figure 7-14. Sound Set-up Options Screen

The details for these options are discussed below.

OPERATION VOLUME

This first sub-option lets you control the volume and nature of the electronic sounds the camera makes. You can use this setting to control the loudness of the artificial clicks that the camera makes as you press the control buttons. You can silence them altogether, or select volume level 1, 2, or 3, as shown on the selection screen in FIGURE 7-15. You might want to silence these sounds with this menu option but still maintain a quiet shutter sound using the next sub-option, so you'll get some audible feedback to let you know when a picture has been taken.

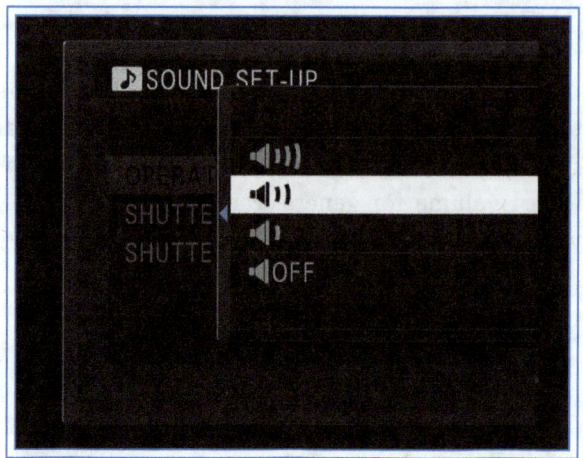

Figure 7-15. Operation Volume Options Screen

SHUTTER VOLUME

This second sub-option lets you control the volume of the electronic sound that is programmed for the X100S's shutter. Although some photographers like to silence the camera as much as possible, as noted above, some also like to be able to hear when the shutter is actually released so they will know they have recorded the image. So, in some cases, photographers may want to leave the shutter sound turned on, but at the lowest possible volume. If you want to maintain that minimal level of shutter noise, this feature serves the purpose; you can choose from three levels of sound, or silence. The selection screen is identical to that shown for Operation Volume, above.

SHUTTER SOUND

Finally, if you like to customize your camera's operational sounds, you can choose from three different types of shutter sound, as shown on the selection screen in FIGURE 7-16.

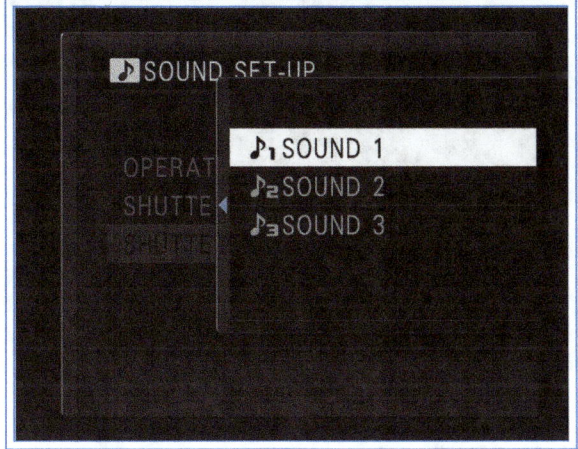

Figure 7-16. Shutter Sound Options Screen

Choice number 1 is the sound of a leaf shutter, which has the advantage of reflecting this camera's actual construction; number 2 is the sound of a focal-plane shutter; and number 3 is the sound of a reflex camera with an internal mirror that slaps as the image is taken. I don't see a great deal of reason for selecting any sound other than number 1, but this is a matter of taste, and some photographers might prefer one of the other, heavier sounds.

Screen Set-up

This menu option, like the previous one, includes several sub-options. In this case, all of the items are intended to let you control the appearance of the LCD display screen and electronic viewfinder and the way in which images are displayed on them. Details for the five sub-options are as follows.

IMAGE DISPLAY

With this first sub-item for the Screen Set-up option, you can control whether and for how long an image appears on the display after you take it. By default, this setting causes your new images to appear for 1.5 seconds. If you like, you can set it to 0.5 second, Off, or Continuous, as shown in FIGURE 7-17.

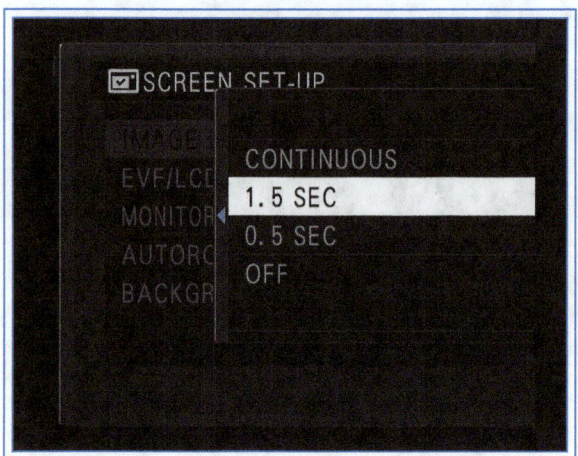

Figure 7-17. Image Display Options Screen

If you choose Off, new images will never appear on the display; the camera will return you to the shooting screen as soon as possible after the image is captured.

If you choose Continuous, the new image will display on the screen indefinitely until you press the OK button or press the shutter button halfway to dismiss the display. While the image is displayed, you can enlarge it using the AE/Zoom-in button, and you can also zoom in on the focus point by pressing in on the center of the Command Control. However, you cannot delete the image or call up an index screen while it is displayed. You also cannot alter the information displayed on it using the Display button; only the image itself is displayed.

EVF/LCD BRIGHTNESS

This next sub-option gives you the ability to control the brightness of the LCD display, and also lets you adjust the brightness of the electronic viewfinder (EVF) display. This option has no automatic dimming or other fancy features; it just presents you with a scale, as shown in FIGURE 7-18, that defaults to the standard brightness of zero and lets you adjust the active display to be brighter or dimmer by setting the level to a positive or negative number from one to five.

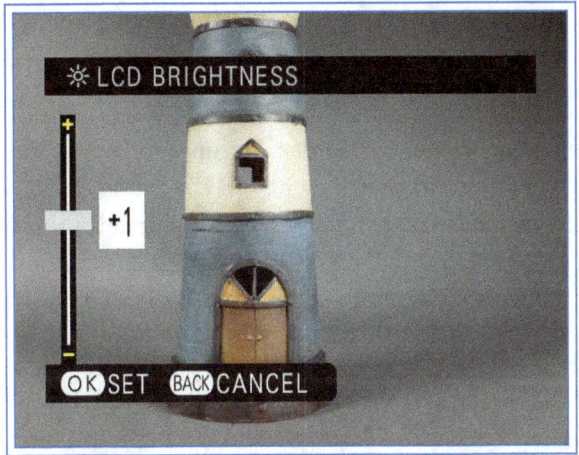

Figure 7-18. LCD Brightness Setting Screen

Note that the menu option affects only whichever display is active; therefore, you can set the two displays (LCD and EVF) to different brightness settings. This makes sense, because you are more likely to need additional brightness for the LCD screen when viewing it in bright sunlight; the viewfinder display is likely to be quite visible even when it is dimly lit, because it is naturally shaded from the sun by your head.

MONITOR SUNLIGHT MODE

This option lets you boost the brightness of the LCD display and the EVF even beyond the brightest setting available with the EVF/ LCD Brightness option. If you select this option and turn it on, the extra brightness may help you make out the details on the screen even in fairly bright sunlight. You also can trigger this setting, which Fujifilm also sometimes calls "Outdoor Mode," by pressing and holding the Q button for a couple of seconds when either the shooting screen or the playback screen is displayed. You can turn the option off by holding the button down again, or by using this menu option. Of course, using this level of brightness depletes the camera's battery quite quickly, so you should use it only when necessary. In most cases, you are likely to be able to use the EVF at its standard brightness level when conditions are too bright for using the LCD at that level.

AUTOROTATE PLAYBACK

This fourth sub-option for Screen Set-up affects how the camera deals with images that were taken with the camera held vertically, so that the image is taller than it is wide. By default, this feature is turned on, which means that the camera will automatically rotate any such image so that it appears properly oriented on the display, as shown in FIGURE 7-19.

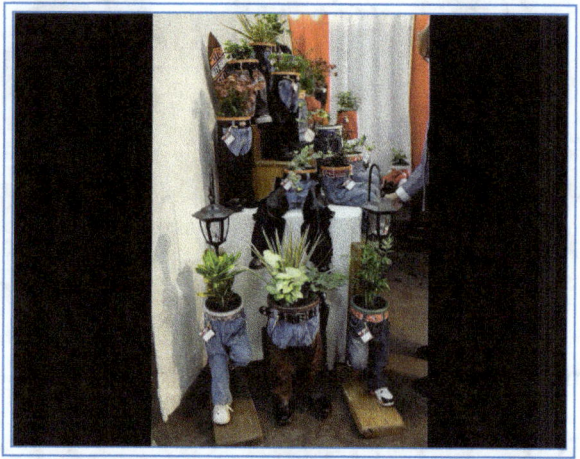

Figure 7-19. Autorotated Image

Of course, this means that the image will be displayed in a somewhat smaller size than normal, because the tall side must fit within the limits of the horizontal display. If you would prefer to have such images display without rotation so that the image, in effect, lies down on its side, as shown in FIGURE 7-20, just leave this option turned off.

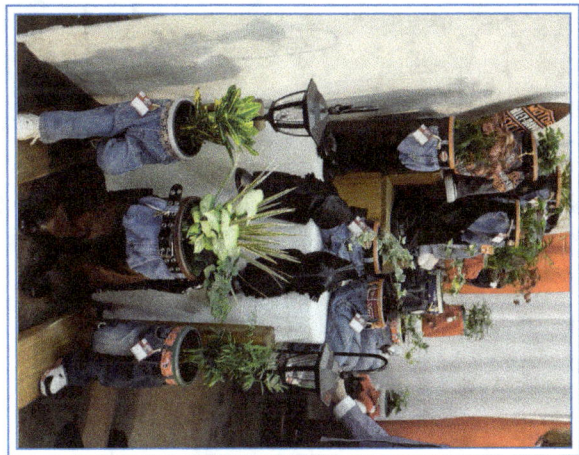

Figure 7-20. Image Not Autorotated

You can always rotate such an image (or any image, except those protected with the Protect feature) manually, using the Image Rotate feature on the Playback menu.

BACKGROUND COLOR

This final sub-option for Screen Set-up lets you select the color that appears on the edges of the menu screens and in the selection blocks that highlight the menu options you select. It might be more accurate to call it the "trim color" or "accent color"; the background color is uniformly gray. In any event, the choices here, as shown in FIGURE 7-21, are silver, gold, blue, yellow, green, and white. To the extent that you want your X100S to be a "stealth" machine that you can wield without attracting too much attention, I recommend sticking with the default selection, white, but you can make a fashion statement if you want to.

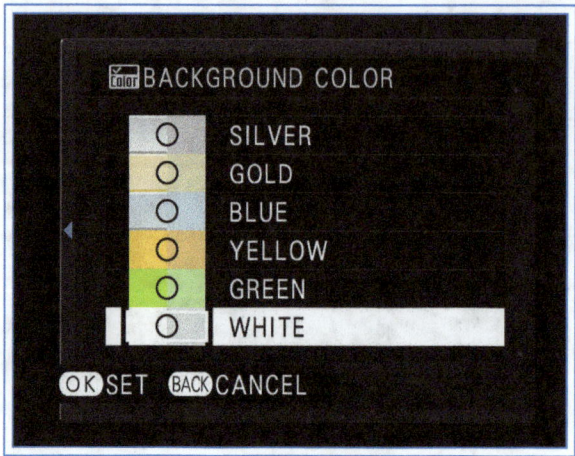

Figure 7-21. Background Color Menu Option

Or, if you find it useful to pick a color that makes menu selections really stand out, you can pick a color such as green, which is almost phosphorescent and really makes the selections pop out at you, as shown in FIGURE 7-22.

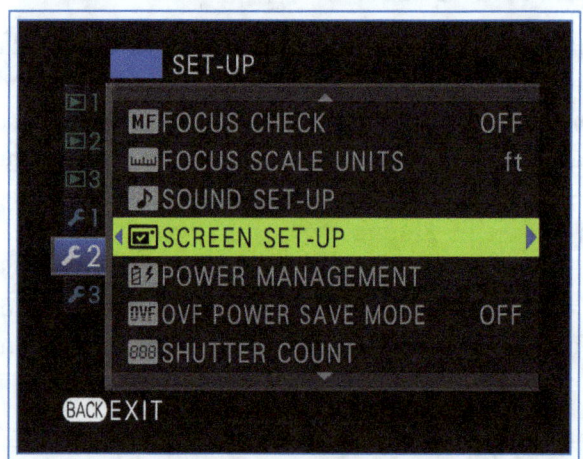

Figure 7-22. Bright Green Background Color in Use

Power Management

This menu option presents you with two sub-options for controlling how the camera uses its battery power, as shown in Figure 7-23.

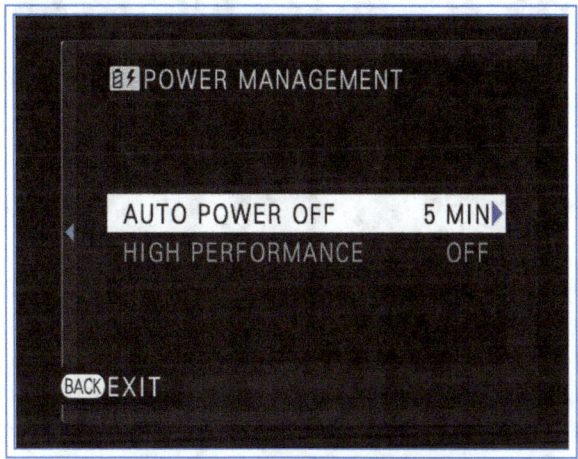

Figure 7-23. Power Management Options Screen

AUTO POWER OFF

This first sub-option gives you a way to conserve power. By default, the camera powers down to save its battery after two minutes when no controls are pressed. Using this menu option, as shown in Figure 7-24, you can change that interval to five minutes or you can turn the feature off so the camera stays powered up as long as the battery lasts. When the camera powers down in this way, you can wake it up by pressing the shutter button halfway. To wake the camera up, you have to give the button a good, solid half-press for about a second; if you just tap it, the camera won't respond.

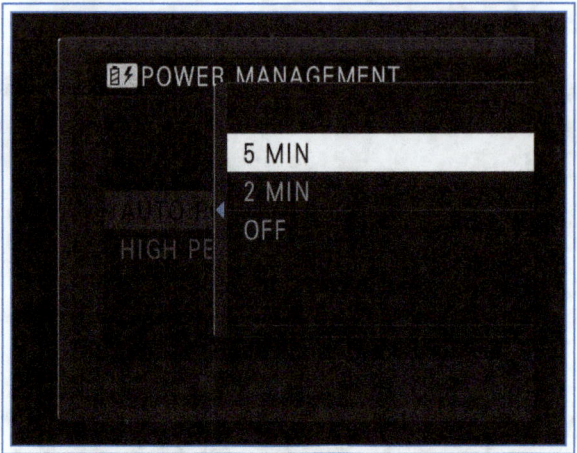

Figure 7-24. Auto Power Off Options Screen

HIGH PERFORMANCE

This other sub-option can be turned either on or off. If it is on, the camera will start up and focus more quickly than usual, at the expense of a faster drain of the battery charge. If you have one or more spare batteries and don't mind running through them a bit more quickly, you might try this option to see if the performance enhancement is worth the extra drain on the camera's charge.

Optical Viewfinder Power Save Mode

This option, as its name indicates, is provided strictly to help conserve the camera's battery power. This feature has any effect only when the optical viewfinder (OVF) is being used. One effect it has is to reduce the automation used by the camera in evaluating exposure. For example, in Program mode, if ISO and Dynamic Range are set to specific values, the camera normally will evaluate exposure and display its selected shutter speed and aperture values constantly, even in the OVF. However, if you turn on the OVF Power Save Mode setting, then the camera will not display those values until you press the shutter button halfway. Also, when this setting is turned on, the Histogram will not appear in the viewfinder, even if you have it turned on through the Display Custom Setting item on the Shooting menu. The camera also is somewhat slower to complete its autofocus process with this setting turned on. Through these savings of battery power, the camera is able to take more shots with a single battery than it could otherwise do when the OVF is in use, according to Fujifilm.

There is one quirk about this feature that you should be aware of. When you turn this feature on, the camera is limited in the settings it can use for shutter speed in Aperture Priority mode. Specifically, if the OVF Power Save option is turned on, the slowest shutter speed available in Aperture Priority mode is ¼ second. So, if you are using Aperture Priority mode in dim lighting and wonder why the camera will not select a shutter speed slow enough to expose the image properly, check to make sure this option is turned off. I routinely leave it turned off, because I always have a spare battery with me, and I don't use the OVF so heavily that this option would make a big difference for my use of the camera.

Shutter Count

This last option on the second screen of the Setup menu has a simple function.

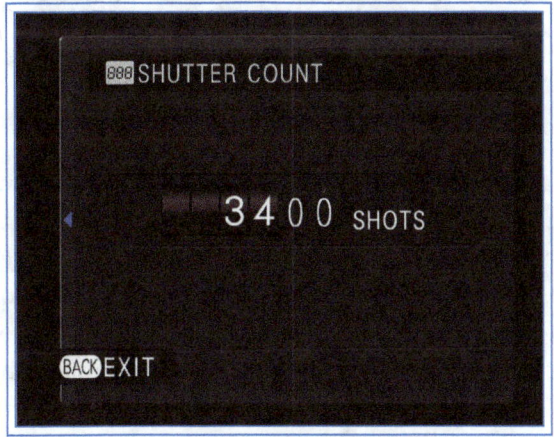

Figure 7-25. Shutter Count Screen

Highlight the item, press the Right or OK button, and the camera will produce a display like that shown in FIGURE 7-25, reporting the number of shutter actuations that the camera has had to date. This count is "approximate," according to Fujifilm, in part because the number is increased for events other than shutter presses, such as switching to the OVF. Also, this option counts shutter presses and other events only to the nearest 100, but it does give you a general idea of how much the camera has been used.

Finally, I will discuss the items on the third and last screen of the Setup menu, shown in FIGURE 7-26.

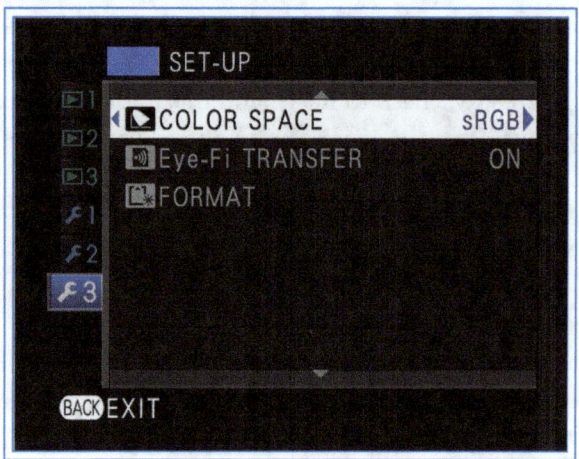

Figure 7-26. Third Screen of Setup Menu

Color Space

With this option, whose selection screen is shown in FIGURE 7-27, you can choose whether to capture your images using the "color space" known as sRGB, the more common choice and the default, or using the Adobe RGB color space. The sRGB color space includes fewer colors than Adobe RGB, and therefore is considered more suitable for producing images for the web and other forms of digital display than for printing. If your images are likely to be printed commercially in a book or magazine or it is critical that you be able to match a great many different color variations, you might want to consider using the Adobe RGB color space.

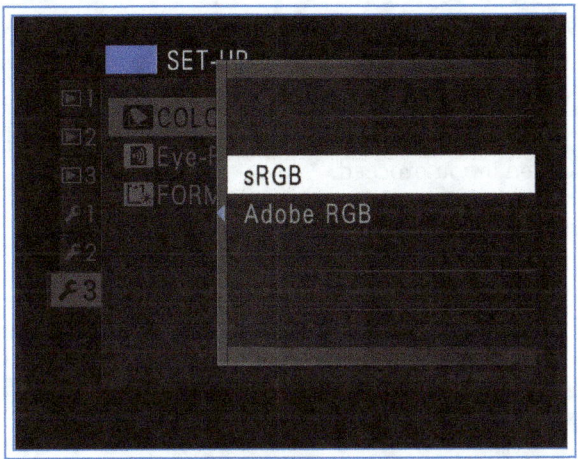

Figure 7-27. Color Space Options Screen

If you shoot your images using the Raw format, you can always select the color space later, using the in-camera Raw Conversion option or your Raw-processing software.

Eye-Fi Transfer

As I discussed in Chapter 1, you have the option of using an Eye-Fi card to store images and videos with the X100S. This sort of card has a tiny, built-in Wi-Fi transmitter that will send your images over a wireless network to your computer or to other devices or destinations. With this menu option turned on, those transfers are able to take place. If you turn this option off, then the Eye-Fi card transmissions are disabled. You may need to turn this option off in areas where such transmissions are not permitted, such as airplanes, hospitals, and some countries. If you are having difficulty with Eye-Fi card transmissions, check to make sure this option is turned on.

Format

This last item on the Setup menu is one of the most important of all menu options. Choose this process only when you want or need to completely wipe all of the data from a memory storage card. When you select the Format option, the camera will display a screen like that shown in FIGURE 7-28, to warn you that all data will be deleted if you proceed.

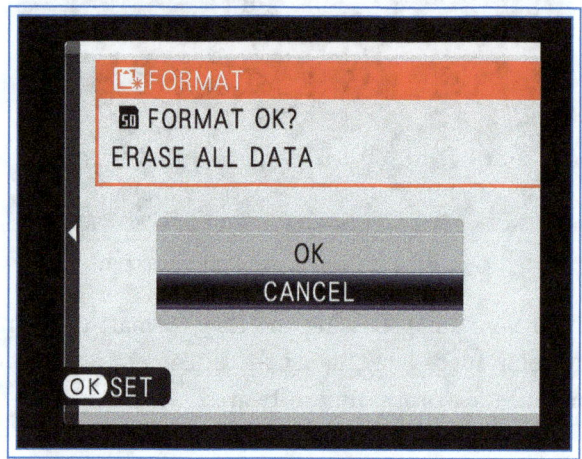

Figure 7-28. Format Confirmation Screen

If you reply by highlighting OK and pressing the OK button to confirm, the camera will proceed to format the card that is in the camera, and the result will be a card that is empty of images and properly formatted to store new images from the camera. With this procedure, the camera will erase all images and videos, including those that have been protected from accidental erasure with the Protect function on the Playback menu. It's a good idea to periodically save your good images and videos to your computer or other storage device and then re-format your memory card, to make sure it is properly set up to start recording new images and videos. It's also a good idea to use the Format command on any new memory card when you first insert it in the camera. Even though it likely will work without that procedure, it's best to make sure the card is set up with Fujifilm's own particular method of formatting.

If you want to format the camera's internal memory instead of a memory card, just remove the card from the camera. Then, when you select the Format command, the camera will format the internal memory.

CHAPTER 8:
Movies

Nowadays it seems to be a necessity for any advanced compact digital or DSLR camera to include movie-making capabilities. Most recently, it's become standard practice for camera manufacturers to incorporate high-definition (HD) video recording into their premium cameras. The X100S is one example of that trend. I will explain the camera's options for movie-making in this chapter. Before I get into the specific settings you can make for your movies, though, I'll begin with a brief overview of the process.

Movie-making Overview

If you've used other recent models of digital cameras for movie-making, you may have seen various approaches to recording movies. With some cameras, you can press a Movie button at any time, no matter what shooting mode the camera is set to; with others, you have to set the camera to a specific Movie mode before you can record any motion pictures. There also is considerable difference among models as to what menu options and other settings are available when you record movies.

With the X100S, Fujifilm takes an approach that is similar to the shooting-mode approach. That is, you have to select the Movie option from the Drive mode menu, after pressing the Drive mode button.

Once you have selected Movie mode with the Drive mode button, you can proceed to a large extent in the same way as you do when shooting still images. That is, you can adjust various settings, though not as many as for shooting still images, using the camera's physical controls as well as the Shooting menu.

It's important to note that the X100S has built-in limitations that prevent it from recording any sequence longer than ten minutes. You can, of course, record multiple sequences adding up to any length, depending on the amount of storage space available on your memory cards. For example, an 8 GB card can hold 26 minutes of HD video. If you want to fit both still images and HD video sequences on a card, you would be better off using a 16 GB card or larger. For any video recording, you should use an SD card rated in Class 10 so it will have enough speed to record the high volume of data generated by the HD recording.

Quick Guide to Recording a Movie Clip

I will discuss the details of movie-related settings later in this chapter. For now, here are some suggested guidelines for quick settings when you just want to record the action, and you don't care about fine-tuning the menu options and other settings. I'll discuss these steps with a bit of extra detail, in case you have turned to this section before mastering the camera's various controls and menus.

1. With the camera powered on, locate the focus mode switch on the left side of the camera and slide it to the middle position, AF-C, so the camera will autofocus continuously during the movie recording.

2. Turn the aperture dial around the lens so that the A setting is lined up next to the indicator line on the lens.

3. Press the White Balance button (Down button) to pop up the menu of choices for White Balance; use the Command Dial or

the Up and Down buttons to highlight the selection for Auto White Balance.

4. Press the Drive mode button on the left side of the camera to pop up the menu of choices for continuous shooting. Use the Command Dial or the Up and Down buttons to scroll down to highlight Movie, the last choice at the bottom of the menu. Press the OK button to confirm this selection.

5. Compose the shot. When you are ready to start recording, press the shutter release button all the way down and release it. When you are done recording, press the shutter button again to stop.

Other Settings for Movies

The steps outlined above will get you started recording video with the X100S using standard settings for White Balance, focus, and exposure. Once you have become familiar with the basic steps for movie-making, though, you may want to experiment with some of the other available settings. There are several items that can be adjusted for recording videos with this camera.

SPECIAL SETTINGS FOR MOVIE RECORDING

If you press the Menu button to get access to the menu system while the camera is set for video recording, you will notice that there are only five items on the Shooting menu screen, as shown in FIGURE 8-1: Movie Mode, Film Simulation, Microphone Level Adjustment, Display Custom Setting, and Wide Conversion Lens. Three of these—Film Simulation, Display Custom Setting, and Wide Conversion Lens—work the same for movies as for stills. They were discussed in Chapter 4. There are just two Shooting menu options—Movie Mode and Microphone Level Adjustment—that are applicable only for movie recording. I will discuss these options here.

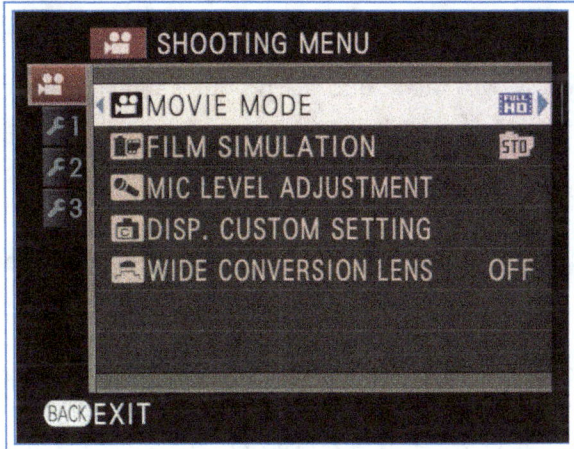

Figure 8-1. Shooting Menu Screen in Movie Mode

Movie Mode

The first of these options, Movie Mode, gives you a choice of two settings for the frame rate (frames per second) of the videos you record—60 fps or 30 fps, as shown in FIGURE 8-2.

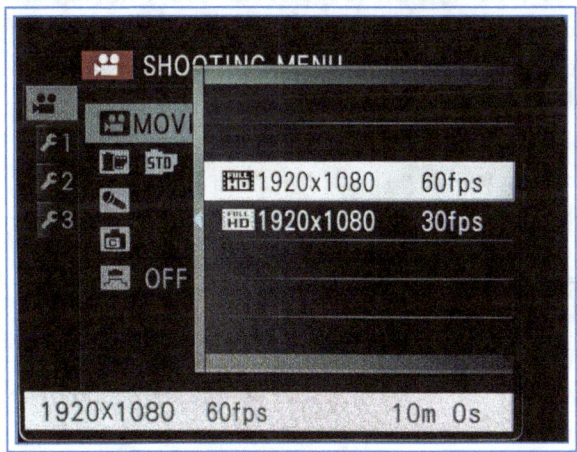

Figure 8-2. Movie Mode Options Screen

This is the only choice you can make for the format for your movies with the X100S. Both Movie Mode options result in movies in the QuickTime format, with a file extension of .mov. All movies on this camera are recorded in Full HD, with a resolution of 1920 x 1080 pixels, a widescreen format in the 16:9 aspect ratio. Both Movie Mode options produce movies with excellent quality, though there are a few factors to consider in choosing between 60 fps and 30 fps. The 60 fps setting is the best choice for maximum quality, if the lighting is adequate.

With 60 fps, the camera records more information about the subject, and, if the subject is one that moves rapidly, like a motorcycle, athlete, or running animal, the recorded footage should appear smoother using this setting. However, when the camera is recording 60 frames each second, that means the effective shutter speed is 1/60 second or faster. That fact limits the amount of light reaching the sensor, which may lead to dimmer images if the ambient light (or artificial light, if in use) is not bright enough.

The bottom line is that you probably will want to use the 60 fps setting whenever possible, to get maximum quality for your videos. But, if the lighting is somewhat dim, you can switch to the 30 fps option and still get excellent results, particularly if your subject does not involve rapid motion horizontally across your field of view. In addition, if you want to use a narrow aperture in order to maximize the depth of field, you may need to use the 30 fps setting to make it possible to get a proper exposure level with that aperture. (Conversely, if conditions are bright and you want to use a wide aperture to blur the background, you may want to use the 60 fps setting.)

Microphone Level Adjustment

The only other menu setting that is unique to movie-making is Microphone Level Adjustment. This option presents you with the screen shown in FIGURE 8-3, where you can set the level of sound for video recording anywhere from 1 to 4. As you change the setting, you will see the volume meters at the right side of the screen react to any sounds that are being made near the camera, so you can gauge the level of sound being received through the built-in microphone, or through an external microphone, if you are using one. (The two openings for the built-in microphone are on the front of the camera, on either side of the built-in flash.) The two bars for the left and right channels rise higher to indicate louder sounds.

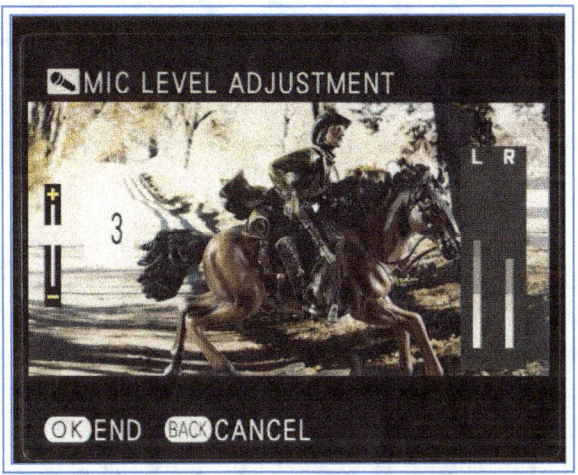

Figure 8-3. Microphone Level Adjustment Setting Screen

If the tops of the bars turn red, that means the sound is too loud, and there may be distorted sound as a result. If they turn orange, they are getting close to the red zone. I have found the default level of 3 to work well, but you may need to experiment, depending on local conditions.

STILL PHOTO SETTINGS AVAILABLE FOR MOVIES

When you are recording movies with the X100S, several of the settings that you make for still photos, either through use of the physical controls or through the Shooting menu, carry over to your movies. For example, if, as discussed above, the camera is set to use continuous autofocus, the camera will focus automatically during the recording. I will discuss below the various settings you can make that will work for movies.

Focus Mode

The first setting that carries over to video shooting is focus mode, which is set using the focus switch on the left side of the camera. For example, you can select manual focus, and you can continue to adjust manual focus during the video recording. There are no manual focus assist options available in Movie mode, though, such as Focus Peaking, Digital Split Image, or an enlarged screen. You cannot switch the camera into manual focus mode once the video recording has started. So, if you want to use manual focus for a movie, select that mode before starting to record the movie.

You also can set the camera to either autofocus mode—AF-S or AF-C. If you choose AF-C, the camera will continually autofocus during the movie recording. This system is useful, because it is likely that the camera, the subject, or both will be moving as the sequence is recorded, and the focus distance may be constantly changing. The camera will select the focus area; you cannot change the location of that area for movie recording as you can for still images. If you choose AF-S, you can focus the lens before the video recording begins and the camera will then use that focus distance for the entire sequence. You cannot re-focus the lens during the video recording with this focus mode, and, as noted before, you cannot switch to a different focus mode once the recording has started.

You cannot use Macro focus mode while recording a movie with the X100S, and you cannot even set that mode while the camera is set to Movie recording mode. If the camera is set to Macro focus before entering Movie mode, the camera will switch back to normal autofocus mode once Movie mode is selected.

Aperture and Shutter Speed

You have some choice as to how the camera handles exposure while recording a movie. If you set the aperture dial to its A setting, for Automatic (that is, setting the camera to either Shutter Priority or Program mode), the camera will handle exposure automatically and do its best to keep the scene properly exposed, even as the lighting conditions change. The setting on the shutter speed dial has no effect when shooting movies; all that matters is whether the aperture dial is set to A or not.

If you would like to control the aperture of the scenes that are shot in Movie mode, you can do so by setting the aperture dial to any of its standard numerical settings. In this way, you can shoot movie sequences with a wide aperture, such as f/2.0, if you want to achieve a blurred background or are shooting in a dimly lighted area. Or, you can stop the lens down as far as f/16.0 to achieve a broad depth of field, keeping subjects in focus at varying distances, à la *Citizen Kane*. You cannot select intermediate f-stops while the camera is set to Movie mode; pressing the Command Control to select those settings will have no effect. And, as noted earlier, the camera will set the shutter speed automatically, even if you turn the shutter speed dial to a particular setting. The setting on that dial has no effect in Movie mode.

Once you have pressed the shutter button to start recording the movie, you cannot adjust the aperture; the entire sequence will be shot at the aperture you initially set. In some cases, the camera may not be able to compensate sufficiently for the aperture setting to expose the scene properly. For example, if you are shooting with an aperture of f/16.0, the lighting may not be sufficient to overcome the narrow aperture, and the resulting scene may be quite dark.

When you set the aperture manually for video recording, the aperture number on the camera's display will turn red, as shown in FIGURE 8-4, if the camera senses that the light is insufficient to get adequate exposure using that setting. If that happens, you may want to switch the Movie Mode setting to 30 fps to maximize the exposure. If the aperture number still is red, you may have to change to a wider aperture, increase the lighting, use exposure compensation, discussed below, or just accept footage that is somewhat dim. (Of course, in some cases that may be the very effect you are seeking.)

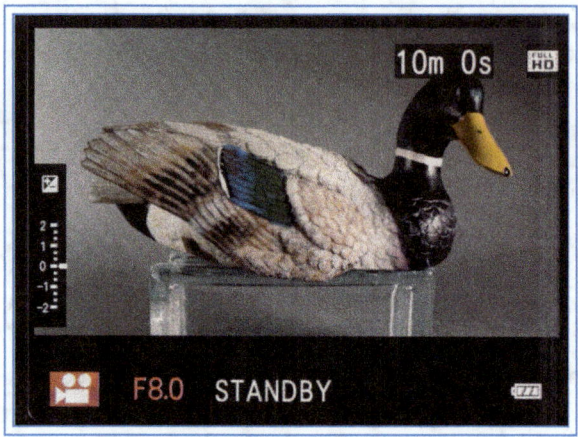

Figure 8-4. Red Aperture Number in Movie Mode

Exposure Compensation

The next adjustment you can make that stays in effect during video recording is exposure compensation. Whatever adjustment you make before pressing the shutter button to start recording the movie, either to brighten or to darken the image, will stay in effect during video recording. You cannot make any changes to this setting during the video recording, but you will see the effects on the screen in the brightness level of the image, corresponding to any level of exposure compensation you set before starting the recording.

White Balance

Another setting you can make that stays in effect during video recording is White Balance. Whatever setting you make, such as Fine (daylight), Incandescent, Shade, Color Temperature, or Auto, will stay in effect throughout your recording. You cannot change it during the recording; you will be stuck with the initial setting. Also, somewhat oddly, the Custom setting is not available for video recording. You cannot set it while the camera is set to Movie mode, and, if you set it before switching into Movie mode, the camera will switch right back out of it. The Auto White Balance setting is quite useful, and I recommend you use it for your video recording unless you have a very specific reason to use some other setting, such as a desire to purposely use a "wrong" White Balance setting in order to achieve an unusual color cast. For example, if you set the Color Temperature option to a high value such as 10000 K, your footage will likely take on an eerie reddish appearance, suitable for some science fiction or horror scenes, perhaps. You also can use the White Balance Shift option when setting White Balance for movies, to tweak the colors along their two axes, as discussed in Chapter 5.

Film Simulation

As noted earlier, if you press the Menu button to get access to the menu system while the camera is set for video recording, there are only five items on the menu screen—Movie Mode, Film Simulation, Microphone Level Adjustment, Display Custom Setting, and Wide Conversion Lens. All of the other items that can be adjusted when shooting still images, including AF Mode, ISO, Dynamic Range, Color, Sharpness, and others, are not available for movie recording. The Movie Mode, Display Custom Setting, Microphone Level Adjustment, and Wide Conversion Lens options are all technical settings that do not clearly change how your video footage looks. Therefore, the only Shooting menu item that you can use to directly affect the appearance of your video sequences is Film Simulation.

The availability of the Film Simulation setting for movies is a considerable advantage, because it lets you add a distinctive style to your video footage. You can shoot in black and white, for example, or you can use a non-standard color setting like Velvia, for a more vivid and saturated color look. If you are taking video of people's faces, you may want to opt for the softer look of the Astia setting. As with other options discussed above, you can make this setting while the camera is in Movie mode, but you cannot change it during the recording of a movie.

Function Button

You can use the Function button while the camera is in Movie mode, though the button will not operate while the camera actually is recording a movie. So, you can press the Function button while in Movie mode and call up a setting before the recording starts, but only if that setting is one that is available in Movie mode, such as Film Simulation.

Another useful setting for the Function button for recording videos is to assign it to the Movie option. With that setting, you can press the Function button to enter Movie mode or to exit from it back to shooting single images. (Even if you were shooting continuous images before entering Movie mode, when you exit Movie mode, the camera will switch to shooting single images.)

If you think you will do much recording of videos, especially in situations when you don't have much time to plan and use menu options, I suggest you consider assigning the Function button to enter and exit Movie mode; that is a very convenient option.

SETTINGS NOT ADJUSTABLE FOR MOVIES

Although, as discussed above, several settings for still photography are available for use during video recording, several others are not. You cannot adjust the ISO, shutter speed, AF Mode (Multi or Area), Photometry (metering method), Dynamic Range, Self-timer, Advanced Filter, or any other Shooting menu settings. Several other settings from the Shooting menu do not apply for shooting movies because, by their very nature, they apply only to still photography (Image Size and Image Quality, flash exposure compensation, and Long Exposure Noise Reduction, for example). You also cannot use the optical viewfinder; only the LCD display and the EVF are available.

If you want to get a quick reminder of what settings are available for recording video, press the Q button to call up the Quick menu while the camera is in Movie mode (but before starting the recording).

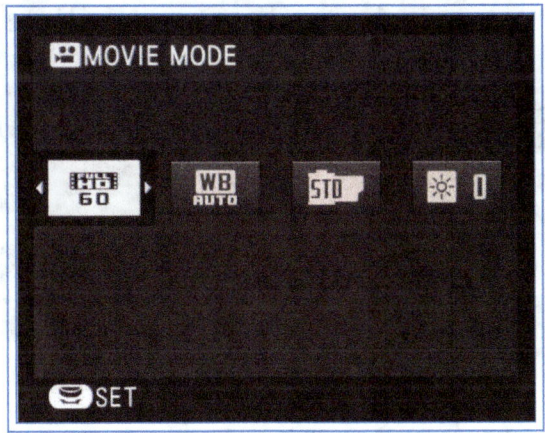

Figure 8-5. Quick Menu Screen in Movie Mode

You will see a screen like that in FIGURE 8-5, which shows that only four items are adjustable using this menu: Movie Mode, White Balance, Film Simulation, and EVF/LCD Brightness.

Movie Playback

In Chapter 2, I discussed the fundamentals of movie playback. Now it's time to go into more detail about that topic.

When the camera is in full-screen playback mode, you can recognize the first frame of a movie by the sets of gray blocks that look like movie film sprocket holes on the sides of the image, as shown in FIGURE 8-6.

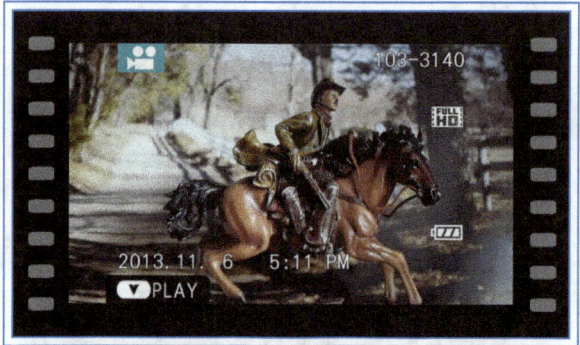

Figure 8-6. Movie Ready to Play, Showing Gray Sprocket Holes

When the camera shows index screens of thumbnails, you can tell which ones represent movies because they are surrounded by gray frames, as shown in FIGURE 8-7.

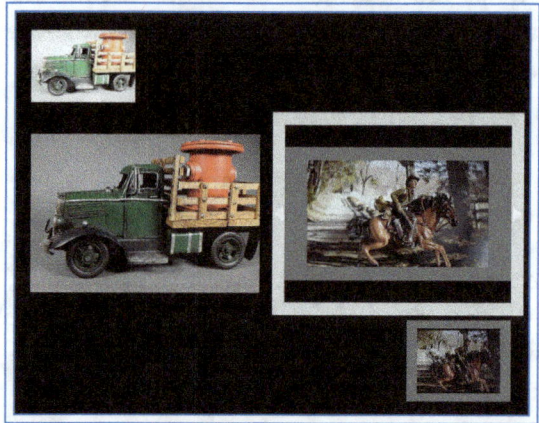

Figure 8-7. Playback Index Screen Showing Gray Frames on Movies

Once you have an individual movie's still frame highlighted on the display, press the Down button to start the movie playing. You will then see a gray progress bar that moves from left to right at the top of the screen, as shown in FIGURE 8-8. You will also see labels at the bottom of the screen showing that you can stop the playback with the Up button and pause it with the Down button. In addition, although no label tells you this, you can pause with the OK button and adjust the volume while paused, using the

Command Dial or the Up and Down buttons. If you pause in that way, you can resume play by pressing the OK button again.

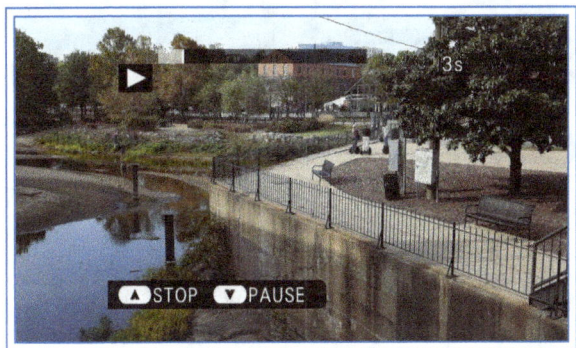

Figure 8-8. Movie Playback Progress Bar at Top of Screen

When you pause the movie using the Down button, you can move forward or backward in the movie one frame at a time by pressing the Right or Left button. To adjust the speed of playback while the movie is playing, press the Right button to increase speed in the forward direction or the Left button to decrease speed, or to increase speed in the reverse direction. You can select from four different levels of speed in either direction, as indicated by the number of right- or left-facing triangles that appear in the top left corner of the display, as shown in FIGURE 8-9, where the four right-facing triangles indicate a rapid fast-forward speed.

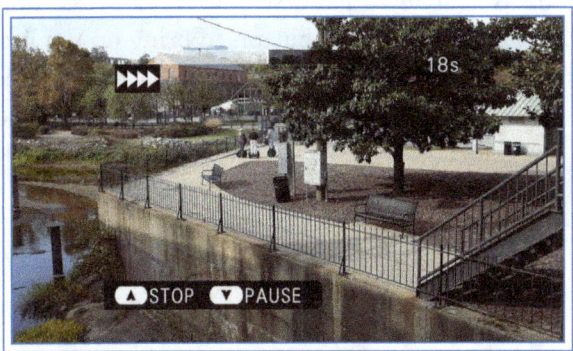

Figure 8-9. Movie Being Fast Forwarded with 4 Arrows

CHAPTER 9:
OTHER TOPICS

Macro (Closeup) Shooting

Macro photography is the art or science of taking photographs when the subject is shown at actual size (1:1 ratio between size of subject and size of image) or slightly magnified (greater than 1:1 ratio). So if you photograph a flower using macro techniques, the image of the flower on the camera's sensor will be about the same size as the actual flower. You can get wonderful detail in your images using macro photography, and you may discover things about the subject that you had not noticed before taking the photograph.

The X100S, like many modern digital cameras, is quite capable of shooting macro photographs. You can set the autofocus system to Macro focus as follows: First, set the focus switch to the AF-S position. Next, press the Left button to bring up the little menu that lets you choose whether to turn on Macro focus, as shown in FIGURE 9-1, then quickly press that button again to select the Macro (flower) icon.

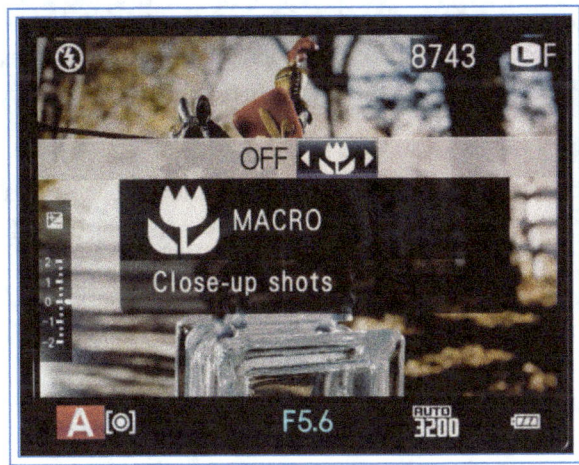

Figure 9-1. Macro Focus Selection Screen

With the X100S, when the focus mode is set to Macro the camera is able to focus as close as about 4 inches (10 centimeters). When you have selected Macro focus mode, the camera puts a flower icon in the upper left corner of the screen, as shown in FIGURE 9-2.

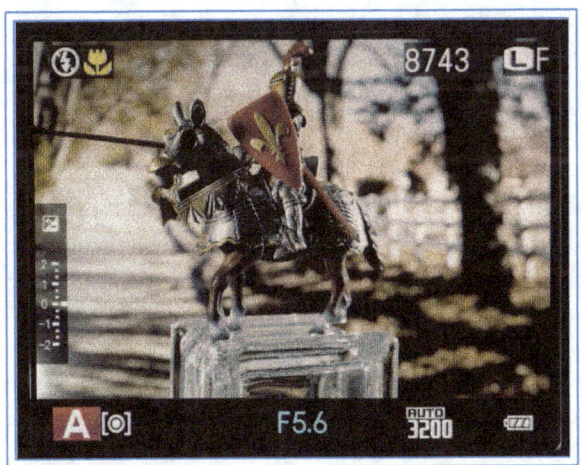

Figure 9-2. Macro Focus Icon on Shooting Screen

In normal autofocus mode, the camera can readily focus only as close as about 2 feet 6 inches (80 cm). However, it can still focus on closer subjects; it just takes longer to focus at that range.

You don't have to use the AF-S setting to take macro shots; if you set the camera to manual focus and then select Macro focus (or even without selecting Macro focus), you can also focus on objects very close to the lens. You do, however, lose the benefit of automatic focus, and it can be tricky finding the correct focus manually.

There's not much point using the AF-C setting for macro shots in most cases, because it would be hard to achieve sharp focus on a moving subject at macro range. However, if you are focusing on a moving subject close to the camera, you might want to try combining Macro focus with the AF-C setting.

When shooting extreme closeups, you should use a tripod if conditions permit, because the depth of field is very shallow and you need to keep the camera steady to take a usable photograph. It's also a good idea to use the 2-second Self-timer or a cable release. If you do either of these, you will not be touching the camera when the shutter is activated, so the chance of camera shake is minimized. If you need the extra lighting of a flash unit, you might want to consider using a special unit designed for close-up photography, such as a ring flash that is designed to provide even lighting surrounding the lens. Another option is to use a piece of translucent plastic, tracing paper, or a similar item to diffuse the flash. You also might want to use an external flash off-camera with a softbox or other diffusing attachment.

For FIGURE 9-3, I used Macro focus mode with the single autofocus setting on the focus switch, in order to get close enough to capture a clear view of a butterfly in an indoor exhibition.

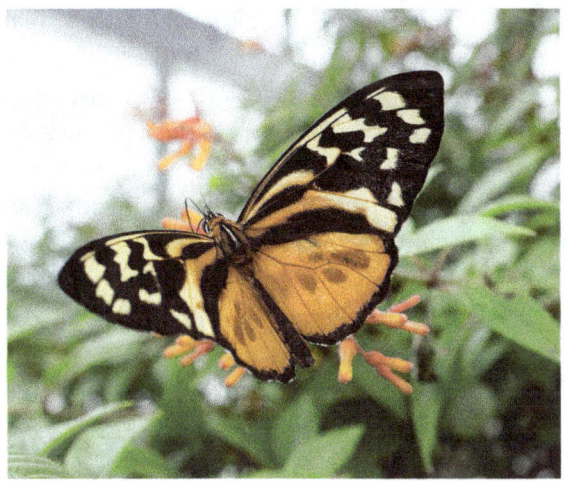

Figure 9-3. Image Using Macro Focus

Using Flash

FLASH MODES

As I discussed in Chapters 2 and 5, pressing the Right button, the one marked with a lightning bolt, gives you access to the various settings for the built-in flash unit on the X100S. There are six possible settings for the flash unit: Auto Flash, Forced Flash, Suppressed Flash, Slow Synchro, Commander, and External Flash. There also are red-eye versions for Auto Flash, Forced Flash, and Slow Synchro; the red-eye versions are activated when the Red Eye Removal option is turned on through the fifth screen of the Shooting menu.

The Auto Flash setting, with or without Red Eye Removal, is available only when the camera is in Program mode. The Slow Synchro setting, with or without Red Eye Removal, is available only when the camera is set to Program or Aperture Priority mode (that is, when the camera is choosing the shutter speed).

Apart from the shooting mode, there are other factors that affect how the X100S uses flash. So, even if the camera is in Program mode, in which you normally have all flash modes available, there are some conditions that will disable the flash. Specifically, you cannot use the flash if you have activated any of the continuous shooting options except Multiple Exposure, including burst shooting, bracketing, panoramas, or movies. Also, the flash is disabled along with the camera's sounds when you activate Silent Mode, either through the first screen of the Setup menu or by pressing and holding the Display/Back button for two seconds. Finally, if you press and hold the Menu/OK button for two seconds, the camera locks out the use of the Flash button, along with the other buttons on the Command Dial. (They still function as direction buttons, but not to activate Flash mode, White Balance, or Macro focus, or to move the AF frame) So, if you believe the flash should be available but you are unable to turn it on using the Flash button, check to see if one of the settings mentioned above has been set.

For now, let's suppose that you have set the camera to Program mode, in which the X100S allows you to choose any of the various flash settings, and that no other settings are interfering with your ability to choose a flash mode. Now, you have to decide whether to choose Auto Flash, Forced Flash, Suppressed Flash, Slow Synchro, Commander, or External Flash. (I'll ignore the red-eye versions, which operate in the same ways as their non-red-eye counterparts except for the Red Eye Removal aspect.)

Auto Flash is a good mode to use when you don't have time to analyze the scene and decide whether flash should be used. With the Auto Flash setting, you are leaving that decision up to the camera's programming, which will take into account the position and brightness of the subject to determine whether to fire the flash, and, if so, how much intensity to use. This mode is likely to be useful when you are at a party or other informal event taking snapshots, or when you are trying to grab action shots of children at play indoors. When the camera is set to Auto Flash, you can tell if the flash will fire under the current lighting conditions, because the camera will display a black lightning bolt in the upper left corner of the screen, as shown in FIGURE 9-4, when you press the shutter button halfway to evaluate exposure and focus.

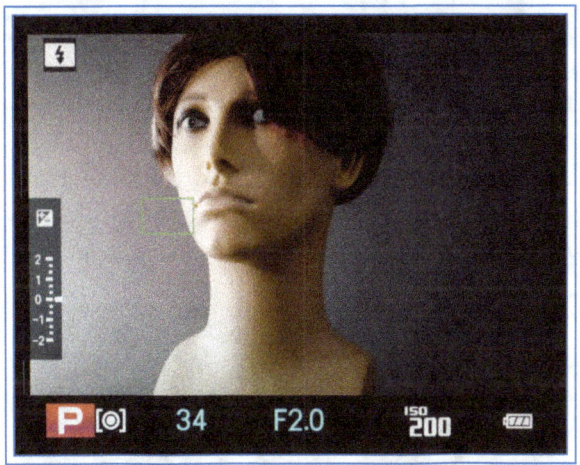

Figure 9-4. Icon Showing Flash Will Fire

Next, when would you use the Suppressed Flash setting? Perhaps you like to experiment with various settings. Maybe you are taking portraits outdoors in the shade, and you want to see how they look with and without flash. If you are using Program mode and have the flash set to Auto Flash, it may or may not fire. If you set it to Suppressed Flash, it definitely will not fire, and you can adjust other settings, such as exposure compensation, ISO, Dynamic Range, and others, to achieve the effect you want without the possibly harsh appearance of flash. In addition, this setting is useful when you are in a museum, religious setting, or other location where the use of flash is prohibited or discouraged. If you use the Suppressed Flash option, you can be assured that the flash will not fire unexpectedly.

What about the Forced Flash setting (sometimes called fill flash), in which the flash fires with every shot? Why would you want to force the flash to fire, when you could set it to Auto Flash and let the camera decide whether it's needed? One case is when there is enough backlighting that the camera's exposure controls could be fooled into thinking the flash isn't needed. If, in your judgment, the subject will be too dark for that reason, you may want to force the flash to fire. Another such situation could be an outdoor portrait for which you need fill-in flash to highlight your subject's face adequately and remove unflattering shadows. You also might want to try at least one shot with the flash in an outdoor setting in order to see what effect the flash has on the White Balance. It may be that the White Balance setting will not compensate properly for the shady setting, and that you will achieve better results with respect to the colors in your image if you use flash.

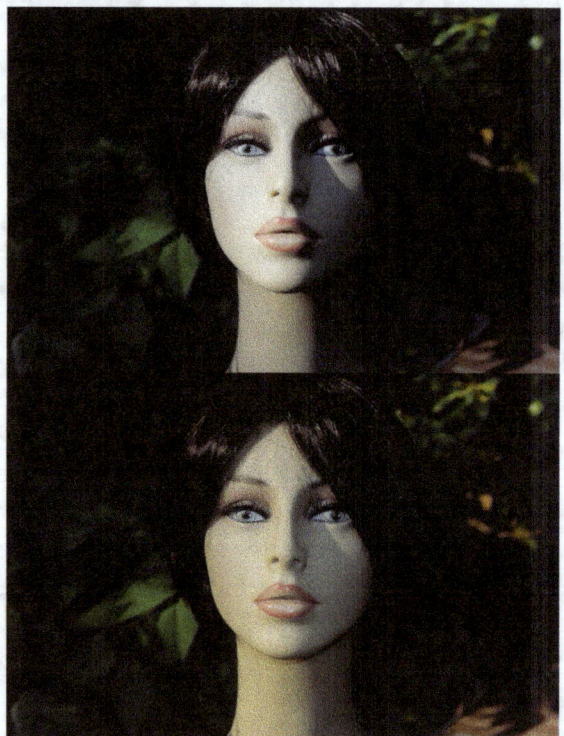

Figure 9-5. Top Image No Flash, Bottom Image Fill Flash

For example, FIGURE 9-5 includes two images, both shot outdoors under the same conditions. The top image was shot without flash, and the bottom one with the camera's built-in flash. As you can see, there is a substantial difference in the overall appearance of the two images. In particular, the one without flash has harsh shadows, while the lighting of the image with fill flash is considerably more even and well distributed.

How about the Slow Synchro setting? With this setting, which, as noted above, is available only in Program and Aperture Priority modes, when the camera chooses the shutter speed, the camera uses a slower shutter speed than it ordinarily would for a given flash shot. Normally, when the X100S's built-in flash fires, the camera uses a fast shutter speed, because the flash provides enough light to expose the image quickly. (The X100S can sync with its flash at shutter speeds as fast as 1/2000 second.) If you use the Slow Synchro setting, the camera will attempt to take the picture with a considerably slower shutter speed, so that the ambient (natural) lighting will have time to register on the image.

In other words, if you're in a fairly dark environment and fire the flash normally, the flash will likely light up the foreground subject (such as a person) quite well, but, because the exposure time is short, the background may be too dark, or even black. If you use the Slow Synchro setting, the slower shutter speed allows the surrounding scene to be visible also.

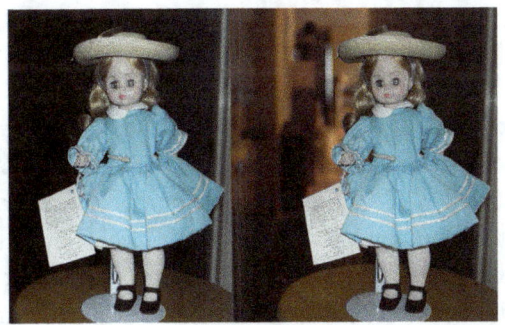

Figure 9-6. Left Image Forced Flash, Right Image Slow Synchro

For example, FIGURE 9-6 includes two photographs taken at the same time and in the same conditions. I took the image on the left in Shutter Priority mode with Forced Flash mode. I set the shutter speed to 1/250 second and the camera set the aperture to f/2.0.

For the image on the right, I set the camera to Program mode and the flash mode to Slow Synchro. The camera set the shutter speed to 1/8 second with an aperture of f/2.0. The much longer shutter speed for the second shot allowed the ambient lighting from the room beyond the doll to show up much more clearly than in the first image.

Of course, you don't have to use the Slow Synchro setting to ensure that the background is properly illuminated. You can, instead, use the Forced Flash mode, and just select a slow shutter speed yourself, as long as the camera is set to Shutter Priority or Manual exposure mode. With Slow Synchro, though, the camera is programmed to do the work for you by calculating how slow to set the shutter speed while still using the flash.

The next available Flash Mode setting is called Commander. When you select this option, the X100S's built-in flash will fire every time the shutter is pressed, but with no pre-flashes. In other flash modes, the camera ordinarily fires one or more times before the actual exposure. It uses these brief pre-flashes to illuminate the subject so the camera's metering system can judge what exposure to use when the flash fires a split second later, to expose the image.

With the Commander setting, the built-in flash fires only once. The reason for this is to let the flash trigger an "optical slave" unit for an external flash. When the optical slave senses the flash from the X100S, the external flash that is connected to the optical slave will fire. If the X100S's flash were to fire a pre-flash, the pre-flash would trigger the optical slave prematurely, before the actual exposure, and the external flash therefore would not fire at the right time to illuminate the subject. As a result, the image would be dark. When the X100S's flash is fired in Commander mode, the flash fires immediately, and the optical slave senses that flash and immediately fires the external flash, so the resulting exposure is perfectly synchronized with the external flash.

The Commander setting also works with Fujifilm external flash units that are compatible with the X100S, such as the EF-20, EF-X20, and the EF-42.

In order to make use of the Commander feature, the remote unit must be either an external flash with an optical slave capability built in, or a separate optical slave unit that can connect to an external flash. I will discuss both of those options in Appendix A.

Here is a final note about the Commander setting. Although the intent of the Commander feature is to trigger an external optical slave, the flash does fire, and it can illuminate your subject quite nicely. Of course, because there is no pre-flash, the camera cannot calculate the exposure, so you would have to calculate the exposure yourself and set the camera's aperture and shutter speed manually. However, you might find it useful on some occasions to be able to fire the flash with no pre-flash, because the exposure is accomplished more quickly, without waiting for the multiple flashes to take place.

The last setting for the Flash mode on the X100S is External Flash. This setting is provided so you can set the X100S to work properly with an external flash made by a third-party company. You don't need to use this setting—and, in fact, it will not even appear on the menu of choices—if you are using one of the Fujifilm external flash units that are designated for use with this camera, such as the EF-20, the EF-X20, or the EF-42. The X100S will automatically connect to any one of them and disable the built-in flash unit.

If you are using any other external flash unit, Fujifilm's instructions say that you must select this Flash mode setting so that the camera will disable the built-in flash and trigger the external one. This process can be a bit tricky in practice, because you have to make sure you are using a compatible flash unit. I tried using a Metz 36 AF-4 flash, a model designated for Olympus and Panasonic cameras. It fired once or twice when I had the External Flash option turned off, and did not fire when I had that option turned on.

I also tried a Panasonic DMW-FL220 flash unit. That one worked as expected; it fired when I turned on the External Flash option, and did not fire when that option was turned off. I had to set the flash unit to its Manual mode to get it to work. I then tried a Canon 430EX II flash unit. It also worked perfectly in its Manual mode, firing when the External Flash option was turned on, and not firing when it was turned off.

Another external flash unit that worked very well with the X100S is the Yongnuo YN560-III. When I attached this camera to the flash shoe on the camera and turned on the External Flash option, the Yongnuo flash fired every time I pressed the shutter button. I had the flash set to its Manual mode.

So, the process of attaching and using a third-party external flash should work well, provided you have selected a compatible unit. You should set the flash unit to its Manual mode, and you should set the camera to Manual exposure mode as well, because the automatic exposure features of the flash will not function with the X100S. When you have the External Flash option activated, you will see an icon of a flash gun in the upper left of the display, as shown in FIGURE 9-7, instead of the normal flash mode icon.

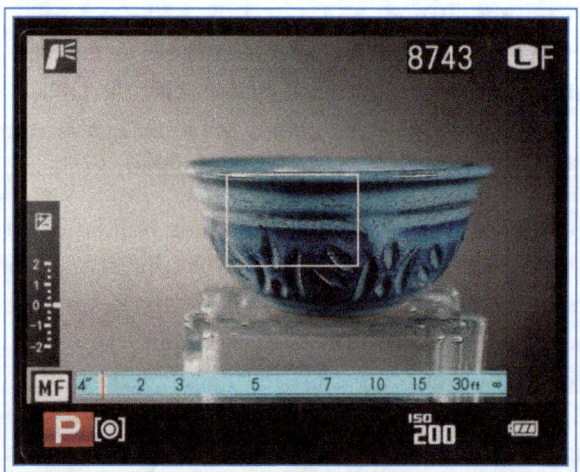

Figure 9-7. External Flash Icon on Shooting Screen

FLASH EXPOSURE COMPENSATION

Another flash-related setting to keep in mind is flash exposure compensation, which is available through the Shooting menu, as discussed in Chapter 4, and is called simply Flash on the menu. The settings screen for this option is shown in FIGURE 9-8.

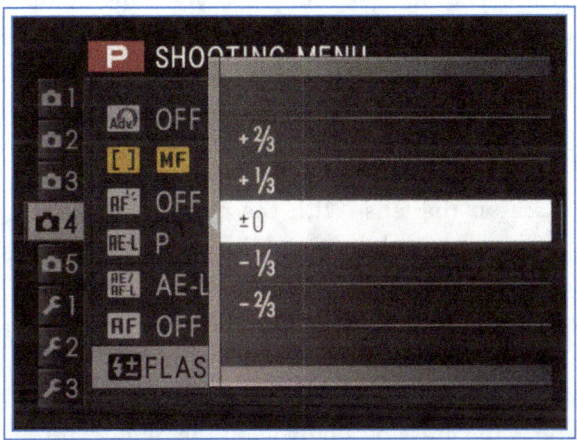

Figure 9-8. Flash Exposure Compensation Setting Screen

The Flash option allows you to increase or reduce the intensity of the flash in increments of 1/3 EV, even when the camera is automatically setting the exposure. Just as with normal exposure compensation, when using flash you can adjust this setting if your test shots appear too bright or too dark. Go to this menu item and set the value to a positive number to brighten the image or to a negative number to darken it. Just remember to set it back to zero when you no longer need the adjustment, so it does not affect other shots when you don't need it.

I have found that this setting is quite useful when taking portraits outdoors if I am using Forced Flash, because the fill-flash, while softening the shadows, sometimes can be too bright on the subject's face. Reducing the intensity of the flash by about 2/3 EV in this situation can reduce the risk of a harsh effect.

Infrared Photography

Infrared photography involves recording images that are illuminated by infrared light, which is invisible to the human eye because it occupies a place on the spectrum of light waves that is beyond our ability to see. In some circumstances, cameras, unlike our eyes, can record images using this type of light. The resulting photographs can be quite spectacular, producing scenes in which green foliage appears white and blue skies appear eerily dark.

Shooting infrared pictures in the times before digital photography involved selecting a particular infrared film and the appropriate filter to place on the lens. With the rise of digital imaging, you need to use a camera that is capable of "seeing" infrared light. Many modern cameras include internal filters that block infrared light. However, some cameras do not, or block it only partially. You can do a quick test of any digital camera by aiming it at the light-emitting end of an infrared remote control and taking a photograph while pressing a button on the remote; if the remote's light shows up as bright white, the camera can "see" infrared light at least to some extent.

The X100S is quite capable of taking infrared photographs. In order to unleash this capability, you need to get a filter that blocks most visible light, but lets infrared light reach the camera's light sensor. (If you don't, the infrared light will be overwhelmed by the visible light, and you'll get an ordinary picture based on visible light.) The infrared filter I normally use is the Hoya R72. It is a very dark red and blocks most visible light, letting in mainly infrared rays in the part of the spectrum that tends to yield interesting photographs.

The next question is to figure out the settings. What I do is set a Custom White Balance, using brightly sunlit green foliage as the base. That is, I call up the camera's White Balance setting screen by pressing the WB button and choose the option for setting a Custom White Balance. To make that setting, I fill the large white rectangle on the camera's screen with the bright green foliage and press the shutter button to record the new White Balance setting.

For exposure, I set the camera on a tripod in Aperture priority mode and let it select the shutter speed, which often will be quite long because of the dark filter. For FIGURE 9-9, the X100S exposed the image for 7.5 seconds at f/11.0, with an ISO setting of 200.

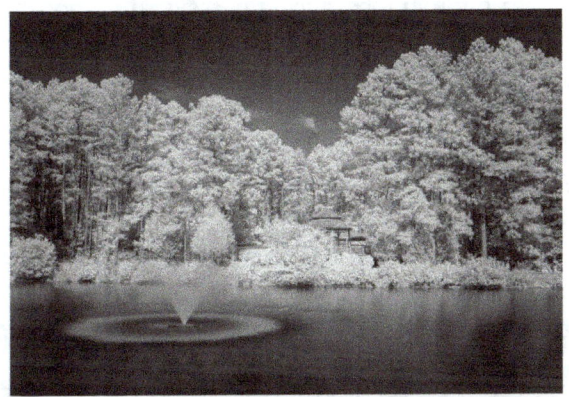

Figure 9-9. Infrared Example Image

The result was essentially what I expect from infrared photography—an image with leaves and bushes that look white, and a darkened sky. This image was taken in early autumn, before the leaves had changed colors, which is a good time to get such results; this sort of infrared photography often is most successful when there is a rich variety of green subjects available outdoors.

Street Photography

One reason many users prize the X100S is because it is great for street photography—that is, for shooting candid pictures in public settings, often without alerting the subjects.

The camera has several features that make it excellent for this type of work: It is compact and unobtrusive in appearance, so it can easily be held casually or hidden in the photographer's hands. Its 35mm equivalent wide-angle lens is excellent for taking in a broad field of view, for times when you shoot from the hip without framing the image carefully. Its f/2.0 lens lets in plenty of light, and the camera performs very well in low light, with high ISO settings available to let you use fast shutter speeds despite the dim lighting. Finally, for those photographers who like to shoot in JPEG format rather than Raw, the X100S offers several in-camera processing options that are ideal for producing good-looking street photographs, including several monochrome Film Simulation settings as well as excellent control over highlights, shadows, noise reduction, and sharpening.

What are the best settings for street shooting with the X100S? I will give some fairly broad guidelines as a starting point. The answer depends in part on your own personal style, such as whether you will talk to your subjects and get their permission before shooting, or will fire away from a greater distance and hope you are getting a usable image.

Here is one set of guidelines that you can start with and modify as you see fit. To get the gritty "street" look, set Image Quality to Fine, Film Simulation to Monochrome, Noise Reduction to Low, and Sharpness to Medium Soft. Set Image Size to L 16:9 to give the wide field of view of the 16:9 aspect ratio. Set ISO to 1600 to give you good image quality while boosting sensitivity enough to stop action with a fast shutter speed. Set the camera to Aperture Priority mode with the aperture at f/5.6 or f/8.0, so you will have a broad depth of field. Set Dynamic Range to 100%.

For focus, if you plan on shooting subjects at fairly consistent distances, such as ten feet (three meters), then you might use manual focus with the lens pre-focused at that distance. You can still press the AFL/AEL button to have the camera quickly autofocus on a subject at a different distance if necessary.

You will very likely want to set the camera into Silent Mode by holding down the Display/Back button for a couple of seconds, to keep the camera's beeps, AF Illuminator, and flash from giving you away, if you're trying to blend into the environment. Also, I suggest switching into viewfinder mode so the image on your LCD display does not attract attention to you, and using the optical viewfinder to save some power.

I generally set my X100S for continuous shooting at its fastest rate of 6 frames per second, because that way of shooting increases my chances of capturing an interesting position or interaction of people on the street.

Of course, there are many variations that you could use; the above settings are just suggestions. For example, you might prefer to shoot in color or with Raw quality to give you more options and flexibility for post-processing. You also might prefer to set the camera to autofocus, rather than relying on the camera's achieving a broad depth of field. If you use autofocus, you could open up the aperture a bit, even to f/2.0, for better light-gathering ability and the ability to blur the backgrounds for some shots.

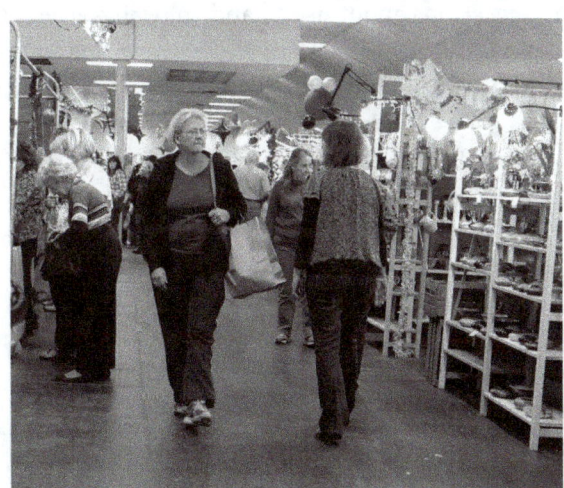

Figure 9-10. Street Photography Example Image

For FIGURE 9-10, I set Film Simulation to Monochrome, turned on continuous shooting at its highest speed of 6 frames per second, and set the camera to Program mode, as I searched for photo opportunities at a large, indoor crafts show. This image was captured at f/2.0 with a shutter speed of 1/60 second at ISO 640.

Digiscoping and Astrophotography

Digiscoping is the practice of attaching a digital camera to a spotting scope in order to get shots of remote objects, generally birds and other wildlife. Astrophotography involves photographing the stars, planets, and other celestial objects using a camera connected to (or aiming through) a telescope.

I can't say that using the Fujifilm X100S is the best possible way to engage in either of these activities; if you want to take closeups of wild animals and birds, you might do better with a DSLR using a long telephoto lens, and for astrophotography you undoubtedly could do better with a special camera or imaging device that is designed for long exposures through a telescope. However, this book is about the X100S, and my goal is to give you some suggestions about useful and enjoyable ways to use this camera, not to find the best possible methods for long-distance photography. That's not to say that the X100S is a bad camera to use for these types of photography; it does have some features that equip it nicely for taking pictures through a scope, including light weight, a large sensor, a high-quality f/2.0 lens, manual exposure, manual focus, Raw quality, a cable release connection, and exposure lengths of up to 60 minutes.

One of the less-helpful features of the X100S when it comes to astrophotography, however, is that it has a permanently attached lens. You cannot remove the lens and attach the camera's body directly to a telescope or spotting scope, as you can with a DSLR. So, you have to use the lens of the X100S in conjunction with the eyepiece and main lens or mirror of the scope. There are many different types of scope and several different ways to align the scope with the X100S's lens. I will not discuss all of the various methods; I will discuss the one approach I have recent experience with, and hope that it gives you enough of a start to explore the area further if you want to pursue it.

I used a Meade ETX-90/AT telescope, shown in FIGURE 9-11 with the X100S connected to its eyepiece.

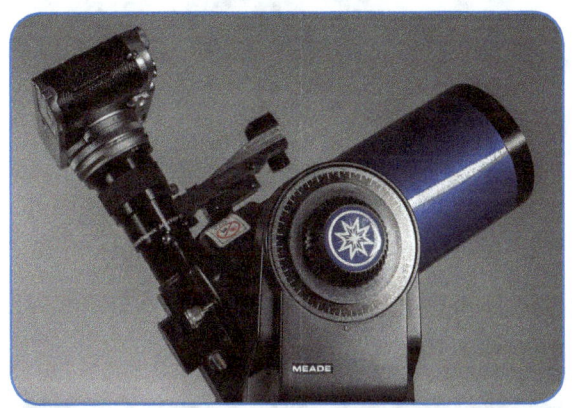

Figure 9-11. Fujifilm X100S Camera Connected to Meade Telescope

This telescope has a diameter of 90mm (3.5 inches), an effective focal length of 1250mm, and a focal ratio of f/13.8. It is of the Maksutov-Cassegrain design, which uses both mirror and lens to focus light into a relatively small tube (compared to the tube of a comparable reflector or refractor).

The challenge in using a camera like the X100S to take photos through this telescope is to find a way to get the image that the eye can see through the scope's 1.25-inch (32mm) diameter eyepiece into the camera's lens. The approach I used was to obtain adapter rings that let you connect the camera directly to the telescope's eyepiece, providing a firm and continuous connection. For this system, you need the camera's filter adapter, model number AR-X100, or the equivalent, as well as adapter rings that let you connect the filter adapter's 49mm ring to the telescope's eyepiece. You can get the proper adapter rings by purchasing the 49mm Digi-Kit, part number DKSR49T, from the online site telescopeadapters.com. That is the setup shown in FIGURE 9-12.

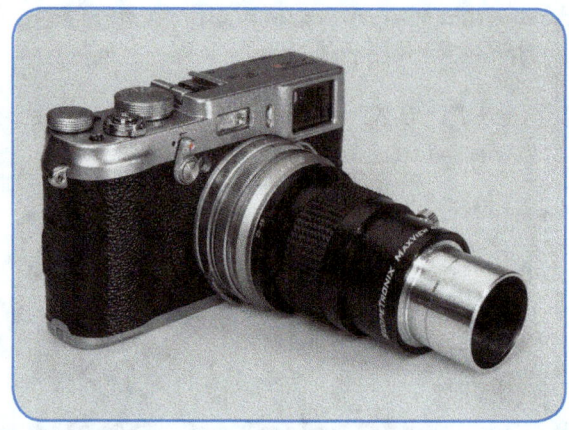

Figure 9-12. Camera With Telescope Eyepiece Attached with Filter Adapter

I took the image in FIGURE 9-13 with the X100S connected to a 40mm eyepiece on the telescope.

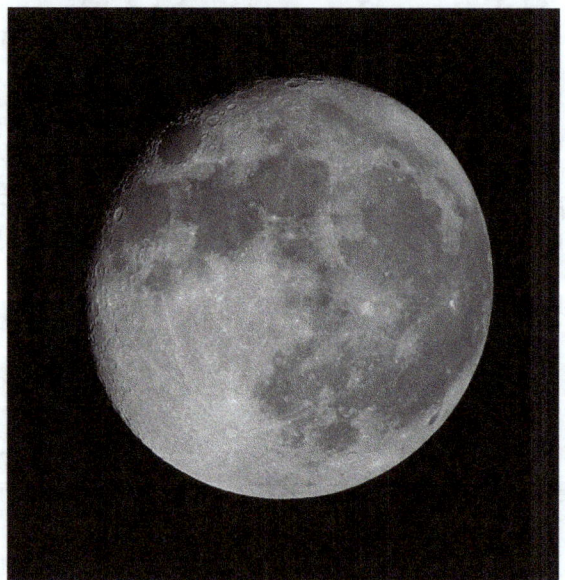

Figure 9-13. Moon, f/4.0, 1/125 Second, ISO 200

I set the camera to Manual exposure mode; through experimentation I arrived at an exposure of 1/125 second at f/4.0, with the ISO set to 200 for maximum image quality. It was somewhat tricky to get the image of the moon in focus. My approach was to use manual focus on the camera, setting the focus point at infinity, and then to use the telescope's focusing control until the image appeared sharp on the camera's LCD display. I then used the camera's manual focusing aids, including the enlarged screen and Focus Peak Highlight, to get the image as sharp as possible.

I used the Self-timer, set to 2 seconds, to minimize camera shake as the exposure was taken and I set the Image Quality to Raw to give some extra latitude in case the exposure seemed incorrect. In the end, the X100S did a pretty good job of capturing the moon. Because of the large sensor and relatively high resolution of the X100S, this image can be enlarged to a fair degree without deteriorating.

You can also use the X100S for digiscoping. I used the same eyepiece and adapter rings, but this time connected the camera to a Celestron Regal 80F-ED spotting scope, as shown in FIGURE 9-14.

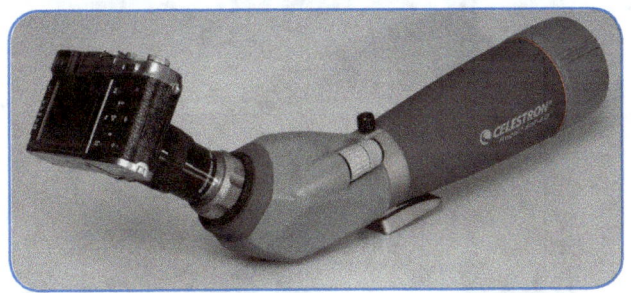

Figure 9-14. Camera Connected to Celestron Spotting Scope

I aimed at a small fountain where birds like to spend some time in the water, and eventually captured the image of a cardinal in FIGURE 9-15. As you can see, the vignetting with this setup is quite severe; only the very center of the image was usable. I used the Self-timer with its 2-second setting to keep the camera steady, and turned on high-speed burst shooting, so I could catch the bird in a reasonably good position. The result is not ideal, but it captured a much closer view of the bird than would be possible otherwise with the X100S.

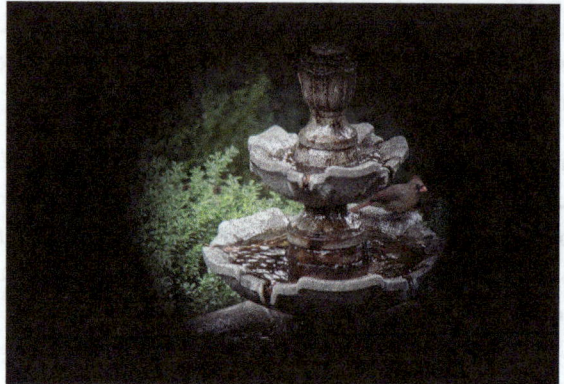

Figure 9-15. Digiscoping Example, Showing Vignetting

For comparison, FIGURE 9-16 shows the fountain taken from the same position with the camera's normal lens.

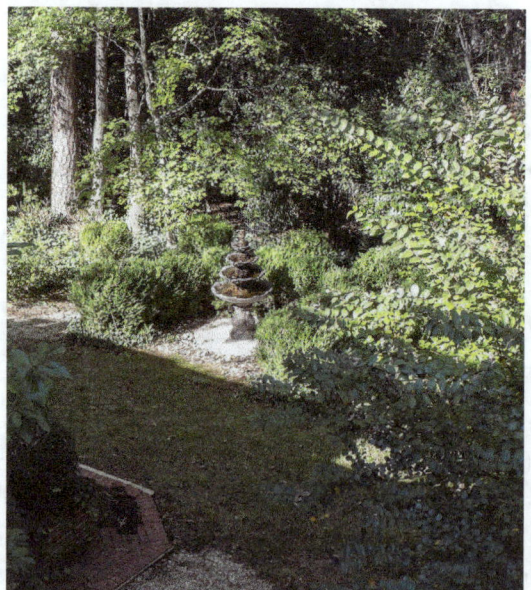

Figure 9-16. Comparison Image for Digiscoping, Taken With Normal Lens

Using Raw Quality

I've discussed Raw a couple of times. Raw is an available setting for Image Quality on the Shooting menu. It applies only to still images, not to movies. When you select Raw, as opposed to JPEG, the camera records the image without any in-camera processing; essentially, it just takes in the "raw" data and records it.

There are both advantages and drawbacks to using Raw in this camera. First, the drawbacks. A Raw file takes up a lot of space on your memory card, and, if you copy it to your computer, a lot of space on your hard drive. Second, Raw files require special software to process them so they can be read by many editing programs, shared by e-mail, and otherwise manipulated. Third, there are various functions of the X100S that won't work when you're using Raw. The menu options and other features that don't work with Raw files include Image Size, Advanced Filter, Red Eye Removal, Multiple Exposure, Panorama, and the highest and lowest ISO settings. In addition, you cannot use the DPOF feature to mark Raw images for printing directly from a memory card.

The main advantage to using the Raw format is that Raw files give you an amazing amount of control and flexibility with your images. When you open up a Raw file (those from this camera have an .raf extension) in a compatible software program, the software gives you the opportunity to correct problems with exposure, White Balance, contrast, color tints, and other settings.

For example, FIGURE 9-17 shows an image that I took on a sunny day using Raw for Image Quality, and for which I purposely underexposed the image and used a White Balance setting that did not match the outdoor lighting. Without any processing, the image looks unusable for ordinary purposes.

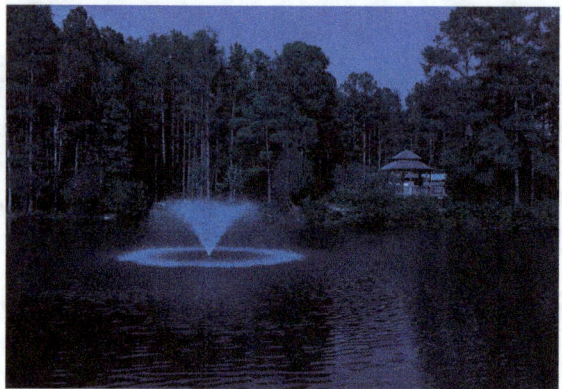

Figure 9-17. Raw Image Taken with Improper Settings

FIGURE 9-18 shows that image being opened in Adobe Camera Raw, the software I normally use to process Raw files from all cameras, including the X100S.

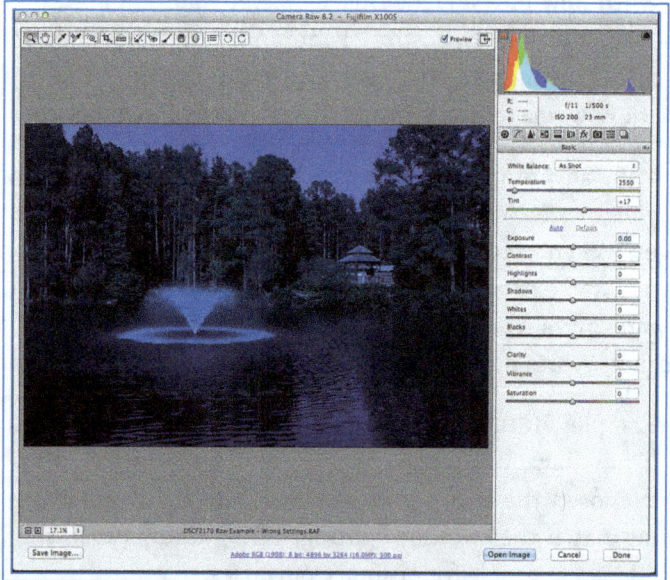

Figure 9-18. Raw Image Being Opened in Adobe Camera Raw Software

Although the image is small in this book, you may be able to see the various sliders that you can adjust to change the settings for Exposure, White Balance, Highlights, Shadows, Clarity, and several other values.

FIGURE 9-19 shows the same image after I finished processing the Raw file in Adobe Camera Raw.

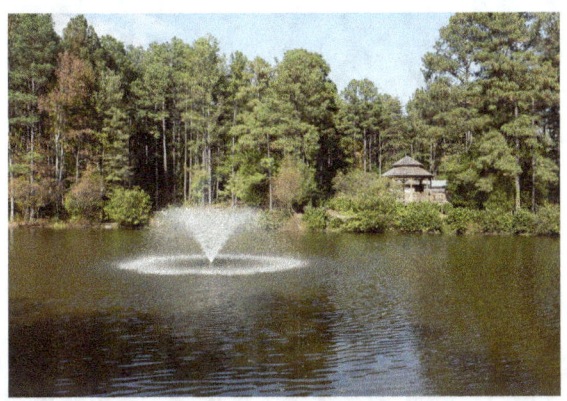

Figure 9-19. Raw Image After Correction with Adobe Camera Raw

As you can see, the adjusted image looks essentially as it would if I had used normal settings when I took the picture. All I had to do was move the Exposure slider and change the White Balance setting to match the conditions that existed when the image was captured.

The bottom line is you certainly don't have to use Raw, but you may be missing some opportunities if you avoid it.

Connecting to a Television Set

The X100S is quite capable of playing back its still images and videos on an external television set. To do this, you need to purchase an optional HDMI cable to connect the camera to the TV. Fujifilm apparently does not offer such a cable, but you can use any generic HDMI cable, as long as one end has a mini-HDMI (type C) male connector, and the other end has a standard HDMI male connector, as shown in FIGURE 9-20.

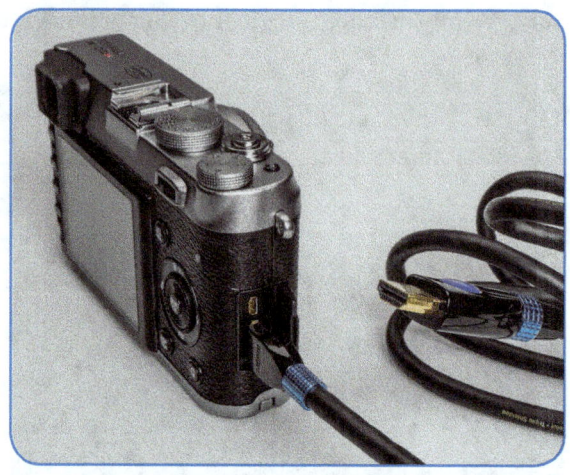

Figure 9-20. HDMI Cable Attached to Camera

Once the connections are set and the TV is turned on with the correct input selected, turn on the camera in playback mode, and you can play back any images or videos you have recorded.

When you have connected the X100S to a TV, the camera operates much the same as it does on its own. Of course, depending on the size of the TV set, you will likely get a much larger image, possibly better quality (on an HD set), and certainly better sound. You cannot control the volume of your movies using the camera, though; you have to use the TV's volume control once the camera is connected to the TV.

You cannot use the camera in shooting mode when it is connected to a TV set; all you can do is play back images and videos stored in the camera's memory or on the SD card. You can, if you want, view the screens of the Playback menu, so you can make use of the camera's Raw Conversion option to alter the processing of Raw images. It might be worthwhile to view the images on the large screen of a TV set while trying various settings for the Raw conversion.

APPENDIX A:
Accessories

When people buy a new camera, especially a fairly sophisticated model like the X100S, they often ask what accessories they should buy to go with it. I will cover the highlights, sticking mostly with items I have personal experience with.

Cases

There are endless types of camera cases on the market. I like to keep a camera in a bag that has room for extra batteries, battery charger, connecting cables, flash, filter adapter, filters, and other items. For the X100S, I also purchased the official Fujifilm-branded brown leather case, model number LC-X100S, which holds just the camera, as shown in FIGURE A-1.

I give this case high marks. It's made from good leather, fits the camera nicely, closes firmly with a magnetic fastener, and comes with an attractive leather strap. To be honest, though, the best features are the classic good looks and solid leather feel of the case. It doesn't let you carry any extra items. If you purchase this case, be careful to get the latest version. When I purchased mine, the first one I received was the older model for the X100 camera; that version does not have the flap in the bottom to give you access to the battery/memory card compartment. If that flap is important to you, you need to make sure you get the later version of the case, as shown here.

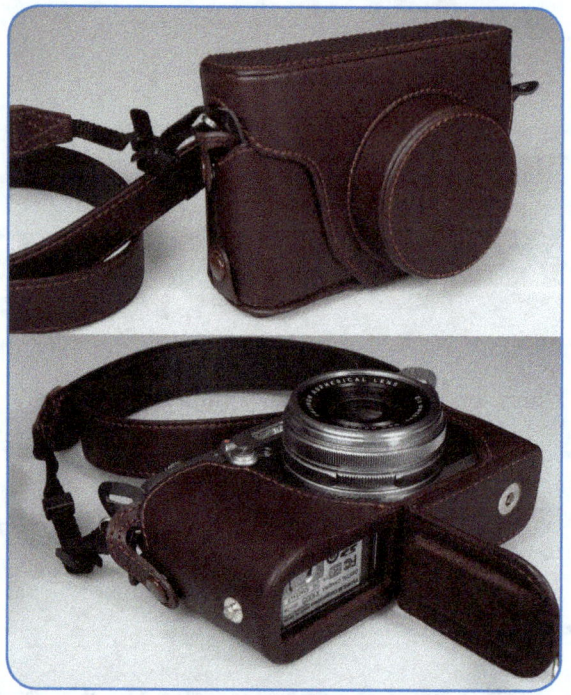

Figure A-1. Fujifilm Leather Case for X100S Camera

When I'm going on a trip specifically oriented to photography, I use a larger case so I can carry along some other items I may need on the trip. I have taken several photo day trips using the Lowepro Passport Sling bag, shown in FIGURE A-2, which hangs on my shoulder comfortably and has several compartments that easily accommodate the X100S, an extra battery, an external flash unit, and filters, and still has plenty of room for items such as trail mix, bottled water, and a guide book for the day's hike. I have also had good success with the Lowepro Inverse 100AW, shown in FIGURE A-3, a waist pack that is smaller than the Passport Sling but still has room for the camera, some accessories, and a couple of small water bottles.

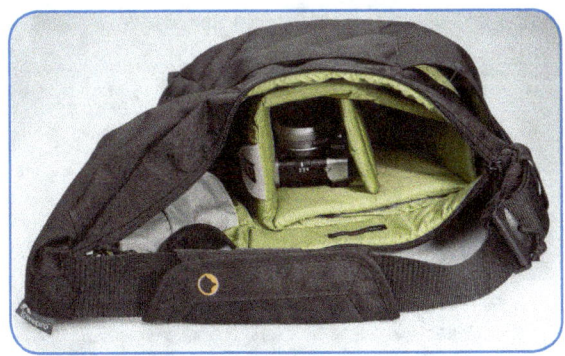

Figure A-2. Lowepro Passport Sling Bag with X100S

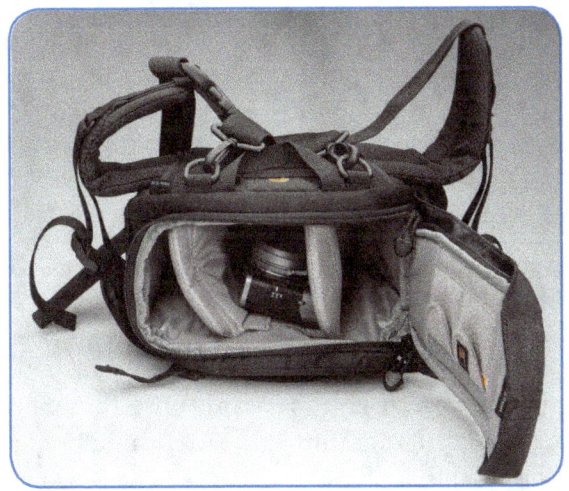

Figure A-3. Lowepro Inverse AW100 Bag with X100S

I also have used the SnapR 35, a combination strap and soft case made by BlackRapid (www.blackrapid.com), shown in FIGURE A-4. With this system, a short strap is screwed into the X100S's tripod socket, and the other end of the strap is attached by a loop to the shoulder strap. That strap is attached to the case, which hangs down at waist level. The camera rests inside the bag until you need it. When a photo opportunity arises, you can quickly pull the camera out of the case, and it rides smoothly up and down the shoulder strap by the loop attached to the tripod socket. I have found this system secure and comfortable. The case has two outer pockets that zip closed; I was able to store two extra batteries in one and a filter in the other with no problems.

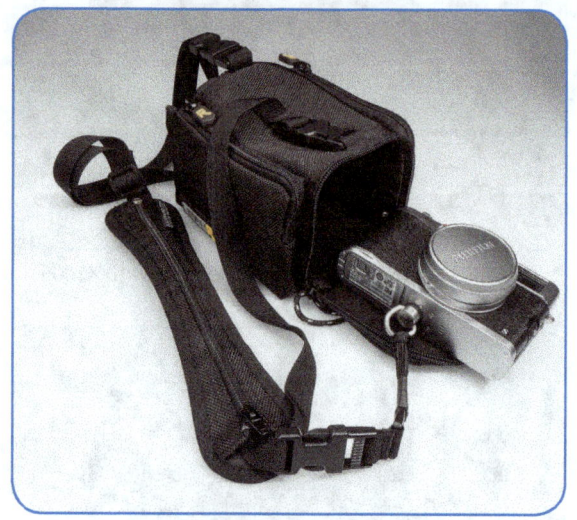

Figure A-4. BlackRapid SnapR 35 Case with X100S

Batteries and Chargers

Here's one area where you should go shopping either when you get the camera or right afterward. I use the camera pretty heavily, and I find it runs through batteries quite quickly. You can't use disposable batteries, so if you're out taking pictures and the battery dies, you're out of luck unless you have a spare battery or two. The model number of the official Fujifilm battery is NP-95. You can get a genuine spare Fujifilm battery for about $40.00 through an online seller as I write this, and you can get replacement batteries of various brands for amounts from about $7.00 to $20.00. I have bought a couple of Pearstone replacements for the NP-95 from B&H Photo Video, a reliable photo equipment dealer in New York City, for about $20.00 each; those batteries have worked well. I also purchased a replacement SterlingTek charger for the NP-95 batteries, shown in FIGURE A-5, for about $20.00 from B&H.

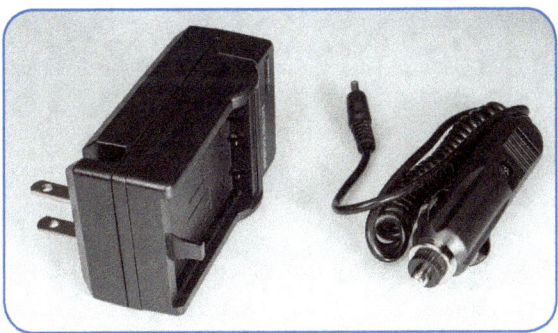

Figure A-5. SterlingTek Battery Charger

Here's one other note about battery chargers for use with the X100S. If you happen to have an Apple MacBook USB wall charger lying around, that charger likely came with a removable piece that plugs into your electrical outlet, as shown in FIGURE A-6.

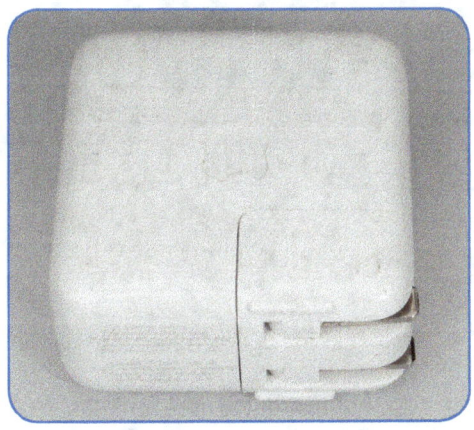

Figure A-6. Apple Computer USB Charger

If you remove that piece from the Apple charger, as shown in FIGURE A-7, it should fit into the Fujifilm charger, as shown in FIGURE A-8, and let that charger plug directly into the outlet without using the power cord.

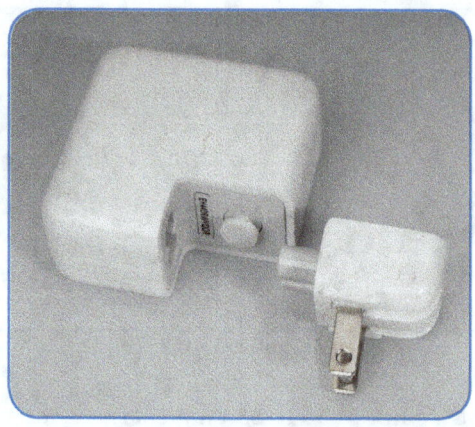

Figure A-7. Plug Component Separated from Apple Charger

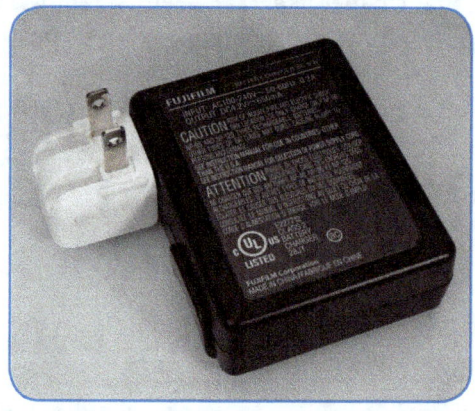

Figure A-8. Apple Plug Component Attached to Fujifilm Charger

If you don't have an Apple charger of this type, you can obtain it from various sellers, including some on eBay. If you search at an online seller's site for "Apple 12W wall charger," you should find the right item.

Add-on Filters and Lenses

You cannot safely attach a filter or other add-on item, such as a closeup lens, directly to the lens of the X100S, as you can with DSLRs and other larger cameras, whose lenses are threaded to accept filters and auxiliary lenses; the lens of the X100S is not designed to accept such attachments.

(Actually, you can attach a 49mm filter if you screw the reverse side of the filter onto the lens after removing the front ring, but that is not a safe thing to do. If you do that, the lens will hit the filter when focusing, and the lens will be subject to damage.)

However, Fujifilm sells an optional adapter, model AR-X100, which lets you attach any filter with a 49mm thread. You can find similar adapters through sites such as eBay. FIGURE A-9 shows a generic adapter that I purchased from an online seller. The adapter is lying next to the camera at the right side of this image.

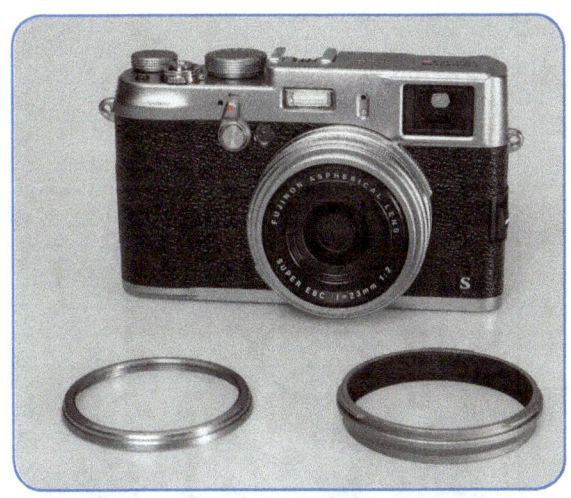

Figure A-9. Front Ring at Left, Filter Adapter at Right

In order to attach the adapter, you have to unscrew the trim ring from the X100S's lens. To do so, hold the camera very firmly in your left hand, grasp the thin trim ring very firmly in your right hand, and turn that ring counter-clockwise until it loosens and comes off the lens. FIGURE A-9 shows the ring lying beside the lens, at the left side of the image.

Screw the adapter onto the lens, as shown in FIGURE A-10. You can then safely attach any 49mm filter to the lens.

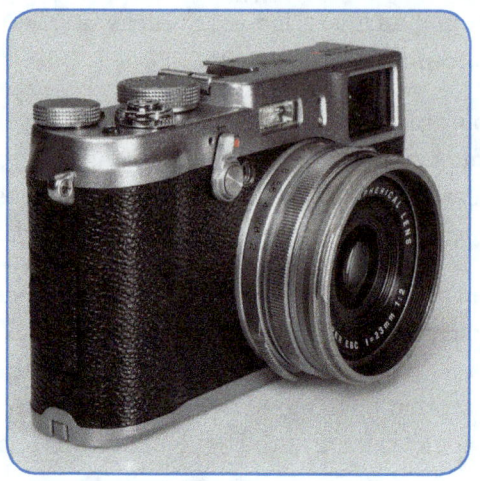

Figure A-10. Filter Adapter Installed on Camera

Also, if you want, you can then attach the Fujifilm lens hood, model LH-X100, which attaches by means of a bayonet assembly on the filter adapter, as shown in FIGURE A-11.

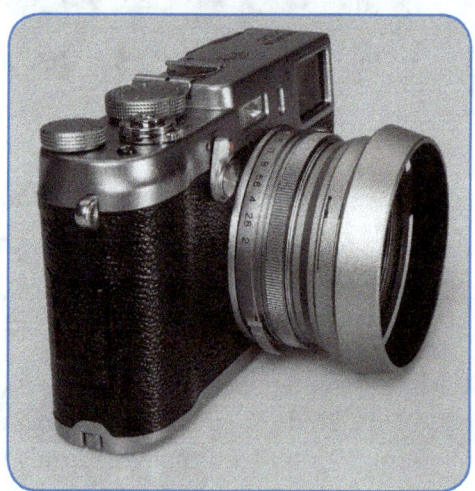

Figure A-11. Lens Hood Installed on Camera

FIGURE A-12 shows an infrared filter attached by means of the filter adapter.

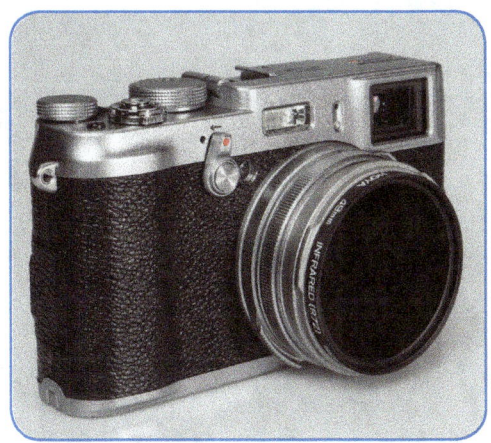

Figure A-12. Infrared Filter Attached to Camera

Having the ability to attach filters enhances the usefulness of the camera considerably. You can use infrared filters, UV (ultraviolet) filters, polarizers, or any of a wide assortment of closeup lenses, and, if the camera's built-in ND filter is not sufficient for your needs, you can use a conventional ND filter with the adapter.

External Flash Units

Whether to buy an external flash unit is very much a question of how you will use the X100S. For everyday images that are not taken at long distances, the built-in flash should suffice. It works automatically with the camera's exposure controls to expose the images well. It is limited by its low power, though, and by the fact that you cannot change its position.

If you need to take photos of groups of people in large spaces, or otherwise need additional power or features, there are some other options for flash. One unit designated to work with the X100S is the Fujifilm EF-20, shown in FIGURE A-13, a small unit that fits very well with the camera in terms of looks and function.

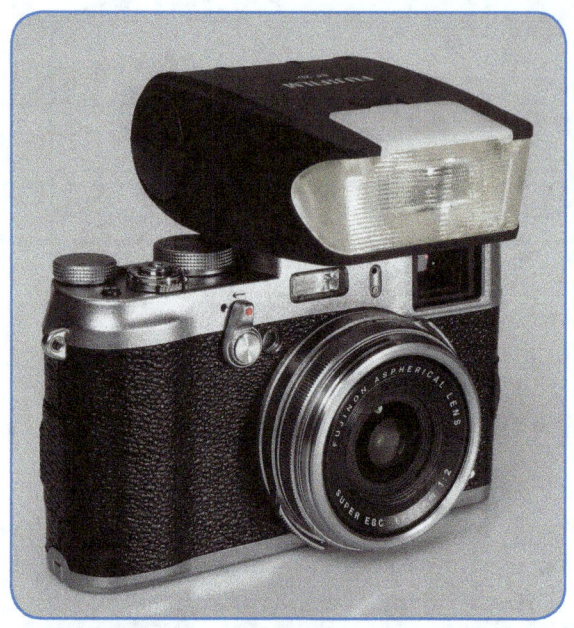

Figure A-13. Fujifilm EF-20 External Flash

The EF-20 fits into the camera's hot shoe and has a head that can tilt up for bounce flash, along with a built-in diffuser that is useful for wide-angle shots. One problem with this unit is that, because it sits low on the camera, it is somewhat awkward to turn the shutter speed dial when this flash is installed in the hot shoe.

A newer model, the EF-X20, shown in FIGURE A-14, is very small, and has a built-in optical slave capability, so it can be remotely triggered by the flash from another camera. It also has a built-in wide diffusing panel that can be switched into place by a lever on the side of the flash.

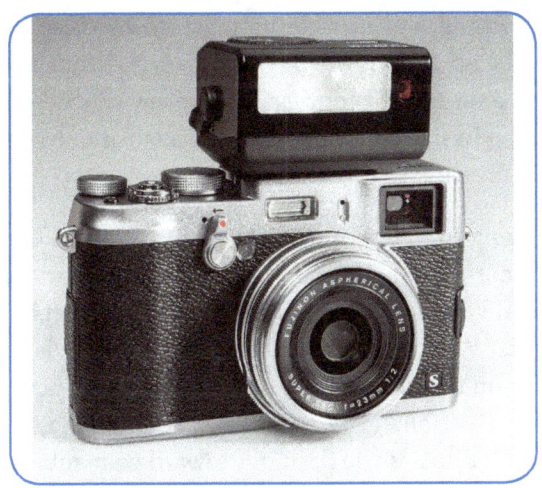

Figure A-14. Fujifilm EF-X20 Flash on Camera

Fujifilm also makes a larger flash that is compatible with the X100S, model EF-42, shown in FIGURE A-15.

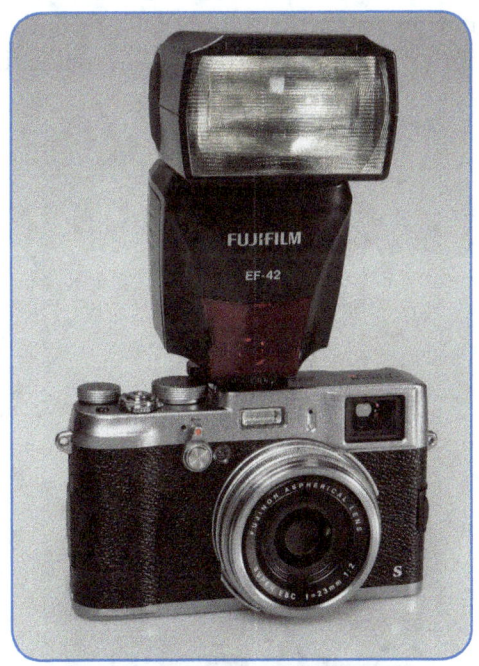

Figure A-15. Fujifilm EF-42 Flash on Camera

This is a powerful and capable unit, which features a head that not only tilts up and down but also swivels from side to side, and which has a built-in diffuser. However, the EF-42 is rather overwhelming in size and weight when attached to the hot shoe of the X100S camera.

If you are going to be shooting indoors in a space you can control (in your home studio, for example) you may want to consider setting up one or more external flash units with separate optical slave triggers. With that system, an external flash is attached to the hot shoe on the optical slave device, and aimed at your subject (or, possibly, positioned to fire into a flash umbrella or through a softbox, which diffuses the flash out toward your subject).

To trigger the slave properly, you usually need to set the Flash mode on the Fujifilm X100S camera to the Commander setting. As discussed in Chapter 9, with that setting the camera does not send any pre-flash from its built-in flash. Then, when you press the shutter button on the X100S, its built-in flash immediately triggers the optical slave, which fires the external flash.

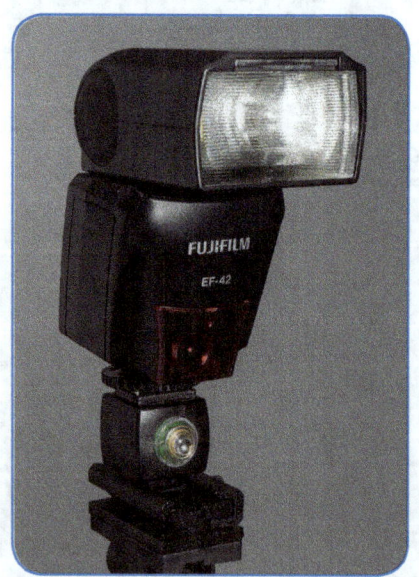

Figure A-16. SYK-3 Optical Slave with EF-42 Flash

I tried this system using the Fujifilm EF-42 flash unit with the SYK-3, an inexpensive optical slave unit sold by Cowboystudio, which I purchased from an online seller. FIGURE A-16 shows the small optical slave unit sitting just below the flash. This system worked well with the X100S, with the camera's flash mode set to Commander. Whenever I pressed the shutter button on the camera, the flash unit fired. I needed to use Manual exposure mode on the camera, because the camera's automatic exposure system would not communicate with the flash with this setup.

The obvious advantage of using a generic optical slave unit is that you can use many different types and brands of flash unit, provided the unit is compatible with the optical slave. Not all flash units are compatible, so you may want to check with Cowboystudio before deciding what flash to use. Of course, if you have the EF-42, that unit is a good choice for this purpose as well as for use in the camera's hot shoe.

You also can use the optical slave system to trigger an external flash that has the optical slave capability built in, such as the Yongnuo YN560-III, discussed in Chapter 9.

Note that, earlier in this discussion, I said that "usually" you have to use Commander mode for the flash on the X100S when using an optical slave to trigger a remote flash. There are some optical slave units that can be adjusted to ignore the pre-flash from the Forced Flash mode; if you are using one of those, you may not need to use the Commander setting.

Finally, one other option that works well with the X100S is a setup involving a radio trigger for the external flash. You can obtain a set that consists of a small radio transmitter that fits in the flash shoe on the X100S, and a compatible radio receiver that attaches to the external flash unit. Then, when you press the shutter button on the camera, the transmitter sends a signal to the receiver, which triggers the external flash.

FIGURE A-17 shows a radio receiver that I attached to a Fujifilm EF-42 flash, and FIGURE A-18 shows the matching transmitter attached to the X100S.

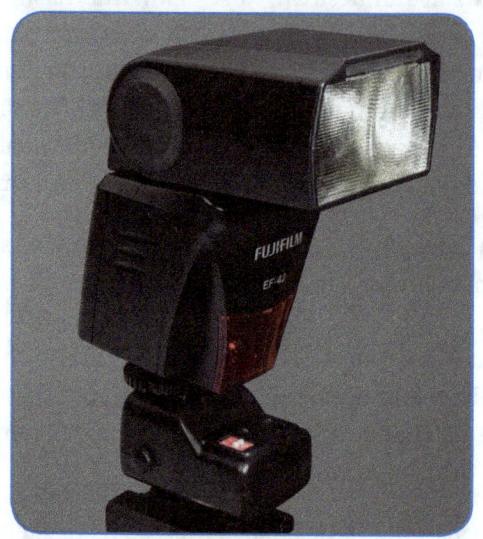

Figure A-17. Flash Radio Receiver with EF-42 Flash

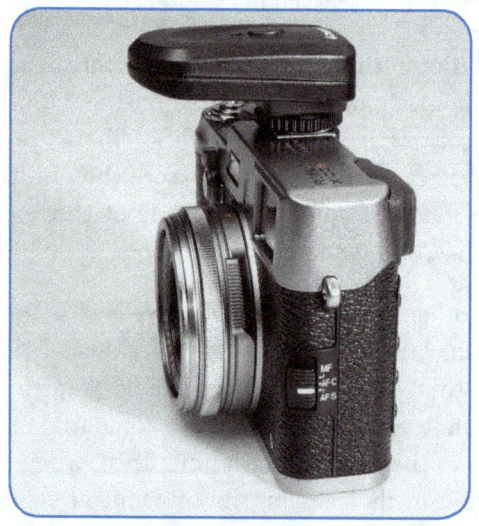

Figure A-18. Flash Radio Transmitter on X100S

The receiver and transmitter are sold together in a set as FM Radio Trigger, model number PT-04, by Cowboystudio. For this setup, I found that the transmitter triggered the flash when I set the Flash mode on the X100S to either Commander or External Flash. With the External Flash setting, the built-in flash on the X100S did not fire, and, of course, with the Commander setting it did fire. With the Forced Flash setting, the external flash fired, but it was not in sync with the exposure.

Wide Conversion Lens

As I have discussed, the Fujifilm X100S is equipped with an excellent-quality Fujinon lens with a 35mm-equivalent focal length of 35mm. This range qualifies it as being a mild wide-angle lens, or possibly a somewhat wide "normal" lens. For many purposes, including street photography, landscapes, and other general applications, this lens will provide excellent results. However, there may be occasions when you wish for a bit more leeway toward the wide-angle side. If so, Fujifilm offers a fine solution—the Wide Conversion Lens, model number WCL-X100, shown installed on the camera in FIGURE A-19.

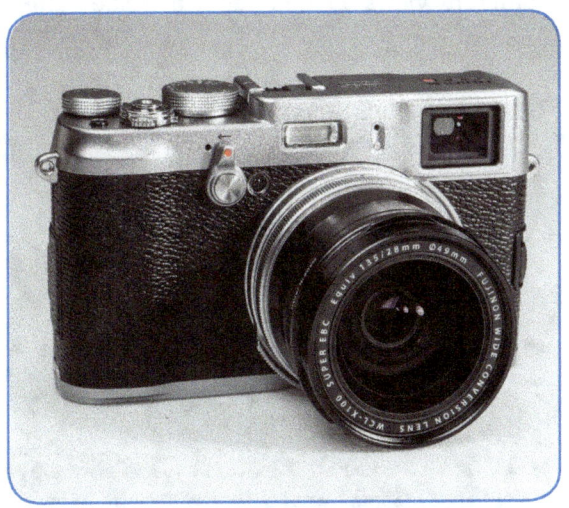

Figure A-19. Fujifilm Wide Conversion Lens on Camera

This lens extends the wide-angle range of the camera's fixed lens to a focal length of 28mm, which qualifies as a more definite wide-angle rating. With this accessory attached, you will be able to photograph interiors of rooms, groups of people, and many other subjects without having to move so far back to get a broad angle of view. The lens integrates very well with the existing lens, and does not make the camera feel bulky or unwieldy. You cannot use the official Fujifilm case with this lens attached, but, as noted earlier, there are many cases that will hold the camera with accessories included.

To install the Wide Conversion Lens, you have to remove the front ring from the camera. However, you do not install the filter adapter; instead, just screw the conversion lens onto the front of the main lens. Once the lens is in place, go to the third screen of the Shooting menu and set the Wide Conversion Lens menu item to On, so the camera will correct its JPEG images for the curvature of the add-on lens. Be sure to turn that option off after removing the lens.

FIGURE A-20 is an image taken using the camera's normal, fixed lens, with its 35mm focal length. FIGURE A-21 is a comparison image taken from the same place using the Wide Conversion Lens. These two different views of the river clearly show the difference that the added wide-angle range makes in your images.

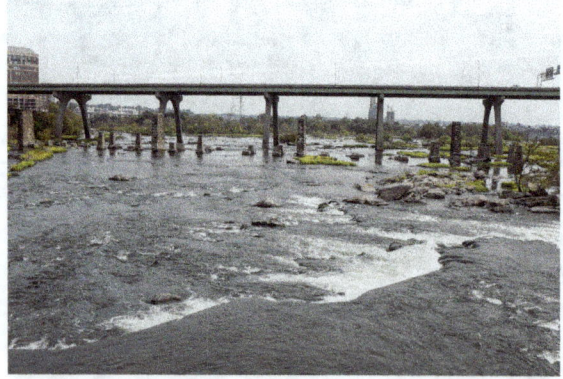

Figure A-20. Sample Image Taken with Normal Lens

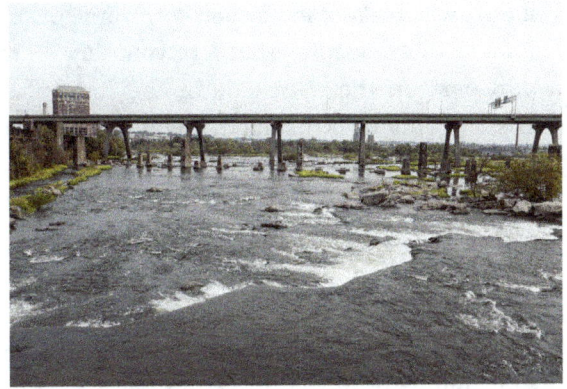

Figure A-21. Sample Image Taken with Wide Conversion Lens

External Microphones

With the X100S, Fujifilm provides a way to attach an external microphone to the camera's hot shoe for use in recording audio for movies. Fujifilm makes one microphone, model number MIC-ST1, that can connect to the camera, as shown in FIGURE A-22.

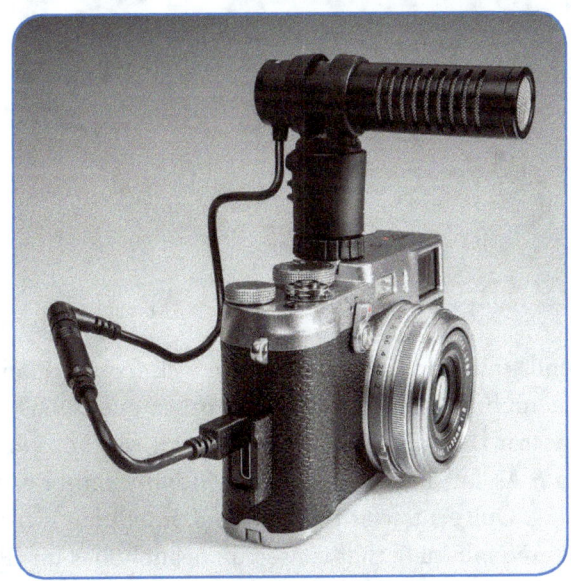

Figure A-22. Fujifilm MIC-ST1 Microphone on Camera

This microphone, which also can be used with some other Fujifilm cameras, comes with an adapter that lets you plug its cable into the micro-USB port on the right side of the camera, as shown here. Once the microphone is installed, it works just like the built-in microphone to capture sound for your movies. It may provide better recording of low frequencies than the built-in microphone, and, because of its structure, it is somewhat more directional. This directionality can be a problem if you want to provide an audio commentary from behind the camera as you record a video; for that purpose, you might do better with the built-in microphone, which picks up sounds from that direction more clearly than the external microphone does.

If you want to use other external microphones with the X100S, you can do so if you get an adapter. The Fujifilm external microphone needs an adapter, shown plugged into the camera in FIGURE A-22, which is provided in the box with the microphone.

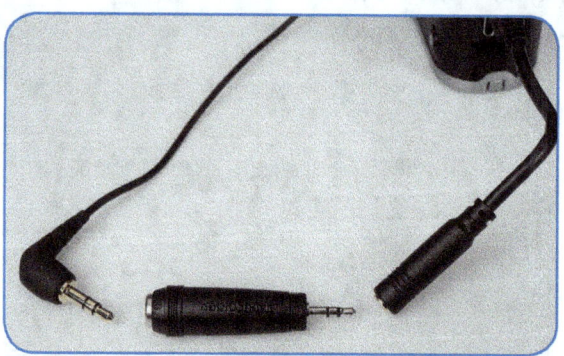

Figure A-23. Connectors for External Microphone

On one end, that adapter has a female jack for the 2.5mm plug on the microphone cable, and on the other end it has a micro-USB connector that plugs into the USB port on the right side of the camera. As far as I am aware, few other microphones use a 2.5mm plug. Quite a few of them use a 3.5mm plug, which is the familiar stereo miniplug that is used on headphones for iPods and many other portable devices. So, you need to find an adapter like that shown at the bottom center of FIGURE A-23, which will let a microphone with a 3.5mm plug be connected to the 2.5mm female jack on the adapter that comes with the Fujifilm microphone. With this adapter, along with the Fujifilm adapter, shown on the right in this image, a microphone that uses a 3.5mm plug can be plugged into the USB port on the camera. If you don't have the Fujifilm adapter, you may be able to find or make an adapter that accepts the 3.5mm plug from a microphone and ends in the non-standard micro-USB connector that fits into the camera's USB port. Here is a link to a discussion of the specifications of the needed adapter by a dpreview.com contributor: http://www. dpreview.com/forums/post/52456072.

FIGURE A-24 shows the Rode Videomic Pro microphone plugged into the camera, using a 2.5mm to 3.5mm adapter from Radio Shack along with the adapter that comes with the Fujifilm microphone. This microphone worked very well, producing a recording with excellent low-frequency sound.

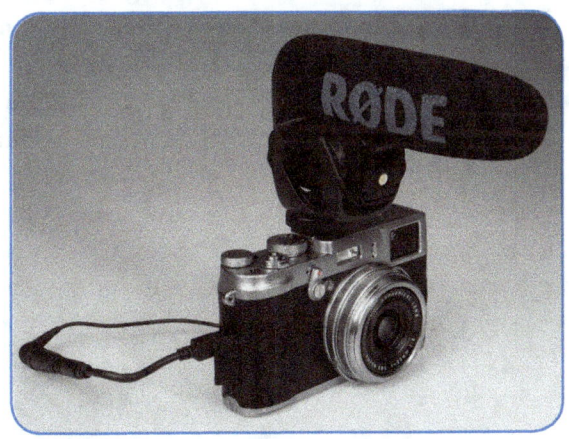

Figure A-24. Rode Videomic Pro on Camera

AC Adapter

There may be times when you would like to plug your X100S into a wall outlet for continuous power, such as for a long time exposure using the Bulb setting, or a long slide show with the camera connected to an HDTV set. Fujifilm does produce the equipment to let you do this, and you also may find compatible versions made by other manufacturers.

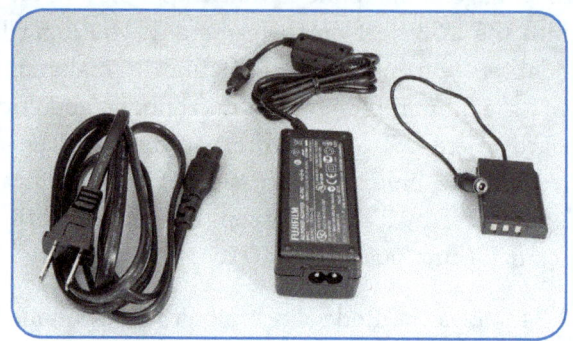

Figure A-25. Components of Fujifilm AC Adapter

You need two separate components, which have even more separate parts, all of which are shown in FIGURE A-25: first, the AC adapter, model number AC-5VX, which plugs into the electrical outlet. That device includes a power brick with a cord going to the power outlet and a thinner cord that ends in a small, round plug. That small plug connects to the second component, which is called a DC Coupler, model number CP-95, shown at the right, which is shaped like the camera's NP-95 battery. That coupler, with the adapter's plug connected to it, fits into the X100S's battery compartment. The power cable extends out of the compartment, fitting into a small channel that you have to uncover by pulling out a gray plastic plug, as shown in FIGURE A-26.

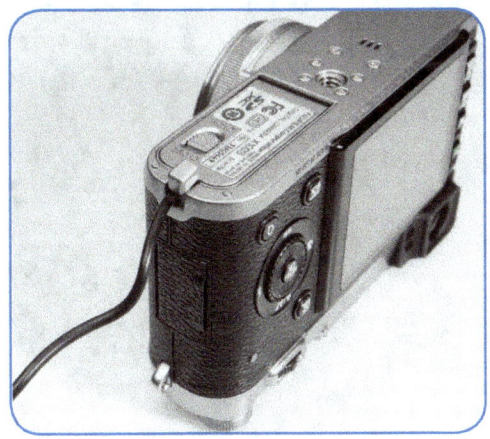

Figure A-26. DC Coupler Cord Connected to X100S

Obviously, this equipment is quite bulky and is a nuisance to set up and use. However, if you are doing indoor work that requires long, uninterrupted sessions with the camera, it is available for your use.

Other Add-ons

Finally, there are a few other items you should consider as accessories for your X100S, depending on your needs. The first item is an old-fashioned cable release, an example of which is shown in FIGURE A-27—the same type that was used on cameras in the days of film and mechanical shutters.

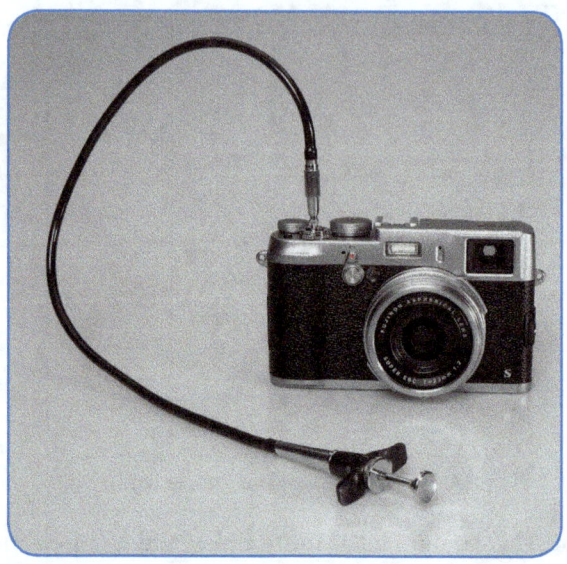

Figure A-27. Cable Release Attached to X100S

One of the nice design features of the X100S is that it accepts this traditional piece of equipment. The cable release lets you trigger the shutter without pressing your finger on the shutter button, which can cause blur through camera shake. It's kind of nice to be able to use a reliable piece of equipment that doesn't need batteries or any electronic circuitry. You should be sure to get a cable release that lets you lock it by twisting a screw or with some other mechanism, so you can press the plunger, then lock the release down. That way, you can start a long time exposure using the Bulb setting and not have to keep holding down the release with your hand.

The last two items to be discussed are both shown installed on the camera in FIGURE A-28.

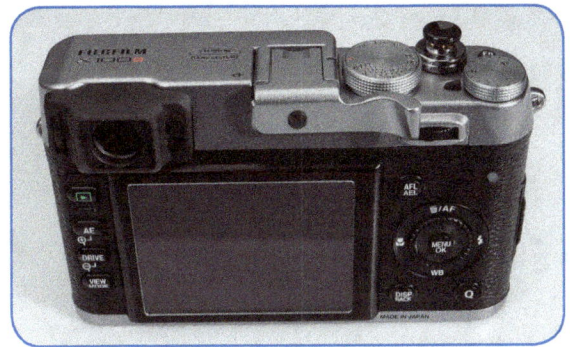

Figure A-28. Thumbs Up and Soft Release on X100S

The unusual-looking device that is inserted into the hot shoe is called the Thumbs Up. It is a custom-crafted item, originally designed for Leica and other camera models, that gives you a place to rest your thumb. The idea is that, when you press your thumb against the curved handle, you achieve a more comfortable and steady grip, and can therefore handhold the camera without much camera shake. It is costly at over $100.00, but some photographers find that it provides enough additional security in their grip that it is well worthwhile. I bought mine from Popflash Photo (popflash.com). You can find more details at matchtechnical.com, the site of the manufacturer.

The other item shown here is a soft release—a small accessory that screws into the shutter release button to give you a smoother, softer surface to press when releasing the shutter. You can find many different styles and sizes of these releases. Some people like to dress up their camera with a colorful one; I went for the basic black model. Again, I bought mine from Popflash Photo, but they are available from many sources.

Finally, although they are not pictured, several useful items are available for the X100S from lensmateonline.com, including a less-expensive filter adapter, an automatic lens cap, and an add-on to make the Menu/OK button easier to press.

APPENDIX B :
Quick Tips

In this section, I will include some tips and facts that might be useful as reminders or as new suggestions. My goal is to provide small chunks of information that might help you in certain situations, or that might not be obvious to everyone. I have tried to put down bits of information that you might not remember from day to day, especially if you don't use the X100S constantly.

Take advantage of the Quick Menu and the Function button. The X100S has excellent options for quick access to important settings. For example, you don't have to use the Shooting menu to set the ISO level. You can assign ISO to the Function button on top of the camera, to the right of the shutter button. Then, you can press the button at any time to call up the ISO menu. If you are using the optical viewfinder, pressing the Function button lets you change the ISO value directly on the viewfinder screen by turning the Command Dial. Several other settings can be assigned to the button or appear on the Quick menu, as discussed in Chapter 5.

Use continuous shooting. The X100S has excellent continuous-shooting capabilities, which can help you catch images ordinary cameras might not. I recommend you consider turning continuous shooting on as a matter of routine, unless you are running out of storage space or battery power, or have a particular reason not to. In the days of film, burst shooting was inconvenient, because you had to keep changing film, and you had to pay for film and processing. With digital cameras like the X100S, it just gives you more options. Even with portraits, you may catch the perfect fleeting expression with the fourth or fifth shot. So, press the Drive mode button, scroll down to the second option, burst shooting at 6 fps or 3 fps, and select it. Of course, you should still take care in your composition and other aspects of shooting; don't look on the burst of shots as a way to improve the quality of the images, but it can give you a few more views to choose from for a given scene, especially if any sort of motion is involved.

Take advantage of the Custom Setting feature. Use this option that lets you store your most important groups of settings. For example, right now I have the Custom 1 slot set up for my latest settings for street photography: Film Simulation = Monochrome; ISO = 1600; White Balance = Fine; Sharpness = Medium Soft; Noise Reduction = Low. All other saved settings are at their defaults. When I am going out to shoot, I go to the Select Custom Setting item on the Shooting menu and choose Custom 1 to make all of the above settings. Of course, I also have to make sure I have other settings the way I want them, including autofocus, shooting mode, shutter speed or aperture if not using Program mode, etc.

Try this other set of custom settings. I could give you long lists of other custom settings to try, or I could even recommend one set as the "best" settings to use. I don't think that makes much sense, because different photographers will prefer different settings, and various subjects will dictate the use of different approaches as well. But people often ask what settings to use, so here is one more set that has been found by some photographers to yield excellent results overall: Dynamic Range = 100; Film Simulation = Astia; Color = Medium High; Sharpness = Hard; Highlight Tone = Medium Soft; Shadow Tone = Medium Hard; Noise Reduction = Standard; other settings at defaults or your choice depending on conditions.

Explore the X100S's creative potential. The X100S is a sophisticated camera with advanced features that give you the ability to explore experimental photographic techniques. Here are a few suggestions: Use Manual exposure mode with its shutter speeds as long as 30 seconds (and Bulb exposures as long as 60 minutes) to take night-time shots with trails of lights from automobiles, storefronts, and other sources. Use shutter speeds as fast as 1/4000 second to freeze moving motorcycles, airplane propellers, and other speedy subjects in mid-motion. Use long exposures (on a tripod) to turn night into day. Try light-painting, for which you keep the shutter open for an extended period in a dark environment, and then "paint" the scene with a flashlight or other forms of illumination, tracing successive bands of light on the image. Use the Multiple Exposure setting to create interesting montages.

Adjust the camera's color settings. The X100S has several settings that let you fine-tune the colors of your images: White Balance, the Film Simulation settings, and the Color setting on the Shooting menu. Try different settings for each of these until you find color combinations that convey what you would like to express with your images. With White Balance, you can achieve unusual effects by purposely setting a Custom White Balance while aiming at a colored surface, rather than a white or gray one, and you can also adjust the White Balance along the red-cyan and blue-yellow axes using the White Balance Shift option, which is reached by pressing the Right button or the OK button when you have a particular White Balance setting highlighted .

Take advantage of the Raw format. If you haven't previously used a camera that shoots Raw files, get to know the benefits of Raw and use it to improve your images. Install and use the Raw File Converter EX software that comes with the X100S, or use other software, such as Adobe Camera Raw, Lightroom, or Aperture, to "develop" the Raw images. Learn how to fix problems with White Balance, exposure, and other settings after the fact, using the flexibility of Raw shooting. You also can use the camera's powerful feature for Raw Conversion through the Playback menu.

Use the built-in neutral density (ND) filter for some shots. There are times when you want a slow shutter speed, but in bright light you can't achieve it because the aperture can only go as narrow as f/16 and the proper shutter speed will still be relatively fast. In this situation, you can use the X100S's built-in ND filter (on the Shooting menu) to reduce the light reaching the sensor, resulting in slower shutter speeds. You might want to do this to slow down a waterfall to a smooth, blended look, or to achieve a motion blur in a shot of a passing runner or walker. You also can use the ND filter to cause the camera to use a wider aperture, such as f/2.0, so you can achieve a blurred background while keeping the foreground in focus.

Diffuse your flash. If you find the built-in flash produces light that's too harsh for macro or other shots, try using translucent plastic pieces from milk jugs or broken ping-pong balls as homemade flash diffusers. Just hold the plastic between the flash and the subject. Another approach you can try when using fill-flash outdoors is to use the Flash setting on the Shooting menu to reduce the intensity of the flash by about 2/3 EV.

Use the Self-timer to avoid camera shake and with continuous shooting. The X100S has a Self-timer that is easy to use; just select it from the Shooting menu and choose 2 or 10 seconds for the delay. This feature is not just for group portraits; you can use it whenever you need to avoid camera shake because of a slow shutter speed. It can be useful when you're doing macro photography, digiscoping, or astrophotography, also. Don't forget that you can set the Self-timer in conjunction with continuous shooting, which can increase your chances of getting more great images. If you find yourself using the Self-timer often, consider assigning it to the Fn button, so you can call it up with one press of that control.

Set zone focusing. If you're doing street photography or are in any other situation where you will need to shoot quickly and want to set the camera on manual focus for a specific zone or general distance, here's one way to do so. Set the focus switch to autofocus-single, then aim at a subject that is approximately the distance you want to be able to focus on quickly. Once focus has been confirmed, move the focus switch to manual focus. Now you have locked in the focus at your chosen distance, and you're ready to shoot at that distance without the need to refocus.

Select Flash mode and Macro focus quickly. When you press the Macro focus button (Left button) or the Flash button (Right button), a small menu pops up to let you make your choice, but the menu disappears very quickly. The quickest way to use these menus is to keep pressing the initial button. That is, to select the flash mode, press the Flash button once, then quickly press it as many more times as needed to get to your chosen flash mode; then just release it. For Macro focus, press the Macro button twice quickly to change to or from Macro focus.

Use manual focus in conjunction with the AFL button. When you're faced with a challenging focus situation in which the camera may not be able to autofocus quickly, turn on manual focus with the focus switch, but press the AFL button (above and to the left of the Command Dial) to make the camera autofocus if it can. Fine-tune the focus by turning the focus ring. Press in on the Command Control to enlarge the focus area to check for precise focus. (This works even if you're using the optical viewfinder, because the camera will switch to the electronic viewfinder to show the enlarged focus area.) Use the other manual focus assist options on the Shooting menu if needed.

Don't forget the intermediate apertures and shutter speeds. When you're using Aperture Priority, Shutter Priority, or Manual exposure as your shooting mode, it is easy to forget the values that don't appear on the aperture ring or the shutter speed dial. Don't forget that, for the aperture, you can set intermediate values by pressing the Command Control right or left, and, for shutter speed, you can set intermediate values by turning the Command Dial right or left.

Pay attention to the depth-of-field scale. Remember that, with some shooting screens, there is a focus scale at the bottom of the display. Besides the blue distance scale and the red indicator for the focus point, the scale contains a white region that expands and contracts to indicate the depth of field—that is, how much of the scene will be in sharp focus. You can use this scale to help you decide if you can shoot without refocusing when doing street photography, for example. It's not precise, but it can give you a general idea. (This scale appears for manual focus on the Standard display screen, and for both manual focus and autofocus on the Custom display screen, but only if it has been selected for either or both of those settings using the Display Custom Setting option on the third screen of the Shooting menu.)

APPENDIX C:
Resources for Further Information

Photography Books

A visit to a large general bookstore or a search online will reveal the vast assortment of books about digital photography that is currently available. Rather than trying to compile a long bibliography, I will list the few books that I consulted while writing this guide.

J. Canfield, *Camera Raw 101* (Amphoto Books, 2009)

C. George, *Mastering Digital Flash Photography* (Lark Books, 2008)

C. Harnischmacher, *Closeup Shooting* (Rocky Nook, 2007)

H. Horenstein, *Digital Photography: A Basic Manual* (Little, Brown, 2011)

H. Kamps, *The Rules of Photography and When to Break Them* (Focal Press, 2012)

J. Paduano, *The Art of Infrared Photography* (4th ed., Amherst Media, 1998)

S. Seip, *Digital Astrophotography* (Rocky Nook, 2008)

C. White, *The Ultimate Guide to Water Drop Photography* (e-book available at www.liquiddropart.com, 2013)

Web Sites

Since web sites come and go and change their addresses, it's impossible to compile a list of sites that discuss the X100S that will be accurate far into the future. One way to find the latest sites is to use a search engine such as Google or Bing and type in "Fujifilm X100S." I just did so in Google and got more than 800,000 results. I will include below a list of some of the sites or links I have found useful, with the caveat that some of them may not be accessible by the time you read this.

DIGITAL PHOTOGRAPHY REVIEW

http://forums.dpreview.com/forums/forum.asp?forum=1020

This is the current web address for the "FujiFilm X System/SLR Talk" forum at the dpreview.com site. Dpreview.com is one of the most established and authoritative sites for reviews, discussion forums, technical information, and other resources concerning digital cameras.

REVIEWS OF AND ARTICLES ABOUT THE X100S

The links below lead to reviews and articles discussing the X100S. The ones listed below seem quite thorough and useful.

http://www.dpreview.com/reviews/fujifilm-x100s/

http://www.photographyblog.com/reviews/fujifilm_x100s_review/

http://reviews.cnet.com/digital-cameras/fujifilm-x100s/4505-6501_7-35566613.html

http://www.imaging-resource.com/PRODS/fuji-x100s/fuji-x100sA.HTM

http://www.cameralabs.com/reviews/Fujifilm_X100S/

http://www.luminous-landscape.com/reviews/cameras/fuji_x100s_review___fallinin_love_all_over_again.shtml

http://www.stevehuffphoto.com/2013/03/25/the-fuji-x100s-review-the-s-stands-for-sexy-speedy-stealthy-by-steve-huff/

http://www.stevehuffphoto.com/2011/06/09/why-shooting-with-just-a-35mm-lens-can-help-your-photography/

THE OFFICIAL FUJIFILM SITE

The Fujifilm company provides resources on its web site, including the downloadable version of the user's manual for the X100S, firmware upgrades, and other technical information.

http://www.fujifilm.com/products/digital_cameras/x/fujifilm_x100s/

http://www.fujifilm.com/support/digital_cameras/models/#x

FUJIGUYS VIDEOS ON YOUTUBE

Fujifilm has produced a series of informative videos on YouTube, featuring two Fujifilm employees known as the Fujiguys, who provide tips about using the X100S, answer questions from users of the camera, and demonstrate the camera's features, using their inside knowledge of its workings. The link below leads to one of their detailed videos about the X100S; from there, you can find links to other videos in the series.

http://www.youtube.com/watch?v=OrUrwrjx6Qw

OTHER X100S FORUMS

These forums are dedicated to discussion of all aspects of the X100S and other X-series camera.

http://www.fujix-forum.com/

http://www.fujixseries.com

INFRARED PHOTOGRAPHY

This site provides helpful general information about infrared photography with digital cameras.

http://www.wrotniak.net/photo/infrared/

Index

V

W

Y

Z

www.ingramcontent.com/pod-product-compliance
Lightning Source LLC
Chambersburg PA
CBHW071247220526
45468CB00001B/27